Dandelion on My Pillow, Butcher Knife Beneath

The true story of an amazing family that lived

with and loved kids who killed

by
Nancy L. Thomas
Terena Thomas
Beth Thomas

Published by Families by Design
Glenwood Springs, Colorado

A special thanks goes out to:

Jerry Thomas for his love and support for all of us and the children
CJ Cooil, for the courage to do this incredible work
Dr. Foster Cline for the foresight to develop powerful therapy to save the kids
Dr. Denise Arehart for her editing and input of critical thinking
Helen Bandarra for her selfless support and love and hours of work and sharing
Ross & Ramona Talbott for sharing their beautiful lodge for our writers' retreat
John Bombardier for loving Terena and sharing her with Nancy and Beth
Jennie, Peggy, Lisa, William & Tim for helping Beth with the details of her life
Lori Wilson, for thousands of hours of teaching and support and love.
And a special thanks to all the children and families throughout the years that
we've helped and learned from!

All the events described in this book are true. Only names, places, and certain
facts not central to the actual story have been changed to protect the dignity
and privacy of the individuals.

****Due to the graphic nature of this book, sensitive readers should take
caution.**

Library of Congress # 2002090035
ISBN # 978-0-9703525-2-1

Drawings throughout the book are by artist David Molinatto, Bahama NC
Back cover Photo by Glenwood Photography Studios

Other Books by These Authors:
by Nancy L. Thomas

When Love is Not Enough,
a guide to parenting children with RAD

The Handbook of Attachment Interventions (co- author)

Videos/DVD's by Nancy L. Thomas

Rebuilding the Broken Bond
Building Brilliant Brains through Bonding
Captive in the Classroom
Give me a Break
The Circle of Support
Mastering Steps to Reach Children with RAD

by Terena Thomas

Not Just Horsing Around with Defiant Kids!
A manual and DVD's with a dynamic lesson plan
for working with challenging
kids through equine intervention

coming soon
by Nancy L. Thomas

Taming the Toddler Before You Have a Wild Child
DVD and booklet

Table of Contents

Forward
by Foster W. Cline, M.D.

This book has a strange title, Dandelion on my Pillow, Butcher Knife Beneath, but it is an honest title which attempts to explain the fact that with many adopted and foster children, what you see on the surface is not what you get beneath! The overt and winsome smile of the child often hides a covert rage that only the parents can fully comprehend.

Nancy Thomas and her daughters, with love, humor and faith introduce readers to the world occupied by thousands of foster and adoptive parents.

This book is an essential book. Accepting disturbed children into a home can be a dangerous, exciting, fulfilling, frightening, heartwarming and heartbreaking experience. In fact, one might take all the emotions associated with child-raising and raise the intensity of those feelings to the 30th power to have some idea of the emotional roller coaster such parents as Nancy experience.

An abusive husband may look "normal" to neighbors and friends of a couple. However, the wife in the privacy of her home lives a hell that few can imagine. Thus it is with seriously disturbed children.

Nancy Thomas' story of triumph over tragedy will, therefore, serve several purposes. It is a handbook of "how to's" where distraught parents who have run out of ideas and energy can turn for insight and invigoration.

And for the rest of the nation..... for those living with normal children who have normal difficulties, this book will help them to understand the issues faced by today's adoptive and foster parents.

And such parents do need understanding:

Foster parents and many adoptive parents have jobs that require a 168 hour work week with no overtime.

Although foster and adoptive parents are entrusted with our most valuable resource, America's children, foster parenting is one of the lowest paid professions in the United States.

Foster and adoptive parents now, at the turn of the millennium, are asked to attempt to cope, in their homes, with children so disturbed that they would certainly have been admitted and treated in residential treatment centers in times past.

To such parents, alarms on the doors, nets over cribs, insight supervision, and tightly controlled environments are the order of the day. Such supervision is not understood by the average parent who may question why such constant surveillance is necessary. "The kids are only playing house." And, the foster mom replies, "Let's just say that my children don't play house like your children play house!"

Moms will find solace and answers here. Nancy Thomas has taught thousands of adoptive and foster parents how to best cope using love and effective techniques to reach the children who would put a knife under the pillow.

I wish that every parent considering adoption and all those who do adopt or foster children were required to read this book so that there might be more tragedy to triumph experiences. From the personal perspective of the mother and her children, here is a guide book to the persistence, love, tools and techniques necessary to survive and triumph.
I have found that many professionals who have never lived with disturbed children simply have no idea of what is actually required from the parents. So this book is an essential look at the adoptive and fostering issues from the personal vantage point of a mother and children who "have actually been around the block".

Introduction

This book is the result of many hours of literally blood, sweat and tears. The events are true. My daughters and I secluded ourselves together during three mountain retreats to remove all distractions and totally immerse ourselves in these pages. We shared laughter and tears as we each "gave birth" to our memories. Terena used her gifted writing skills to create much of this written account as I told it. Beth wrote her story straight from her heart. Our goal is to share the stories of a few of the amazing children we have had the privilege to share our lives with. We, the authors, selected these few cases over many others. They did not all fit into one manuscript and we felt to include them all would be overwhelming to readers.

This book is our gift to all traumatized children, that they may be understood. It is our gift to the mothers and fathers trying to help these wounded ones, that they may be lifted up, supported and honored for their efforts. It is our gift to mental health professionals, case workers and those who are considering adopting or becoming foster parents that they may have their eyes opened and be more prepared to help the children. It is our gift to you, the reader that you may have a deeper understanding of mental illness and the fallout caused by abuse so that we may bond together to do all we can to help.

There are more than one half million children in the foster care system of the US today. Most of them got there by being abused or neglected. Our country brings in tens of thousands of orphans internationally that have not had their needs met. One out of five babies is born too soon and may suffer weeks or months of medical trauma away from their mothers. The number of children with Attachment Disorder is estimated to be 800,000. Not all adopted or foster children have emotional illness! We have added some technical information at the back of the book and a list of suggested reading if you would like more details.

A portion of the proceeds from *Dandelion on My Pillow, Butcher Knife Beneath* is being donated to SAVY Inc. a nonprofit foundation established to provide funding for treatment for traumatized children, scholarships for therapists wanting training in this field, and information for new mothers on the importance of bonding right from the start. We believe it is a donation well worth our investment and commitment to Stop America's Violent Youth.

We hope you will enjoy this book as we lay bare our lives to you.

Chapter 1

The Incineration

I was lovingly pulled from the lull of sleep by my husband's rough, work- worn hand gently shaking my shoulder. He leaned over our bed and softly said, "Babe, wake-up! There's been a fire". My eyes shot open and strained to focus as my mind raced to make sense of what had just hit my ears. I searched his weary blue eyes and saw only concern. Lifting up on one elbow, I replied with a disbelieving, "What?!," while blinking the fog of sleep from my consciousness. My heart began to race as Jerry stood beside the bed in his cowboy hat and work jeans, his supportive hand still resting on my awakening body. Although he wanted to explain, all I yearned to do was to pull a bathrobe around me and see the damage for myself. I stopped and patiently waited.

After twenty years of marriage we knew each other well. Although he tried to hide it his eyes told me he was overly concerned about my reaction. Had I been so fragile lately? He lowered his lean, strong form in order to sit on the bed and explained, " I went out to feed the animals and when I came around the corner of the garage I saw that the guest house had burned. The storage shed that held all of Terena's stuff is gone too".

I couldn't wait any longer. I rushed from bed, grabbed a warm robe to ward off the September chill and took the stairs leading up from our room to the front door two at a time. I threw open the door with barely a pause. The acrid smell of smoke assaulted my nostrils as I raced down the porch and across the gravel driveway. The sight of the blackened rubble stopped me dead in my tracks; the remains of our guest house, all 500 square feet of it, was now a pile of smoldering ash about thigh high.

In total shock, I stood there in disbelief that all of this could have happened while my husband, myself and all five children peacefully slept through the night. One day it was there, the next day it was all gone. In a daze, I shuffled to the house, looking for the phone to call the fire department. The flames had nothing left to consume, but smoke still swirled and danced above the wreckage. Wondering how long it would take the fire fighters to reach our remote mountain ranch in the Colorado Rockies, I worried that the propane tanks might still be able to blow. The black ash surrounded them. Were we still in danger? How could this have happened? I trudged up the stairs to the room of my daughter, Terena. I had to wake her, but my heart was burdened and heavy knowing the pain and sadness it would cause her.

She had come home from college for the summer and had brought only some summer clothes and essentials to her room; the rest had been placed in the storage shed, neatly packed. Every worldly possession she had now lay incinerated in the yard or floated as ash through the morning air. Outside of her closed door, I said a little prayer to God that my only biological daughter would be strong enough to handle such a loss. With a deep breath, I hesitantly opened her bedroom door. I.Q., her German Shepherd dog, greeted me with a warning woof as I stepped into her room. I approached Terena's nineteen-year-old body and watched her sleep in peace, her satin gold hair shimmering across the pillow as if angels had placed it in a halo about her face. As I gently woke her, she looked up and I saw her father's blue eyes looking into mine. Before I could say anything, Jerry joined me. We glanced at each other in acknowledgment of the painful moment we must share and joined hands before Jerry said, "Terena, wake up. There's been a fire". My voice broke as I added, " I am so sorry but your stuff is gone."

She shot upward in order to see us better in the soft morning light. "Huh? What?" quickly escaped her lips while I could see confusion and disbelief filling her soul. "What do you mean all my stuff is gone? Where was the fire? What's going on?" Her bombardment of questions was answered with warm hugs and apologies. Softening the blow by using her nickname, I continued, "I'm sorry, Smiles, but a fire took the guest house and the storage shed. It's all gone. Why don't you get dressed and come downstairs. We'll be waiting for you".

A moment later, she was stumbling down the stairs. The smell had penetrated the house, so reality washed over her even before she opened the door to go outside. Her body was tense; her eyes were wild with fear and misunderstanding. She stepped outside and rushed to the edge of the porch. She freely allowed tears to roll down her cheeks. I grabbed her and held her as sobs wracked her body and strength left her soul. My heart was breaking for her so I just held her tighter and allowed her to bury her head against me. My plump body cushioned her muscular, trim form as she leaned into me for comfort.

My senses were alive and more sensitive than normal. I could hear our creek rushing past as if nothing unusual had occurred. The birds sang from their perches of the trees behind our home as they do every morning. The farm animals were anxious and confused as heard by their bleats and whinnies. Breakfast was late and their people were acting strange. They were feeling the effects of the thick; smoke filled air by coughing occasionally and drinking more than usual. The metallic, grittiness of soot was in my mouth as well.

I gazed out over the remains and noticed for the first time that the big twenty foot tall cottonwood tree that had shaded the garage and guest house had been burned from top to bottom on one complete side. Fear replaced the ache as I began to realize how close we had all come to death. Had the whole tree been destroyed, the garage too would have caught fire. Propane tanks, welding fuels, compressed oxygen, oils and paints, and miscellaneous farming mixtures stored in the garage would have exploded too easily and wiped everything out within a hundred yards- including the home where we had all been sleeping unaware.

Still holding Terena, I began to wonder how could this have happened without any one of us hearing it? Fires are noisy. The explosions of canisters and other flammable objects within the heart of the fire would have surely caught the attention of someone. Why didn't anyone drive by and see it? The neighbors, although a quarter mile away, didn't notice either. Our three dogs never alerted us to anything strange, nor did their sensitive noses or ears pick up any signs of danger throughout the night. Relief spread over me when I realized how blessed we were that the guests that had occupied the dwelling only a few nights before were safe, and far away from all this. I was still wondering how this happened. What started it?

Terena didn't step out of my arms until the sirens of the fire engine echoed through the valley. We watched as they rounded the curve before turning into our driveway. A little too slowly I thought, one truck holding four men came down the drive and ground to a halt. Their yellow jackets looked sleek and wet under the morning sun. Each assessed the situation and began their individual responsibilities. Terena sunk into one of the porch chairs and cried softly as she observed the dedicated men sift through her possessions and hose down the areas still smoking. I noticed that they where speaking in hushed tones as they surveyed the sight. Intrepidation began to overwhelm me, because I needed answers to my questions and wanted to put my concerns to rest. Approaching one of the men I asked, "Is my family safe? Can the propane tanks still blow? What should we do?" At first he laid my fears to rest with his confident, assuring answers, but when he finished with, "We've called an arson investigator, Ma'am," a whole new fear entered my heart. What would have caused someone to drive the long distance from town just to light a fire in a house that had nobody in it? What kind of whacko would do something like that?

I went back into the house just as the yellow school bus drove past. Was it only 7:00 am? I had been so preoccupied that I had forgotten to wakeup the children, but as I stepped into the dining room, I saw that Beth, my thirteen-year old daughter, had taken care of the other three. She hadn't always been so level headed, perceptive and caring, but this morning it was greatly appreciated. All four sat quietly eating cereal while eyeing me to see how I was reacting to the devastation. I knew that they must be scared, so I sat with them and assured them that their day would stay as normal as possible, and that dad would be driving them to school in a few minutes. I gave them each a big hug, and as I was wrapping my arms around Beth the investigator knocked on the door. We all jumped and the dogs excitedly announced his presence.

I opened the door to a young, friendly investigator. Our green eyes met for an instant and I could see his objective concern for our family. I led him into the living room. He asked for details out about the fire, and the whereabouts of every household member during the incineration. "May I question everyone privately?" he asked me. I escorted him to a quiet area and instructed one of the girls to join him for some questioning. I returned to the living room and sat down with Beth and the other two. It was then that I had a chance to think about the histories of the children in my care.

The two younger girls had no track record of fire obsession, nor did Beth or Terena. Damon, the only boy in my care at the time, did. When I realized this the hair on the back of my neck stood on end. He had proven capable of such destruction years before. Had our therapeutic environment and pro-active intervention been wasted? I quickly decided that seeing the fire truck and excitement of it all might feed his already excited emotional pathology, and might encourage the past to rear its ugly head once again.

In an attempt to distract him and keep him away from the hectic situation, I asked Damon to fold some laundry in my room downstairs. While he began his task, I walked into the master bathroom to freshen up and prepare for the day. I leaned against the washbasin and looked into the mirror. For a moment my mind hoped I was looking into a carnival mirror that makes your body seem exaggeratedly fat or thin. The pain of all the emotionally disturbed children who had come through my life was manifesting itself as insulation. Somewhere inside this body was a younger, thinner me, but this mirror wasn't going to reflect that image. My eyes were encircled with dark shadows and I looked so much older than my forty- three years. It didn't matter. My work helping kids and families was my passion and it seemed a fair trade.

I turned away from the mirror and took one last minute to wash my face, brush my teeth and pull my light brown hair into a bun. My family needed me. Damon seemed compliant enough to stay on task, so I left him and closed the door behind me. The locked gun cabinet behind the door, full of the hunting rifles and ammunition Jerry had inherited from his father, was the last thing on my mind.

While I was downstairs taking care of Damon, the investigator had finished talking with the first child so Beth sent the second in for questioning. Since the girls all seemed ready for school, I called out the door for Jerry, "Pa! When the investigator is finished, will you please take the girls to school? They are already so late, I think I'll keep Damon home today since he hasn't been in with the investigator yet." Jerry agreed and set out to start up the maroon Dodge Caravan. Having been preoccupied by the huge pile of ashes, he wasn't prepared for the damage he found when approaching the automobiles.

Jerry's blue Dodge pickup was parked about 15 feet from the fire and yet it had fire damage. My Caravan was parked closer at about 5 feet while Terena's Honda CRX was parked directly in front of the storage shed. Both were extensively damaged. The Honda was literally melted to the ground and had the most severe impairment. The firemen recommended not starting it, since the wiring was melted and could short out causing the gas tank to explode. It would have to be towed straight to the garage to see if anything could be salvaged. The Caravan's paint had bubbled and cracked so badly that the primer and metal was showing through. All the windows on the side of the fire had imploded and sprayed the entire van with splinters of glass. The metal frame holding the window in place had bowed and melted, making it sag about a foot. Jerry's pickup, although scarred, was the only drivable machine left. Being an engineer, he quickly assessed the situation and pulled the truck around the fire engine, up to the porch.

When he came inside his face was sallow, and his eyes even more tired than before. Not really wanting to hear more bad news I asked him if he was all right. "Babe, your van and Terena's car are both destroyed. My truck is drivable, but it will need a new paint job, new tires and all the light caps on the passenger side replaced. But that's not the worst of it." I braced myself for what could possibly be coming next, "Since we had just finished paying off both of our vehicles, I dropped the comprehensive coverage from our insurance a couple of months ago. Terena doesn't have comprehensive either so it looks like we'll all be saddled with car payments. We'll have to start all over again with different vehicles."

Everything began to feel surreal. The investigator asked for Beth, so I had the other two girls get their book bags and shoes on while I prepared sack lunches. I was as removed and distant as if this was happening to someone else, and I was just an observer. My senses became numb and my brain just stopped. The only thing I felt passionate about at that moment was getting back into bed, pulling the sheets over my head and sobbing. Had there not been so many people depending on me to hold it together, I would have acted upon that desire, but instead, I focused on the external situation and tuned out my feelings.

I walked both girls over to the fire scene and explained that the firemen were putting it out so there was nothing to worry about. I then gave them hugs, handed them their lunches and had them get into the truck. Beth followed suit shortly after and although her facial expression was asking me to let her stay, I simply gave her a hug and helped her into the truck. "I love you girls! Keep your heads up and your hearts soft. We'll be waiting here for all three of you when the bus brings you home. Try to have a good day." I wanted to say so much more but I couldn't muster up the strength for the pep talk that I knew all three needed.

Jerry pulled himself into the big Dodge Ram and waved goodbye to me as he pulled down the drive. I watched them until I couldn't any longer, not because I wanted to, but because I knew when I turned around, I would have to face the disaster. Worse yet, I would have to look into Terena's pain-filled eyes once again. I kept telling myself, "Keep it together, Nancy. Your family is depending on you. Pull your shoulders back, take a deep breath and lift your chin. You're not the only one going through this!"

I finally turned around to where Terena sat, staring vacantly at the now reduced version of her things. "Has anyone noticed if the cats are all okay, Mom?" she finally asked after not blinking for several minutes. She no longer cried, yet dried tears stained her face, her long beautiful eyelashes were matted together. Her eyes were swollen as she squinted against the bright Colorado sun. She hadn't moved until the investigator came out on the porch to talk to her. Startled back into reality, she tried straightening her hair and wiping the salt from her cheeks. They both stepped back into the house to finish the questioning.

I was alone for the first time since this happened and it stressed me further. I began second guessing myself. Was this ultimately my fault? Terena's stuff wouldn't be gone had I not encouraged her so hard to give up her apartment to come home for the summer. Is the arsonist still nearby watching his carnage? I walked inside and began busying myself with cleaning the kitchen, hoping the domestic work would quiet my mind.

Terena and the investigator joined me in the kitchen a few minutes later. He stated, "I interviewed your husband before coming to the door this morning, so I only need to talk to the boy now. What is his name and what is his relationship to you?" I replied, "I am a therapeutic Mom. That means that I stay home full time and devote my day to helping emotionally disturbed children heal. Damon is a twelve-year old child from Littleton, Colorado who is living with me. He has Reactive Attachment Disorder also known as RAD." He quickly jotted down the pertinent information before leaning forward with a quizzical expression. Seeing the typical confused look that people give me about this mental illness, I explained, "RAD is an emotional disturbance that makes it difficult or impossible for people to establish relationships. They typically have little or no empathy for other people or animals and often have delays in conscience development. Damon's been in and out of treatment for almost five years now. He recently had a major setback." I paused as he scribbled in his notebook. When he looked up again, he asked cautiously, "Is it okay if I talk to him?" I said, "Sure" and left to get Damon from downstairs.

It never entered my mind that any of us were suspects. I thought the investigator was looking for eye witnesses or evidence that the children may have seen or heard, but when he was through with Damon he called me over and said, "There are some things that aren't adding up with Damon's story. First of all, he said he awoke in the night and watched the flames from his window. When I asked why he didn't immediately go tell you, he stated he thought you had it under control and that the fire engines would be coming soon. The second area I'm concerned with is that Damon said he went back to sleep when the trucks didn't arrive." The wheels in my mind were spinning in high gear by this point.

I excused myself and quickly ran up the stairs to Damon's room. Pressing my head against the screen in Damon's window yielded a view of only half the driveway. The flames would have been hidden from his view. My heart sank as I realized he couldn't have seen the fire from there. He had lied.

I returned to the living room where the investigator sat making more notes. "I just went upstairs to Damon's room. No matter how far you push on the screen, you can't see where the fire was from his window." I told him. He looked back down at his notebook before commenting, "Let me make a quick call and I'll meet you at the social services office in Glenwood Springs. It will be easier there because an interrogator they employ is very good with kids. As soon as you have a vehicle, please make your way there." I felt defeated. I had to look at the facts, but in my heart I couldn't believe that Damon would do it or even could do it. I wanted to believe that he was innocent. I thought he had come so far and worked too hard to burn away his chances of a successful and happy future. I was afraid that it would be the final blow that would forever break my heart.

Terena came from the upstairs bathroom where she had finished freshening up. She said in a flat, emotionless voice, "I see the firemen are still here sifting through the ashes. I thought I'd start making myself useful and begin a list of everything I can remember that was lost." I asked her to come sit with me so I could help her begin the list. I couldn't tell her yet about the investigator's suspicions of Damon. It was still too difficult for me to think about, let alone verbalize. I thought it best to just let the investigator do his job before stirring up any unnecessary emotions in anyone. I was also praying that he was wrong.

We spent the next half hour making a list of everything that went up in smoke. Her new queen mattresses she hadn't even slept on yet, a Macintosh computer with all her school work, an immense collection of horse figurines from all over the world, photo albums with baby pictures that could never be replaced, spices, jewelry, her mementos from being rodeo queen and prom queen nominee, a mountain bike... We had over three pages before a knock at the door pulled us back to the present. Damon was there quietly reading while the dogs barked incessantly at the intruder wearing yellow. It was one of the firemen. The fire was fully extinguished and was no longer dangerous so their job was over and they were preparing to leave. Their kindness was greatly appreciated so I thanked them and walked them out to the truck.

Jerry was pulling into the driveway just as the firemen started up the engine. They patiently waited while he drove the tenth of a mile and stepped out. He walked over to the mighty truck and thanked the volunteers profusely for the couple of hours they devoted to helping us. They tipped their hats and drove away.

I quickly updated Jerry on the happenings of the last hour and requested that he drive Damon and me to the office. I asked Terena to stay home, to work on the list and await the school children, as I had no idea how long this would take. Damon walked to the truck as I watched in utter denial that this head full of auburn curls with a cute, helpful and lovable attitude could destroy so much so quickly. Before climbing into the truck he turned his sad green eyes to meet mine and I could feel his concern. This child was too caring and gentle to cause the turmoil of the morning, I thought to myself. I gave him a tired but reassuring smile before he broke his gaze with me.

The drive to Glenwood was a quiet and tense ride. Jerry tuned the radio to a local country station, but my nerves had become too raw to listen to its melody. I asked him to turn it off. As we neared the social services office my heart beat faster and my hands became clammy. I felt as if I were the one being interrogated. Damon and I got out of the truck and nervously waved goodbye to Jerry so he could search for a new car.

Once in the building, everyone introduced themselves before taking Damon to the interview room. I was escorted to a small adjoining room with a video monitor where I could watch the proceedings without actually being there. The room was restricting as it was a converted closet, but my heart was in my throat and I was already extremely uncomfortable. The size of the room was the least of my concerns.

I watched as Damon sat quietly, not willing to give the investigators the information they wanted. Frustrated, the interviewer came out of the room and said, "We're not getting anywhere in there." I offered to help and was instructed thoroughly not to put words into his mouth before being led into the room. I sat next to Damon and gently guided him over onto my lap so he was lying in my arms. With my face close to his I said softly, "Damon, if you did this you need to tell the truth. A bad secret will hurt you as long as it is locked in your heart. You need to be strong and let it go." I was so afraid that he might have done it that tears were streaming down my heart because they couldn't show on my face. I finished with, " You need to let it go Damon." His eyes locked onto mine as he calmly said, "Mom, I didn't do it. I'm so afraid they think I did and Terena will be mad at me. I don't want Terena to be mad at me." He stopped talking and let out a low sob. I hugged him and rocked him gently as the investigator interrupted, " I need to ask Damon a few more questions. Mrs. Thomas, would you please step outside?"

Because Damon was still refusing to admit to anything, the investigator finally gave up. "He's not talking and I can't see any good coming from us badgering him for more information. Maybe he didn't do it." I knew though, in my heart, he was guilty.

I nearly sank to the floor, unable to carry the burden of it all. I sat down and tried to concentrate on breathing. My whole body ached with pain. My head throbbed and my eyes stung with every blink. The lights seemed to shine more intensely and the air had become oppressive and unwilling to fill my lungs. My limbs had turned to stone as I sat there unable to move.

The investigator must have sensed how crushed I was so he brought me a cool glass of water. I wasn't sure I could swallow with the growing lump in my throat. "You can take Damon home now", he stated. I urged my eyes to look up, to focus on the man addressing me, still lost in knowing Damon was guilty. "I need to call his therapist and my agency.", I murmured almost inaudibly. Seeing how ashen my face had become, he followed with, "Mrs. Thomas, are you okay?"

I was losing Damon who had become like a son to me. My daughter was wounded. Tens of thousands of dollars of property was destroyed and I felt like a horrible mother. I couldn't tell this to this poor man only trying to do his job, so I looked to heaven. I prayed to God to fill me with the strength I needed to endure the rest of this awful day. Within minutes I had gathered my composure and found my second wind. "No sir, I'm not, but I have a lot to do", I replied to the investigator.

Through the phone calls I was instructed to get Damon to Denver as soon as possible so he could be closer to his therapist and his adoptive family. Maybe there he would be strong enough to tell the truth. Strength was something I didn't have at the moment and I was facing a one hundred seventy mile trip one way, and I had no car- yet.

Jerry picked us up a little after noon and informed me of some good news. "I found a car for you at the dealers. They are expecting you and will have the paper work ready". I sighed with relief, "Thank you, Pa.! Do you mind if I look around a tiny bit before you show me which car you think is best. We need a little fresh air and the walking will do us some good". We pulled onto the lot, I took Damon's hand and I began searching. In the row a few cars back I saw a, blue Toyota station wagon. "Pa, did you look at that one back there?" I asked. Jerry smiled his knowing grin and said, "That's the car I picked out for you, Babe! The paper work is ready, all you have to do is sign on the dotted lines and we'll be out of here in less than ten minutes." I love that cowboy!

Jerry was right. It was the most pain-filled, yet painless car buying experience of my life. I had Damon get in the new car and wait as I explained to Jerry that I had to drop him off with another therapeutic foster Mom, Lori, in Denver, and would be back later that night. I also asked him to overnight express a list of items Damon would need during his stay with Lori. We gave each other an extended embrace before I opened my car door and got behind the wheel. Jerry headed home to pick up the girls after school.

The three-hour drive was quiet. I was numb and worn out, tired and grieving, yet somehow I kept all four wheels on the road and arrived safely at the home of my good friend and co-worker, Lori. She met us in the driveway and hurried Damon into the house before he knew what was going on. I stood in her driveway, eyes drooping and spirits falling lower. She came back from the house and offered me some ice tea, which I gladly accepted. I wasn't thirsty, but I knew the caffeine would help for the long drive back over the Continental Divide. As I stood there, I started to break down. I knew I had to keep it together and get home. She empowered me with a love filled hug and turned away to deal with Damon.

As I drove west on Interstate 70, headed for home, my mind was overflowing with thoughts. Lori loved me so much that without any hesitation she had taken in Damon, the probable arsonist. She had just rebuilt her home from a devastating fire the previous year when faulty Christmas lights had created an inferno. I knew then that there was not a greater or more loving thing that she could have done, not only for me, but to help Damon as well. What a blessing she was!

Exhausted, I longed to crawl back into my bed beside my cowboy's warm body only to wake up to find that this had all been a nightmare. Instead, I thought for quite sometime as I drove. How had I become so burned out that it manifested as being burned up? When did this whole thing start? How had my destiny come to this?

Martha and I are looking at our new baby sister Maxine. Maxine, looking up at her big sister, Martha, is certainly not being greeted with smiles.

Chapter 2
The Early Days

The still, quiet air of Oklahoma was broken by my screams as I took my first breaths of air on December 30, 1951. I relaxed and smiled as I was placed in my mother's warm embrace. Mom gazed at me and lifted her weary head to address the nurse, "She just smiled at me!" The nurse coldly replied, "It must be gas pains." The nurse came closer and pulled me out of my Mother's arms. My mother never forgot those cutting words.

I learned a lot from my mother while growing up. She was classically beautiful, and although she cared about us children, she spent much of her time keeping up her appearance and watching her TV shows devotedly. My mother's dark hair framed her eyes that reflected the color of the summer sky; always staying blue but regularly changing in hue depending on her mood.

Her constant obsession with physical appearance often left us children feeling sad or rejected. I quickly internalized that caring for yourself so fully left others feeling neglected. In my young, malleable brain, I learned that superficial beauty got in the way of what was really important. Parenting was one such important priority that was nearly excluded.

My Mom's standard parenting response to my challenges to her authority was, "Wait until your father gets home". His response was regularly an angry, " Woman, can't you control these kids?!", which entered my ears as, "You can't control these kids!" I began to believe it. I had to test her to see if it was true. Was I so powerful as a little girl? When she would attempt to discipline us, she would wait until her emotions were so extreme that her patience would be gone and her actions illogical.

Being the strong-willed middle child, I was constantly looking for leadership. Because Mom was naturally meek and believed she had a learning disorder, her self-image was never strong enough for her to have the confidence to establish authority. The safety of clearly set limits, which I craved, was not available from her. My mom was reluctant to make decisions; I on the other hand was overly decisive and impulsive.

In yet another act of defiance when I was nine years old, I stuck my tongue out at my mother. I was fighting with my sisters and she demanded I stop. In my usual manner, I gave her sass. She straightened up and squinted her eyes with a stern and proper, "Don't you talk to me like that, young lady. I'm your Mother and I said stop!" In my usual rebellious manner, I stuck out my tongue. Out of nowhere, her hand stung my face and my jaw clamped down on my protruding tongue. I stood there in disbelief of what she had done, stunned so thoroughly that I simply allowed the blood to run down my face to drip on the floor. Our relationship was never the same after that, because I saw the expression of victory come over her at finally being able to get my attention.

Arguing was so commonplace in my family that I learned to love fighting. The adrenaline rush and excitement filled the air and fed our hearts that yearned for communication and touch. My sisters and I would spend hours scratching and biting and pulling each other's hair; sharp words accompanied every battle. As I grew older and began parenting tough children, instead of fighting with them, I fought for them.

I also learned to have high tolerance and more patience because my Mom had little of both. While living in Tucson during my preadolescence, I remember locking myself in the attached laundry room when Mom tried to confront me. There I made faces and ridiculed her. Out of desperation and exhaustion she grabbed a nearby broom and bashed it through the glass window. Stunned and covered in glass, I looked out at my Mom. She dumbfoundedly looked at me and shrieked, "Now look what you made me do!", before she ran back into the house, sobbing. I stood there in bewilderment as I pondered the amount of power I must have to make an adult do something as radical as that. I realized I would never want to feel so powerless or intolerant, and I decided then that I would develop my patience and tolerance unlike my poor mother.

She would threaten us daily with spankings. Because she seldom followed through with any of the warnings, I saw her as a liar. Her core being was honest, but as a child viewing the world as I did, her empty threats were far from truthful which encouraged me to view her as weak. Looking back on my childhood as a young adult, I gained insight as to how vital honesty was in parenting children. I had learned how essential follow through was in building trust.

My Father, Maximilian, didn't threaten us. He was a man of action. As a test pilot in the Air Force he worked long hours and was gone from home quite often. He commanded respect, not only because he was a military officer, but also because he was a leader and a hard worker. As a powerful six foot two, muscular blonde, he dominated any room he stepped into. I adored him. He showed me how important feeling special was in the eyes of a developing child.

As an expert pilot, he was a flight instructor for people all over the world. At the end of each training he would host a dinner party at our home where my sisters and I were expected to be on our best behavior. Our 1950's style party dresses fascinated us. The layers and layers of lacy petticoats filled the skirts and made us feel like ballerinas. Our freshly polished black and white saddle shoes reflected the patio lights decorating each party. Dad's enormous chest, covered with military awards, would swell with pride as he would introduce each of us. "This is Martha, my oldest daughter. She's the brains of the family," He would step over to where I was standing, his hazel eyes twinkling and announce to all, "This is Nancy with the laughing face. She never walks, she always runs." My eyes would light up each time he would introduce me and I became more determined to keep smiling and moving quickly to always stay special in his eyes. He finished with, " And this is

Maxine. She's the beauty of the family." We each felt special by his introduction.

He was a brave man. Flying a B-52 in World War II, he landed each run with a full crew. His plane, the Anita Marie, had to be retired after he safely brought it back from a mission. It had been riddled with over six hundred holes from the Nazi bullets in his final flight. The pain from the war stayed with him, even after it was long over.

When he came home from work, he would be wearing his flight uniform. It left a contrail of jet fumes lingering wherever he went, which was usually first to the fridge for a cold beer. Dad would start each evening, after changing, with a bottle of Bourbon next to his place at the head of the table. I didn't realize that alcoholism was something I should have been ashamed of. I thought every father came home from work and kept his glass filled with the burning liquid, repeating the same war stories night after night. Knowing what I do now, I realize that drinking was his way of handling the echoing pain of the war.

As much as my father loved me, he too added to the stress and learning of my childhood. I had long, thin arms and legs that never seemed to move where I wanted, so there were many times when I would trip or fall or knock something over. One night while we were all sitting at the table, my gangly elbow bumped my half full glass and sent it tumbling. Sitting to the right of my father, he easily reached over and backhanded me in the chest and arm. "Watch what you're doing Nancy", he said as I began wailing in astonishment. I cleaned it up slowly vowing to try harder next time.

The next night, I concentrated being careful as we sat around the table eating. Again, I bumped my milk and watched in horror as it spilled across the table. Wham!!! I was smacked, again. I cleaned it up, watching the milk swirl with my tears.

The more Dad smacked me, the more I tried not to knock my cup over. The harder I tried, the more I spilled and the more I spilled the more Dad hit. I was caught in this vicious cycle that didn't make any sense. I actively decided after the fifth or sixth time of trying to wipe up the mess, that instead of hitting my kids when they spilled I would just teach them how to clean it up and go on with dinner. I truly was going to teach my kids they didn't have to cry over spilled milk.

I also knew that when I got older, I didn't want a relationship like my Mom and Dad had. For the first six years of their marriage they were like honeymooners. Then my older sister Martha was born and the spell was broken. The rest of the time they fought and argued. He regularly would say to her, "Anita, you're fat, sloppy and lazy!" The covert message to me was that I needed to be thin, organized and hard working in order to be worth loving.

Martha was the first-born, and became Mom's favorite. She suffered from Bipolar Disorder that went undiagnosed and untreated. She overreacted to most things and was nonsensical at the height of her episodes. To appease and help her to settle, my mother constantly took her to the movies, shopping and traveling without the rest of the family. Mother and Martha were the best of friends, which created a lot of resentment from myself and Maxine, my younger sister. In retrospect, I can see that their relationship emotionally crippled my oldest sister by enabling her to avoid uncomfortable, yet important learning opportunities in social situations.

Martha was extremely intelligent. She was treasured and loved by my Mother and yet, she wasn't protected against mental illness. She was honest and gentle hearted but the mood swings would overtake her personality and consume her rationality. I learned to love and accept her the way she is. She is my sister and she is wounded and suffering with this invisible affliction.

I've now seen others with Manic Depression (or what is now called Bipolar Disorder) treated so successfully with medication and therapy that those afflicted with it now have a happy, full and stable life. My dream for Martha is for her to someday have a life so filled with love and laughter that it will heal all the pain and loneliness of her past. She has a bright mind and good heart. I believe in her.

During our childhood, while Mom and my older sister were out, I stayed with my younger sister, Maxine. She was beautiful and sensitive. We shared laughter and bickering, fights and hide-and-seek; she was one of my best friends growing up. Being a child is difficult anyway, but poor Maxine suffered from Tourette's Syndrome. The disease wracked her whole being with occasional full body tics that isolated her from the rest of her peers. It was so severe that her teachers seated her at the back of the class and placed a screen around her. She felt crazy, dumb and alone.

She was in her late thirties before I learned about the disorder in a workshop. The presenter was explaining about the difficulties of living with such involuntary muscle movements and the more she discussed it, the more I realized she was describing my little sister. I was so energized by finding a reason for Maxine's odd behavior that I immediately left the room to call her. It was such a revelation that tears flowed from my eyes as I hurriedly dialed the pay phone. When I heard the voice of my little sister I excitedly said, "Maxine! You're not crazy!" There was a pause on the other end of the line before she replied, "I'm not crazy?!" I quickly told her that Tourette's was a genetic disorder characterized by body tics. "All those exaggerated blinks, the bending over to pull up your socks every few steps and the sideways jaw movement that pulled even your nose to the side. It's all a characteristic of this disorder!" She was quietly crying with relief when she replied, "There must be others like me. Where can I learn more, 'Nance'?" I gave her the number to the Tourette's Syndrome Association, told her I loved her and hung up the phone to hurry back to the workshop to learn more.

A few weeks later she called me up and enthusiastically exclaimed, "Not only am I not crazy, but I'm not suicidal either!" Confused, I waited. She continued, "I just received a newsletter from the association and it covers mental tics." I was still baffled so I blurted, "I didn't know you wanted to die!" She spoke so quickly; I had to think fast to take in all she was saying,

"Whenever I leave my husband or children I always hug them goodbye, thinking I would never see them again. I start driving and my brain repeats 'drive off the road. Drive off the road'. I don't want to die by going off the road! It is hard work to stay focused and I have always thought it was crazy. But I am not crazy! It is a mental tic, 'Nance'! It's a repetitive thought that you can't control or stop!" I was so happy for her that she was finally able to understand what went on in her own head. We were learning about Tourette's Syndrome together and the more I learned, I realized I had it too!

Her self-image was finally able to repair itself from all the damage done to it during her childhood and adolescence. The waitressing job she had held for over fifteen years at a wonderful Mexican restaurant didn't seem to fulfill her anymore, so with the recommendation and encouragement of her daughter, she applied at a fortune 500 company. They looked at her work ethic. They recognized her loyalty. Her intelligence was obvious during the interview and they hired her immediately.

Through our childhood, I had watched Maxine being teased, tormented and rejected. She was a great friend, yet other's viewed her as strange due to her tics. She was a tortured child but now she has blossomed into an awesome woman, great friend and exceptional mother! I am so proud of my baby sister! Watching her struggle taught me to be understanding and empathetic towards other's pain, especially the hidden pain of an emotional disturbance.

That understanding was compounded by the insight I received from my soft, floppy eared, sable colored mutt known as Princess. The shoulder I cried on was hers, and her warm hair and wet kisses comforted me when nothing else in my life was tender or sympathetic. I would spend hours telling her my secrets. She was my confidant. She never repeated one to another soul- not one! Princess was never too busy for me. Her unconditional loving heart was powerful enough to love me even though I was clumsy and made mistakes. Never once did she get angry if I spilled the milk and would even willingly help me clean it up. Her wagging tail always reassured me. The moments spent with her were the most peaceful of any in my childhood.

When I was five years old I thought I was a brilliant dog trainer. The training was only brilliant because Princess nearly read my mind. We often won local pet shows because she knew so many tricks. My early experiences with that sweet, forgiving and intelligent dog helped me to later grow into a successful dog trainer and dog enthusiast. She was with me and loved me throughout all of my elementary and high school years.

Princess would always lie at my feet as I completed my homework. I enjoyed school. Sometimes, the teachers would ask each of us girls what we wanted to be when we grew up. My ambition had always been to be a mom. When it was my turn to answer the question of what career I wanted to have, I felt ashamed to admit that I wanted *only* to become a mother. To avoid humiliation in front of my classmates, I would quickly and enthusiastically reply, "I want to be a baby factory!!" The class would break out in laughter and the subject would be dropped. I learned then that humor was a quick and easy way to skirt issues that were too painful or embarrassing for me to address.

I wanted a child so badly that often on Sunday, when I would go to church, I would press my little hands together as tightly as possible before praying to God to send me a baby girl. At 5 and 6 years old I had no idea where babies came from, so I thought that the more firmly I squeezed my hands the more serious the request would become. Each Sunday night I would sleep very still so that if God granted my wish, I would not disturb the baby that He would lay next to me while I slept. Monday morning would come and with it came my deepening sorrow that I must not have prayed hard enough, because there would be no baby for me to love.

Throughout my elementary school years, Dad's career caused us to move often. The only place where I felt truly at home was in the desert of Tucson, Arizona. I reveled in the sunshine. Its warmth soaked through my bones and sunk deep into my soul. I spent thousands of hours hiking and exploring the hidden treasures the desert held in order to escape the chaos of my home.

Hawks, snakes, tarantulas, cottontail bunnies and javelinas inhabited the desert near our home. While exploring the contours of the land I would sometimes come across injured or orphaned creatures so I would carefully bring each one back to my home where I would tend to their needs. They stayed in my care until they were strong enough to be freed. It was a great outlet for my need to nurture.

The animals allowed me to learn that I was lovable and capable of returning such love, so when Steve entered my life as a freshman in high school, my heart was ready. It was his Mom and Dad that showed me how a loving relationship was supposed to work. They kissed and hugged and laughed and helped each other. Even though they had been married for twenty years she still sat on his lap and made him giggle. I thought of one time in particular that I went to their home to visit. She greeted me with her usual warm, cheerful hug and asked if I'd like to see the pies she was making for the church bake sale. I followed her into the kitchen where I saw the entire table covered with pies! I gazed in amazement at her and the kitchen. Her hair was perfect. There was no flour on her face. The stylish outfit she wore had no evidence of baking. The kitchen was spotless and she was just beginning to put the pies into the oven to bake. She was beautiful, talented and organized.

Who was I to believe I could come close to such perfection? I loved him, but I knew with my upbringing that I could never even come close to being the phenomenal woman that she was. I told him yes, when he asked me to marry him when we were seniors but in my heart I believed I could never make him happy. If I had known what fate held for me around the next corner, I would have jumped at the chance to marry such a wonderful man. But I didn't.

A drawing I did of Butch participating in his favorite hobby.
He signed it.

Chapter 3
Duck and Cover

It was a wonderfully hot summer after I graduated from high school with the class of 1969. Steve and I spent much time together as we knew that once summer was over we'd both be headed off to different colleges. August was a hard month for both of us; we knew it would be the last time our lives would ever be so connected. Packing up my things, I reflected on the wonderful memories we had created over the last four years. I thought I had matured so much. My understanding of what life could offer was much deeper after having known him and his family. It was a bittersweet time with endings and new beginnings.

Dad helped me load my things into his sedan as I prepared to depart for college. Soon we were on the road to new horizons. The dorm building looked ominous and uninviting thus I hoped the inside was more friendly. My room was on the second floor giving it a nice view of the mountains. Dad helped me bring up my stuff, gave me a reassuring hug, some words of encouragement and left. I was alone with four big boxes waiting to be unpacked and my classes ready to begin.

The semester was zipping by and before I realized it, Homecoming was a week away. Steve was supposed to drive the five hours from Denver to take me to the dance and I was looking forward to seeing him. My bubble of excitement quickly burst when he called to say he couldn't make it. Already in a slump, Dad called an hour later to inform me that his mother had passed away. I loved my grandmother very much and the news struck a blow deep into my already fragile psyche. I went to class the following day, but my mind was still mourning.

Later that same day, Mom called and told me Princess had joined Grandma in heaven. I hadn't even finished hanging up the phone when I collapsed in a chair and sobbed. Steve wasn't coming and I'd never see Grandma again. These things really hurt, and losing my beloved dog, Princess, was the final blow.

Stumbling back up to my room, I just got into bed and didn't move until a soft knock at the door awoke me. Whoever it was knocked again, louder. I hid deeper under the covers. "Nance! Can we come in? We're worried about you!" said the voice behind the door. Silence. The door slowly opened and I heard several sets of feet shuffle in. "Please, Nance. Come out from under there," they pleaded. "We brought you some dinner and we have a special treat for you". I slowly came out of hiding. The smell of spaghetti filled the room, which made my mouth water, and I quickly gobbled down the sustenance. "Thank you" I quietly said. Two girls left while two stayed with me. "Let's fix your hair and do your nails. Maybe if you look better, you'll feel better", encouraged my friend. I didn't balk, so they looked pleased.

Two hours later, my hair was ratted, teased and sprayed into the popular flip hairdo of the sixties. My nails were buffed and polished and from somewhere my cutest outfit appeared. "Put a little make-up on and get dressed, Nance." With that, they all left the room.

As I pulled on my suede coat, the girls came back in. "You look too good to stay hidden up here, so we've invited some guys from the next dorm to come play cards with us. Let's go!" With one on each side of me, our arms linked, we went downstairs to the lobby where the tables, couches and chairs were. The guys were already there.

I started feeling better as we played cards. The laughter and companionship did me good. Knowing that I had such compassionate, caring new friends lifted my heart and helped me feel more optimistic as the hours passed. Butch, the handsome student across the table had flirted with me and was now asking me if I would join him for a walk. Hesitating briefly, I accepted.

We talked and laughed while walking around the campus. The moonlight made his dark hair appear blue while making deep shadows across his handsome face. He was twenty years old and had already been in the Vietnam War. When I asked him more about it, he painted a picture of himself as an injured war hero that had shown bravery in battle. He was a veteran just like my dad. As we neared the double doors leading into the lobby of the girls dorm, he turned to me and said, "You are perfect, Nancy! I have been looking for you all my life. You are going to marry me, you know." I informed him that I was already engaged to someone else, but was flattered by his attention. He winked at me and said, "I will have you as my wife!", and with that, he kissed my hand, opened the door for me and said good night.

Walking back to my room, I did indeed feel flattered. His approach was a bit strong, but his powerful, decisive manner was appealing to me in my loneliness. He was direct, strong, brave and willing to die for his country. That night, although still grieving, I went to bed with lighter spirits.

The next night we all met downstairs to play cards again. Butch sat next to me this time. His mustache tickled the sensitive lobes of my ear whenever he leaned over to whisper sweet things to me. Looking into his big, brown, sad eyes I would politely smile and say thank you, the whole time eating up his affection. He again asked if I wanted to go for a walk. I agreed and out the door we went. "I have something to show you", he said to me as we were leaving the building. I was curious as he reached into his pocket for a strange shaped box. Opening it he said, "These are my war medals. This one is a purple heart since I was injured and this one is a bronze star for killing the enemy." I looked with respect and awe as he held the box open for me. I admired his military background and these awards simply proved he must be a good, honorable man. On our way back to the dorm he again said, "You are perfect for me, Nancy. You will marry me, I'm sure of it!" Opening the door for me like a real gentleman, the words sunk into my soul a little deeper this time.

The Homecoming dance was two days away and I decided to go with my girlfriends since Steve would be unable to join me. Butch called and we talked a few times over the phone, as I was too busy getting caught up on schoolwork to go out. I received a love letter from him posted to my door after class. Upon opening it, fresh rose pedals tumbled to the ground, filling the room with the sweet smell of love. I read each word, wondering if this man was for real.

Saturday arrived and along with it came the frenzy for the upcoming dance. My girlfriends and I spent the whole afternoon preparing with facial masks and bubble baths. Make-up was spread from one end of the shared bathroom to the other and laughter echoed from the tiles as we tried different looks on each other. The co-mingling of perfume was so thick that at the end of the preparations, when I inhaled, I choked on the taste left behind in my mouth.

One last look in the mirror and I knew I was ready to go. The music was making my legs move to the beat even before I entered the big dance hall. Once there, I nearly ran to the open floor to set my body free to the beat of the music. Not long after I got there, Butch arrived and danced with me the whole evening. Any other guy that got near me was glared away by him; I felt so special and desired.

After the dance he walked me back to my dorm and asked how I liked his letter. I beamed at him, took his hand and said, "It was the sweetest thing! Thank you!" We held hands for the rest of the walk and I knew I would have to end it with Steve. As if reading my mind, Butch said matter of factly, "I'm going to marry you. You need to break up with that other guy."

I got back to my room and thought about what I had to do. Calling Steve the next morning, to tell him that we were over, would be difficult for me. I dreaded it! Remembering all our wonderful times, I cried as I fell asleep.

Dialing his number the next morning, I was still crying. He answered and I told him I was lonely. I told him that he was very special to me but I needed more than what I was getting. I told him I would always love him and that I didn't believe I could make him happy. I told him everything. Crying together, we hung up. I knew I had just broken his gentle heart.

I married Butch the day after my eighteenth birthday. We had dated for four wonderful, fun filled months. It was a beautiful ceremony with five brides maids and a custom made wedding dress. My father was handsome and proud of me as he walked me down the aisle. Butch looked sharp in his tuxedo; his bronze Cherokee skin was in stark contrast to his white collar. His thick, straight French Canadian hair was combed to perfection. He was so handsome that I began to doubt whether I could keep him happy. Shoving these premonitions from my mind, I happily said, "I do" and took his hand in marriage.

He became drunk at the reception and I drove us back to our tiny apartment in Denver. We were on a limited budget as we were both still students so we didn't splurge on a honeymoon.

The first dinner I prepared for him was chicken Parmesan with marinara and angel hair pasta. It smelled wonderful. I wanted it to be special. While setting the table with everything just right, I hummed happily. "Butch, dinner is ready. Please come sit down to eat!", I cheerfully said. He got up from the recliner where he was watching the Broncos play football and sauntered over to the table. Scratching his belly and yawning, he pulled out his chair to sit down. I placed his meal in front of him proudly and sat down in front of mine. As I bowed my head in prayer, Butch rudely demanded to know where the salt and pepper was. Without even pausing long enough for me to answer, my beautiful meal was thrown across the kitchen. Wham! The plate shattered as it hit the wall and the red spaghetti sauce oozed down leaving streaks. I turned to look at him and before having a chance to even focus; I felt the sharp sting of his hand across my face. "Don't ever have me come to the table when it's not all ready!", he growled. Stunned, I watched as he strolled back into the living room to watch the rest of the game. I choked back tears as I numbly got up for ice.

Making a cold compress for my lip I soothed my swelling mouth as I thought about what had just happened. I should have walked out right then, but I was not a quitter so I made up my mind to help him to see how much I loved him so he would be more patient with my mistakes. I lifted my eyes and silently asked God to tell me what lessons this attack held and to please help me be a better wife. Afterward I started cleaning up the tomato sauce from the wall. Little did I know that the red juices were a mere prelude of what was to come.

Butch never could hold down a job. He worked as a hospital orderly on and off or as a delivery boy for local businesses. After a week or two at each job he would just stop showing up. Instead of working he would hangout with his friends doing any drugs they could get their hands on or he would over sleep and then decide not to go at all. Knowing that we needed the money, I would try to wake him. He would get angry when I disturbed his rest, so I quickly learned to leave him alone and make do with what little we had.

As it is with abusive relationships, Butch began to close in the walls around me. I was forbidden to leave the house if he wasn't at my side. I wasn't allowed to even attend church on Sunday. Seeing my friends was strictly off limits and getting a job meant that I was beyond his grasp of influence. It wasn't an option. I was only allowed to visit my parents if he joined me. He told me, "I don't want you to go out because some one might steal you away. You're too special!" I wanted to please him, and not realizing that he was gradually taking more and more control of me I complied without reserve.

Since I wasn't allowed to get a job, he was in charge of paying the bills. I found out he was neglecting our financial obligations when we received an eviction notice a couple of months later and the shelves in the kitchen became bare.

To make matters worse, I became pregnant within the second month of our marriage. I was highly affected by morning sickness and I vomited the whole time we searched for a place to live. Butch had relatives in Wichita, Kansas so we drove there to stay with them while my husband tried finding a job. Janice and Frank's house was posh and immaculate, so when I learned she had a daycare there, I was surprised.

The next morning I watched as she repeatedly opened the door with a warm cheery smile, chit chatting with each parent while taking into her manicured grasp the tiny hand of each child. Saying goodbye she closed the door and immediately whisked the child away to the basement where they were expected to watch television all day. Before the children went home in the evening, she went down the stairs with juicy popsicles and played with them briefly to get them smiling. Minutes later, their parents' would come to pick up their happy, smiling children unaware they had been basically left alone all day.

Here was a middle class, clean-cut home with people that seemed warm and friendly, yet the children were neglected and left to fend for themselves. It was this experience that made me decide I would never place my children into the care of a baby sitter. I made the extreme decision that I would rather give them up for adoption than hand them over to strangers to raise them all day.

Butch couldn't find a job there so we drove back to Denver. It was a long drive and I was still very sick. I called Dad and told him of our problems with finding a place to live. He offered to cosign on a loan for a trailer home so I moved our possessions into our new house trailer the following week. I was the only one packing and hauling boxes because Butch was useless. He had received some heroin from some friends in Vietnam and it was one of the few times he was wonderfully mellow and sweet.

Sex was always an obsession for Butch, but I was grossed out to learn that he regularly attended XXX rated porno films. After one such movie, he came home and excitedly told me he had something to show me. Taking me by the hand, he led me into the bathroom saying, "This is a new thing I learned about, it's supposed to get you horny. Take your clothes off." Not sure what he was going to do, I slowly got undressed. He instructed me to lie on the floor where he proceeded to urinate all across my body. I lay there, appalled and disgusted! I thought to myself, how could anyone find this a turn on?! He interrupted my thoughts with, "It's called a golden shower. Do you like it?" Like it? I couldn't even validate what he had just done with an answer. I felt demoralized and lower than nothing. As he walked away leaving me on the floor dripping, I rolled over and rushed to the shower.

The hot water could wash the stench off my skin, but no matter how hard I scrubbed I felt dirty and repulsive. I felt like I must have done something really unjust for God to punish me like that. Maybe it was because of my arrogant attitude with my mother that I was now being taught humility. Is that what I was supposed to learn from this? I got down and cleaned up his urine that was now spread throughout the bathroom. That night I prayed harder than ever for God to help me. "Please God, let him start treating me better." On my knees with my hands together in prayer talking to my heavenly father I still felt filthy on the inside for what I had allowed him to do.

❧❀❧ ❧❀❧ ❧❀❧ ❧❀❧

As our marriage aged, the level of abuse he inflicted on me escalated. I soon learned what truly happened in the war after one evening he was choking me while screaming, "I have to kill you, you fucking 'Gook'!" Sitting on the couch in our trailer Butch told me how he had been high on pot, cocaine and acid for the majority of his time there. During a night air raid, the alert sirens were confusing his stoned mind so he left his bunker while wearing nothing but his boxer shorts. Stumbling around in the smoke filled dark, he fell head first into a foxhole. Landing right next to a Colonel in combat attire, he felt safe and serene thus he relaxed back into his drug induced high. Moments later, with his legs still high in the air, a mortar landed next to the officer, which blew his flesh all over Butch's mostly naked body. His legs were injured with shrapnel from the blast, which explained the Purple Heart he received upon reaching American soil. The image I had of him as a brave soldier and courageous war hero was being chipped away with each word he shared with me.

The bronze star was for bravery in battle. My heart rose a little with hope at the prospect of him truly doing something brave. I leaned forward earnestly waiting for this tale of fortitude. He had told me while at Adam's State College he had earned the honorary medal for killing enemy soldiers to save his fellow men. I was now learning he had embellished that story immensely. Grimly, I listened while the war hero in my mind was being whittled down to nothing but a peon. "I had swallowed a mescaline tab as we walked through an open field. Hallucinating, I began dancing about wildly. I stepped out of line and fell into an enemy rat hole. When my eyes focused in the dark, I saw three 'Gooks' staring, confused, back at me. It was either kill or be killed, so I lifted my rifle and sprayed the whole dugout with bullets. I felt like G. I. Joe. Popping my head back out of the hole, my buddies whooped and hollered cheering for me at my victory. I shot more bullets into the air and felt bigger than life." As he told the tale, I could see his eyes turn black with pride at killing the unsuspecting Viet Cong. He then admitted that he had been discharged from the army after spending many months in the Army psychiatric ward without much improvement.

I forgave him for choking me and leaving huge bruises around my neck because I felt he couldn't help it with the trauma of the war. I held him close and did all I could to soothe him. I now understood his frequent nightmares. I naively believed that since he had talked to me about it, he had healed from the experience and would not need to reenact it again.

I was often sad while pregnant because Butch was so cutting and cruel. I was alone and isolated from the world. We couldn't afford a phone. To fill the otherwise empty days, I would sometimes sit and gaze at a beautiful statue we had received as a wedding gift. It was Saint Michael the Archangel. He stood tall and proud with his wings open and a sword in one hand, a chain in the other. His foot was on the head of a reptilian looking Satan. He was athletic with lean, trim muscles and I would look at him hopefully and wish that my baby would grow up to be valiant and strong like him. I dreamed that he would have the same washboard stomach and muscular body.

Butch's parents, Gilbert and Neva, were living in a motel room while their plumbing was being repaired. We went to visit them periodically because they usually fed us and Butch could steal money from his father's wallet and drink free beer. I didn't like the way he treated them, but our budget was getting tighter and tighter so I was left without food more often. I ate the meals gratefully, knowing I was eating for two.

One afternoon, after we had finished eating, Butch and his father were headed to the dog races to gamble. He insisted I stay behind in the motel with his drunken mother. She was slurring her words and leaning out of the chair precariously. I pleaded with him to take me along because I didn't want to stay in the dirty, smoke filled room with a woman on the verge of passing out. He harshly said, "No, hippo! You're staying here with my mother!" Angry and empowered with his parents there, I stood my ground. "Butch, please take me with you!" I said in a strong, clear voice. He turned, backhanded me and bitterly said, "Look wench, I told you you're staying here, and so that's what you'll do!" Confidently, I looked him straight in the eye and slapped him back. "Get in the car. NOW!", he seethed. Thinking I had won, I wobbled to the car in my bare feet, careful to avoid the broken glass in the parking lot. An instant later he joined me in the car and we drove away leaving both his parents.

Stopping a few blocks away, at an open field, he left the car running with the radio on. Ike and Tina Turner were singing the duet 'I Want to Take you Higher'. Opening my door, he grabbed me by the hair and dragged me into the field. My screams mingled with the music playing in the car. "Hey, hey, hey, hey the beat is getting stronger.", they sang. He dropped my heavy body into the cold snow. "Beat is getting longer, too. Music soundin' good to me." I felt both fists pounding into my body. Hostility emanating from his icy glare. "I wanna, I wanna, take you higher. Let me take you higher." He kicked ferociously into my belly. "Baby, baby, let me light your fire. Oh yeah, little bit, higher. Ooohhh." His kicks and punches were hard and repetitive hitting my face, shoulders, legs... whatever they could. I curled into the fetal position to protect my innocent baby from his possessed rage. Blood stained the white snow. "Boom shaka laka laka. Boom shaka laka laka. Boom boom!" Guarding my unborn baby as best I could, he continued to punch and kick until he was close to exhaustion. I couldn't feel anything anymore. "Hey! Hey! Hey! Hey!", Tina and Ike sang. Butch stood over my beaten body and wiped the slobber from his mouth with the back of his hand. He barked, "Don't ever embarrass me in front of my family again you God damn bitch!" I closed my eyes as he gave me one last emphatic kick. "Beat is gonna get ya!", was the last phrase from the song that rang in my ears as I heard the car door close and away he went.

I laid in the snow, feeling the pain wash over me. I felt guilty that I had brought such a beating onto myself by hitting him. I was afraid he was going to kill me the next time. I was trapped. I had no money, no skills. I believed I was huge and sick, ugly and stupid and I had nowhere to go. Looking down at my unborn child, I whispered, "Poor baby! I'm so sorry I did this to you. I'm so sorry." With that I started sobbing, still holding my protruding stomach with both hands. I knew I could take the abuse, but my tiny infant could not. Rocking myself and sobbing, I sat in the snow for a long while thinking how I could be a better wife to avoid this kind of thing once the baby was in our life. Knowing I had to walk back to the motel before it was dark, I made a snowball and began washing the blood from my face and body. I didn't bother going back to where his mother was and instead hobbled the three miles home.

All my bruises couldn't be hidden this time, so for the next week, I stayed inside. I was ashamed of the way I looked. I didn't want anyone to know. I forced the memories to the back of my mind and when they came forward I had to make each incident smaller to be able to tolerate staying there. I was trapped. I did everything I could to keep from provoking him again.

>✸< >✸< >✸< >✸<

I was four weeks past my due date, when I felt the first twinge of a contraction. After a thirty-seven hour labor my son, R.B. was born. On November 9, 1970 they held him upside down by his slippery calf and showed my newborn to me. I tried counting his fingers and toes, but the glimpse I got of him wasn't long enough so I took the doctor's word that they were all there. I was ecstatic at knowing he was a healthy baby boy. Then they whisked him away.

I waited in the hospital room for them to bring my son for what seemed like hours and hours. I waited patiently at first. The longer I sat in the sterile bed, the more agitated I became. Out of desperation, I finally rang the nurse's buzzer. "Excuse me, ma'am. I haven't seen my newborn son yet and he was born hours ago! May I see him?" I asked, trying to sound calm. She curtly retorted, "No, it's hospital policy to feed the babies a bottle of glucose water before allowing the mother to see them." Worn thin, tired and exhausted I sadly said, " But I'm going to be breast feeding him! " She replied, "It is hospital policy". I replied through clenched teeth "If you don't bring my baby to me right now, I'll start screaming like you've never heard before!" She ran out of the room. A few minutes later an orderly brought in a rocking chair and behind him was the nurse holding a tiny bundle. "This is your son, ma'am," she said. Sitting next to my bed, she rocked him in the chair and fed him the sweetened water mixture. I yearned to hold him. When she finished and he was sleeping she gently placed him in my arms. I looked at his long silky black hair and tiny fingernails. "So these are what you used to carve your initials in my womb, huh R.B.?" I rubbed noses with him and smiled at how beautiful he was. I played with his long hair, funny sideburns and gently stroked his soft skin. There were big swollen, purple bruises on each side of his head where forceps had been clamped about his skull and seeing these made me sad. R.B.'s hunger was satiated so he lay, peacefully sleeping in my arms. Having not slept for two full days, I too was beginning to nod off. The nurse gently pulled his drowsy form from my arms and left to put him in the nursery.

The next morning I waited for my son to join me for breakfast. When he didn't show, I buzzed the nurse again. "My son must be hungry. When can I nurse him?", I asked frustrated. "Your son sucked fluid into his lungs while in the birth canal yesterday. He has pneumonia now and will have to stay here," she said nonchalantly. Lowering my eyes, I swallowed the impending tears away. "The good news is, you can go home today!", she said trying to cheer me up. I only felt worse! I was supposed to leave my baby there and go home with empty arms!

Upon my return home, I found that the guy who was supposed to care for my dog, Moaf, had never come by. It didn't surprise me that Butch hadn't cared for him either. Three days he'd been locked in the house without any food or anyone to let him outside. Trash was strewn throughout the house and he had eliminated in various places. I passed the baby nursery as I picked up the trash and held in a sob that threatened to escape my lips. I tried to busy myself with scrubbing the floor where poor Moaf was forced to go to the bathroom. Having the mess cleaned up and the house aired out, I went back to his nursery. Not knowing what to do, I picked up a little teddy bear and sat in the rocking chair. Rocking the bear, I looked out at the gray winter sky and sobbed into its plush fur missing my baby.

Five long days later I carried R.B. through the door to our house for the first time. I was so happy; I didn't know what I wanted to do with him first. I fed him. I sang to him some more. I held him. I talked to him nonstop about everything. I decided to bathe him. Filling the kitchen sink with luke warm water, I carefully put his little body into the bath. I gently wiped him with a cloth and washed his pretty hair with the special brush the hospital had given me. When I was done the water was cover with his soft hair! I held my bald baby close and kissed him over and over, apologizing for the horrible mother I must be. I thought I had ruined him for life!

While at the hospital they had circumcised him using the new method called a bell circumcision. His little foreskin was pulled over a plastic ring and tied off. It was supposed to fall off evenly and all at one time, but there was one area that didn't release. This caused him severe pain, so R.B. would wail inconsolably at times. Butch didn't want the baby to become spoiled or too dependent on his mother, so he wouldn't allow me to pick him up when he was around. Since his healing circumcision wound hurt and I wasn't allowed to hold him, he would sometimes cry for long periods of time. Butch, in cold frustration, placed white surgical tape over his tiny mouth. Stepping from the room he looked at me and said, "I got him to shut up. You're just not a good mother". I walked over to the crib and caught my breath when I saw his lips forced shut and his eyes wide with fear. I didn't think he could breath, so I knew I had to pull it off. As gently as I could, I removed the strip from his mouth and watched part of his tender skin come with it. He immediately began bawling. "What a stupid bitch you are! Shut that baby up!", Butch bellowed from the living room. I took little R.B. into my arms, closed the door and got into the closet. Sliding the door shut behind us to muffle his cries, I rocked him in the dark sitting on the floor until he fell asleep.

I spent a lot of time in that closet with my son crying. Butch worked nights so he slept throughout the day and if the baby or I woke him, one of us was in for a beating. He had learned not to hit either one of us in the face, as people would ask too many questions, so the punishment was always below the neck. No matter how hot it got, R.B. and I wore long pants and sleeves to our wrist in order to cover the bludgeoning marks from the abuse. I was a stubborn young lady. I wouldn't admit to myself that I had made a mistake by marrying him and I couldn't accept the failure of this marriage. Divorce was against my religion and a mark of shame. I kept hoping that it would work out. I believed that if I was a good enough wife, loving and patient that he would start to value me and begin to treat me better.

We usually ate dinner at the same time so Butch could go to work on a full stomach. He had been working the same job for a couple of weeks, but I hadn't, as usual, seen the fruits from his labor. We had no milk or butter so I prepared a box of macaroni and cheese using just water. Being sure the proper spices were on the table, I called him to dinner. He carried his beer from the living room where he had been watching T.V. and sat down. Looking at me through slits for eyes, he said, "You know I eat with bread and butter!" He was getting so predictable by this point that I flinched and waited. The glass dish went flying. This time though, instead of just slapping me, he dragged me to the floor.

The television was blasting in the background and as he swung first with the right fist then the left, he was hitting me in time with the speaking on the show. He punched and punched. I lay, pinned to the floor by his weight, unable to protect myself, the smell of cheese wafting through the air. "I hate having to straighten you out! When are you gonna get it you stupid bitch?", he would demand between driving punches. I closed my eyes and waited until I couldn't feel it anymore. I suddenly felt pain free with peace and quiet settling over me. Surprised, I opened my eyes to see that he was still using my body as an outlet for his anger, but I wasn't there. Looking from a detached place I objectively noticed that he looked less mad and that he would be stopping soon. Yes, his face was softening a little, so I knew he was almost done. I couldn't feel the pain of the blows anymore. My mind had learned to dissociate. My flesh and bones were his punching bag, but my mind was free from it all.

Standing above me, he kicked my soulless body one more time before spitting, "I got to get out of this nut house! You better get it straight you moron. Next time I'll kill you." I watched him storm out and slam the heavy metal door of the trailer. I lay amid the macaroni noodles covered in gooey cheese. Glass was everywhere and blood dripped in puddles around my body, but I was okay. My spirit was okay. Hearing R.B. cry, I was instantly transported back to my broken body where I picked myself off the floor and went to pick up my son.

><*>< ><*>< ><*>< ><*><

Each time he beat me, I declared I would leave him. I had nowhere to go. I was terrified if I went to friends or family they would be killed along with myself and my son for betraying him. Yet, as a threat to hopefully get him to stop I would begin packing my things. He would sob and plead that he couldn't live without me and that if I stayed he would try harder, promising to never hit me again. He would then lock himself in the bathroom where he would slit his wrists, saying he was no good and might as well be dead. He had just beaten me and here I was worrying about him. I would pound on the door begging him not to kill himself and then guilt would fill my soul because I had made him do it. He would open the door, dripping his blood everywhere, as I would plead with him. This happened each time he would seriously beat me and I would prepare to leave. Before I knew it, I had become encircled by the insanity and sucked up into its vortex.

Butch lost his job again and I knew that we couldn't keep going without money. R.B. and I would go days without eating and when we did get food it was sometimes just noodles. I didn't think I had any job skills, but I was able to get a wonderful job caring for an elderly lady with terminal cancer, who allowed me to bring my son to her house while I worked. She loved him as if he were her own, so I felt comfortable there with him and it kept him safe from his father.

Butch came home one night in a rancid mood and he told me he was leaving me because he had gotten his girlfriend pregnant. "I'm going to marry her!" he claimed. In confusion, I asked how that was possible when he was already married to me. He didn't answer but went on to explain, "I'm a connoisseur of sex and I can't settle for just one flavor. I have to sample from many vines." I questioned why he had married me in the first place. His answer sickened me further, "I only married you because I thought you were a rich bitch. I wanted your Dad's money!" Repulsed, injured and feeling hopeless, I got R.B. and left him with a friend. Coming back to the house, I took every pill we had. Mike and Butch were dropping acid in the living room, so I sat on the couch and waited. Mike noticed I was droopy and asked, "Are you all right, Nancy?" I replied, "I will be soon," and with that I passed out.

I woke up in the hospital with a tube down my throat. I hadn't died. It hurt so much to live that death had to be better. I was told they wouldn't release me until I talked to the hospital psychiatrist. He was young and clueless. He had no idea what was going on nor did he make an attempt to try. The only thing he had me do was to promise never to try killing myself again. They released me and I went home to learn that Butch had broken up with the girl and was going to stay with me. I didn't care one way or the other anymore. I was numb.

A month later, as I entered our house, Butch ambushed me, beat me bloody and then raped me. He screamed over and over, "You're mine, nobody else would have you anyway, I would kill you before I'd let you go!" It was on that night that I conceived my second child.

>֍ ֍ ֍ ֍

To try to keep peace at home, I worked for the kind elderly lady for several months before she became too ill and had to be hospitalized. My younger sister, Maxine knew I was out of a job and asked her employer if she had anything I could do. Sure enough, there was and the boss, Betty, even offered to allow R.B. to come to work with me; I was thrilled.

I enjoyed the companionship of Betty and Maxine. Having somewhere to go everyday was refreshing and uplifting. They loved R.B. and as he was almost a year old, he added personality to the dog grooming shop. After a few months of working as a dog bather, Betty offered to make me an apprentice groomer. I learned to groom using scissors to get the looks of the different breeds of dogs. I loved the work, was able to buy food for R.B., and I was learning a valuable skill.

Butch didn't believe the child I carried was his so he would regularly punch me in the stomach. Doubling over as much as I could, I would try to protect my unborn baby. This tiny human was traumatized long before entering the world and I believed there was little I could do about it. At that point I was beaten down. Butch used my baby to keep me with him. He told me over and over what a horrible mother and wife I was. He had me convinced that if I called social services for help, they would take my son away from me. I was willing to endure the pain to keep from losing my child.

>֍ ֍ ֍ ֍

I worked right up until a few days before I delivered my second baby. I wanted to save enough money to stay home while I breast-fed. While at home those few days before going into labor I explained to R.B. that he'd be having a new little brother or sister. His eyes widened when I told him it would come from my tummy and he spent much time talking to his unborn sibling. I laughed and snuggled him up into my arms. I was happy that at least two thirds of the family wanted this baby.

While I was in the hospital giving birth, Butch went over to my father's house to celebrate. He drank until he was well drunk before returning home. Once there he slit his wrists, called the ambulance and laid, bleeding on the couch waiting for them. We were both in the hospital at the same time. Twenty-seven hours lapsed before a healthy, long, lean baby boy was born to me. It was March 22, 1972. They took my second son, Clint, to the nursery where he waited for a bath in a heated glass box.

There were not enough beds for all the patients in the 'poor people' hospital, so I walked the halls waiting for one to open up. I was tired and sore so I went to the nursery to look at my son through the glass partition. He was so peaceful yet he constantly moved and stretched. It must have felt good to finally be out of the cramped quarters of my womb. I stood in awe at what a beautiful baby he was and ached to hold him in my arms.

Clint was soon washed and dressed, so I held him and rocked him in the nursery rocking chair until a room opened up. I kept him with me. I breast fed him and kissed him. Two days later they released both of us and I headed for home with my active, healthy baby boy.

I returned to the house to find that no one had cared for poor Moaf-again. He had eaten the sofa where Butch's blood had dripped and found some noodles in one of the cupboards. The house was a mess again and I spent the first day of Clint's life at home cleaning up the urine and piles of dog excrement. Welcome home, son!

When my mom dropped R.B. off at the house after having watched him while I was in the hospital, I introduced him to his new baby brother. "R.B. this is your new brother, Clint." I told him. "Okay, Chucky!" he quipped. "No, R.B.! His name is Clint," I said again more slowly. "Chucky", he said sweetly. For two days he called his new brother Chucky while I called him Clint. Finally, while changing his diaper I looked at his shiny blonde hair and decided that R.B. was right. He did look more like a Chucky than a Clint, so Chucky he became.

The in-utero trauma Chucky had endured was evident right from the start. Whenever he was placed in his crib, he would inevitably move about using a swimming motion. I would check on him and find him missing. My heart would jump into my throat in fear at first and then on closer inspection I would spot a little leg or arm under the mattress bumper. Big dents would show on his head from where the bars of the crib would stop his forward motion. His tiny elbows and knees would become red and sore because they were his source of propulsion. From the first night I brought him home, he slept through the entire night. Never once did he wakeup and cry to be fed.

I wasn't home with Chucky for more than a week before Betty came to my home begging me to come back to work. She offered me a managerial position and Butch encouraged me to take the offer. Not sure that both boys would be able to join me in the shop, I balked so my husband offered to watch the boys while I worked. I agreed to go back when Clint was a month old, but the pit of my stomach ached when I thought of Butch caring for my sons.

Work was busy and the shop was filling with clientele. My hands were getting strong and steady as I used scissors all day and the dogs were prancing out looking better and better. I dreaded coming home each night, because I knew Butch would be drunk or drugged while my children were left unattended and unchanged. Clint's little bottom was sore and raw from sitting in a dirty, soiled diaper all day. He cried whenever something touched it. His wails aggravated Butch, so he would spank him so hard that the whole crib mattress bounced along with his little body. I felt helpless as I watched him attack my month old son just as he had beaten R.B.

It hurt me more to watch my children get hit than it did to get punched myself. I could have taken the beatings for the rest of my life, but I knew he would kill my boys. I knew I had to leave. I knew I had to get far away. If he found us he would kill us. I was terrified of the thought. I didn't think I could make enough money to support the three of us but I would have to find a way soon.

Leaving my children with my husband as I worked didn't last long. It had been less than a week and I was caring for my last dog of the day. It was a half hour before closing time and I knew the dog's owner would be coming by soon to pick him up. The phone rang. It was Butch's screaming voice, "If you don't come within 15 minutes, I'll put this baby in the freezer." I hung up the phone, not knowing what to do. He was crazy enough to do it! If I left the dog, I would surely be fired. Terrified, I paced the floor and prepared to leave hoping the dog's owner would show up quickly. Thankfully, she arrived just then and as the dog left with it's owner, I raced home. I was terrified. Waiting outside of the trailer door, I couldn't bring myself to open it. I visualized his little body, frozen in an eternal cry suspended in the coldness with his arms reaching for his absent mother. I cried even before I knew the conclusion. Butch opened the door to see my wet, terrified face. He laughed, dragged me inside and said, "You dumb bitch! You knew I was just kidding." I thought to myself, "no, I didn't know. You really are capable of doing it". He had Chucky in his other arm. "This kid has been screaming all day. Now you shut him up!" My shaking arms were outstretched to take him but instead, Butch lifted his tiny body and vaulted him across the room. I watched, horrified, as my infant son hit the top of the wall and slid to the floor in a heap. The crying stopped. As Butch slammed the door in departure, I rushed to Chucky and picked him up. His eyes were huge as he blinked up at me. I was so happy he was still alive! As his amazing brown eyes looked into mine I made a promise to him right then: "I will never allow this to happen to you again! We will pack up our stuff and leave." With that, I called a cab, gathered my sons and some things and headed to my boss Betty's house, never to turn back.

I had been afraid we would not survive without Butch. I finally realized we would not survive with him. I didn't know the dark days of my life were now behind me and my future was bright with hope and promise.

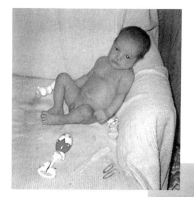

Chucky at age one month, his eyes filled sadness and the expression on his face tells the story of the overwhelming trauma he has already endured. His knees are red and sore from his constant "swimming" in his crib.

Chucky, seven months, RB, almost two. Chucky's eyes still clearly express his inner pain.

The passage of time hasn't eased Chucky's pain.

Chapter 4

Enter - the Cowboy

The trauma and abuse inflicted by Butch didn't leave my mind as quickly as it took to physically leave him. For years beyond his beatings, I would flinch and immediately relive the trauma when any man raised his voice, got angry or lifted his hand above his head. By the time I left, he had tried to commit suicide thirty-two times. The scars from each attempt were horizontal white streaks from his wrists to his elbows. I didn't count the number of severe beatings he gave me, but since he usually tried to kill himself when I threatened to leave, it must have been at least as many scars as ran down his forearms. The echo of the abuse would stay with me for the rest of my life.

The time from December 1969 to May 1972, although it was a living hell, gave me insight into pain that I would have never had. I learned what it felt like to leave my body in order to find a sanctuary where there was no pain or fear. I quickly figured out that violence wasn't the answer and that hitting someone yielded nothing but submission and fear. No lessons could be taught using aggression and intimidation. Patience was another skill I further developed as was shutting my mouth and listening. I was able to now understand the humiliation and terror of being abused and the shame the victim feels in allowing it to happen. I learned that talking about it was taboo and only added to the already existing guilt. I understood how easy it was for the perpetrator to make the prisoner feel responsible. The power that one person can have over another and the amount of emotional destruction that one person can inflict were eye-opening lessons for me. The memories and the feelings were seared into my mind. I knew what it felt like to see death as a viable option. I could understand suicide as a way to end the pain of living.

I no longer needed to see dying as an option to escape the degradation and dehumanization of sexual and physical abuse. Leaving Butch opened up other doors that closed the door of death even though he continued to try to invade my new life without him. He tried to kidnap RB. Moaf mysteriously died. Butch threatened to kill me so I had to get a restraining order after he was arrested outside of my house when he threatened me with a gun. We moved often, hiding in terror from one home to another. He would call me at work and imply that he knew where I lived and what I had been doing. I was still terrified of him, but I was getting stronger by the day. I was on my own. I was caring for my sons by myself and we always had something to eat, even if it was a can of beans split three ways. We were making it!

The divorce was final in September 1972. I didn't want to ask for child support because I didn't want Butch in our lives anymore, but my attorney insisted that I needed the financial help. I never saw a penny from him, so to survive I worked two full time jobs. I worked at the grooming shop during the day and as a cocktail waitress at night. I was burning the candle at both ends and rarely got more than four hours of sleep, but I was taking care of my responsibilities and we were happy.

I had always told myself that if it came down to having to put my boys with a baby sitter all day, I would put them up for adoption first. I couldn't live without my children; I loved them both too much. They were a part of me. I was too selfish to give my sons up to a better home so I stared at the ugly face of "child care". I searched out a baby sitter that I thought would suffice. I found an old retired couple that loved children. When I drove up to check the place out, there were kids playing on the swing set outside and toddlers splashing in a baby pool. The whole time I interrogated the kind, gray haired woman, she held an infant, lovingly, in her arms. The kids were amply fed nutritious, well-rounded meals with milk or juice. I decided, Mrs. Spoonie was kind and would care for my children almost as I would. We agreed she would start caring for my boys the following week.

Because I worked nights, I hired another sitter for the later hours. I would see the boys in the evening after picking them up from 'Grandma' Spoonie's while they played in the yard behind the shop as I finished up. We would eat dinner together before the sitter arrived and off to my waitressing job I would go. It wasn't ideal, but at least my family was still together!

Grandma Spoonie sewed buttons onto their jumpers and patched the knees that had become thin or worn through. She potty trained Chucky. Then she got very sick. While she was in the hospital, I took the boys to her neighbor's home that was highly recommended by Grandma Spoonie. Four months later, she was back on her feet and our baby sitter was available again. R.B. and Chucky were moved back to her care. My mom and Martha, my older sister, spoiled them rotten on Saturdays while I worked and provided family continuity to their greatly disrupted lives.

I moved far from the town so I could hide out and find serenity. At night, after I had tucked the boys in bed, I would run out into the alfalfa fields until I could no longer see our little cottage. I would look up at the dark night sky before tightly shutting my eyes and releasing my problems to the heavens in the form of screams. I would breath deeply before allowing a long wail to escape from the deepest depths of my being as loudly as I could, again and again. It released so much pent up anxiety, frustration and anger that it would resound for several minutes into the darkness. It felt wonderful to let go. The floodgates of emotion would just open and leave me feeling clean and free, before I turned to walk back to the house, unburdened from the weight of emotional baggage.

Since I couldn't go running through the fields every night, I would sometimes sit and cry on the couch. My life had been so full of misery and broken dreams that, at times, I just couldn't hold back the sadness that occasionally overwhelmed me. Once, while crying, RB came up to me. In his two-year old speech he asked, "Tammy bite you?" She was our dog at the time. I shook my head no. "Chucky bite you?" Again, I shook my head and looked at my concerned son. "Need Kleenex?" Finally receiving an affirmative to his questions, he trucked into the bathroom. I laughed when I saw him bringing one square of toilet paper to me. Wiping my cheeks, I pulled him into my arms and hugged his chubby little body.

>̶⊶̶ ☀ ̶⊷̶< >̶⊶̶ ☀ ̶⊷̶< >̶⊶̶ ☀ ̶⊷̶< >̶⊶̶ ☀ ̶⊷̶<

While living in the trailer with Butch, I had made friends with our neighbors, Mike and Rose. They were happily married and had a son that was a month younger than R.B. They would come over at night to play cribbage with us. Several times they called the police when my screams became too intense for them to handle. They were wonderful people that loved each other very much. I would watch them talk and laugh with each other, as our sons played together in their baby pool. Running around tickling one another made laughter echo throughout their home. They were happy. Marriage without violence was working for them. They inspired me to believe that such relationships did exist. When I left my abuser, I missed seeing them, so I invited them out to our little cottage. Having met Mike's family and seeing how sweet and compassionate they all were, I half jokingly asked, "Are there anymore at home like you?" He smirked and looked at Rose before replying, "Yes, I have an older brother living in Phoenix, Arizona." I started asking him question after question about him and before I knew it, his mustached smirk had spread into a full grin. He continued answering my barrage of questions as he picked up the phone and dialed. "Here, why don't you ask him yourself!", and with that he handed me the ringing phone and laughed.

Jerry, Mike's older brother, and I talked for a while. He was kind and funny. Intelligence emanated from his quick responses to my inquiry and before we hung up I had agreed to go on a date with him when he came for Christmas. It was to be my last blind date.

It was my twenty-first birthday when Jerry and I met face to face. I drove to Mike and Rose's house where I left the boys and headed off in his yellow Scout. He was a handsome blonde with the popular side burns of the seventies. Many years of reading engineering books in college caused him to wear glasses and his soft hair was hidden by his cowboy hat. His soft manner of speaking matched the soul I saw reflecting from his azure eyes.

Memories of watching the family on the TV show "Bonanza" flooded my mind as we drove. As little girls, my sisters and I used to dream of marrying the three sons on the show. My older sister, Martha was going to marry "Adam". My little sister, Maxine would marry "Little Joe". I said I planned on marrying Hoss. The truth of the matter was I wanted all three of those cowboys! Here I was, twenty-one and dating with someone who just might fit those qualifications! I smiled at the thought and watched this man drive carefully and purposefully through the delicate snowflakes that had just started to fall.

Opening the car door for me, he reached for my hand and escorted me from his Scout to the dance club. The loud, twangy music hit my ears the moment he cracked the door. Barrel cactus and the three armed Saguaro cactus lit up the walls with their neon luminescence and reminded me of the desert I loved as a child. Multitudes of cowboy boots danced on the floor in a counterclockwise circle while others mingled in every other conceivable area. The band was playing country western music and I reveled at how new this experience was for me.

I had not been a drinker, but as it was my birthday, I thought about having a light cocktail. Not knowing what to get, Jerry recommended the sweet and tangy Moscow Mule. Since I was the birthday girl, it was on the house.

We tried talking over the blasting music, but it was too difficult so he accompanied me to the dance floor where we danced the night away. While attempting to learn the two-step and the cowboy waltz I stepped on his boots a million times and kept tripping over my own feet. We laughed and started over each time. It felt good to be with a man that didn't try to impress me with his record collection or his slick moves. This man wasn't afraid to be himself. At midnight, he gently took my face in his hands and kissed me. "Happy Birthday, Nancy!", he exclaimed. The twinkle in his eyes sparkled as we left the club laughing.

It had snowed about eighteen inches since we had entered the place only a few hours before and the snow was still coming down heavily. On our way back to Mike and Rose's house, we stopped by a diner to eat a piece of pie. The snow didn't seem to bother Jerry as he had grown up in Colorado and had a four wheel drive, so we laughed about my dance skills and talked about our dreams and aspirations for about an hour before heading back out into the winter storm.

The headlights reflected diamonds as the flakes fell in front of our sled with wheels. Pulling into Mike and Rose's driveway I saw my car was beyond buried. The only sign of a vehicle was a slight mound in the otherwise beautiful, pristine white snow. It looked as if I wasn't going anywhere until morning.

Jerry and his brother, Mike, pulled the hide-a-bed from its compartment in the couch while Rose and I found sheets and a nightgown for me to wear. I checked where the boys were fast asleep and tiptoed in to kiss them goodnight. I changed in the bathroom. Walking back to the living room, I noticed Mike, Rose and Jerry had already made up my bed and had Jerry's sleeping bag rolled out on the remaining small area of carpet.

I quickly slid into bed and pulled the sheets up around my chin. Jerry whispered goodnight to me before turning off the lights and slipping into the silky bag on the floor. I had dated before and found that most men would often attempt sexual advances, so as I lay there, I thought of how I would react to Jerry's attempts. I deliberated telling him I wasn't interested or that I didn't know him that well, but neither seemed exactly right. I pondered other responses and finally decided on saying "I'm not that kind of girl!" In the dark, I lay there waiting for him to get fresh, so I could turn him down. I waited and waited. Out of desperation, I peeked over the bed to find that cowboy already sleeping with his arm over his eyes.

I spent the next half hour wondering what was wrong with me. Had I said something stupid? Did he not like me or was I not pretty enough? Knowing there was nothing I could do about it, I rolled over and finally fell asleep myself.

The next morning Jerry was awake long before me. When I got up, I found my car already shoveled off and scraped clean of the thirty-two inches of snow that had fallen throughout the night. The driveway was mostly clear as well, and the snowplows had moved the snow from the roads. When he came in, I tried not to laugh as his glasses fogged all up. His eyebrows and sideburns were covered in frost and icicles and his nose was as red as Rudolph's. Before I got a chance to thank him for his hard work, my boys came running into the kitchen.

We all sat down for breakfast and discussed the winter wonderland that had appeared outside. R.B. wanted to go outside and I worried that I might never find him again. I told him he'd have to wait until I was done, but just as soon as I finished that sentence, Jerry asked if he could take him. Wondering if this man had any experience with children, I hesitated just long enough for his nephew, Michael to jump into his arms. "I come too?" he pleaded with Jerry. With that interaction, I knew my son would be fine and we began to bundle up both boys to ward off the icy cold.

I drove home that afternoon with thoughts of the wonderful man I had just met. I had absolutely no intention of ever getting married again, but the periodic, adult companionship would be nice. I knew that Jerry lived far away and only visited during the holidays, so I held little expectation of seeing him again soon. As his image was warming my heart though, the sun broke through the heavy clouds and reflected rainbows across the snow banks. To me, God was sending hope to his children and I was lucky enough to have witnessed it.

The grooming shop was growing and Betty was spending less and less time there, which meant I was running it more and more. I had hired more people and Maxine was no longer working there. Everything was going well so when Betty approached me with a workable offer to purchase the business, I quickly accepted. I was a single mom and an entrepreneur. I had come so far is such a short time and I knew if I worked hard, the sky would be the limit.

I still worked two jobs, so I moved closer into town to save time and money. I rented a house with two bedrooms, so my sons and I shared one bedroom while I prepared the other to rent out. It had a big fenced yard where the boys and our dogs could romp and play safely.

While working at the shop one evening, a man I had never seen before came through the door. His gaunt frame stood at least 6' and his pale cheeks were hollow. When I approached him from behind the counter his tired eyes followed me as he started to speak, "I need some help with my daughter. I've checked it out and you're the only one who can help me!" Confused, I told him I thought he must be mistaken. He repeated, "You're the only one who can help me. Please, help me with my daughter, Ava!" The deep concern I could see in his eyes told me this was no joke. I had taken in many stray dogs but this was very different. The man's intense desperation for his child touched my heart. I didn't know what, if anything, I could do to help. I remembered the feeling of desperation I had felt in my past and how hard it was to find someone to trust enough to ask for help. I could not refuse someone's plea. So, I agreed to help him.

He went to his car and came back holding the wrist of a beautiful Navajo girl about fourteen years old. Seeing they were clearly different races, I concluded that she probably was adopted. Her eyes stayed on the floor and her shoulders slumped more when he introduced us. Ava made no attempt to acknowledge me. The pink frilly shirt she wore didn't match her dark complexion and her beautiful ebony hair was cut blunt and short. Her powerfully built form looked as if gravity had more effect on her than it had on others. She shuffled and rarely lifted her head. This pitiful child appeared afraid and ashamed of who she was. I felt like she might just need a safe haven and some love so I agreed to take her for a short time to see if I could help.

Feeling that her self-image must be seriously damaged, Ava, the boys and I went shopping that night and purchased some maroon fabric. My first mission was to get her in touch with her heritage and help her to be proud of who she was. As I had spent summers in an Apache reservation in Arizona as a child, I decided to make her the only Native costume I had seen. In front of the sewing machine, she and I spent hours talking and laughing as we made a beautiful top for her. Proudly she pulled it over her strong shoulders and I finished the outfit with a concho belt I had kept since I was a little girl. Ava looked beautiful and for the first time, I could see she felt good about who she was. Mission one accomplished, her self-esteem had grown a tiny bit. Another thing I could do with this injured young adult was to be her friend and a nonjudgmental ear. We spent a lot of time talking and sharing.

A few days into her stay with me, Ava's father brought her Scotty dog to her. I felt like it would be a comfort to her. Chucky was able to walk now, so I watched while talking on the phone as he immediately went to the dog. All I saw was the back of his head as the dog attacked him. Dropping the phone, I quickly picked up my now sobbing toddler and rushed him into the bathroom. He was bleeding so badly that I couldn't tell if he had a face left. My heart was pounding as I tried to run water over his wounds. The entire bathtub, filling with water, turned red with my youngest son's blood. I was trying hard to stay calm. Finding a huge gash across his forehead, I pressed his head into my breast as I grabbed a towel to absorb the blood. He'd have to have stitches. I ran to get RB when I noticed Ava in the corner. She was like a zombie with no facial expression. Her little dog was trapped in the corner as she kicked it over and over. I called her. There was no movement from her except the repetitive movement of her foot swinging at the dog. I called her again and this time clutched her arm. Finally getting her attention, I asked her to get in the car.

All four of us raced to the hospital. A blood soaked towel was still wrapped around Chucky's head as I carried him into the emergency room. "Please, someone, help my son!", I urgently begged. A doctor came to our aid and started caring for the wound. I trusted that the doctor knew what was best, so when he said he wouldn't be using anesthesia, I didn't balk. He said the anesthesia would make the tissue swell causing the injury to heal more slowly creating more scarring. They tied my little son to a board while three of us held him down. The doctor stitched. My son screamed in fear and pain and I helped hold him down so his scar wouldn't be bad. Each cry of pain broke my heart. I wasn't strong enough to stand up to the doctor, so I just held back my tears of disgrace and remorse and tried to calm my son as best as I could. I wish I had been strong enough to have said, 'I don't care how big the scar is, don't let him hurt anymore'. I wasn't and my poor Chucky suffered because of it.

A few nights later, as I slept in our room with my white shepherd, Star, I was startled awake by her low growls. A fireman was standing in my doorway and I grabbed Star's collar to keep her from attacking him. "Ma'am do you live in that apartment over there?" Frightened and still groggy with sleep, I said, "What's going on and what are you doing here!?" He replied, "We got an emergency call. Is that room there, part of your apartment?" He gestured behind him to the room where Ava had been staying. Dazed, I replied, "Yes, why?" He proceeded to tell me that the girl that I had laughed with talked with and given a hug that night had attempted suicide. I didn't understand. She had been just fine when she went to bed. I threw on a bathrobe and walked outside to find an ambulance, two police cars and a fire engine parked on my front lawn. Ava was in the ambulance with gauze around her wrists and next to her was the maroon outfit we had made together. We looked into each others eyes as the doors to the emergency vehicle closed. I waved a confused farewell as she was taken away. I turned to the officer and asked what had happened. He told me that she had apparently slit her wrists and then phoned for help. Mystified, I stammered, "Well, why didn't she just talk to me? I was right here. If she was upset I would have helped her. I don't understand. This doesn't make any sense to me. I thought these past few weeks we had become friends." His reply, "Maybe she needed more than a friend," left my mind churning for the rest of the night. I searched my memory and didn't find even the slightest indicator that she had been upset that evening or that this was coming. I called her dad and shared the sad news with him before cleaning up the trail of blood. I never saw her again. It was then that I learned that some emotional disturbances can't be cured with just love and kindness, no matter how hard you try.

⤞✸⤝ ⤞✸⤝ ⤞✸⤝ ⤞✸⤝

For my twenty-second birthday, Jerry took me out again. We went to the same country western bar with the neon cactus lights and the Moscow Mules. We laughed and tried to talk over the loud band and again, when we became tired of hollering at each other, we hit the dance floor. This time I only stepped on his toes a half million times and I tripped mostly over one leg instead of both. When we got dizzy from going in the same direction, we left the club, twang still reverberating in our partially deaf ears. There was no snow this time, so we stopped by the same cafe for dessert again. We talked and laughed for hours.

Instead of kissing me at midnight, we touched lips about 1:00 am, before I picked the boys up from Mike and Rose's. He helped me carry their limp, sleep filled bodies to my car and again, we kissed. I drove home from that second date feeling warm and fuzzy because he was so kind, considerate and gentle.

With Jerry pushed to the back of my mind I went through the next year still working long hours. I rented the other room in the house to an employee from my shop and charged her minimal rent in exchange for watching the boys after work. This saved on the cost of hiring another baby-sitter and allowed me to save some money. The boys could sleep in their own beds without having to be awakened to be brought home.

⤞✸⤝ ⤞✸⤝ ⤞✸⤝ ⤞✸⤝

The business was getting so big that it was time for us to expand. In 1973 I was only twenty-two so when I went to my first bank to ask for a quarter of a million dollar loan, the loan officer looked at me and laughed. He informed me that someone would have to be stupid to lend money to a young single mother like me. My Irish blood took those words as a challenge so I set out to prove him wrong. I put together a powerful business proposal. I searched out banks that had a reputation for listening to their clients and being open minded. I approached a number of investors. Two months later, and with a partner, I had my money and the business moved to a bigger facility. I had proven to that man that I could do it, but more over I had proven to myself that if I wanted something bad enough, I could get it if I set my mind to it.

⤞✸⤝ ⤞✸⤝ ⤞✸⤝ ⤞✸⤝

Much of the damage Butch had done to my self-confidence was healed within the first two years I was on my own. Even though R.B. and Chucky would still spend their days with Grandma Spoonie, they often played with big wheels and the other toys in the huge yard behind the shop while I watched from the window. During the summer, I would fill a baby pool and they would splash and keep cool there. The girls helping me bathe or clip dogs would often comment about what a patient and caring mom I was, which made me feel good all over. Being a good mother was one of the most important things in the world to me.

Everything was just as I had hoped. My boys were adjusting well to their various sitters. My business was booming and I was succeeding in life. I felt like I had it all. Little did I know that all the time I spent away from them, while they were being watched by others, would come back to haunt me years later.

As was becoming tradition, Jerry took me out for my twenty-third birthday. He no longer lived in Arizona because the Forest Service had needed his engineering skills in Salt Lake City, Utah. Again we headed toward the cowboy club. We had a great time together. We both looked at each other and laughed when we stepped from the loud club later that night to see snowflakes starting to fall. "Uh-oh! We'd better hurry home before another blizzard snows us in!", Jerry said with a wink. He grabbed my hand and we ran for the Scout. On our way back, we stopped by the same little cafe as had become our yearly tradition. We laughed and shared stories before heading out. I wanted to see this man again, so as we carried my sleeping sons to the car and said our goodnights, I invited him to dinner the following night. It had been a long time since I celebrated the New Year and it had been an even longer time since I had invited a man to my home. He accepted and I drove home humming Patsy Cline's, 'I Go Walking After Midnight'. Looking at my clock when I got home, I smiled, because it was well after midnight.

The next day, because the shop was closed for the holiday, I prepared a meaty stew. The house smelled warm and inviting and I spent the rest of the day cleaning and preparing for Jerry's arrival. He was punctual and brought flowers for the table. I hugged him warmly and taking his cowboy hat from him, I carefully placed it upside down on the top of the refrigerator just high enough to keep it out of the hands of fascinated little boys. Knowing I wasn't a big drinker, he brought a six-pack of soda along with the flowers. As I finished the last minute preparations, Jerry played with R.B. and Chucky in the living room. Calling them all to dinner, they all tumbled through the doorway in a frenzy of excitement. We all sat around the table eating the hearty stew and slurping soda, dipping homemade bread into the broth. I intentionally left the spices off the table and I was relieved when he didn't even look for them. We enjoyed our evening together and he headed back to Salt Lake City.

I was flattered when he wrote to me and said that he admired my "pioneer spirit" and that he thought I was a good cook. We talked often on the phone and as it was long distance, the cost was getting out of hand. "I figured out a way to cut these phone bills and as I can't seem to stop calling you, I think you should hear me out," Jerry said. I listened as he continued, "If we get married and I move you and the boys to Utah with me, then we won't have any long distance bills." I thought that was a practical solution, but that was a huge decision and I wasn't sure I was ready. I told him I would have to think about it. "Call me tomorrow and I'll let you know what I think!" I replied. We said goodnight and ended the call.

That night, I slept restlessly. I was tired of working so hard and not spending much time with my children. Even though I had only been on four dates with him, I knew his family and felt they were good people. I had met his mom and dad several times while over visiting Mike and Rose. They had always been considerate, respectful and loving with each other. Mike was a good man. Jerry had been a good man so far, but from my experience, they could be good until the vows were said, then they could turn into monsters.

I thought about Jerry and how he had been working with the Forest Service for years. He had a strong work ethic. He had done his duty in the Army, but didn't go to Vietnam. He loved animals and was kind and patient with my boys plus he hadn't been in a mental hospital.

The more I thought about it, the more I realized that Jerry was a good and honest man. He was the man I had been hoping to find the first time around. I wasn't ready then apparently, but this time I was ready and I wasn't going to spoil this chance for a happy, strong and loving relationship. Would this be my chapter of Bonanza? The one where I live happily ever after? I would accept!

I met with my business partner, Bob, and shared with him my dreams of being able to be a full time mother for my sons, to have a real home and family with dinner on the table when my loving husband returned from work. I was proud of our business accomplishments, however, I knew the best thing for me and my boys was to leave. I offered to give him my share of the business in exchange for me keeping my share of the building. He accepted and we promoted an employee to manager.

My Cowboy, Jerry.

Jerry and I had a small wedding at a chapel in the Rocky Mountains. May 21, 1975 was a beautiful spring day. R.B. and Chucky, in matching tan jackets, walked side by side down the aisle, carrying ring pillows. Jerry took a rose to my mother and thanked her for creating me and raising me to be exactly right for him. I gave his mom, Bobbie, a rose and thanked her for being the great mom that she was so that I could now have a great husband. We lit candles and said our vows with God smiling upon all of us.

The next day, Jerry and I packed up his new pickup truck with all of our belongings. Jerry and I, with RB, Chucky, Freddie the dog, our cat, our mother ferret and her week old kits were all loaded into the front of the truck to "ride off into the sunset". With all of us packed like sardines, we sang as we drove across Colorado and into Utah where our new life awaited.

Chapter 5

It's a Wonderful Life

Jerry's mobile home had bunk beds that he handmade for the boys in one of the two bedrooms. The first morning we awoke in Utah, my husband called for us to join him outside in the glowing morning sun. There, we witnessed hot air balloons rising high into the sky. The boys, still in their pajamas, squealed with glee from the highest perch they could find, their parent's shoulders. Looking at the colorful sight, I absorbed the symbolic meaning of our new life with Jerry. We were on our way up to a vibrant future!

The boys soon became hungry so we all piled back into our new home for the first breakfast we all had together. I poured milk and cereal into bowls. Asking R.B. to set out spoons, we all sat down and said a prayer before eating. I watched as the boys dug in. Chucky had a difficult time using a spoon, so his three-year old fists grabbed as much as they could from the milk before shoving it into his little mouth. I realized, while watching him eat, that I had been so busy working and trying to survive, he had never learned manners at the table. He had no idea what was expected of him. Sadly observing my children eat, I decided my goal would be to give them the mom they deserved and the skills they would need to be successful in life. Being home full time I now could fulfill my dream of being a mom. I was so excited about the time I could now spend teaching, guiding and playing with my sons.

It took a couple of weeks to unpack all the boxes from the move. The trailer was starting to feel like home and the boys were quickly learning. Jerry would come home from work every evening at the same time, so I began having dinner ready when he walked through the door. I felt safe with the consistency, but with the experiences of my past life I couldn't allow myself to fully trust this man.

The first night, he asked that Fred, my red and white Collie/Beagle mix sleep on the floor. He had been a part of my life for over a year and he was accustomed to sleeping on the bed with me. I didn't know if he'd understand why he was being displaced, but I agreed with Jerry and made a dog bed on the floor for him. Looking into Fred's soft, devoted eyes, I stroked the top of his silky head before turning off the lamp, purposefully not inviting him up. Several hours passed before Freddy finally jumped up to snuggle between us. Jerry awoke and guided him off our bed and over to his dog bed. Getting back into bed, Jerry curled up around my sleeping body. A few minutes later, Fred jumped back up. Patiently, Jerry removed him. This happened several times that night, and each time, Jerry calmly asked him to jump back down.

The second night was very much the same. Jerry would just get comfortable and start to nod off before my four-legged friend would jump up to make his nest between us. Jerry would calmly ask him to jump down. The third night, he gave up trying to keep him on the floor and just required that he stay near the foot of our bed instead of near the pillows. This interaction helped me to see how peaceful and caring Jerry really was. He didn't get angry. He never hit Freddy. He never even raised his voice out of frustration. For the next fifteen years, that would be Freddy's spot.

Four months into our marriage, we decided to have another child. I had desperately wanted a daughter, ever since kneeling in prayer in church as a little girl. Soon we were expecting our new baby and I was as happy as I'd ever been.

While we awaited the birth, I sat with RB and Chucky at the table teaching them their alphabet and colors. RB would be in kindergarten soon and I wanted him to be ready and the teachers to see just how smart he was. Chucky had a brilliant, quick mind but couldn't sit down long enough to actually learn much. Because he wasn't interested in sitting to color, draw or learn things his little active body would often disrupt the teaching, so out of frustration, I would often send him to his room to play where he proceeded to bounce off the walls. I worried about his future.

During one school lesson, I asked R.B. what kind of baby he wanted for a sibling and I was thinking he would probably prefer another brother to a sister. He contemplated this for several minutes with a seriousness that was unusual for such a young child before replying, "I wanna Chinese baby!" Laughing, I grabbed his growing body and set him on my lap. "Wouldn't daddy be surprised! You know, your little brother or sister can hear you. Do you want to talk to her?" His eyes widened with wonder as he started teaching my unborn child the alphabet.

I also taught R.B. to cook scrambled eggs on the stove when he was five years old. He would happily help me prepare meals and felt very important when I asked him to set the table. He was a hard worker, but passionate about control.

He was also fascinated with trains while Chucky found pleasure in tractors. Knowing this, Jerry went to an antique store and purchased an old beat up tricycle tractor and parts for a pedal powered locomotive. Each night after we tucked the boys into bed, he would saw, hammer, bolt and sand pieces of wood and metal. I watched this loving father as he took the raw materials and created two remarkable, handmade treasures. He had spent many hours perfecting each design and adding little details so they would both be perfect. My love for him was growing as I saw how much he cared for two children that weren't really his. On Christmas morning, each child was given their few wrapped presents from under the tree before being led outside where Jerry waited with their custom built vehicle. The boys were delighted at such wonderful gifts and spent the whole holiday riding them.

Within months both toys had been destroyed, so when the Forest Service promoted Jerry and transferred him to Denver, we left the pieces of the totaled tractor behind. We packed all four of us, the dog, cat and the now grown ferrets back into the front seat of the truck and returned to Colorado. Being very pregnant, I spent the long hours during the road trip knitting a special blanket for the child doing flips inside of me.

In an attempt to save money to purchase a house, we rented another mobile home in Aurora, a suburb of the capital. While on our way home to pick RB up from school, Chucky and I were in a car wreck on the interstate. Waiting for the police, I watched as the time ticked away. I was worried that .B, being only five years old, would be scared and worried as he walked home from kindergarten and entered an empty house. An hour later, I raced home. Opening the door, I smelled eggs and saw the table was set. "Hi mommy! I saw you were running late, so I made dinner for us!", he said wisely while smiling at me from where he stood on a chair at the stove. I was relieved to see how strong he was and delighted in how caring he could be. I was even more relieved he hadn't burned down the house or hurt himself! We all ate the eggs happily as I calmed down and shared the story of our mishap on the road.

Jerry accompanied me to Lamaze classes where I learned to breathe and work with the contractions of birth. The odds of having to have a caesarean were one in ten. There were ten mothers in the class and having already given birth twice, I figured it would happen to one of the others. I was wrong.

Walking down the hall on the afternoon of June 6th, 1976, I felt my water break. Excitedly, Jerry rushed to get R.B. and Chucky over to the neighbors. Dropping the boys off, we sped to the Aurora Hospital. They confirmed that my water had broken and decided to induce labor. I was hooked up to an I.V., a heart monitor and a fetal heart monitor.

A nurse came in for my first contraction and immediately left to get the doctor after watching all the screens. Observing my second contraction, the doctor informed me my tiny infant's heart was stopping each time my muscles tightened. Growing terror filled my heart as they told us our child, conceived out of gentleness and love, could be born blind, retarded or dead if the medical community didn't intervene. I asked what our options were. "We're going to do you Hollywood style." Knowing what they meant, but not wanting to face it, I asked what exactly that meant. "We're going to give you a smiley face incision. You're baby is going to be born C-section! Don't worry, we have an ambulance standing by to take your baby to Children's Hospital." Feeling an overwhelming panic fill my mind I started to worry they'd cut my precious infant in half. Was that why the ambulance was waiting? Before I could become more stressed, they knocked me out late that night in the cold, sterile operating room. The loving man I needed at my side was relegated to a room down the hall to wait.

"Pa! Pa! Is the baby okay?", I would ask as I was coming out of the anesthesia. Not hearing the answer, I would fall back under the lull of medication. "Pa! Pa! Is the baby okay?", I repeated over and over, frightened that he wasn't answering me because things weren't okay. Jerry sat by my side and continued to answer, "She's fine! Our little girl is beautiful and healthy!", but each time I would lose consciousness before hearing him. Finally, as the effects of the drugs wore off and the pain from the incision began to enter my mind, I heard his words. They were like hearing a songbird singing after a storm. Falling back to sleep, finally able to relax, I knew that God had answered my prayer at last.

They handed me my daughter with olive complexion and mink brown hair. We decided to name her Terena after my best friend from elementary school. Her head was round, not having been squashed through the birth canal. She looked around thoughtfully, peace shined from her dark eyes. I nursed her often and seldom set her in the bassinet while in the hospital. Noting this, the doctor asked, "Don't you ever put that baby down?" I tried to hold back the floodgates, but his decisive work had saved my little infant and I wanted him to know I recognized his effort. Crying all over him, I thanked him profusely. Later that day, I introduced Jerry to the nurse. Upon learning his name, she straightened up and looked uncomfortable. When alone, she stepped into my room and whispered, "I think you should know. While you were coming out of the anesthesia, you were calling for someone named Paul." I thought that odd as I didn't know anyone named Paul, until I laughed and told her I must have been calling for Pa, the nickname for my husband. She breathed a sigh of relief and Jerry and I chuckled about it later when I told him of the misunderstanding.

We stayed in the hospital for five days and before they released us to go home, I had to have the staples removed from my abdomen. I felt like Frankenstein, afraid that my guts would spill from the still fresh wound. I didn't want Jerry to see my big scar because I worried he would find my body repulsive and ugly now. He smiled and shook his head that I would think that way and responded; "I will love you forever, no matter what! Besides, you could never look like a monster!" My mind was full of fear, but I was on my way home with my baby and that gave me hope and happiness.

I loved being home with my children and because Jerry took good care of us, I had time to sew. Getting the pattern for a snugly, which was a baby pack that kept my infant in front of me, I sewed one soon after coming home from the maternity ward. Keeping Terena in my arms and close to me felt good and safe. Both boys learned to change her diaper as I felt it important they feel invested in the child. RB was proud to be a big brother and would often talk of the things he would do with his new little sister when she was old enough. Chucky was very jealous and saw the infant as a nuisance and an intruder. Within the first month, her soft fuzzy brown hair started growing in blonde. Her two toned hair was so fine and soft that it would stand on end making her look like a dandelion in seed. It seemed that one heavy breeze would send all her hair dancing in the wind so we called her 'Little Miss Dandelion' for most of her first year. She was a happy baby and I loved being with her all the time. Sadly, I realized how much I had missed of Chucky's younger days.

Jerry felt that it was important that the boys have stability. By then we had not heard from Butch for several years. He owed thousands in back child support, having not paid any. Jerry made it clear he wanted to adopt my sons and proudly share his last name with them. Butch seemed happy to sign the relinquishment papers and be relieved of the financial burden, never asking how the boys were or if he could see them. At that time he had not seen them in over five years. The day we stood before the court and requested that the adoption be finalized and their names be changed forever, the judge said it was his favorite part of being a judge. Dressed in his black robe, he reached down from his bench and handed lollipops to our beaming boys. RB was so awed by this powerful man, that years later he asked about the day the "President of the United States" reached down and handed him a sucker.

Our menagerie of children and pets was outgrowing the mobile home and Jerry was great at saving the money we would need for the down payment on our first home. The wind would roar past our trailer and rock it. The washing machine and dryer caused all the walls to shake, so I was euphoric at the thought of having a home without wheels. Jerry and I searched throughout the metro area until we found the perfect house. It was a ranch style on a half-acre in an animal friendly neighborhood. When I first walked into that house, I knew it was home. It was within walking distance to the elementary school; so being active with the school programs would be easy. We packed up our things, caged up the critters, buckled in the children and set off to our new home.

RB was seven years old and starting the second grade. Chucky was five and a half and preparing for a half day in kindergarten while Terena was only about a year old. Our family was complete. We were all safe and happiness filled much of our day.

When Terena was about twelve months old I was teaching her to brush her few teeth. She had often sat in the bathroom as Jerry or I prepared for the morning, so she had seen it done many times. As we finished and she rinsed her brush, I watched in amazement as she very purposefully tapped her toothbrush three times before stretching her little chubby arms to deposit it in the toothbrush holder. That night, I sat in the bathroom talking with Jerry as he prepared for bed. Sure enough, after rinsing his brush, he tap, tap, tapped, before placing his brush in the holder. My young daughter had imprinted this same behavior. I began wondering what other things were imprinted on my childrens' impressionable young minds.

Terena's nickname was changed from Little Miss Dandelion to Smiles. By the time she was two, her smile was so prominent that even strangers commented on what a happy toddler she was.

We purchased a plastic pony on springs for Terena's second birthday. Her little two-year old body would spend hours galloping to imaginary places. Squeak, squeak, squeak, I would hear her on the porch knowing her little blonde ponytail was bouncing to oblivion. I would watch as she would dismount and walk over to where Chucky would be playing. Pow!! He'd hit her and she'd straighten up indignantly, toddle back over to her loyal mount and jump back on for another fanciful adventure. Even at that age, riding horses was her outlet and release. I could see her little face squeeze up in total ecstasy as she bounced on the back of that little plastic steed. Someday, I knew she'd ask for a real pony. Pushing that thought aside, I found contentment in knowing she had found her life's passion.

When she wasn't out riding, R.B. would be pulling her around the yard in the wagon. Sometimes, RB's strong body would pull both Terena and Chucky. I seldom saw him getting a free ride, as he was usually the one pulling or pushing the other children. Even when he was so young, I knew he was going to be a strong, giving man.

RB was also always working on the farm with me. Within weeks, our half-acre was plowed and planted with oats. Calling up my friend Linda I asked, "Do you want to go get in trouble with me?" Knowing I often had wild ideas, she enthusiastically agreed and so we drove in her station wagon to a little farm. There I purchased Esmeralda, a dairy goat. Her long pendulous ears and Roman nose were spotted with black, brown and cream markings. Jerry came home that night to the sounds of a lonely, bleating goat and was not happy that I had purchased this animal when he had said absolutely not the previous night. I waited; with my heart pounding and my mind ready to escape, as he spoke to me in anger. He was right, I shouldn't have bought this farm animal, but we had the land and the milk would help the kids grow to be strong and healthy. I wanted to show him I truly had a pioneer spirit like he said and I needed goats' milk to make cheese, ice cream and soap. I knew he had forgiven me when I caught him out talking to her the next morning. I breathed a sigh of relief and opened up to trusting him a little more. Ezzie, as we began to call her, was officially part of our family.

RB and I would milk her twice daily, and as his hands got stronger he was able to do it all on his own. Within two years, his daily chore was the milking. Chucky's chore was to feed the rabbits and chickens while Terena's was to collect the eggs every day. Being two years old, she would get the bucket that was almost as big as she was, and tenaciously make her way past the loose tom turkey into the chicken coop. I told her regularly how responsible she was for remembering to get the eggs. Whether she broke them or not was not the point of her chore. After having seen how easy imprinting was, I wanted to imprint in her young mind that she was capable.

As part of that scheme, I became active in the Parent Teacher Association, PTA, and was often at our elementary school for meetings. I was also a participant in a baby-sitting coop where we traded caring for each other's children on occasion. Because it was so hard for Chucky to be able to sit still during the PTA meetings, I would have him stay with other parents in the coop so he could play.

Ever the great actor, while at one lady's home, he convinced her that he hadn't eaten in two days! His soft, dark brown eyes looked at her pitifully and pulled her into the lie. When I showed up to get him I found his dark hair plastered to his head with sweat as he raced about the house, out of control. Meeting me at the door, with a glare of condemnation, the sitter told me how she "had to" let Chucky to eat all the cookies in the house because he was so hungry. Watching him dart about like a humming bird on speed, I lowered my head in embarrassment and mumbled a thank you. As he ran another lap of her living room, I quickly grabbed his hand and left. Driving home, I thought about the big breakfast of farm fresh eggs and the snack of homemade bread I had made for him. I realized right then how easily people could be conned by a child, and vowed to find a sitter that was stronger and less gullible in the future.

At the meetings I noticed another mom, Lori that was there as often as I was. I noticed her face was highlighted with long beautiful eyelashes that framed her honey brown eyes. Her quiet, gentle yet powerful way of handling situations fascinated me. This chance meeting of this amazing woman would be a turning point in my life. I didn't know it at the time, but in the near future I would come to rely heavily on her and her expertise with difficult children.

Chucky was seven-years old when I began working with Lori as a parent in the PTA. We spent hours preparing newsletters, organizing fund raising programs for playground equipment and school supplies and gaining community support for our elementary school. While sitting in the lunchroom one day, Lori and I sat across from each other collating the pages for an upcoming bulletin. I asked her what she did when she wasn't helping the organization. I was intrigued when she replied, "I work with emotionally disturbed children." I asked if that meant she worked with crazy kids. "Well, yes, but I also have kids with other problems like ADD. Mostly I work with children with Attachment Disorder." I looked at her children across the room that were helping and wondered what their stories were. "That sounds interesting!" I quipped. "Yes, it is," Lori, said with a knowing smirk. My curiosity was piqued, so I investigated further. "What exactly is Attachment Disorder?" She pulled her lean body from the bench and grabbed her purse and pulled out a brochure that explained it. In her confident way, she handed the folded paper to me and said, "This should answer your questions."

That night, after we had finished our project, I read her brochure. Reading through the symptoms it dawned on me as I absorbed every word that Chucky wasn't a "bad kid" he might be emotionally disturbed! His charming nature was superficial and seemed to only appear when he wanted something. He could literally "turn on the charm". I checked the box next to that symptom. I thought back to when I received eye contact from my little active son. He seldom looked into my eyes except when there was something in it for him. I marked that box. I read how these children are sometimes indiscriminately affectionate with strangers. No, that wasn't Chucky. Was he unable to give or receive affection? I thought about all the times I had wanted to cuddle him and if I was able to catch him, he would happily oblige. No, he didn't have that one either. I sighed in relief. Maybe he didn't have the full-blown disorder, I thought.

I checked the next box because he had extreme control problems and was the sneakiest child I had ever met. I continued to struggle with him over doing chores, finishing his homework or trimming his hair. These weren't battles because he didn't want to do them; they were disputes over the control involved in each task. I nodded in understanding as I read further. He wasn't cruel to animals so I skipped to the next symptom. I had watched him hit and smack around his little sister for no reason since she was old enough to leave my side. Although he didn't actively try to hurt himself, he did intentionally break his toys and anything that happened to get in his way. I checked next to the symptom of destructive to self, others and things. I circled the box several times that represented chronic crazy lying. Boy was that right on target! His stealing was a lack of impulse control. He didn't want the actual items usually, but the excitement of getting away with such dishonesty fed his pathology. Check. Chucky had an exceptional mind, so I fought with him over his continuously flunking grades; he had a learning lag! Check. He was unable to relate causes and effects to his behaviors and consequences. I understood then why star charts and the coupon system didn't work for Chucky. He lacked cause and effect thinking! Check.

I pondered whether my young son had a conscience for a long while. I really wanted to believe he had one, but as I reflected on his delight in stealing and exhibiting extreme behavior, I realized he had no remorse or empathy for anyone. I sadly checked the symptom: lack of conscience. He didn't eat abnormally or have poor peer relations, so again, I felt like maybe he wasn't too sick. The three fires in one week made me check the box for preoccupation with fire, blood or gore. Our home always felt chaotic and stressful because of his incessant chatter. It seemed as if his mouth was only closed when he slept. Check. And his sleeping, was it disturbed? All those nights I would see him sleeping restlessly, but he did at least sleep. No, I decided he probably didn't have that one. Was he demanding and clingy? I think if he was, his energy level prohibited him from being still for longer than a few seconds, so I read on. Did he continue to repeat 'what' or speak so I couldn't hear or understand him? No. Did he falsely accuse individuals of abusing him? I nearly skipped right past that symptom before I remembered the incident with the baby-sitter where he claimed he hadn't eaten in two days. I supposed then that if the allegations would yield something he wanted, he wouldn't hesitate to cry wolf. I checked the box.

I thought back to his parent teacher conference when he told the teacher he never had enough time to do his homework because he had too many chores to do at home. I sat, as this kind woman lectured me on the importance of his take home assignments, thinking how hard I worked every night to get him to finish his work. Triangulation of adults was definitely a trait Chucky exhibited and if it wasn't between the teacher and his parents, it was between Jerry and me. Check!!! I read the last symptom and before I could confirm it, I wanted to look in the mirror. Yes, the reflection I saw was a tired, hostile woman with anger hidden behind her eyes. How did I get this way? I wasn't a naturally angry person, and the hostility must have arisen from feeling as if I were under attack each afternoon when Chucky came home. I checked that box too. He had fourteen of the twenty-two symptoms and I was confused as to whether I should be happy that we might have found out what was wrong with my son or saddened at the fact that he might be suffering from Attachment Disorder.

How did he become this way, I thought to myself. What had created this? As I read through the causes I became overcome with sadness, shame and guilt. I thought back to Chucky's first thirty-two months of life, when bonding and attachment were at high risk for becoming damaged. I had wanted Chucky from the start and although he was conceived through rape, he was my child and I loved him very much. Butch hated him from the moment he found out I was pregnant, so I wondered if his feelings of my pregnancy would affect Chucky the same way as maternal ambivalence did. I then thought of how many reality-altering substances Butch had consumed which may have damaged his half of the genes passed onto my son. The beatings I endured and the trauma inflicted on my unborn son was another cause of Attachment Disorder. He had in-utero abuse as well as physical abuse while still a newborn, but his birth was normal without trauma. When I left my first husband, I was forced to work two jobs that could translate into a sudden separation from his primary care giver- me. He didn't have any undiagnosed pain or illnesses, so I read on. The daycare I thought he was adjusting so well to was actually a huge reason for this disorder surfacing in such fierceness. He started too young and changed providers more than once. I hung my head in shame when I realized my misinterpretation of his adjustment to the situation, as a toddler was simply his withdrawing from the painful break in the vital relationship he needed from me and me alone. The last cause definitely applied to him. I was a very devoted mother for the few hours I was with my children, but the lack of consistent care and parenting had clearly hurt his connection to me deeply. But I did not want to believe he didn't love me and was not connected. I could feel how much I loved him. I could feel that love through my entire being. I decided to believe he did not have the disorder. He would out grow this bad behavior. I would just love him and try harder.

My thoughts turned to my oldest son, RB. He had been loved and wanted from the start, but had suffered in-utero trauma as well. His birth had been traumatic and he was separated immediately from me because of the pneumonia. Enduring the physical abuse of Butch's beatings couldn't have helped facilitate his attachment with me either. He had stayed with me during his whole infancy and the start of his toddler hood, but after his first two years, he was placed into daycare with Chucky. I scanned the list of symptoms and was relieved that R.B. had only two. He had control issues and lack of eye contact. He did many loving things for me so I was sure he loved me. I knew we were attached. I was much more worried about R.B. and his temper than Chucky and his lying and manipulating so I decided to focus on helping my oldest son learn to be more tolerant and patient.

I then thought back to my pregnancy with Terena and her first couple of years. I had wanted her even before her conception. She had no stress or trauma while in-utero, but her birth trauma was evident by the scar I carried from the caesarean. The only abuse she'd ever endured were the jealous punches from Chucky. Never was she separated from me, unless she was napping. She had not been moved around in daycare or even been to a baby-sitter. While nursing, she did have colic for a few weeks, so I became concerned when I saw that was a potential cause under chronic pain or illness. I was proud to say I was prepared for motherhood and had been able to develop my skills as a parent. I felt slightly reassured in knowing that at least I had started one of my children without much trauma. If the saying 'third time's a charm' was ever fitting, this was the time.

Later that night, I showed the brochure to Jerry and as he read over it, I wondered how such a hard working, trustworthy and integrity filled man ended up with a child that was his absolute opposite. We had worked so hard to be the role models for our children and honesty was a moral we both highly valued yet Chucky hadn't taken in our values. We discussed the options. We both vowed to take more parenting classes and do all we could for our children.

As part of that vow, I asked Lori how worried I needed to be about my children. She said that a child needs to have half or more of the symptoms of Attachment Disorder to be diagnosed with it and at least one of the causes. A few weeks later, I drove the mile to Lori's house to work on the upcoming monthly mailing for the PTA. She greeted me pleasantly at the door before offering me an ice tea. She led the way into her house and asked one of the children to make two glasses of the instant drink. I sat on the couch and noticed her long sable hair glistened and cascaded like a waterfall down her back. Pulling her long hair out of the way, she sat opposite me and called all the children to the room. I quietly watched as eight kids replied 'Yes Mom!" and trampled into the living room before being sent to bring in the groceries from the car. I sat, wondering silently as we addressed the topics needing to be covered in the PTA newsletter, whether these kids really had Attachment Disorder because I didn't see any of the symptoms. Most had seemed sweet and kind, giving me hugs or complimenting me on my hair or outfit. It was then that I recalled the symptoms of being superficially charming and engaging as well as indiscriminately affectionate with strangers. I had been conned and manipulated into believing these children were healthy because they knew all too well how to play the game.

My belief of this was compounded when a thirteen-year old boy with a crew cut and broad shoulders entered the room and informed me that it was his birthday and he was planning on opening his presents at that moment. No impulse control and control issues blinked across my mind as if on an electronic message board. Lori, looked at me and said, "This is Alex. He's only been with me for a few weeks, so he doesn't know the appropriate way to act when there are guests here."

With her gaze directed at Alex she calmly replied, "Alex, we're going to have dinner first. Then we'll all eat cake. Then you can open your presents!" I saw his glassy eyes turn cold and menacing. He pierced everything he glared at with the rage that glowed from them. The energy in the room changed and my heart began to beat faster. His five foot six form straightened and he walked up to tower over Lori, who was now standing in all her five foot two glory. His jaw tightened and he spoke through gritted teeth, "They are my God damn presents and I'll open my God damn presents when I damned well want to!" Without even wavering, Lori looked lovingly into his eyes, pointed up to him, stepped closer and quietly retorted with no hint of anger, "You'll open your God damned presents when I say you'll open your God damned presents and not a minute before! Got it?" I tried to sink deeper into the sofa, knowing that this big young man would surely retaliate by pounding this little woman into the floor where she stood. He was cold and calculating. I could feel his angry energy like liquid volatile hate, from where I sat and I knew that after he had finished off Lori, he'd start on me. My jaw hit the floor in amazement when he backed down and replied, "Got it!" Lori told him to finish helping with the groceries and he walked off with a "Yes, Mom!"

I was awestruck with the level of power and presence this person had. I saw no fear. Her body language was strong and confident displaying a clear message of loving leadership. She had quelled the storm even before it had started. I sat, stunned at how she had smoothly handled the potentially dangerous situation. I attempted to make sense of what had just happened, but fear still gripped my soul. I asked what this child had done to be placed with her and she confided in me that he had stabbed a classmate over a place to sit in the cafeteria. My fear tightened inside me, so I thanked this determined woman for her input and left while my life was still in my own hands.

A few months later I was honored with being chosen the President of the PTA. I was proud to preside over my first meeting. Punch and cookies were donated for the night. Much was gained from the evening and as I thanked everyone for coming and sharing, I looked out over the lunchroom. It was a mess so the few folks that stayed behind to help were greatly appreciated. Grabbing a wet rag, I began scrubbing the punch spilled across parts of the floor while still in my good skirt and suit jacket. Mumbling to myself, I thought 'I'm the President of the PTA! I shouldn't have to clean up the floor!" Lori heard my muttering and came over to where I was kneeling. In her confrontive wisdom, she bent down to my level and said, "You should be thankful you can even get down there!" I stopped scrubbing and thought how right her statement was. Yes! There are people not this strong who could neither get down here nor get up! I needed to spend more time on my knees. With that simple comment, my whole mindset changed and I became humbled. I respected this woman even more for putting me back on track when I needed it. This was a person who I could trust to be honest and real about things. If only I had consulted her before having a weakness of excess compassion.

While shopping in the mall, I visited a pet store. In the far back I saw a sick, baby raccoon hiding under some filthy rags in a wire cage. The little creature pulled at my heartstrings and I knew if I could just nurture her and love her she would be okay. I immediately ran to a pay phone to call Jerry. "Please, Pa! There's a little raccoon for sale and she's very sick. She needs some goat's milk to settle her tummy. Can I get her?" Frustrated at our already exploding animal farm he responded, "No! We don't have the money and we don't need another animal. Besides, where would you keep it?" Disheartened and feeling like this little animal was destined to die I resisted the urge to buy her and left the mall.

I tossed and turned that night with thoughts of this little masked 'coon lying in her own feces. Her little black eyes were dim and hopeless. The next day, I kissed each of my sons as they headed off for school and hugged Jerry as I handed him his lunch and watched him drive off to work. Waking Terena, I pulled a dress over her weary eyes and jumped into the car. "Mommy, where are we going?", Terena asked curiously. "We're going to the pet shop!", I confidently replied.

That night, Jerry came home. He warmly and lovingly embraced me, but I was unable to fully appreciate it. I knew that when he found out I had defied him yet again, he would be angry and saddened at my obstinance. I didn't mean to disobey him, but I could never live with myself had that little, ill animal been left without the resources she needed to get healthy. Jerry went outside and grabbed each boy in a bear hug before coming back in. He went to where Terena was still napping in our room. Sitting on the edge of our bed, he began changing out of his work clothes. Having felt the bed move, Terena stirred and noticed her Dad sitting nearby. "Hi Daddy!" she sweetly said. He leaned over to give her a kiss and about that time, a little masked face popped out of the covers. Shaking his head, he looked at me and asked, "What is this?" Not knowing how to tell him that I couldn't leave her in the pet shop, I looked at him pleadingly and said, " This is Paddy Cake McBeamish. She's cute, isn't she?" He looked back at the tiny little face. Shaking his head he muttered "The guys at work are going to have a real laugh tomorrow. They all made bets about whether you'd buy it or not. I can't believe I lost the bet!"

Beamish drank the goat's milk with gusto. Her bed was a carpeted box close to the ceiling that Jerry had made for her. A carpet covered pole led to the floor that she would climb down in order to join the family. Her skinny body filled out as she matured and her silver tipped fur grew thick and glossy. Although she was a wild animal, she loved being petted, snuggled and held. She was true to who and what she was. There were no pretenses in our relationship. She broke things and ate anything she found appealing. A trail of broken stuff was left wherever she had been. Sleeping during the day meant that her waking hours were at night. She ransacked our home nightly. When threatened, her big silver body stood its ground fearlessly. No matter what she damaged or got into, I loved her for being her.

Beamish by this time had grown so heavy; I decided to put her on a diet. After a few days, with hunger motivating her actions, she climbed up onto the counters and pulled the refrigerator door open. The next morning, Jerry awoke to find broken egg shells all across the floor and the door to the fridge wide open. Understanding her hunger, I couldn't get mad at her. She didn't do it out of anger or revenge, she did it because the response was primal and compelled by her desire for food.

Knowing how to open the door to the magic food well, she would often browse through the cooler to find delicacies. I had been out picking purple grapes one day, and being tired, I simply put the whole ten-pound paper sack in the bottom of the fridge. I planned on making jelly the following morning. Big mistake.

The light switch for the kitchen was through the room, on the opposite side from where the bedrooms were. Jerry regularly woke up before the sun and would put his coffee on before jumping into the shower. He slept 'au naturel,' and knowing that none of the children would be up so early, he would walk through the kitchen, in the buff, to turn on the light and start the coffee. This particular morning was no different for his routine than any other. As he walked through the dark kitchen, he slipped and fell on something slimy on the floor. Trying to get up, he fell again. The sludge-like substance was across the entire floor, so crawling on his hands and knees; he reached the far side and flipped the switch. Having heard his thuds, I came rushing to see if he was okay just as he turned on the lights. Bracing himself against a wall was my purple husband. Grape skins were spread everywhere. Trying not to, I burst out laughing hysterically. There was my sweet, gentle husband, in the corner looking like a deranged smurf, screaming obscenities. I quickly helped him to the shower where we both scrubbed for twenty minutes. We didn't have to wonder who had done the deed as little purple raccoon prints covered the counters, the carpet and the wall leading to her box, where she slept, content and full of the soft insides of sweet grapes.

My children were growing up. Terena strolled up to me, in her four-year old saunter, and asked, "Mom, what is rich?" Not quite sure how to answer her, I told her we should both think about and discuss it later. Not more than ten minutes passed when she skipped through the kitchen and announced, "I know what rich is, Mommy! It's when you have two pennies and people that love you!" That was as good a definition as any I had ever heard, so I agreed with her and contemplated that thought for the rest of the day. The youngest minds can come up with some of the most profound things.

Both boys were fighting their own battles, as they got older. Jerry would try to correct them and they'd ignore him. They were often disrespectful and rude to the man that had taken them in, adopted them and treated them like his own. RB's moods were becoming more hot-tempered and impulsive. Chucky, at 8 years old, was out of control.

RB had always been a hard worker, so the summer of his tenth birthday, he started his own lawn mowing business. He paid to have business cards printed and went door-to-door offering his services to the neighboring community. The special wagon he built to carry the mower and weed whacker was pulled from yard to yard as he earned spending money. He was cautious about saving his cash so it was a big surprise on Mother's Day when he took me out to Red Lobster for dinner. Here was my ten-year old son, sitting across from me, wearing a shirt and tie. His blonde hair was combed to one side. His eyes still showed sadness, but that day, with pride and love he wasn't sad at all. I was so honored to have such a wonderful son to share the day with. For my birthday, he snuck my new Corgi puppy to an artist and had her portrait done. I awoke that morning to find this huge beautiful picture with a red bow tied to it. The card said, "To Mom. With much love and devotion, your oldest son, R.B." Many years later that painting still hangs where I can see it everyday and each time I look at it, I feel my son's love.

For Father's Day, RB made Jerry a homemade cheesecake topped with cherries. He was always doing amazing and thoughtful things for us and although he and Jerry butted heads often, he was a great child.

The following year, my oldest son's business was so successful, he subcontracted the edging and weed whacking to other neighborhood kids. He continued to do the milking as a chore, but as he got older, we also added a house chore to his daily duties. He was such a hard worker that I never had to worry if his responsibilities were fulfilled. His homework was finished and his classes were a breeze for him. When he was old enough to be on the honor roll, there was seldom a quarter that his name wasn't on the list.

He excelled on the swim team and played baseball with ease and participated in the school talent shows. He was a good sport with an honest heart.

RB wasn't perfect though. He had trust issues because of the abuse he had witnessed and endured. I worked such long hours when he was little that many of the normal feelings and experiences little boys have were either repressed or neglected. I would have to buy him new shoes all the time because he would sit and peel the rubber of the sole from the leather upper. No matter how often I lectured him, his picking never stopped.

His temper was quick to surface and he struggled to control his outbursts in school. There were times the principal would call and ask me to pick him up. I'd drive up to find my handsome boy disheveled, bruised and bloody. His eyes would be on the ground, ashamed of himself for not handling the situation appropriately. His buttons were easily pushed and I'm sure the other kids soon learned that too. I didn't spank him for fighting, because I couldn't justify punishing his violence with more violence. I tried taking away everything he owned. I figured that if he wanted to act like a animal, reacting with aggression rather than talking problems out, then he should live like one and animals don't own things. That didn't work. I talked with him, repeatedly, to no avail. I grounded him. For short periods at first and when that didn't work, we tried grounding him for a longer time. I worried so much about how this would affect his life as an adult.

But RB wasn't the only one I worried about. Chucky's contagious grin and wild sense of humor often had the whole family rolling with laughter. He was stubborn and strong willed just as I was as a young girl. I loved his spirit. He was the most like me of my three children, yet he was suffering. I yearned to calm his agitated body. I didn't have the tools. I had no idea what was wrong with him. I had missed much of his first years. I started his journey to healing with lots of prayer and a doctor, then a nutritionist, a therapist, an herbalist, military school, laying on of hands, vitamins, herbs, special diets, star charts, all of it would prove not enough in my quest to save my son.

Chucky had always been hyper, but the problem grew worse the older he became. His thin, ever moving body would crash into things causing injury to himself and others. Without hesitation, he would pick his injured self up off the ground and begin buzzing around again. He seemed to feel trapped when I pulled him into my arms to snuggle him. He would writhe and pull away. It would sadden my heart, as I wanted so much to hold and rock him. I loved to smell his soft hair. His quicksilver actions were hard for him to calm as he was only able to settle and self soothe when he sucked his finger. We couldn't get him to sit still at the dinner table, in church or at school and since Ritalin wasn't available then, we dealt with it as best we could. He struggled with this malady.

He would talk incessantly and create elaborate tales. Not knowing what was true and what was made up, Jerry and I struggled with finding some way to help him become honest. The more he lied, the more I began to doubt anything he said was true.

Chucky was becoming more and more disobedient and belligerent. In order to give him a haircut, I would have to chase him around the house while he screamed in defiance, his arms flailing high in the air. Around and around we would run until I would finally out smart him and grab his little active body. Still screaming and wiggling, I would cut his hair into the popular style of the season. He always looked so handsome when I was finished and was happy at what he saw reflecting back from the mirror. I never could understand his response when I pulled out the scissors each month.

My older sister, Martha, went to the New York Institute of Fashion Technology, so she would use her amazing sewing skills to make western shirts for my boys. Chucky would remove his handmade shirts by grabbing the shirttails and tugging them apart quickly. The snaps, holding the shirt together, would pop loose and shoot throughout the room sounding like a spray of bullets. One shirt would last him a few washings. It made me sad to see such disregard for the loving effort my sister had put into the many gifts she sewed for him.

He would destroy his clothes, whether they were handmade with love, handed down from R.B. or brand new from the store. His pants would often have huge holes in the knee after only a week. Ink or marker would stain them from the belt loops to the pant hems and no matter how I laundered the stains away; they'd be re-stained and ruined shortly after receiving them. His shirts would mysteriously unravel or rip within days. He was hard on his clothes and our pocket book was becoming stretched because of it.

My son's behavior spiraled more out of control. Stealing became a severe problem for Chucky. During the winter of Chucky's seventh year, he stole $60 from his Grandpa's wallet and hid it under the neighbor's lawn mower. My father was angry and hurt, and I was shocked that my son would do such a thing to his own grandfather. I would find toys in his room that weren't his and when confronted, lies would spill from his mouth. The more I tried to make him stop, the more he stole.

I attended some more parenting classes, thinking the problem must be in the way I was dealing with him. He earned coupons for good behavior that could be redeemed for great prizes. I designed fabulous star charts and enthusiastically stuck each little gold star that he earned to the poster board. I did all the things the parenting class taught. What I didn't realize then was that the class was designed for normal, emotionally stable children and Chucky had suffered too much trauma. He was wounded and needed more help than normal parenting classes could offer.

As I saw Chucky's problems escalate, I desperately searched for better answers. After he stole the money from my dad I decided to take him to our pediatrician where tests were run. I was told our little over active boy suffered from hypoglycemia. I learned that Chucky's young pancreas would fail and cause his death within five years if he continued eating the typical American diet. I was terrified I would lose my son! I acted swiftly and decisively to removed all traces of sweetness from our home. Worried about how difficult it would be for him and how it might make him feel left out, I changed the whole family's diet in order to keep him from feeling different. I tried everything to make him happy with the changes needed to keep him alive. Chucky's favorite food was cheese. He loved cheese. So, instead of a birthday cake, he had candles burn in a big huge round of Swiss cheese. His eyes lit up with joy when he saw the feast.

Concerned about losing my son, I studied voraciously about vitamins, minerals and nutrition. I took every class I found and changed our eating habits accordingly. In my efforts to help Chucky to become healthy, we all got healthier. We all took daily supplements and changed our lives drastically.

Chucky craved sweets intensely. In search of sugar, my seven-year old son would rummage through the neighbor's trash looking for the sweet foods his body craved. His head would be so deep in the barrel that his feet would dangle without support. This reminded me of the bears at Yellowstone. I lectured him incessantly about the problem, but had no idea how to help him or get him to stop.

We would be walking down the sidewalk and I would see him chewing gum. Knowing how much sugar it contained, I would be horrified, and ask where he got it. "I picked it off the cement when I bent over to tie my shoe!" Totally grossed out, I would have him toss it into the nearest trashcan. The harder I tried to keep sugar from him, the more he would lie, cheat and steal to get it. He thought it was a game of catch me if you can just like his other stealing. I was terrified this game was going lead to his ultimate death.

For a birthday present, Jerry and I gave Chucky a male, champagne colored rat. He loved him very much. The two of them spent their days together. When I would tiptoe into Chucky's room at night to pull up his covers and check on him, there would be "Hot Rod", curled up in bed beside him. I was surprised to see the little furry body scamper down the side of the bed onto some newspaper, where he was potty trained to eliminate and then return to his warm spot beside his best friend. When Chucky shared a piece of candy with him one day, the blood on the paper the next day was obvious. The vet informed us that Hot Rod, the rat, had diabetes, a pancreas problem, just like Chucky. Knowing they had something in common bonded the pair even tighter than they already were and they were nearly inseparable. Tenderly caring for his small buddy helped calm my son.

Since I had noticed an improvement in Chucky's excess energy level, I continued on the special diets but after a year it was evident more had to be done. I had been learning so much about what our body needed to fully function, so I turned to an herbalist for more answers. For another year, I made Pao D'Arco tea for him and encouraged him to take multiple capsules of herbs. While I worked so hard at home to give him the things the professionals said he needed, Chucky would go to school and trade lunch with other children. He was miserable on his special diet and would steal their lunch money and find even more ways to feed his sugar addiction.

I thought exercise would release some of his pent up energy, so I enrolled him on the swim team and the baseball team. I was hoping the organized sports would teach him discipline and control. To my chagrin the baseball coach had him sit on the bench each and every game. It was heart breaking, seeing my little son feeling rejected. On the swim team, however, his slender body would rocket through the water. We would all cheer him on as my son, sleek as a dolphin, claimed his ribbons.

Lori and I continued to work together on school projects but it took me over a year to work up enough courage to go back to her house. I drove the short distance with thoughts of the boy who looked evil enough to kill someone for the fun of it. The anger from his eyes penetrated my memory and I hoped he would no longer be there. I walked up to her door and knocked. My heart nearly jumped when Alex answered the door. I asked to see my friend. "She's not here right now, but she'll be back in a few minutes. My mom said to have you come inside." Resisting the urge to run in terror, I looked back towards my car and thought to myself, 'I'm an adult. I should handle this like one and not let this boy know I'm afraid of him.' I turned back to face this now six foot tall young man and took a deep breath. "Sure, I'll wait." I stiffly followed his powerful form into the living room where he offered me a chair. "Would you like me to make you some iced tea?", he asked nicely. My mind filled with all the things he could do to me while I sat alone with him in the house. I then thought about what he would do to my tea. Spit? Poison? Salt instead of sugar? I didn't know, but I knew that if he was in the kitchen he wouldn't be trying to kill me, so I replied "sure". I listened as he opened cabinets and drawers, wondering what his sick plan might be.

I was expecting the worst when he strolled into the room carrying two full glasses of ice tea. He gently smiled as he handed mine to me then set the other glass by the couch. "This one is for my mom!" I figured he had done something to the drink, so I set mine aside and made a note not to touch it. He stood in front of the door as he spoke to me, "I'm lookin' to get a job detailin' cars and for the interview they're gonna have me do a car to see how hard I work and how fast I can get it done. Can I clean your car out for you?" I started thinking about my stereo and the items I kept in the glove box. I didn't trust this boy in the slightest, but I knew if he was out "cleaning" my car, he wasn't inside hurting me. I agreed to let him practice on my car.

As he was stepping outside, Lori came in followed by six children. Each carried a sack and quietly walked to the kitchen while my friend came and joined me on the sofa. Alex peeked his head in the door, "Mom, I made you some tea. It's next to your spot on the couch!" He closed the door and as he did so, I breathed a sigh of relief.

When Lori and I finished our PTA business she walked me out to her driveway. Alex was nowhere in sight and as I open my car door I was relieved to see my stereo and change still there. Sliding inside, I quickly realized all the pet hair, dog nasal art, dust and grime was removed from my seats, windows and the floor. The interior looked brand new! Shame filled me. I waited as Alex stepped from the garage, expecting him to charge me fifty bucks for all his hard work. I told him my car looked great and asked what I owed him. He smiled, "Ma'am, you don't owe me nothing'. I appreciate you let'n me practice on your car." I figured he was just saying that so I tried again with: "No, really, how much do you want?" Again, he insisted I owed nothing and refused to accept the bills I held out to him. I thanked him, gave Lori a hug and drove home in my very clean, nice smelling car with confusion filling my mind.

I was up all night wondering what happened to the rage filled boy I had encountered so many months before. Alex was hospitable, thoughtful, hard working and generous now. What had Lori done to help him so much? I had never seen her hit or yell at her kids. What was her secret? I had to know. I needed help with my boys and hoped maybe she would teach me. The next morning, first thing, I called Lori. "I have to know what you did to Alex! He is so different from the way he was!" She explained that she didn't know exactly, but invited me to come and sit on her sofa to watch whenever I wanted.

That afternoon, I arrived at her home armed with a note pad and pen. Her children were expected home from school soon, so I sat and waited. Lori made me an ice tea and we sat chatting before the arrival of the group. I watched as each child filed through the door, removed their shoes, placed them neatly by the wall, walked through the room and waited for a hug from Lori. She stood and wrapped her arms around each child and smiled into their eyes. As she let go, they trotted off to their room where they deposited their school bag, changed into play clothes and began collecting tools for their various chores. Mops came from the closet, brooms began sweeping corners, the vacuum started sucking up debris from the floor and the laundry was folded. She didn't say a thing to the kids and yet they were all busy with household tasks. It was as if the queen bee had wagged her antennae silently and sent all the bees to work caring for their hive.

Lori's quiet power and love illuminated her home and I could see its effect on all the children. There was no arguing. No fighting or yelling filled the air. She didn't have to browbeat them into getting their chores finished. I watched in amazement as one child said to another, "I got done with my chore. Can I help you finish yours?" I tried to pick my jaw up from the floor and put my eyes back in my head. I was stunned to hear such kindness and cooperation between children. It took several attempts before my mouth was in working order and I responded with, "Lady! You have got to know, it's not like this in other homes!" She quietly replied, "Well, it should be!"

I thought about that statement as I sipped my tea. I flashed back to the struggle my mother had with getting us to even pick up our things. I then remembered the difficulty I had with my boys. Every attempt at getting them to clean their rooms, pick up their toys or even do chores was met with obstinance, aggression and a screaming match. I found it easier to just do it all myself than to try to get them to do anything.

I sat, drinking the tea, absorbed in my thoughts when I noticed the children finishing their chores. Two got a board game and began playing quietly on the floor. Three went outside and played catch. One drew pictures.

All the children were entertaining themselves, laughing and enjoying the company of their siblings- quietly and under control. I slowly scanned the house from where I sat and wanted more than anything to have my house be as calm, collected and under control. This lady had a magic touch with kids and I wanted it too!

I drove home that evening with thoughts whirling around in my mind. I arrived at my doorstep with only one thought- my priorities were going to have to change if I was going to have a family like Lori's! I wanted a home filled with peace, joy, cooperation and love. Boy did I have a lot of changes to make!

Proud Dad

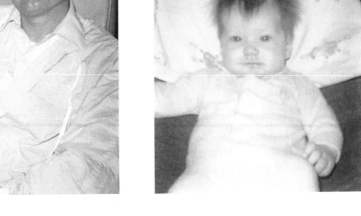

Little Miss Dandelion

RB and Chucky, happy!

Terena, two years old, performing
her daily chore, collecting eggs.

Beamish and RB having dinner.

Chapter 6

Smoke Gets in Your Eyes

The herbal remedies were not curbing Chucky's impulsiveness as he lit three fires in one week. I walked out of the back door because I smelled smoke and found him gazing at our wooden garden gate engulfed in flames. Screaming at him, I grabbed the garden hose and sprayed the partially burned gate with water. I told him he was grounded for a month. I made sure to hide all the rest of the matches and lighters. Two days later, Terena came into the house with no eyelashes, bangs or eyebrows. The stench of burnt hair surrounded her. When I asked her what happened, she stammered that Chucky was lighting candles in the underground fort R.B. was building. With dread filling my mind, I walked out to see smoke pouring from the opening. Again, I yelled at him and Jerry spanked him when he returned from work.

Three days later I became concerned when I hadn't heard from Chucky for a while. I called for him and received no answer. Walking around the yard I saw clouds of smoke billowing from the crawl space under the house. I panicked! I raced to the door and yanked it open to see Chucky calmly sitting with a fire he had built in the two and 1/2 foot high space! The flames were licking the floor joists. While our ninety-year old grandmother, Iva Lou, Terena and I made lunch in the kitchen, Chucky had stolen the lighter fluid from the outside grill and started a fire with cardboard right underneath us. All the flammable Christmas decorations and stored boxes of other items were within inches of him as he watched the flames. Having tried everything I could think of to teach my son that starting fires was not acceptable, I called the police and had him arrested. I sadly watched, exhausted and without answers as they tried to hand cuff his thin wrists, while hate looks shot at me from his cold eyes. His nine-year old mind couldn't comprehend that I had done this for his own good. The vision of my son burning himself to death while he torched our home haunted me. I had to find a way to stop this dangerous game. My hope was that the shock of being behind bars for a few days would scare him enough to make him stop before he burned himself to death. He stayed behind the steel bars throughout the weekend. Jerry and I arrived on Monday morning to get him. Before walking to the temporary holding cell, I prayed to God to help my youngest son.

The sugar free diet, herbs and other concoctions had backfired. It had increased his craving for sugar to the point that he was now stealing and eating much, much more of the sweet stuff than he had before we started taking it away from him. After more than two years of the constant battle I admitted defeat with the diet. Even by adding some sugar into our diet we were still eating much healthier than we had before.

I studied with Lori for months and then made some dramatic changes to my parenting style. I was stronger and more secure in the boundaries I set down for my children and felt comfortable giving them consequences instead of trying to deal out punishment when they tested the limits. I continued to sit on Lori's couch watching and learning new techniques whenever I had a chance.

I began implementing daily chores for all three children. RB had already been milking the goat twice a day, so I added one small household chore to his routine. Chucky attempted to feed the chickens, ducks and rabbits, but because he neglected his duties the majority of the time Jerry had opted to do it himself. I reassigned Chucky to folding the laundry. Terena was bringing in the eggs. I told them all, that as soon as their chore was completed, they could have playtime. That meant that if it wasn't done by dinnertime, they had missed playtime. RB and Terena had no problem accomplishing their tasks. Chucky tested me the first day I imposed the new plan and spent the afternoon sitting on the couch looking at the laundry instead of folding it. The next day, he came home from school and immediately folded the two days worth of laundry. I smiled at his newfound focus and gave him a reinforcing hug. My hopes began to build for my family.

That fall of 1981, Terena was enrolled in kindergarten. Her first day, I curled her fine platinum hair and dressed her in a cute blue jean skirt and vest. Taking pictures of her, I smiled and gave her a hug. R.B., Chucky, Terena and I walked, hand in hand to the elementary school. I hugged R.B. and Chucky when we arrived at their classrooms and waved to them as they skipped to their respective desks. Terena was excited and her grip tightened around my hand. "Can we go to my room now?" she asked. We walked down the corridors to where her class was assembling. I waited, anxiously for her to cry or sob or act as if the lack of daycare had negatively affected her. She watched, still holding my hand as a few other children threw temper tantrums or wailed in terror when their mothers left. She looked up at me and asked, "Mommy, why are those kids crying?" I smiled down at her innocent face and answered the best I could, "They will miss their Mommies because they don't get to see them as much as you get to see me. I will miss you, Smiles, but I will be here at noon to get you!" She hugged me again and trotted off to meet her new friends. The lady had said this class would be a nightmare for Terena, but what I think she meant was that it would be traumatic for me. I left my baby girl there; in the large carpeted room with a Mary Poppins look alike. I looked through the outside window and watched her smile and laugh with the other children, before walking home to an empty house to cry because I missed her so much.

With Terena in school I had more time to read and research. I was curious about the history of Attachment Disorder so I reread the story of Helen Keller. I had read it in high school, but didn't realize her famous story was caused by the fact that she suffered from this disorder. I read John Bowlby's book on the research sponsored by the World Health Organization from 1948. He studied children separated from their mothers during the war and called them" affectionless thieves". Confused, I wondered why none of the psychologists or therapists I had been to ever mentioned the malady. It had been scientifically documented so many years before. I was appalled that the information wasn't more available or more public than this! Reading through the many books by Foster Cline, M.D., I gathered valuable information about helping these tough kids. It made so much sense, I eagerly awaited my chance to use the tools I had been gathering!

Lori's little girl, the one that had ripped the door off the washing machine, quickly stopped the pity party with me when she realized I wasn't falling for it anymore. Instead of the sad, puppy dog eyes, I now received cold, menacing looks from across the room. She was having a hard time one day with being respectful, responsible or even any fun to be around, so Lori asked if I would watch her while she stepped out to get some toilet paper. "Candy, I want you to show Mrs. Thomas what strong sitting is." With that instruction, the little girl sat cross-legged on the floor with her hands folded in her lap and her head looking straight ahead. I was impressed by her straight back and ability to resist the urge to look around. Lori explained that the strong sitting gave Candy an opportunity to think about her actions and decisions. It wasn't punishment and was helpful for times of transition and to assist her brain to function better. I remembered taking yoga a few years before and was surprised by the similarities of the posture. I had always felt rejuvenated and more clear thinking after the class, so I easily related to her explanation of the exercise.

She asked me to find an area in the room that was against a wall (with no wallpaper or an electrical outlet) that would distract Candy. "I'll be back shortly, so just have her strong sit to think about what kind of day she would like to have when I get back," Lori said before giving her a hug and stepping out the door.

I was honored that she trusted me with her child, but I was also terrified that I'd mess up the hard work she had spent helping this child. Would I be the one to disrupt the miracle? I didn't want to wreck it, so I pulled a chair from the dining room and placed it a few feet behind the sitting girl. Sitting there, staring at the little eight year old breathe, I thought about how lucky this child was to be able to just sit and think. So many children her age had their senses assaulted with a constant barrage of noise, images, and ideas that their brain rarely had an opportunity to peacefully focus.

It seemed like Lori was only gone for a few minutes when she stepped back through the door. I smiled in accomplishment and enthusiastically told her that Candy was still, straight and strong; and, I had watched her the whole time. Lori gave me a hug and said, "I knew you could do it. I wouldn't have left her with you if I didn't feel you were ready! Candy's a good sitter, so I knew you wouldn't have any problems." Lori called Candy over to where she stood and gave her a warm hug. "Did you have enough time to think about what kind of decisions you'd like to make for the rest of the day?" Candy replied with a respectful "Yes Mom!" and asked Lori if she could do a chore for the family since she had not been a good helper earlier. I smiled, knowingly, at Lori and knew that strong sitting would be a useful tool to add to my repertoire.

Having built my confidence, I volunteered to do more respite relief for Lori. She gave so much of herself that I felt she needed a break sometimes. I was only allowed to have the children during the day until I had fingerprints and a background check completed. Within months, I was able to keep a child in respite for longer than a day. Jenny was my first overnight child. She was tall and lanky for her eleven years, but the head of curly hair was cared for like a toddler. A tangle of knots encircled her head and I understood why it was cut short. She was charming and affectionate, but the facade didn't trick me. I was aware of her illness, and appreciated her attempt to at least pretend she was normal, since this was my first overnight watch.

Terena had always wanted a sister, so when she asked me if Jenny could stay in her room, I agreed without really thinking. That night, after Terena's bath, I laid a sleeping bag out on a cot in her room for Jenny. Terena's excitement was hardly contained as she quickly kissed me good night and closed her door. She and Jenny were alone. I heard them chatting for an hour or so and watched as the light under the door went out. Fifteen minutes later I heard a ruckus in the room and Terena calling for me. Rushing to the room, I opened the door to find Jenny standing on Terena's bed naked and Terena cowering near the cot. "Mommy, she wants to get in bed with me, but you told her to stay in her own bed! She's been chasing me around my room and no matter where I try to go to bed, she tries to sleep with me!", my little five year old daughter whimpered. "I don't want to have a slumber party with her naked. Can I come sleep with you and Daddy?" I was glad she asked, because I didn't want her with Jenny anymore. I told the naked child to put her nightgown back on and to go to sleep. I was relieved when she happily complied after saying, "Yes, Mrs. Thomas!" I walked to our bedroom, with Terena's hand in mine before tucking her in. I turned off the light and immediately went to call Lori.

I asked her why Jenny had removed her nightgown and had insisted she sleep under the same covers as my young daughter. As I asked, a sinking feeling filled my mind. I knew the answer, but I allowed Lori to tell me anyway. "Jenny has been having a hard time in therapy. She's keeping a secret and it's making her sicker. I think you just found what she's been trying to hide for so long. Jenny must have been molested as a child and Terena was a potential victim for her. I'm sorry! I didn't know because she hasn't had an opportunity to sleep with any of my kids as they all have separate rooms for just such a reason." I hung up and was glad that I had been able to intervene before Terena had been traumatized. I vowed then, that I would never take in a child that was bigger than any of my children again! But sometimes I didn't have a choice as to the child's age or size; Chucky was one such instance where age and size just didn't matter.

Several tons of sun dried grasses and straw bales were stored in our barn so when Terena came in and told me smoke was coming from it, I immediately rushed out the door. I came around the corner of the enclosure and caught Chucky, at ten years old, smoking cigarettes and dropping hot ashes in the barn with his friend Jed, leaning against the twenty-foot high stack. I shrieked as I asked him what he thought he was doing. His cockiness and brashness surprised me so I grabbed his arm and instructed Jed to walk home immediately and tell his mom what happened. Chucky repeated over and over that I was over reacting that it was no big deal and everybody does it and he knew how to handle fire.

As I marched him into the house, I fumed about how he could be so self-centered to put his best friend in such danger. I was thinking how he must not care for Jerry or the hard work it took to get all that feed into the barn. He was willing to sacrifice the barn, the animals, his friend and our family to fire, all for a quick thrill. My mind raced, as I thought how he didn't care that right at that moment, my father, his grandfather, was dying of lung cancer in the hospital from smoking tobacco. He was willingly and happily inhaling the same toxic poison, the matches and ashes falling into the flammable dried feed. I imagined seeing his burnt corpse, like the scene in the driver's education film of the crispy human form being pulled from a wrecked car. How could he not have learned from the jail experience after the last fire? Did he just not care for anyone or anybody including himself?

Beside myself with anger, I went over the edge. I struck him hard, not to help him to learn, but because I was so furious. I screamed in his face at the top of my lungs, "You have to stop this! You don't care about your grandfather! You don't care about me or your father! First you burn the gate, then you burn your sister's hair, you try to burn the house down! When are you gonna learn? Go to your room right now and don't come out until I tell you!"

As I finished unleashing my fury I sank to the floor and sobbed. I was horrified. I had turned into my mother. I had allowed the anger inside of me to build until I could no longer control myself. I had shrieked in her tone of voice, I had said the things she would have said and I had lost it, just as she used to. Afraid, ashamed, appalled at what I had done to my poor son, I searched for the phone. "Pa...Pa? I need you to come home and help me!" I sobbed into the receiver and told him everything. He told me we would make an appointment for Chucky with the best psychologist we could find, and we would get better help than what we'd had so far.

I hung up still feeling desperate, so I called a friend and told her what happened. Crying again at what I had done to my child and how I had lost control, I felt a little better when I had shared with her what I had done and how awful I felt. When I hung up I got down on my knees and spent a long time in prayer. I went to Chucky's room and opened the door. I tried to say how sorry I was and tell him I would not tolerate fires in our home. He didn't listen. I rushed into Jerry's arms when he came home and sobbed as I told him what I had done. We made a plan.

I was looking for more answers. I wanted help. I knew Chucky had bad genetics and a bad foundation from early abuse and from being away from me so much at a young age. I didn't know if or how I could heal the pain he had suffered during those beginning years.

The psychologist told me I was doing the star chart wrong. I thought to my self " How much intelligence does it take to put stickers on a chart?" He also told me to set out a bowl of fruit and everyday Chucky didn't steal any of it, I was to give him a piece of candy. So, everyday, I would count the grapes and plums. The apples and oranges were always there, so I would walk into his room, praise him profusely and give him the candy. He was still stealing from everywhere else and lying to cover up the stealing, but I gave him that candy, because he had left the fruit alone. It seemed ridiculous to me, but I had spent $150 to see this highly trained individual, so he must know the right things to do. Chucky was denying his theft problem. He took no responsibility for his actions. He felt no shame or guilt about what he was doing and his story changed every time he told it. He had a very bright mind and delighted in outsmarting those around him. I was scared he would end up in prison and I only knew of one mom who could save children like Chucky. I had more to learn and time was ticking; off to Lori's I went

Lori's every waking moment was focused on leadership and love while being dedicated to the children and the other moms struggling with tough kids. She spent hours on the phone, after tucking in her recovering demolition crew, supporting, helping and giving hope to the many moms needing her wisdom.

One such mom was an alcoholic. I watched as Lori would answer the phone, say nothing but, "Oh!...... Uh huh..... Well sure!..... Uh huh..... I'll be right there!" As she instructed me on what to do in the event of an alarm going off on one of the bedroom doors, she shared with me that the mom had been drinking and couldn't handle her five year old anymore. Apparently this had happened for years, and each time, Lori would drop whatever she was doing in order to help this mom. I waited while she went to pick up the child. When they returned, I saw the most beautiful girl walk through the door. "Stephanie, I would like you to take your shoes off before walking through the house", Lori stated assertively from behind her. The little Shirley Temple look alike, turned on her heel, put her hands on her hips and screamed, "No! I won't and you can't make me!" Lori smiled, picked the defiant little one up and carried her off to her room while stating, " Holler all you want. Get it out of your system. When you're quiet, I'll come to get you so you can try it again." She left the fit throwing Stephanie in a room and walked back to the couch.

She didn't judge or condemn the mom. She didn't blame the little girl's behavior on the mother. She just loved the mother where she was in her life and accepted that the only way this mom knew how to deal with life was to self medicate with alcohol. Sometimes it would take a few days for the mom to get in shape to come get her daughter. Sometimes it would be weeks, but each time Lori would welcome the mom back with a warm hug. She would then bring in Steph and encourage the mother to hug and rock her little girl. Lori would feed them both and wish them good luck before they left to start over.

The more I saw of Lori, the more I wanted to be like her. I admired her tremendous amount of love, knowledge, patience and power. This five foot two inch tall woman had made a huge impact on so many lives. I felt honored to be in her presence and delighted that she allowed me to oversee her work. She was unlike anyone I had ever met or heard of. The things she accomplished with these tough kids were nothing short of miracles, and I was blessed to be a part of it! I knew that she didn't do this amazing work all on her own. The children attended weekly attachment therapy sessions that were intense. Without Lori, though, the therapy would be wasted because the day-to-day interactions with the children were just as important as the weekly therapy sessions. Lori was the catalyst for their healing.

The more I learned, the more my family changed. I had Chucky sew his own western shirt to learn how much work and time went into making such a garment. He never again popped the snaps from his tops and proudly wore his beautiful black shirt with silver yokes. It was very flashy. His clothes lasted longer and he put more effort into caring for them.

R.B. made his own pair of knee-high moccasins out of leather. Instead of going out and purchasing new shoes when he picked at the bottoms, he simply replaced the soles with new leather. He loved his boots so much that he wore them often. He was deeply saddened when he finally out grew them, but we never again had to purchase new shoes because of his destruction.

I continued to reinforce Terena's responsibility in remembering her chore. Lori mentioned how important it was to have an event preceding the chore in order to help jog her young memory. We set her egg collecting time for right after lunch and if the eggs were used in the meal, I was sure to announce how important her job was. "If you weren't here to collect the eggs, we couldn't make these muffins! I'm so glad we have you." I empowered Terena to believe what she made a difference and was important for the family to function. I brainwashed her (Why do only the bad guys use it?!) by telling her daily, "You are so responsible! You always know what needs to be done!" I didn't remind her to do her job, but if she forgot, I simply asked her to bring her basket to me for washing. The little tip would trigger her toddler brain into remembering. "Okay Mommy, but can I go get my eggs first?" I would smile, give her a big hug and reply, "Oh! You are so responsible. You always remember what needs to be done!"

Later, when Terena was in college, she called and asked why I hadn't pestered her about getting her homework finished like her classmates had been complaining so much about. I smiled and told her that I had taught her to do her homework when she was two years old. She accepted this for about ten seconds before she replied, "I didn't have homework when I was two, Mom." I told her she had work at home and didn't need reminding to do it. "Smiles, you were always responsible! You always knew what needed to be done and you happily did it!"

I also quit confusing my children about school issues. Instead of focusing on their grades I put my attention into what they were learning in school. I started asking them everyday what new things they had been taught and how it related to everything else. Their grades would come in and I let them worry about them. I watched smugly, as their grades increased without me nagging them about homework or marks anymore.

While in a study group during Terena's second year of college, she became upset and phoned me. "Mom, why am I so different? My study group told me they wouldn't invite me anymore if I kept trying to learn the stuff the instructor said wasn't on the test! They didn't seem to like my reply when I told them I didn't study for the test and instead studied to learn the subject better!" I smiled into the phone. She had clearly learned that it wasn't the grade that was important but what she learned. Taking the bull by the horns, I decided to make some other changes as well.

Bedtime had always been a struggle. I would consistently remind the kids to start picking up their toys and belongings an hour before bedtime. I would continue to prompt them into cleaning up and getting ready for bed non-stop until way past bedtime. I would scream and yell at them nightly. By the time I read to them and shut their light off it was late, Jerry would often be sound asleep, and I would be pooped!

Something had to change, so instead of fighting with the boys to get into bed at a reasonable hour, I decided to assign chores for every minute they were up past their bedtime. Terena was still too young to tell time, so I started her on a nightly routine that was completed by the time the boys were to be in bed. I would put her in a bath to relax her little active body. We'd sing tub songs and play with her little rubber toys. The evening was finished with me reading a story to her. Sometimes, before turning the light off, she would ask me to smell her eyes. Laughing I would watch as she scrunched her little eyes and pink nose together. "Smell my eyes, Mommy, smell my eyes!", she would squeal as I touched her little lashes with my nose. "They smell like sunshine and rainbows, Smiles!", I would say before kissing her one last time and turning off the light.

The first night, R.B. proudly complied without fuss. At 7:30, his door was closed and he was in for the night, just as he was supposed to. Chucky on the other hand, had to test these new boundaries. He was out of his room playing until 8:15 and I didn't say a word to him. When he finally went to his room, I noted the time and began making a list of chores for him to accomplish. The next morning he came to the breakfast table still tired from having gone to bed well after bedtime. As he sat to eat his eggs, I laid a list of forty-five chores down in front of him, and without saying a word, I left the vicinity. After he was done with breakfast, I told him that I would expect two chores to be finished before he had lunch and another two finished before having dinner. It would take him twelve days to finish off the list, and our house would be sparkling and clean. Hugging him, I told him that I loved him very much and thanked him for staying up late. "I hope you're late often so we can have a super clean house! Won't that be wonderful?", I asked rhetorically.

I now had bedtime under control, so I decided mornings should go as well. Having been in the habit of waking them up three or four times, telling them to get ready over and over and coaxing them into eating their breakfast, I dreaded the morning routine. In an attempt to change the typical morning, I had the boys both earn money for an alarm clock and I told them they were now in charge of getting themselves up and ready for school. Dr. Foster Cline called my parenting style the "helicopter mom" because I hovered around my children. In order to quit hovering about, giving reminders and orders I decided to stay in bed and read until they came in for a hug before leaving for school. It worked well the first morning, but Chucky had to test to see if I meant business. He didn't get up when his alarm clock went off, so he was late. The natural consequence of his behavior was that he was tardy for school and would have to enter his class late and deal with it. This new parenting stuff was fun and it was working! But all the parenting in the world couldn't compare with the high Chucky felt each time he got away with stealing.

Chucky still craved excitement. The rush of adrenaline was like an addiction for him. We were baby-sitting a pony for a year for my sister, Maxine. Chucky delighted in riding that little horse. He knew that when he got her going fast enough she would plant her feet and screech to a dead halt, causing him to fly over her head. He got so good at reading her body language that he would prepare for the flying lesson and was able to do a midair flip and land on his feet. It was amazing to see! Not once did he get injured and over and over he would run with her, waiting for her to stop so he could fearlessly orbit off. As his feet touched down safely my heart would begin to settle back into a normal rhythm. His arms would fly over his head for a huge "V" for victory as if he were an Olympic athlete. His face would have a huge smile of accomplishment. It still warms my heart as I think back to it now.

Chucky's extreme hyperactivity, defiance, stealing and lying continued to escalate. He was failing school and the repeated calls from teachers had us gravely concerned. After much soul searching Jerry and I decided to have a complete evaluation done to see if they could diagnose what we had obviously missed. The psychiatric hospital, after hearing his symptoms, recommended a two-month stay for him. I thought they would be doing all kinds of psychological evaluations, ink blot tests, timing him with blocks and mazes, brain scans and blood tests checking for imbalances or toxins. I was wrong. At just over a thousand dollars a day they had people with little training observing his behavior. There were no therapy sessions, no evaluations, no blood tests run. Still overactive and receiving no help while there, we saw no change in our sick little boy and wondered what our money was really being used for. When we came to pick him up, the psychiatrist told us that children steal because they feel deprived. We took Chucky home and did as the psychiatrist told us: we implement a weekly allowance program.

Years later we would find out that the $80,000 we had paid them for their useless advice had made Chucky a victim of molestation at the hands of another child with a history of molesting others. These "mental health" professionals had housed Chucky in a room, alone with another child, unsupervised at night. While I trusted them with my son he was abused at the hands of another severely disturbed child. Sending Chucky to this psychiatric hospital proved to be the most destructive decision we ever made.

The weekly allowance system we implemented taught R.B. and Terena to save and manage money, but it only enabled Chucky to steal more. Not knowing what we had given him as allowance and what he had stolen, became a game of "catch me if you can". The harder I tried to catch him stealing, the more sneaky he became. He delighted in outsmarting me.

To make matters worse, my father, Maximilian, succumbed to cancer in 1984. He had been in the intensive care unit for a very long time and his once strong body was withered and gaunt. I visited him everyday in the hospital until he died. The day of the funeral, I held the wake at my house. Before the ceremony, I made sure everything was in order. I was an emotional wreck inside and was only holding it together by a thin thread. I asked R.B. to put the plates out on the table and when he griped at me for having to do it, I cracked. I calmly stepped over to where my teenage son held the plates and took them from him. Not taking my eyes off of his, I purposefully dropped the whole stack of glass plates on the floor between our feet. "There! Now it doesn't matter who puts them on the table. Go to your room!", I said without raising my voice. Confused, scared and hurting too, my son shuffled off to his room, his chin to his chest. I watched as he closed the door behind him before I called Lori. I was sobbing so hard into the phone, she asked several times, who was calling. I finally stammered out my name coherently enough for her to understand. "Nancy, I'll be right over!", she replied before hanging up. Five minutes later, she opened the front door to find me crumpled into a heap on the sofa. A pile of tissue surrounded me. My swollen eyes met hers and she sat by my side and held me. I later watched, distanced from the harsh reality, as she assigned jobs to her children and mine in order to finish preparing the house for the coming mourners. R.B. swept up the mess I had made, walked over to me to give me a hug and an apology.

She was a great friend and I loved her even more after that day. She taught me to speak with more authority when addressing my children. Instead of saying, "I need you to clean your room, okay?" I changed it to, "I want you to clean your room. Got it?" I empowered my requests and made my expectations clear by saying, "I want" instead of "I need". I expected all of my children to be respectful of themselves and others, responsible for their actions and their work and fun to be around. These three things were the goal for my children to work towards. My life's dream was becoming a reality!

RB's hot temper was getting him in a lot of trouble, so I started having him do push-ups until he began cooling off. He was in charge of how many he needed to do and it was interesting to hear his counting change from a seething, aggressive tone to a more mellow and controlled manner. By encouraging him to release his anger through physical exercise, he built an incredible upper body and delivered his hate looks to the floor instead of toward me. I would watch as his furrowed brow and tight jaw relaxed into the rhythm. To this day, R.B. still holds the unofficial record for the highest number of push-ups at Rifle High School!

Chucky was acting more responsible, but he was still lying and stealing. The consequence for his sneakiness was to pay back double the value of the stolen item to whomever he stole from. I would catch him with a stolen article and feel so sorry for him when he would sob and cry that he'd never do it again. I felt terrible for missing out on so much of his early childhood that I would allow him to slide by. I would find myself letting him off the hook for the compensation of his dishonesty because I felt guilty for missing his first words and first steps. I had stayed in an abusive relationship and allowed him to be hurt when he was so tiny and helpless. My guilt got in the way of parenting him. I seldom followed through with his consequence. His manipulations of me were brilliant. I was helping him learn to play the game better and was making him sicker by using idle threats. My weakness was to become Chucky's downfall.

>m※⁄w >m※⁄w >m※⁄w >m※⁄w

Another time of weakness (when I broke down and brought Beamish home from the pet store), was turning into a victory. The little baby that nearly died was aching for freedom after being with us for six years. Although she had never been caged, she was becoming less friendly and more agitated with each summer. Out of desperation, she climbed into the attic to make a nest. The fiberglass insulation penetrated her delicate paws and so she spent hours licking her raw feet. In turn, her tongue became inflamed and she began losing weight. When she fell through the ceiling, crashing to the kitchen floor below almost killing herself, I knew she would have to leave our family soon. We spent one last Christmas with her before taking her to a program for rehabilitating wild animals. The wild is where she truly belonged. It was a sad day, but I knew I had tried to domesticate her long enough. I also knew when it was time to let go, so my family said goodbye and with heavy hearts, we left her in capable hands. I had learned much from living with a wild animal that would serve me well in later years as I began working more and more with children suffering from RAD.

One afternoon in the summer of 1985, I received a phone call from the director of the Attachment Center at Evergreen (ACE), C.J. Cooil. "I've heard about the good work you're doing with children", she told me. Flattered that my efforts had been noticed, I listened as she continued, " We have a little girl in Texas that needs to come into the program. I feel like you could do a really good job with her! She's six years old and in big trouble. She really needs help!" Caught by surprise, I asked if I could call her back the next day after discussing it with my family. I hung up the phone and tried to calm my mind. Was I ready for such a task? I thought about the vow I had made a few years earlier about taking a smaller child than my own and was reassured because she was two years younger than Terena. Surely she'd be smaller! Fear entered my heart then, not of the six year old, but of failing her. What if I messed this child up more than she already was? I wasn't nearly as wise as Lori and I had limited experience! I called CJ back and shared my fear with her. She chuckled soothingly before replying, "Oh you don't have to worry about that! She's so sick she can't get any worse!" With an odd sense of relief, I hung up the phone.

That evening, I called for a family meeting after dinner. I explained to my husband and three children that a sick little girl in Texas had her heart broken when she was little. I shared with them that she was very mad and did a lot of bad things and that her parents wanted to know if we'd help her. "She needs a family with big brothers and a big sister that can show her how to act right. Will you help me? I think she can get better if we all work together. What do you think?" R.B. thought for a moment before telling me he could be a good big brother to her. I smiled at him warmly because I expected that response from him. Chucky hesitated too long, so Terena responded, "Sure Mom, I'll help you!" Chucky finally quipped, "Will I have to share my stuff?" Jerry looked over his family before meeting my gaze. "Where will we put this child if we bring her here?" he asked logically. I had been thinking that very question all afternoon, so I quickly told him of my plan to divide the large living room into two rooms: a bedroom with a walk in closet and a smaller living room. He thought about that for a moment before agreeing to it. My heart began to pound as I asked for confirmation. "So... are we going for it?" R.B and Terena replied, "Yes" in unison, Jerry nodded and said, "yes". Chucky mumbled, "I guess so."

The next morning, I called ACE to tell them we were willing to open our home to this child and do all we could to help her. CJ was excited and told me she'd be sending out a file of information and dates for an upcoming training workshop that all new therapeutic parents had to attend. She asked us to sign up for the first available class and ended the conversation with, " This girl needs to be moved right away! Your help will be needed soon because she has killed a litter of kittens!"

ReactiveAttachmentDisorderisaconditioninwhichindividualshave
difficultyforminglovinglastingrelationships.Theyoftenhavean
earlycompletelackofabilitytobegenuinelyaffectionatewithothers
.Theytypicallyfailtodevelopaconscienceanddonotlearntotrust.T
heydonotallowpeopletobeincontrolofthembecauseofthistrustissu
e.Theycanbesurfacecompliantforweeksifnolovingrelationshipisi
nvolved.Withstrangerstheycanbeextremelycharmingandappearlovi
ng.Uneducatedadultsmisinterpretthisasthechildtrustingorcarin
gforthem.Iftheycannottrustandlovetheirownfamilythatlovesthem
,thentheywillnottrustandloveacasualacquaintance!!Theydonotth
inkandfeellikeanormalperson.SomefamouspeoplewithRADwhodidnot
gethelpintime:Hitler,SadamHussein,EdgarAllenPoe,JeffreyDahme
r,TedBundy.ReactiveAttachmentDisorderisaconditioninwhichindi
vidualshavedifficultyforminglovinglastingrelationships.Theyo
ftenhaveanearlycompletelackofabilitytobegenuinelyaffectionat
ewithothers.Theytypicallyfailtodevelopaconscienceanddonotlea
rntotrust.Theydonotallowpeopletobeincontrolofthembecauseofth
istrustissue.Theycanbesurfacecompliantforweeksifnolovingrela
tionshipisinvolved.Withstrangerstheycanbeextremelycharmingan
dappearloving.Uneducatedadultsmisinterpretthisasthechildtrus
tingorcaringforthem.Iftheycannottrustandlovetheirownfamilyth
atlovesthem,thentheywillnottrustandloveacasualacquaintance!!
Theydonotthinkandfeellikeanormalperson.SomefamouspeoplewithR
ADwhodidnotgethelpintime:Hitler,SadamHussein,EdgarAllenPoe,J
effreyDahmer,TedBundy.ReactiveAttachmentDisorderisacondition
inwhichindividualshavedifficultyforminglovinglastingrelation
ships.Theyoftenhaveanearlycompletelackofabilitytobegenuinely
affectionatewithothers.Theytypicallyfailtodevelopaconscience
anddonotlearntotrust.Theydonotallowpeopletobeincontrolofthem
becauseofthistrustissue.Theycanbesurfacecompliantforweeksifn
olovingrelationshipisinvolved.Withstrangerstheycanbeextremel
ycharmingandappearloving.Uneducatedadultsmisinterpretthisast
hechildtrustingorcaringforthem.Iftheycannottrustandlovetheir
ownfamilythatlovesthem,thentheywillnottrustandloveacasualacq
uaintance!!Theydonotthinkandfeellikeanormalperson.Somefamous
peoplewithRADwhodidnotgethelpintime:Hitler,SadamHussein,Edga
rAllenPoe,JeffreyDahmer,TedBundy>ReactiveAttachmentDisorderi
saconditioninwhichindividualshavedifficultyforminglovinglast
ingrelationships.Theyoftenhaveanearlycompletelackofabilityto
begenuinelyaffectionatewithothers.Theytypicallyfailtodevelop
aconscienceanddonotlearntotrust.Theydonotallowpeopletobeinco
ntrolofthembecauseofthistrustissue.Theycanbesurfacecompliant
forweeksifnolovingrelationshipisinvolved.Withstrangerstheyca
nbeextremelycharmingandappearloving.Uneducatedadultsmisinter
pretthisasthechildtrustingorcaringforthem.Iftheycannottrusta
ndlovetheirownfamilythatlovesthem,thentheywillnottrustandlov
eacasualacquaintance!!Theydonotthinkandfeellikeanormalperson
.SomefamouspeoplewithRADwhodidnotgethelpintime:Hitler,SadamH
ussein,EdgarAllenPoe,JeffreyDahmer,TedBundy.

Chapter 7

Our Bottomless Pit

My stomach churned as if an alligator were inside of me doing a death roll with a victim clenched in its jaws. I read through the girl's file and began wondering if I was the right mom to help this very sick child. She had murdered seven helpless, fuzzy kittens. After removing their tiny heads the girl methodically aligned each little body next to the other and placed a head at the bloody stump of each neck. She then returned to finish sweeping the front porch as if nothing had happened.

The record showed a similar incident had occurred several months before with a different cat. The adoptive mom, Elaine, and dad, Todd, thought learning about the magic of birth would be interesting for their new six year old daughter, Alicia, so they purchased a two year old pregnant cat. They excitedly awaited the birth of purebred Siamese kittens. Six little balls of tan and black fur were born to the new mom who immediately went to work licking and nursing her family. The mother seemed to be appropriate and nurturing, so when all her offspring were found torn to pieces, the family vowed to never breed her again and took her to the vet for spaying immediately. They assumed the new mom had become confused and killed her own babies. When the second litter was discovered the same way from a different cat all carefully lined up, Todd and Elaine knew something was terribly wrong.

Alicia had been born in Dallas, Texas to a thirteen year old runaway. The two moved from one rundown, condemned home to another for the first year, but the baby was often left with other runaways or strangers. Her tiny body was used as a bargaining chip for the purchase of drugs. Sexually violated and neglected before she was even able to walk, Alicia was removed from her mother and placed with her grandparents after a drug bust shed light onto her dark little world.

They were an elderly couple and her hyperactivity and destructiveness left them exhausted. The constant stress began creating serious health problems. At three years old, Alicia's grandmother brought her to Social Services and asked the agency to find her a new home.

Todd and Elaine experienced and successful parents with four grown children had adopted a beautiful daughter from Korea and were delighted with her loving heart and gentle ways. They felt they had room in their hearts and in their home for another needy child. So, Todd and Elaine, a prominent Houston family adopted Alicia in the spring. Confident in their parenting ability, the lawyer and social worker, believed they had a lot to offer a young child. Wanting to spend a lot of time with their new daughter, Elaine put her career with Social Services on hold.

Within the first month, Elaine found a therapist to help her new daughter transition into the new family environment. Alicia's development was so delayed she started kindergarten when she was six. Her intelligence was tested and found to be in the fifties. Not specializing in mental slowness, the therapist referred the family to a different center that could better meet the needs of her low I.Q. So off to therapist number two they went in order to find help and answers.

Alicia was very polite and gentle at first. She was helpful and sweet, so the couple was surprised when she started acting like a wild animal after a couple of weeks. She ate with her hands and refused to follow any rules the struggling couple tried to set. She screamed and threw things at her adopted family, breaking any item in her path. When confronted with her behavior, she would sulk and detach from her physical body causing her to shut down. She would not let her new mom hug her or tuck her in at night. Drawing pictures of angry black scribbles or demons, or blood covered knives, she would hide her drawings in her mom's bed for her to find at night.

In the therapy sessions, her behavior was angelic, just as it had been when she first came to her new family. She spoke slowly and politely, claiming that her parents were too mean. Her eyes teared up and she would whimper as she told the therapist how they didn't feed her enough and spanked her often. Being out of the room, Elaine didn't know what lies her new little daughter was telling the adult supposedly trained for handling such manipulation, but when the expert called her into the room, she could see nothing positive had been accomplished. She was told to lighten up on her daughter and to love her more. "Alicia is a very charming little girl. Don't hold such high expectations and everything will be fine." Lighten up? How could she lighten up? She had not disciplined her harshly or yelled at her, nor did she expect more than respect and manners! Love her more? Alicia was rejecting any love she tried to give!

Determined to find useful help, she went to a psychologist. Elaine was able to watch from a closed circuit T.V., as an academy award-winning act was played out for the adult by her six year old for the professional. She was told the same thing: don't be so hard on sweet little Alicia, just love her more, she's so charming, she just needs more time to adjust.

Frustrated, Elaine searched for more help. She wondered why it was so difficult for her to help her daughter? She had worked in the field for years and had more resources than most! She felt that she was a patient and loving mom and had lots of experience. Searching the Internet, she finally settled on a therapist three hours away. If he could help her daughter, she would be willing to drive to the ends of the earth, so again, they transferred her growing file to a new 'specialist'.

The first consultation seemed hopeful as mother and daughter sat together and shared problems and goals with the new expert. He thought the little girl was 'charming' and discussed some reasons for Alicia's behavior. He recommended they start Alicia on Ritalin and said she needed time to adjust. It had been six months of defiance, destruction and rejection. Elaine, committed to her daughter, religiously drove six hours each week for her sessions, but when the second litter of kittens turned up dead, she called the therapist in desperation. It was then that the specialist told Elaine that he was no longer able to help Alicia. He told her he would contact a center in Colorado that was trained and equipped to handle such serious pathology.

I quit reading the file and began doubting whether I was able to really help this child. I didn't have the level of formal education that these people had, and they couldn't make a difference in Alicia's life! Where was I coming from in thinking I could make a difference?

I thought back to my great great Uncle, Clyde Beatty, who tamed lions and tigers for the circus. Beasts that many thought were wild and savage slept in his room with him. His tenacity and patience helped to develop trusting relationships with the huge man-eating cats. Taming wild creatures was in my genes.

I reminisced about my upbringing. I had learned such powerful lessons from each of my family members that I hoped the early training would add to my skills and understanding of this girl. I thought of all the pain, fear and trauma of my first marriage. All those times I had endured beatings and rapes I had questioned God's plan for me. I smiled now, and closed my eyes in understanding. This little girl had been raped and abused as well, and maybe, by my firsthand experience of knowing what that was like, I could relate to her on a level others had been unable to.

The report said she had broken things and acted like an animal. My thoughts turned to all the lessons Beamish, the raccoon, had taught me. Materialistic things were nothing but just that- things that could be replaced if necessary. Beamish had destroyed a lot of the items I had held dear, so my house was cleared of most valuables or breakables already. Because she truly was a wild animal, I had learned years before to live with the characteristics of the untamable. I loved her for being true to her nature and I returned my thoughts back to Alicia. She was taught to fend for herself in a world full of darkness and turmoil. She was being true to herself when she tried pushing everyone away, because up until she was six, nothing but pain, rejection and heartache accompanied her relationships with others.

I was beginning to understand God's plan for me now, and although it had taken me many years to build up the lessons I needed, I allowed Him to lead me down the path. I prayed, as the open file lay in my lap. "Father, is this what you want for me? Am I supposed to take this child? Do I have the skills I need to help her find your love? Am I the person she's supposed to learn from?" My eyes were still tightly closed when the phone rang. It was C.J. "I know you just got Alicia's file, but have you gone through it yet? I know you'll be great with this one, I can feel it! Two spots just opened up for the training class starting this week. Can you and Jerry make it?" I looked to the heavens as I told her yes, I had gone over the file and was prepared to begin the training class. Hanging up the phone, I chuckled at how mysteriously God worked in my life.

That Monday, Jerry and I apprehensively entered the small classroom that was to teach us the needed skill to help this sick little girl. Three hours each week day evening had been dedicated to learning about pro-active and reactive approaches for dealing with the toughest children in our society. Twelve couples filled the room and as the requirements for becoming a therapeutic parent were laid out, the class began to thin out.

The biggest cut in participation occurred when we were instructed that one parent had to stay home full time with the child in order to be considered a therapeutic family. When we learned that the $600.00 each family received per month had to cover meals, clothing and damages several more families dropped out. I calculated my hourly wage and realized the $1.43 wouldn't go very far in providing what this child would need. This certainly wasn't a profession where I'd get rich, but I believed the rewards beyond money were going to be well worth the effort.

On weekends, the whole family helped build the room where our new family member would sleep. The beautiful plush carpet was torn out and replaced with tile. The instructor told us these children often had elimination problems and would urinate or defecate throughout their rooms and I silently thought of a wild animal marking its territory. Instead of drywall and plaster, the walls were constructed of fireproof plywood brushed with biologically friendly paint. Apparently, these children loved to punch and kick, so preparing for this behavior saved much repair time and expense down the road. The glass in the window was replaced with shatterproof Plexiglas and I sewed new curtains. The cheery red, white and blue striped hot air balloons I painted on the wall matched the window coverings and the solid red comforter on the twin bed. The room had shelves for her toys and a little white dresser with red knobs. It was ready for Alicia, just as soon as we finished the class.

Jerry and I spent an entire weekend taking a course in how to safely restrain a child who was a danger to themselves or others. A therapist trained us on how to respond to fit throwing and obstinance. Lori came in and taught us how to clean urine and feces from carpet, houseplants, and wooden and porous surfaces. We learned CPR and First Aid, paperwork and record keeping, nutrition, and respite care. By the last class, only two couples remained. The fear of being attacked, assaulted, having your house destroyed, and dealing with false allegations of abuse was apparently too much for the others so the four of us sat, awaiting our certificate of completion. Along with our diploma was a list of necessary items we had to purchase before our home could be inspected and a child could be placed in our care.

Walking in to Radio Shack the following morning, I thought of how different my perspective on child rearing had become. The children that would be place in my care would not see me as working for or with them. They would see me as the enemy, another individual that must be warded off in order to stay alive. I was preparing for a battle, very similar to strategic planning for war. I was going to fight for this child's life and it was going to be tough, challenging and often times, frustrating, but I was getting ready to win the battle for their lives! I purchased two motion detectors, one for the door and the other for the window. If this was a war, I needed to know where my little trooper was at all times and alarms would alert me to her whereabouts.

I walked across the street to the hardware store. With several padlocks and clasps in my shopping cart, I thought about having to lock up all the medicines and valuables. I wanted everything to be in place before she came, so I could focus on her healing instead of what things she could get into.

At the grocery store, I purchased a baby bottle, hot cocoa, chamomile tea, and sweet caramels and ice cream. At the health food store, I found lavender and chamomile oil. I had read about the soothing properties of both essential oils, so I added them to my growing number of methods for calming upset minds.

The night before we were to meet Alicia, I read through an article about family pets and the unattached child. I thought about all our critters. Freddy, my dog, stayed at my side all the time. Hot Rod, Chucky's rat was in the far end of the house in his room that now had a hook and eye latch too high for a young child to reach. The barn housed our two cats, and four goats. The rabbits, and poultry were safely kept in a different outbuilding and were only loose during the afternoon when I was out gardening.

I still worried for them. Alicia had already killed and our home was full of potential targets. I didn't want our family pets to be her next victims, and as they were unable to tell me of her perverse actions, I would have to work extra hard at keeping them all safe. Supervision at all times would be required when there was any chance for her to have access to them. I also decided to make touching and interacting with the animals a privilege she could earn as she got healthier, because I knew how healing animals could be, but I also knew that the benefits couldn't be obtained until she was ready.

I felt armed and prepared for this child who was capable of scaring her parents, murdering kittens, and manipulating trained adults. I imagined her tough appearance, ripped up jeans and dirty face. Her body would be big and strong with powerful arms and legs. Visualizing her menacing glare as she would twist her face and squeezed her left eye shut to contain some of her fury to spit venom into my face. Sure she's only seven year old, but I pictured tattoos and piercings. Her teeth are bared to show slime and slobber oozing from her mouth. Animal blood drips from her clenched fists. I wait, ready for her first challenge, and I haven't even met her yet!

The next morning Alicia stepped over the threshold of my home followed by her parents, Elaine and Todd. I nearly laughed when I saw the image of the fierce belligerent child in my mind morph into the frail, wide eyed, little girl in front of me with the Barbie backpack strapped across her back. I had been worried about this child? She didn't weigh more than forty pounds and she was hardly taller than my waist! I looked past her to where her parents stood. Todd quietly set down two large suitcases. He looked tired and defeated. Elaine looked scared and nervous. Dark rings of exhaustion circled her sad eyes. I understood that look. They were here to leave their child with people they didn't know. They had nowhere else to turn if this didn't work. The fear, tension and pain they bore was palpable.

I stood to meet them and saw the deep lines of concern in the face of the father. "Hello! I'm Nancy Thomas. I'll be the therapeutic mom Alicia will be staying with! Is this your first time in Colorado?", I asked cheerfully to the couple. Out of the corner of my eye I watched as the young girl inspected the room. "Yes, it is." Elaine stated in a soft Texas drawl. Her pretty face was easy to read. She felt defeated since her parenting skills, which she had taught as a social worker to so many other families, weren't working. I could see she wanted to be hopeful, but skepticism clouded her expression. This caring woman had successfully placed over sixty children in adoptive homes and over saw the placements. She had watched her own as they grew up to became successful adults. I knew she had dedicated her life to the care and welfare of children, and now, her own little girl was having to be placed with another mom because she needed special help. My heart ached for her.

I turned away from her pain filled eyes, and addressed Alicia. She looked me straight in the eye, shook my hand politely and said, "Nath to meet you, Ma'am!" before flashing a charming, sweet smile at me. I wasn't charmed, but I was beginning to doubt whether this tiny human being was even strong enough to kill a flea much/less an animal. Were they mistaken about her history and actions? I certainly didn't see a killer standing in front of me. Her little hand reached out to pet Freddy and I found myself wanting to reach out to hug her. She seemed so pitiful and sad. I turned to give the family a tour of our farmhouse. Alicia came to her mom when she was asked and seemed very compliant. The first room we went to was Alicia's. The parents seemed to breathe a little easier when they saw how cute it was. I instructed their little girl to stay in the room to unpack while I gave the rest of the tour. "Yeth, ma'am!", she drawled as she spun on her heel and busied herself with exploring her new room.

Elaine pulled me aside, when we got out of earshot. "I know you've read Alicia's file, but you should know that she called all those therapists stupid and they called her charming. While she was seeing them she molested 5 school children!" I thought about all those other kids that were now traumatized because Alicia had inappropriately touched them. I thought of the humiliation this social worker must feel. "Elaine, I know this must be hard for you! Your daughter will have tight supervision because if she's able to hurt others, it will only make her sicker. Thank you for letting me know about her behavior, I'll be sure to keep an eye on her when ever there are other kids around!" I gave her a big hug and continued showing them our farm.

It was nearing lunchtime when I suggested to Todd and Elaine that they go on a picnic before the afternoon therapy session. I made some sandwiches for them and let them say their goodbyes to Alicia. She didn't seem shaken that they were leaving and I thought that was odd, but I kept my thoughts to myself as we closed the door behind them. Peeking through the curtains, I saw Elaine collapse into the arms of her husband. Sobs wracked her athletic body as he held her for a while then helped her to their car. As they drove away I felt helpless to comfort them and resolved to do all I could to help their child.

I prepared two more sandwiches while Alicia finished unpacking. I could hear her humming a happy tune as she placed her toys on the shelves and her clothes in the dresser. Waiting until she was finished, I showed her to the bathroom and had her wash her hands for lunch.

We ate quietly and I noted her manners were impeccable at the table. After each bite she would wipe both corners of her mouth. "May ah pu-weeze have thum mo' mewk ma'am?", she asked. I got up to pull the glass gallon jar of goat's milk from the fridge. "Wow!! I ne-vo theen mewk wike da-at be-foe!", she exclaimed with surprised eyes. I explained to her that we owned dairy goats; so all our milk was fresh. I told her how the bread and cheese for her sandwich was homemade. "Wow!! My ma-ma don't make thtuff lack da-at!" I winked at her and told her she'd be helping me make it if she got strong enough.

I thought as I drove into the mountains for Alicia's psychological evaluation, what a waste of time the therapy in which my children had participated had been. I knew Lori said this therapy helped her kids tremendously, so I trusted that the three-hour weekly drive wouldn't be wasted. We walked into the therapy room where I saw a big squishy couch and a few chairs already occupied by her adoptive parents. Dr. Foster Cline motioned for me to sit down in his chair as he moved to the couch. "Alicia, I would like for you to come sit next to me", he invited. She eagerly pranced over to the big man and sat down near him. He introduced himself and began the questions.

Holding up a green crayon, he asked Alicia what color it was. "Wed, bwue, yewow, bu-wack, pink, ow-ange, bwown", she continued naming every color but green. Dr. Cline grinned and set the stick down. Showing Alicia the yellow, he again asked what color he held. Green. Blue. Red. She continued down the list of colors, but did not say yellow. Trying the exercise one more time, he held up the blue crayon. Again, Alicia named every other color she could think of. He looked up at the three of us in chairs and shared his wisdom, "Even a child who is quite mentally delayed would accidentally name the right color. She obviously knows her colors so what we're seeing here is pure resistance."

Moving to the next test in the assessment, Dr. Cline noted the previous report claimed auditory processing difficulties. "I see Alicia is able to repeat what I say when I say it slowly. What I'm going to do here is differentiate between whether this is neurological based or resistance based", he said as he began the test. He asked Alicia how things were going at her new home. She smiled sweetly and blinked in mock confusion. Dr. Cline asked rapidly, "How do I want answers, fast or slow? Fast right?" She grinned and said, "Wight!"

Wanting her to speak in complete sentences, he asked her to repeat her response. Silence filled the room so Foster gave her the phrase, "You want me to go fast!" Looking up at him, she stated, "Ya wan' me fa-yast!" He tucked her in closer to him, "Good! Almost perfect. Try it again! You want me TO GO fast!" She squeezed her face and licked her lips, "Ya wanna go fa-yast!" Curling his arms around the girl he said, "It's hard isn't it? Let's lay you down here so you can do it better when you look at me!" Lying across his big lap, she smiled and began playing with his bolo tie as her head rested on one of his strong arms. Dr. Cline repeated the phrase to her and when she finally said it perfectly he cheered and hugged her.

Looking at her parents, he explained, "We're going to lengthen the sequence to see how the processing advances." His attention focused back on the little girl cradled in his lap he said, "I want you to repeat after me. You want me to go fast all the time. Go!" Alicia looked woefully at her parents. "Alicia, I know this is hard, but I want you to repeat after me. You want me to go fast all the time. Go!" She faced the friendly man and slowly started, "Ya... wanna..me.....go to......" He interrupted her attempt, "You want me to go fast all the time. Go!" "Ya wan' me to go fa-yast...on ya!" Dr. Cline patiently repeated what he wanted the little girl to say. Blinking exaggeratedly she said, " Ya wan' me to go fa-yast powta da time!" Smiling in understanding, the expert looked at the three of us and explained the problem we were seeing was definitely resistance based. "She's making one mistake, in a different way, each time!"

He backed out of the head butting Alicia was creating by talking with Elaine and Todd. Discussing the control battles and game of hassle Alicia used to dominate situations, he enabled her to sit and rest. I watched her as he was preoccupied with clarifying her behavior to the adoptive parents. Her hands climbed up the bolo straps and tightened around the turquoise concho at the base of his neck. She started tightening it to choke the therapist before he calmly loosened the tie. When he asked her again to repeat the phrase, she was able to say it exactly right! It was concluded at the end of the session that a new I.Q. test would have to be administered after her healing in order to reflect Alicia's true intelligence without the variable of resistance.

Alicia contracted verbally to willingly work on her life in therapy while staying with me as her treatment home. Knowing this would be the last time she was to see her parents for a long time, she mechanically hugged them both. After hugging her daughter Elaine reached out to hug me and sadly looked into my eyes. Trying not to sob, she pleaded with me," Please help my little girl. We love her very much!" Grabbing my hand, Alicia smiled sweetly at her family before we turned to leave. I noted the little girl never turned back once as we got in the car, but her mother's aching eyes followed us as we traveled down the road.

We drove the hour and halfback to the suburbs of Denver. I hurried, not wanting the kids to walk home to an empty house. Pulling into the drive, I was relieved to see we were twenty minutes early.

Chucky and Terena came home from school that afternoon. Terena looked at me for approval before running over to her and introducing herself. I watched them as Alicia showed her the Barbies and pink car she came with. My daughter connected with her new sister quickly when she saw the Barbie palomino horse. They were both horse lovers. They played happily in the living room as I helped Chucky with his homework at the dining room table, aware that Chucky hadn't made any attempt to introduce himself.

R.B. walked home from the high school bus stop several minutes later. He gave me his usual hug before furrowing his brow and gesturing with his eyes towards the pair in the living room. "Yes", I exclaimed, "that's your new sister, Alicia." I called his new sibling from the living room. The pitter-patter of her little feet changed tone when she stepped from the carpet onto the hard wood floor of the dining room. "This is your new brother, RB" She smiled, shyly at him and averted her eyes before lifting her hand to shake his. I was amazed at how my son's paw engulfed her tiny palm. Because Chucky didn't want to feel left out, he turned abruptly in his chair and said, "I'm Chucky!" He turned back to his homework and I smiled approvingly at my growing family. So far, everything was going better than planned.

After the boys finished their homework, they began doing their chores. Terena stopped playing and went out to check the eggs, leaving Alicia to play alone on the carpet. Running in, Smiles exclaimed, "Mom! I got almost a dozen eggs today!" Interested, Alicia jumped up to look into the basket," Way-ya did ya git doze eggs?" Laughing, Smiles explained how the chickens and ducks make them. Her eyes became as big as saucers and before she could speak, Terena asked what her chore was. "Ah don't have one!", was Alicia's reply.

I assigned sweeping the kitchen to my new charge. Explaining that work completed in my home was to be A+, I showed her how to clean the edges and corners using the hand broom. Pointing out where the trash can was, I gave her the instruction to have it finished in twenty minutes. With a hug, I went back to assign another chore to Terena.

She was nine years old now, so bringing in the eggs was too simple. Asking her to vacuum the living room, she skipped away to find the upright. I sat at the table, sorting mail where I could watch Alicia sweep and thought how nice everything was. Chucky was folding the laundry, R.B. was mowing the back yard, Terena was singing while vacuuming and Alicia was busy with the broom. I expected Jerry, my cowboy, to be home soon so I left his pile of letters at the head of the table where he would sit for dinner.

Fifteen minutes later, Alicia stepped over to where I was reading at the table. "Ma'am, I'm aw done!", she said proudly. I smiled at her and gave her a hug. "Alicia, thank you for finishing so quickly! In this house, when you're done with a chore, I want you to let me know by doing strong sitting where you can see your job. That way, you're not interrupting what I'm doing, you're letting me know you're finished in a respectful way, and you get an opportunity to look over your job to make sure it's done right. Let me show you what strong sitting is... Terena!" Turning off the noisy machine, Terena joined me in the dining room and demonstrated strong sitting for Alicia. Imitating Terena's position, she worked hard to straighten her thin body and to fold her hands properly in her lap. I exclaimed, "Oh my gosh!! You are such a quick learner today!! Come over here and get a hug then hop over to your chore and strong sit to let me know you're done!" Her skinny torso was pressed hard into me as I rubbed her back and gently squeezed her. She hopped back over and sat up straight and proud and strong. I wrapped my arms around her again before thoroughly checking her job. She had done it well and had even put the brooms away.

Jerry interrupted my checking of the floor as he stepped through the front door. "Daddy!" Terena exclaimed as she ran to greet him. With Terena under one arm, He walked through the living room to where I stood in the kitchen. "Hey Babe!", he said as he hugged me. "So this is our new family member, huh?" I stepped out of the doorway, so he could get a better look at Alicia. "Nath to meet you, Thir!", she politely said before placing her hand in his. Jerry replied with the response taught to us by the instructors at the training class, "Nice to meet you too, young lady. I hope you choose to work on your life while you're here with us!" Her big brown eyes softened as she smiled and replied, "Oh, ye-ath thir. I will!" He made eye contact with me as if asking the same questions I had. This is the sick little girl that killed kittens? You've got to be kidding me!

He tousled Chucky's hair and said, "Hi, son" before going to change out of his office clothes. I began preparing supper. Having finished her chore correctly, I sent Alicia to go play on the swing set with Terena and Chucky. I watched from the kitchen window as my two daughters swung like pendulums in opposite unison. Chucky immediately left to help R.B. build the fort and I sliced cucumbers from the garden to add to the salad. Sighing with relief, I thanked God for the wonderful day.

The next couple of days were harmonious. R.B., Chucky and Terena woke themselves and prepared for school. Giving me hugs before leaving, R.B. walked with Terena and Chucky until he reached his bus stop. The other two continued walking the half-mile to the elementary school. I would get Alicia up have her use the toilet with the door closed and then she and I would wash our face, brush our teeth and brush our hair together to give her a routine to imprint. She would then go to her think spot and do her strong sitting for five minutes. I would cheer on this vital exercise with loving encouragements of " Oh! Your back is so straight and strong! or, " Oh, your hands are perfectly still!" or " I see you still, straight and quiet! You must be getting stronger!" as I made us a nice breakfast to eat together. She acted cheery and helpful, so after breakfast, she and I would make bread. I taught her how to measure the flour and sugar while I broke the eggs and warmed the water and yeast. Her pencil thin arms had a hard time kneading the dough, so I would finish. We watched as the bread would rise, and I would explain how the yeast was eating the sugar resulting in the formation of little bubbles.

In amazement, she would sit at the table where she could watch it grow while drawing with crayons. Her file had contained horrific pictures. I was surprised when she handed a beautifully colored rainbow to me with the caption: To my mom with love, Alicia. I embraced her fragile body in love and thanks. My ego grew as I thought we must be giving her what she needed. The bright colors and promising subject matter reflected none of the evil in her previous drawings with her adoptive parents. I was convinced I had been right when I thought all she needed was more love, even though I had read her file and seen the tremendous capacity for love in her exhausted parents. I justified their failure by telling myself they just needed a break.

After drawing time, I would allow her to punch the bread down, believing the aggressive act would enable her to release pent up feelings. Again, I helped her finish kneading the bread before forming loaves and putting them in the oven. With the house smelling of fresh baking bread , I taught her how to do various other chores around the house. Each time, she completed the job exactly as I had asked while keeping a happy spirit and each time, I was more convinced it was my open, nurturing nature that was healing her. I hugged her and told her what a good helper she was becoming.

After she did her strong sitting for five minutes before lunch, I gave her a hug before we sat to eat the warm fresh bread I had made into sandwiches. I reinforced what a great chef she was. Smiling and dabbing the corners of her mouth after each bite, she would puff up with pride. We'd work on learning new stuff until the kids got home from school. Since she had already completed her chores, Alicia filled out her Feelings Book. Her writing was very primitive, so I had her draw a picture of the best and worst things that happened that day. She worked diligently at drawing the figures and actions, and then colored the whole picture. When she was finished, I would see her strong sit. Calling her over to the couch, she sat on my lap and told me about her drawings while I wrote her explanations on the back. I noted that her drawings each day showed no indication of missing her adoptive parents. Giving her a big hug, I laid down a big beach towel and got the bucket of Legos for her to play with until supper.

Having laid out the towel, I set the boundaries for her playtime. " You may play with the Legos as long as you are quiet and you and your toys stay on the blanket. What is it I want you to do?" Her big brown eyes looked up at me and blinked a few times. I waited. "Pu-way quiet on da bwanket an don't git off!" "Right!! Good listening!" I would tell her, thinking how absolutely darling she is. I walked away wondering whether this child could really kill in cold blood. She is just too cute! Two minutes later she had to test the limits and her lego time was over.

When dinner was nearly ready, I again, had her go to her think spot to strong sit for five minutes as I finished preparing the meal. If Terena and Alicia set the table, RB and Chucky washed the dinner dishes. If R.B. and Chucky set the table, Terena, Alicia and I would clean the kitchen. Afterwards, I would hug each child and they would all go outside and play in the cool spring air while I worked in the garden with a watchful eye. Bedtime was shortly thereafter.

The neighbor from up the road came to pick up some unfinished PTA brochures one morning while Alicia was strong sitting before breakfast. I invited her to stay for eggs and toast, but she declined and hurried off to her car. That evening, she came by before dinner to return the completed brochures. Alicia was doing her five minutes of strong sitting for supper. At the next PTA meeting, I watched as the neighbor threw glaring glances my way as she whispered to Lori. She shared with me later that the woman had asked if I knew what I was doing and wasn't it cruel to have the child sit all day. "I was there at 8:30 in the morning and that little girl was already sitting. Then, when I showed up later that evening, the poor little girl was STILL sitting! She hadn't moved at all and I could tell because she was in the same spot!" Lori did a great job of explaining the importance of having them strong sit for a few minutes. She told the distraught woman that the child sits in the same place every time and that this unique disorder causes the children to become very agitated when daily transitions arise. Strong sitting helps them to settle and calm their nerves. It gives them time to think, plan their day, or even to pray. It is not a punishment like sitting in the corner and its not because she had done something bad. It's just quiet time to think. It is actually an exercise to help their brains to heal. Lori and I exchanged knowing glances and I thanked her and hugged her in appreciation for her wisdom in handling the situation.

Alicia had been with us for five fabulous days. It was Saturday, so the routine was changed, and I wondered how this would affect her. All the children were finishing their chores, so when I saw Alicia strong sit to have her sweeping checked; I hurried over to inspect the kitchen floor. In the dead center, I found a clump of dog hair and several pebbles. Pointing them out to her, I watched as her button nose flared, her lips tensed and her eyes narrowed to slits. She cried and muttered that it wasn't her fault. The chore was too hard and I was being mean. I resisted the urge to grab her sad little body into a big hug and instead asked her to hop off to her room where she could throw a fit as long as she needed. I told her I would come get her when I heard it was quiet for ten minutes.

I listened as her heart wrenching wails filled our home. I was pacing and feeling like an ogre at making this poor abused child stay in her room all by herself instead of reaching out to her. I was following the protocol for a child throwing a fit, but I felt cruel and mean. The little one was in there, crying, alone and surrounded by the ghosts of her past. She probably missed her family and I was making her deal with it in isolation.

Beside myself, I broke down and called CJ. Pulling her out of a therapy session, I cried into the phone. "I can't do this! She's howling in her room, but she needs me and I'm having a hard time with leaving her in there all by herself. Can't I go in and comfort her?" CJ quickly responded, "I know how hard it is, Nancy. But you have to be strong! This little girl needs for you to be her anchor right now, and if you give in to her, she will feel like she successfully manipulated you. It will keep her sick! Try putting some music on and encourage her to howl to the rhythm. I'll see you both for her therapy session on Monday. Stay strong Nancy! I know you can do it!" I thought, "I can clean it myself. It was only a little bit of stuff on the floor. It's not worth hurting her over this!"

With those directions and short pep talk, she hung up the phone and I shuffled over to the stereo to pull out my Beatles album. Placing the needle on "Yellow Submarine" I prepared for battle. Without opening her door, I told her to try howling to the rhythm of the song. I felt like a horrible mother and began to hurt for what she must be going through. Pacing back and forth in emotional pain for her, I kept telling myself to be strong for Alicia. R.B. walked through the front door and stopped with a worried look on his face. "Mom, what's wrong?" I stopped pacing and looked up at my son. He had startled me out of my thinking and I stared at him blankly for a moment. "Mom! Are you okay?", he repeated. I gave him a hug and cried, "I can't help this little girl. She's in her room sobbing and wailing and I'm not supposed to go to her. I'm sure she's curled up on her bed with no one there to comfort her and I can't stand it!" R.B. grabbed my shoulders and held me at arms length. "Mom. I just looked through her window. She's just fine. She's playing with her Barbies in the pink jeep and racing them all around the room!"

Incredulously, I ran out the front door and around the house to her window. Sure enough, there she was, her face totally calm and without emotion, mouth wide open howling as loudly as she could. She was pushing the Barbie jeep around her room and playing with the dolls. In disbelief, I watched for several minutes. The heartbreak sounding cries were nothing more than a ploy to get me to feel guilty for sending her to her room! I had allowed this little seven-year old girl to manipulate me. This was a lesson I took to heart and referred to often. She was not like a normal child. She didn't think like a healthy child and she certainly didn't act like a sane child! I had entered the Twilight Zone of emotional disorders.

It took several hours for Alicia to get bored playing in her room and howling. When I heard it was quiet for ten minutes, I opened the door and asked her if she was ready to be part of the family. She smiled sweetly and replied, "Ye-ath, ma'am! I'm we-dy!" I gave her a hug and directed her to finish sweeping the floor. "Ye-ath, ma'am!", she said as she skipped off to find the broom.

I had nearly lost that battle by retreating. I vowed to be stronger and to identify maneuvers like that more quickly in the future. It was my first real test and although I had nearly caved in, I had won and I found comfort in that.

Her howling became a normal occurrence in our home after the tiniest correction or the word "no" from me. The once sweet, little Alicia transformed into the monster I had read about in her file. I made a mental note to avoid the trap of believing that the drastic and immediate behavior change was due to my special nurturing. I laughed when I realized her first five days were a honeymoon period exhibited by most of these children. It had nothing to do with me. She had sucked me in!

☙❀❧ ☙❀❧ ☙❀❧ ☙❀❧

Monday morning, I was exhausted as I loaded Alicia into the car and began the drive up to Evergreen for therapy. I was hoping for a lot of help. When we walked into the therapy room CJ was sitting in the corner of the sofa and patted the couch next to her, gesturing for Alicia to sit down. Pretending to be sweet and compliant, Alicia happily sat next to the woman, gazing expectantly into her eyes. They exchanged introductions and Alicia politely shook CJ's hand and told her it was nice to meet her. I was asked to pull the chair over next to the couch so I could hold Alicia's hand during the session. The therapist and I discussed how Alicia responded to the absence of her parents. I explained how concerned I was that Alicia hadn't mentioned them once or displayed sadness at their leaving. With that knowledge, CJ started off by asking the six year old how she felt about her new family? "I don't know", was her reply. "What do you feel about your family leaving you?" CJ asked. "I don't know".

CJ gently lifted Alicia over onto her lap with her head cradled on CJ's arm, looking up at the therapist. I was still surprised at how similar the position was to the way loving parents nurture and hold infants; Alicia's legs were just longer! It began making sense to me. By holding them like a tiny baby, it was easier for the child to get in touch with the feelings of their abandonment and abuse in infancy. Trying to get through the resistance of this little girl, CJ asked, "What's my name?" "I don't know." "My name is CJ. What's my name?" "I don't know." "My name is CJ. What's my name?" The first few minutes were filled with CJ asking this simple question and Alicia continuing to answer, "I don't know". I held her hand for encouragement. I didn't understand why she didn't just answer when it was so easy!

When Alicia's eyes wandered, CJ lovingly guided the little girl's chin closer to CJ. The expert then said, "Alicia I want you to say 'You are CJ' in three words". In a contrary manner, the tiny girl replied, "You are C and J!" The verbal exchange occurred again, and Alicia responded with "You are A CJ!". I was amazed at how many creative ways Alicia could say it wrong, She did it every way except for the way CJ had requested it. Periodically, CJ would have the child rest while she explained things.

This was only the second attachment therapy session I had seen, so I had many questions. "This child believes that if she says it exactly my way, she'll be giving up control to me. She learned early on in her little life that if she relinquishes her control, she is not safe. She learned not to trust adults, so she believes if she trusts us or anyone, she'll die!", CJ looked lovingly down at the little girl and brushed aside the shiny black curls obstructing her face. "It's very important we work through this, because if she can't learn to trust us, her chances for becoming healthy are slim. This resistance served her well in the abusive environment she had as a baby. If she didn't have it, she would have given up and died. Alicia has a strong will!" She squeezed the girl in a warm embrace before continuing on, "Now, her strong will gets in her way. We want to shape it, not break it! She has to learn to trust in order to learn to love. Without trust and love, she can not develop a conscience", CJ clarified. Looking down at Alicia, she smiled and said, "I'm glad you were so strong! The world has a lot of beauty and love to offer you. I know you haven't seen much of that, but you have to open up enough to let it in!" Kissing the girl's forehead, she began encouraging her again to simply say, "You are CJ".

For the next hour this continued. When she finally overcame her own resistance and said "You are CJ," we excitedly cheered Alicia for overcoming her "stuck spot" and saying it as she had been asked. Both of us clapped and hugged her. "Say, 'you are CJ,' again!", CJ solicited enthusiastically. With a triumphant smile, Alicia repeated it exactly as requested. "Look at Mom Nancy and say, 'You are Mom Nancy!" Stuttering slightly, she spilled out the exact phrase. We gave her a hi-five and ended the session with me rocking her in my arms, feeding her a bottle of sweet milk and singing and laughing together.

Driving home I reflected on the session I had just seen. It astonished me that such a little child would put up such a battle over saying someone's name. I then realized she had not used our names at home over the last week. It was one of her ways of keeping us at a distance. It was a way to make us "things" instead of people.

The next morning, I woke up my little trooper. She looked up at me, grinned and said, "You are Mom, Nancy!" I beamed back at her and cuddled her tiny body. We had won another battle, and to me, we were that much closer to being victorious for the whole war. I was beginning to love this little one. What a spirit she had!

I had a hard time believing this child was mentally slow, so during the afternoon, we continued to have school lessons. I didn't want her to feel like she was being left out, so as long as my children were in school, Alicia would have lessons to complete. One of her work sheets required her to color the drawing after figuring out the story line. She looked up to where I was making Jerry a new leather belt at the far end of the table. Her speech abnormalities persisted. "What colo' monkey ith?" she asked. I smiled at her cuteness, and corrected her poor grammar before I asked her to repeat it correctly. She said, "What color is a monkey?" Five minutes later, she said, "I haf a go bafroom!" I told her to ask nicely and emphatically repeated "baTHroom". "Mom Nancy, may I please go to the bathroom?" spilled from her lips and I sat, dumbfounded at her ability to speak clearly. It was then that I began thinking her poor speech patterns were fabricated and a topic to discuss later in therapy.

The next week, I learned her father was quite hard of hearing and relied on lip reading to understand conversations. I watched in amazement as she spoke her baby talk without moving her lips which made it that much more difficult to understand. I knew she was capable of speaking correctly so the forty-five minutes spent in therapy helping her to say bathroom instead of bafroom made me understand her pathology and control issues better.

Her manners at the table also declined after the honeymoon period. I thought how sad it was that she didn't know how to use a fork, so I would show her. The more I demonstrated, the more gross her eating habits became. She was continually excused from the table to finish eating in the laundry room for picking the food off the plate with her hands and placing it on her fork. When she did stab food properly with the utensil, her fisted hand would turn the fork sideways so her mouth had to open as wide as it could. It had to open pretty wide anyway, for the size of forkfuls that child tried to chew. A full serving of steak could be consumed in fewer than four bites, but her full mouth disabled her from chewing with her lips closed. That was reason for leaving the dinner table early. For such a skinny kid, she could sure pack it in. I began calling her my Bottomless Pit because she could out eat even my fifteen-year old son. The slurping and snorting coming from her end of the table reminded me of the sounds of pigs eating slop. She was excused often for her ill manners at the table, but I was always surprised when, after each bite, she would still wipe the corners of her mouth with her napkin.

My mother was visiting and had been charmed by our little trooper. Alicia had offered to put milk in Grandma's tea. She had offered to paint her nails. She even tried to lend a helping hand bringing in the many bags from the car. Right off the bat, my mom was sucked into the game, so when I excused Alicia from the table for eating grossly, my mom questioned my parenting in front of Alicia. Alicia's dramatic, pitiful, basset hound expression only fed Grandma's misguided compassion. When I shared why it was important for our little child to eat respectfully, my mom was judgmental. She did not understand the manipulation techniques of these kids even though I tried to teach her many times. She felt she "just needed more love". It hurt me deeply that my own mother could not see the dedication and commitment I had. She didn't see the many hours I held and rocked Alicia. She only saw the facade of pity Alicia hid behind for Mom's benefit and quickly dropped when she was gone. She took the side of the sick child against me. My own mother did not see I was on the child's side. She had not seen the impeccable manners the first five days. I knew Alicia could do it!

Alicia's howling and fit throwing substantially decreased for a few days after each therapy session. She began to handle eating at the table and if she was excused, she was much more accepting. The most amazing thing I noticed was her ability to speak clearly and correctly. I was intrigued at the amount of difference attachment therapy made in her behavior!

I was totally grossed out by the green snot she often had running down her face, past the corners of her mouth. Having tissue in every room, I was astounded at the amount of mucous one child could produce. She wiped her mouth after every bite while eating and yet she would walk around for hours with this glop stuck to her tiny face. It was an area of constant struggle for us. "Honey, please wipe your nose", I was finding myself saying repeatedly. Calling CJ, for ideas, I became armed with a new way of handling her gross behavior. I didn't have to wait very long before witnessing the gooey sludge dripping from her chin. "Alicia, hop off to your room", I announced. Five minutes later, I opened her door to see if she had figured out the problem. "I don't know", she said. I smiled at her and told her I'd be back in ten minutes to see if she knew yet. "Think about the areas you're working on. Are you being respectful, responsible and fun to be around? You think about it and I'll be back in a little bit to see how you're doing!" I closed her door, but not before I saw a clump of boogers drip to the floor.

The next time I entered her room, her face was clean. "So, what was the problem, Sweetie?", I asked her. "I had boogers running down my face" she said. I asked her what she thought was a better way to handle the problem. "Blow my nose!" I gave her a huge hug and reinforced how smart she could act when she wanted.

The next time I saw nasal discharge dripping down Alicia's face, I immediately sent her to her room. Using this method, within a few weeks, it was a non-issue. I called CJ to tell her the good news and asked why a child would do such a thing. "I bet it bothered her Mom! She must have gotten a lot of negative attention for it and learned that it was a way she could annoy Elaine." Understanding the cause of action, I made a point to really focus on the things I wanted from her instead of so many of the things I didn't want from her.

R.B. was cleaning the bathroom one cold afternoon and came across crayon marks behind the door. Calling me over to see the artwork, I summoned the rest of the crew. Three more bodies packed into the small water closet and I asked who was responsible for the defacing of the wall. Chucky was the first to say, "It wasn't me!" Terena quickly followed suit and Alicia parroted the response three times, each time becoming more adamant about it. Looking down at my beautiful raven-haired daughter, I said, "Alicia, go get the crayon!" With strong eye contact, she replied, "Yes, Mom!" and trotted off to her room to get the contraband. Terena giggled at how easy that was, "She didn't even argue, Mom!"

>~*~< >~*~< >~*~< >~*~<

The kids were in their last week of school when Jerry got the news of a job opportunity in the mountains. I listened intently as he told me he'd get a promotion from the Forest Service and we'd be living near the town of Glenwood Springs, Colorado if he accepted the offer. I had always wanted to live in the Rocky Mountains and I felt the city was no place to raise a family. I called ACE to see if Alicia would be able to move with us. "As long as you're willing to drive the three hours each way three times a month for her therapy, I'll drive up the other time!" I was relieved to hear the response from CJ. Happily we called a family meeting to share the news.

The following week, we all piled into the car and drove west on I-70. I thought of my grandmother the first person to ride a bike from New York to San Francisco clear back at the turn of the century. I pictured her pedaling across the rugged mountains. We were so lucky to have the smooth pavement and powerful engine to carry us over the twelve thousand foot high peaks. Go west young family- go west!

The further west we drove, the more I felt like I was coming home. Had I realized I would be driving past this same scenery almost weekly for the next ten years, a damper may have been placed on my excitedness, but the freshness of it all filled my senses. The construction in Glenwood Canyon enabled all of us to step out of the car to absorb the beauty of the sheer rock walls. When not witnessing the shadows on the walls change, we passed the thirty-minute wait by watching the huge commercial rafts tear through the churning white water of the Colorado River. Screams of mock terror filled the air as the patrons became soaked by the cold snowmelt of the Rocky Mountains at each class three rapid.

The little town of Glenwood Springs lay at the confluence of the Colorado and Roaring Fork rivers, two minutes from the end of the five hundred foot walls of the canyon. The striking beauty of this place just about took my breath away. We were all wide eyed with wonder as we drove around and inspected potential homes to buy. I saw Terena's eyes welling up with tears in the back seat between her two older brothers. Asking her what was wrong, she sniffed, "I was hoping we'd have", sniff, " enough land for a horse."

Not finding any properties we liked, we searched the surrounding towns. Back on I-70, we headed west to New Castle. We passed the smoking mountains and learned from a memorial next to the road that a coal mine had blown sky high in 1913, killing many miners of the little town. The mine had been closed, but the fire within the mountains still smoldered and consumed the huge coal vein. Seventy-three years later, thin plumes of smoke seeped into the open air from the barren scars on the mountains sides. I was saddened at the town history, but excitement soon replaced my blue mood.

New Castle was a quaint little western town with friendly people and hundred year old bullet holes in the walls of the few storefronts. Driving eight miles north of town, we found our home. A quarter mile from the White River National Forest boundary, the seven acres contained a big house with lots of bedrooms, separate two car garage, barn and mountain. A creek ran at its base and large cottonwoods and aspens drank from its contents. R.B, Chucky and Terena already had their rooms picked out. Terena became worried when she learned it had a well. "Mom! I don't think hauling buckets of water from the well to the house, is a very good idea!" Jerry and I laughed at her Little House on the Prairie idea of a well. Explaining it was modern with a pump, she joined in our laughter. "I'm so glad. Hauling five gallon buckets full of water isn't my favorite thing to do!", she exclaimed in her usual sunny manner before trotting off to explore the tall grasses in the front pastures with Alicia.

Three weeks later, we packed up all our belongings and prepared all the animals. The moving van came and we spent hours loading everything. The baby grand piano that Jerry and R.B. played was loaded. The kitchen appliances, furniture, farm machinery and clothes were neatly packed and put in the semi trailer. The children and animals were loaded into my Toyota

Tercel, Jerry's new Scout and the rented stock trailer he pulled. I felt like Ma and Pa Kettle or the Beverly Hillbillies with all the critters strapped to every conceivable place. The caravan behind the semi was headed to our new home!

Settling in quickly, our routines were soon established. Alicia's room was remodeled with the floor tile and special walls with fresh paint. I felt better knowing her room was on the same floor as my room and was close enough for me to hear her if she needed something.

A small abused pony soon came to live with us, so Terena's equine dream was satiated for the time being. His name was General Electric, GE for short because his poor untrusting soul would jolt in fear like he was electrocuted whenever anyone touched him. She taught him to trust her. Thus her career with horses began. With the help of the new neighbor, Joyce, she was able to ride him within a few months and his wild, wounded spirit was mended.

As I continued to take classes and learn from the books, my parenting skills improved. I excused Alicia more quickly from the table and I watched as, over the weeks, as she was able to sit at the table longer and longer before eating grossly to test me. The first night that she lasted the whole meal at the table, we threw a party with cake, ice cream and lots of pizzazz. The trivialness of nice table manners didn't escape me, especially when this child was capable of killing, but when I was consistent with the little things the bigger problems didn't surface.

The three-hour drive to Evergreen for Alicia's therapy became a weekly routine. Her language was becoming consistently normal and more understandable. The fits were occurring less and her manners at the table were becoming more appropriate. Her facial expressions were so far off, she had no idea how to look mad, so I taught her the different faces that reflected various emotions. She was still having a hard time with sharing her feelings, but in the overall scheme of things, she was healing.

After a while her therapy sessions focused less on resistance and more on being honest with herself and others. She told the truth about killing the first mother cat. When her adoptive mom put her dinner bowl down on the floor, the cat never came so they assumed her neurotic tendency had caused her to run away. The new cat was already in the home, so they wrote off the first cat's disappearance as jealousy. Alicia had been out sweeping the porch when she heard its meows from behind the screen earlier that day. Letting it outside, which was not allowed, she pinned it against the wooden fence and kicked it until it no longer moved. Knowing she would be punished, she threw its lifeless body into the next street and watched as a passing car flattened it. Describing her satisfaction at seeing the cat's intestines explode, she told us how she raced back to finish her chore.

I listened in horror as this sweet, innocent looking girl shared the details with us. There was no expression on her face and her robot explanations made chills run up my spine. I was convinced at that point that she truly was capable of cold-blooded murder no matter what charm radiated from her outward appearance!

Her demeanor was gentler and more honest after the sessions. Whether it was Dr. Cline conducting the Attachment Therapy or CJ, her chores were finished speedier and she acted more intelligent for days afterward. Having had her for over four months, I learned through experience that the more angry she became, the more mentally slow she acted. I had seen her do complicated math problems for her age. I had heard her memorize and present Bible study verses with little effort.

This point really hit home when, one afternoon, she asked what the black and orange signs had written on them that we were nailing on the fence posts. I had her sound it out. "What does the first word say, Alicia?" I heard her say 'no', so I asked what 'h-u-n-t' sounded like. She quickly replied, "Hunt!" I asked what 'i-n-g' sounded like, and knowing she had read bigger words ending in -ing, I was surprised when she proudly said, "It says no hunters!" Asking her to reread it and say it correctly, she insisted it said no hunters. I told her we would finish hanging the signs and she could think about it. When we got home I gave her one of the signs to look at as she sat in a chair. I told her when she was ready to tell me what it said to say "ready". For two long hours she persisted in saying "It says no hunters".

Elaine called while Alicia was so stuck. I thought some reassurance and encouragement from her mom might do some good, so I handed the phone to Alicia. "Hi Mom! I'm having a hard day because I won't read the no hunting sign right. I keep saying no hunters!", she chirped into the phone. Here I had been thinking maybe she was truly retarded and I had asked her to do something too difficult! She had known all along exactly what it said!

I talked with Alicia's mom and realized her kind, loving spirit was being torn apart. The outside world had seen her little daughter as a shy, cute six year old, and the community that strongly supported the adoption of the inner city child, now turned their back on the struggling family. Blaming Alicia's maladjustment on her parents, everyone but her close friends had judged and condemned them when they sent their little girl away to Colorado for treatment.

I listened as this gentle woman, who loved children so much that her life was dedicated to helping them, told me of her heavy heart. She sobbed. She missed her little girl. She mourned over the fact that she couldn't heal her daughter herself, even with the many years of education and experience she held. She cried about feeling like the town outcast. Their longtime congregation where Elaine and Todd had married welcomed them coldly because of what they saw as the 'abandonment' of their child.

I comforted and encouraged her. I empathized with her, because I had felt similar withdrawal by the community when I tried to explain Chucky's problems to them. I championed her strength and endorsed her difficult decision of placement. I understood where she was coming from and supported her. She was in deep pain.

Hanging up the phone, I asked Alicia to strong sit to think about the sign. Giving her the direction to say a loud "Ready" when she figured it out, I waited at the table thinking about Elaine. Two minutes later, a vigorous "ready!" filled my ears. "It says no hunting, Mom," she said proudly. "That's right! You can do it if you want to!" I proclaimed in support before picking her up and twirling her around with glee.

The true test of her healing was to come when she stole a steak knife from the dishwasher. I had been out gardening all day as she searched the woods behind our house for kindling. The cats were safely locked in the garage, so she had no access to victims. Finding the knife missing that night at dinner, I asked all the children if they had seen it. When I asked Alicia about it, her response of 'I don't have it!' escalated into a shriek. Her over reaction to the simple question told me she did indeed have it and I knew that with her history, lives could be in danger.

Sending her to her room to think about the truth, I vigilantly watched her retreat before going downstairs after her and turning her door alarm on. Pacing the floor in distress while I waited, I tried to think of when she might have had an opportunity to steal such a weapon. I knew she hadn't hurt any of the animals with it. I had noticed that when she did something 'bad' her behavior went right down the toilet, and I had not seen any drastic changes throughout the day.

Praying outside of her closed door, I asked God to give me strength to help the little armed six year old in my care I would soon be confronting. Opening the door, I saw her sitting on the bed with her tiny arms crossed in front of her and the shiny knife laying at her side. I asked, "Are you strong enough to tell me the truth?" Nodding her head, I saw tears fill her eyes as she looked into mine, "I stole this knife this morning while you weren't looking. I hid it under my pillow because I wanted to kill you with it, but I chopped a tree down instead." Taking the knife from her outstretched hand, I gave her a hug and shared how proud of her honesty I was. She hadn't tried to kill and she was strong enough to be tell the truth about her plan.

My nerves were on edge and my mind had a hard time not reacting with anger and blasting this little child with a screaming lecture. I shut down my over active brain and got a grip on myself. Asking her to show me the tree, we walked hand in hand to the edge of woods. There, in the one area I was unable to monitor behind a pile of wood, stood the stump of a tree four inches in diameter! Sap freshly dripped down the remaining trunk and its dismembered body lay fallen in the tall grass. The fury and determination it must have taken to saw through that tree with a steak knife was amazing. I was sad she had stolen the knife, but I was glad she didn't have more casualties than this poor aspen.

She couldn't replace the mama cat or kittens, but she could give back a new tree. Although she had been honest about the knife the importance of there being a consequence was still vital. The replacement and planting of a baby tree not only allowed her to learn a lesson, but it gave her something to nurture and call her own. Since she had told the truth, she only had to pay for half of the sapling.

Alicia stayed with us for six months that first time. Her parents were devoted to her healing, had done their homework and wanted their daughter home as soon as possible. Alicia was still healing, but her level of improvement was astounding. She was respectful eighty percent of the time. She acted intelligent the majority of the time and was honest about her thoughts and feelings, no matter how ugly they were. Daily chores were finished with speed and accuracy; she was a hard worker with a wonderful attitude. Her parents started a support group with other parents and invited me to come out and speak at a fundraiser for their group. I was honored and had a great time. Over one hundred parents showed up. Tom and Elaine were no longer suffering alone with their emotionally disturbed child. There were so many!

Her dedicated parents had been learning the specialized parenting techniques. Flying out as the mountains were gilded in shimmering gold by the aspen trees, they spent a week with us to transfer the loving bond between Alicia and me, to Alicia and her Mom. The rocking chair I had used so many times to rock and hold her, was now being used by Alicia and her mom. I watched as a twinkle formed in Alicia's eyes while she gazed into her mom's loving eyes. It warmed my heart when I listened to the stories and songs Elaine shared with her daughter as they connected. To see Alicia relax in the arms she had fought for so long, gave me a sense of hope for their future together.

I had done my 'job' and although my heart was breaking because I had grown to deeply love the little girl, I was sincerely happy that their family could be complete. We agreed for her to come back the following summer, but my feelings were still those of intense loss. That October day, Terena and I cried in each others arms after their car pulled out of the driveway. We would miss our little Bottomless Pit!

Beth and her Mama laughing and loving together.

Chapter 8

Roots of Violence

Beth: April of 1989 was the first time I laid my icy blue eyes, turned cold from the six years of pain and anger that saturated them, on Nancy Thomas. I was sent to live with her when the task of controlling me became too overwhelming for my adoptive parents and the only answer they had found was in Colorado in the form of a Therapeutic parent. But wait, I'm getting ahead of myself. Let me take you to the point at which this tale begins . . .I learned of many past incidents that had occurred before my birth and during my early years from my sisters. I am now 19 years old as I look back on my life and share it with you.

It was a sunny afternoon on that hot and muggy day late in July that I was born in the little town hospital of Stanley County in Albemarle, North Carolina. It was common to see the women sitting on front porches trying to fan away the stickiness left behind by the characteristic humidity of North Carolina and the men wiping their sweaty brows while working between the rows of corn or tobacco plants during that year of 1982. That day was no different.

Late enough to have the doctors induce labor, I was born to a young, beautiful woman with gentle blue eyes and straight shoulder-length brown hair usually seen pulled back into a pony tail. She had a smile that could move mountains and a gentle heart of gold. Known as an intelligent woman and well loved with a happy-go-lucky personality, she caused much confusion when she married Ronald, the tall, lanky, domineering man that was my birth father, not long after she'd divorced her previous husband.

When she first married Ronald, my birth father, in June of 1976 he seemed too good to be true. He was an ex-Ft. Lauderdale cop that worked in parks and recreation. He was remarkably loving and gentle at first before his facade faded and his true colors began to show. He would continually call my mama a failure as a mother, using her oldest daughter as his proof, since she had left and returned to live with her birth father. He would compare her to his "perfect" mother and describe my mama as dirt beneath her. The abuse he inflicted upon her began shortly after they were married. When Ronald wasn't at his job, then he was at home saturating his senses with beer and turning more and more nasty.

One of my older sisters, Cora, came home from her first grade class, and opened the door to a scene that wrenched her heart: Mama was hanging off of the couch while Ronald sat on top of her screaming obscenities between each blow. His abuse was not only directed toward Mama. He continually kept an devilish watch on Cora. If things were not done according to his standards she'd pay with a smack across the face or a belt whipped across her back end. After one such incident, Mama noticed a four inch purple welt on the back of Cora's leg and a wound where the belt buckle had punctured her skin. Heart broken, Mama tried to convince Ronald to let her punish Cora in the future. When Cora was only five he began to use her as an outlet for his sexual pleasure. Disgusted, terrified and ashamed, Cora kept silent.

When the family moved from Florida to North Carolina in 1978, he cached Mama away and kept her hidden from everyone, like she was his private possession, not allowing her to leave the house unless she was with him. In the beginning, if she ever went anywhere he would grill her about where she'd been, who'd she'd seen or what she had done. It became so irritating that she finally submitted and remained at home. She was forbidden to attend her second daughter, Joy's, high school graduation and he barred her from the church she loved. He had by this time made her feel useless with his continual accusations that she was a horrible mother. If she ever thought of leaving him, he'd use us kids as his bait. During this time Mama got the strength to leave him twice; however both times she returned, apologetic, and promised to never leave him again. He threatened her that since she was such a bad mom he'd get custody of the children and she'd never see us again, so she'd better rethink her plan. Mama could never handle being away from her children so she stayed and suffered the ongoing beatings.

While Mama was pregnant with me she decided to leave Ronald one last time. She gathered all the children and went to stay at a battered women's shelter. Once Ronald discovered where she was, he apologized profusely and promised he'd never lay a hand on her again. He swore that life would be good if she'd only come home to him. So she returned. Two nights later the abuse began again.

✦ ✦ ✦ ✦

I was the seventh child born. Each of us children had all been blessed with our grandfather's Scottish blue-eyes, which he'd passed along through our mama. A chubby, beautiful little baby with dark hair sticking straight up, I would have made Alfalfa from "The Little Rascal's" proud!

Cuddled in my mama's arms I was taken from the hospital to a dilapidated cabin my parents called home. Quite secluded from everything and everyone, our closest neighbor was about a tenth of a mile away. Our cabin was set back about a block and a half and because of a scattering of trees, not easily seen from the road. This stark wooden house held a small kitchen, a living room, two bedrooms and one bathroom. Four children slept in one bedroom on two beds shoved together and I slept in the crib. Cora slept in the utility room that was technically outside the house. When the cabin was locked up at night she would be locked outside.

Ronald did not hold onto jobs very well and many times he would have Mama call Grandma and Grandpa and beg for money to help them. They seemed to constantly be in debt. The money he earned from working on a chicken farm wasn't much and the money received from welfare seemed to disappear as soon as it came. We are not sure what exactly he did with the money but it was quite rare my mama and us children would see any benefit from it. Our most common attire was usually cloth diapers or underpants. Thankfully Mama was a receiver of the WIC program, (Women, infants and children), and was able to get the important food she needed for all of us kids.

Though money was tight, and Ronald was harsh and nasty. Mama's love had no end. She loved each of us more than anything in the world. She constantly was holding and snuggling with all of her children. We were all still her babies, whether we were babies or grown.

Mama and Ronald had named me Cheryl-Ann but she lovingly nicknamed me her little "Squig". I was a shy little girl, and it was rare of me to be seen even climbing into my grandparents' laps when they visited. Everywhere Mama went around the cabin I would be right there, my little hands clutching her skirt or snuggling in her soft loving arms. When I wasn't in her arms I would be in Cora's.

The beatings continued except now Ronald acted out not only on his wife and oldest daughter but on my other siblings and I as well. Almost every night he would get drunk and pound on Mama. He would drag her through the house by her hair, screaming words us children were never allowed to use. When he drug her from the bedroom to the kitchen and back that meant he had to pass through our room. The wails would echo against the walls and our hearts would pound in our ears as the silent tears fell for our mother.

It became too cold to sleep outside, and Cora had been moved into our already cramped quarters. Sadly the screaming and fighting became such an often occurrence that us little ones eventually learned to sleep through it. Cora would be the only one who awoke during these beatings and, feeling horrified, she would try to devise a plan to end it. One night she lay there, fists balled at her side, tears of anger streaming down her cheeks and imagined what she could do to stop him. If she could grab the lamp and smack him over the head and knock him out then he'd stop, but what if he didn't pass out? He'd turn on her! Every nerve within her shrieked to do something but her fear held her at bay.

✦✦✦✦

Mama got pregnant with my little brother when I was only three months old. It was at this time she began to get sick. She had been told before I was conceived that she shouldn't have any more children and she was having them too close together; it was making her weak. However, without the financial resources, the means to acquire birth control, and with a self-centered, controlling, lustful husband she was left with few choices. Therefore, the last five of us children were born nine to 12 months apart.

She started seeing the doctor frequently, complaining of lower back pain. The doctor's diagnosis was kidney problems. She was admitted and released from the hospital over and over. Each time she'd return home she'd pull us children into her arms to hug and hold us but I'd turn and run from her. Eventually I'd warm up to her again and snuggle in her arms. A few days later she'd have to go back into the hospital and the next time she came home I'd run from her again. In the process of giving birth to my youngest brother in August of 1983, her kidneys failed. She'd turned 40 only two days before.

She was placed on a home dialysis machine. She would not only change the IV and try to take care of herself but also the rest of us; the responsibility fell heavily on ten-year old Cora to help with us kids.

During this time Ronald barely spoke to any of us except to punish us. At one point Mama, in her sickness, let my older three-year old brother have a toy to play with and when Ronald returned home that evening she'd forgotten she'd given it to him. The sickening sound of the belt buckle smashing him across the face and his howling sobs wracked the entire house. Terrified I clutched Cora, looking for a safe haven, and felt her own heart thumping against my little one-year old body. I looked up and saw that her face showed no fear yet, I could feel her arms shake around me. Later, she stroked my hair and whispered to me of her plan to run away but she couldn't leave Mama and us children. "I hate that man," she said, her voice caught in her throat as she finished, "but I love you guys too much to go."

The hassle to Ronald of constantly berating Mama every evening because she couldn't fulfill his sexual needs finally took its toll. He then turned even more to eleven year old Cora to fill his sexual wantings. Even if she were tucked in bed with us he'd drag her into the living room to use her little body. He always found a place and a time.

The dialysis machine was failing to do the job and in February of 1984, Mama went into the hospital for the last time. Ronald, angry with Mama's parents for not sending money when he demanded, never told her parents she was sick or being hospitalized. My grandma and grandpa discovered their only daughter was gravely ill and in the hospital from my great-aunt who had gone to visit a friend in the ward and had been informed by the staff that my Mama was a patient. She quickly phoned my grandma and grandpa in Florida. They immediately flew to North Carolina to help take care of us and to be at Mama's bedside.

When Mama went into the hospital that last time, a gentle-hearted African-American woman named Annie Mae came to take care of us. We children grew to love her and we will always thank her for her selflessness. She cared for each of us as if we were her own and would even help clean around the house even though it wasn't her job. She would come during the day, so Ronald could go to work, and then she would return home to her family each evening.

Mama stayed in the hospital for a month, her life slipping from her with each breath. During that time children were not allowed in hospitals so we were unable to even visit. In her last conversation with my sister, Joy, she spoke of Ronald's sexual pressuring and how much she ached to see her children. She told her that being in the hospital she was safe from him and she was so very tired. It was then my older sister realized how much damage Ronald had done. Her dedicated mother had finally been broken and did not want to be repaired. She had remained with a man who had tortured her for too many years. She loved each of us so much that she had endured as much as she could in order to spend each precious moment watching us grow. She had finally been pushed too much, and too far. She died in the early hours of February 29, 1984 of kidney failure. I *was seventeen months old. She left behind her eight children, ranging in age from six months to 24 years, her only brother, her father, stepmother and Ronald.*

꧁ ꧂ ꧁ ꧂ ꧁ ꧂ ꧁ ꧂

After Mama died, it shocked my grandparents when Ronald would not allow any of us children to attend the funeral service. He forbid it, claiming it was too much trauma for us, even though we longed to say good-bye and begged to go. It happened to fall on my older sister's sixth birthday. Ronald wouldn't allow her to eat the birthday cake that grandma and grandpa had brought her.

Ronald had believed his company would pay for everything when Mama died, but he was laid off a few weeks before her death and the company paid nothing.

Thankfully, not long after she died he was rehired, so he could have the money to feed us children.

Social services contacted my grandparents and expressed their concern that Ronald had a past history of sexual abuse and they were worried for the children's safety. Having nothing to convict him with they were unable to help the children until actual allegations were made, that is if anything was happening. Grandma took Cora aside and had her promise if Ronald tried anything inappropriate she was to tell her school counselor or call Grandma and people would make him stop. Before Grandma had spoken with her, Cora had already debated telling on Ronald. Mama was gone. There was nothing to stop him from hurting her every night now. She had thought about it and once again couldn't bear to leave us children. She stayed just like her mama did and took more and more of his filthy pervertedness.

Grandma and Grandpa needed to return home to maintain their jobs. My Grandpa, a big, intelligent and loving man had his Ph.D. in education and taught school. Even though he and my grandma wanted to stay and care for their grandchildren they were unable to remain any longer and had to return home.

A few days after Grandma and Grandpa left Ronald hurt Cora again. This time she didn't care; she wasn't going to put up with it anymore. First thing Monday morning she found the courage and told her school counselor. Ashamed it had happened for so many years, she lied and said he'd only done it that past weekend. She and two social workers went to the house and waited for him to return from work. Annie Mae, shocked to learn what had just unfolded, took all of us children into the kitchen and did her best to calm us and to keep us out of the room when Ronald came home. When Ronald was told of the allegations he acted as if he'd been too drunk to remember it had happened. Sickened, Cora sat there; she knew that he knew what he was doing. Someone who doesn't know what he's doing wouldn't ask if she'd had her period yet and always remember to put on a condom.

Cora was taken away and placed with a foster family. For two days we were without our sister, our protector. Confused, I didn't know who to turn to. My mama wasn't there and neither was Cora, my rock, my comfort. We were all taken from Ronald then and he was arrested and convicted of sexual abuse of a minor. He was ordered never to see Cora again or to contact her in any way. The last anyone heard from him was when he contacted my grandma and asked if she

Dandelion on My Pillow, Butcher Knife Beneath

wanted to purchase Mama's wedding rings for sixty dollars because he had no money.

Social Services wanted to find a home where we could all be placed together. So they sat Cora down and asked if she wanted to live with us or be by herself. Shocking the workers she firmly stated she wanted to be by herself. They didn't understand that at only eleven-years old she'd already been an adult for too long. She was sick of washing diapers and cleaning. Many times she had suffered the painful consequences if she didn't get it done right. She needed a break. No one understood how it tore her heart to choose to give up living with her family but she'd had enough. She couldn't do it anymore!

For a weekend four of us were placed together and then the following Monday we were separated. A stranger came and took my baby brother and me to an unfamiliar car to be taken away. Numbly I stumbled to the car but then I was scared and I cried out. In terror I turned to look at what was left of my family, my world. I sobbed and reached for them out the back window as they faded from view in the distance. I felt helpless and hopeless. It would be many years before we would ever be all together again.

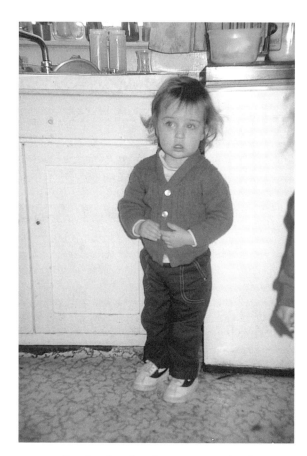

Beth, the day her Mama died.

ReactiveAttachmentDisorderisaconditioninwhichindividualshave
difficultyforminglovinglastingrelationships.Theyoftenhaveane
arlycompletelackofabilitytobegenuinelyaffectionatewithothers
.Theytypicallyfailtodevelopaconscienceanddonotlearntotrust.T
heydonotallowpeopletobeincontrolofthembecauseofthistrustissu
e.Theycanbesurfacecompliantforweeksifnolovingrelationshipisi
nvolved.Withstrangerstheycanbeextremelycharmingandappearlovi
ng.Uneducatedadultsmisinterpretthisasthechildtrustingorcarin
gforthem.Iftheycannottrustandlovetheirownfamilythatlovesthem
,thentheywillnottrustandloveacasualacquaintance!!Theydonotth
inkandfeellikeanormalperson.SomefamouspeoplewithRADwhodidnot
gethelpintime:Hitler,SadamHussein,EdgarAllenPoe,JeffreyDahme
r,TedBundy.ReactiveAttachmentDisorderisaconditioninwhichindi
vidualshavedifficultyforminglovinglastingrelationships.Theyo
ftenhaveanearlycompletelackofabilitytobegenuinelyaffectionat
ewithothers.Theytypicallyfailtodevelopaconscienceanddonotlea
rntotrust.Theydonotallowpeopletobeincontrolofthembecauseofth
istrustissue.Theycanbesurfacecompliantforweeksifnolovingrela
tionshipisinvolved.Withstrangerstheycanbeextremelycharmingan
dappearloving.Uneducatedadultsmisinterpretthisasthechildtrus
tingorcaringforthem.Iftheycannottrustandlovetheirownfamilyth
atlovesthem,thentheywillnottrustandloveacasualacquaintance!!
Theydonotthinkandfeellikeanormalperson.Somefamouspeoplewithr
ADwhodidnotgethelpintime:Hitler,SadamHussein,EdgarAllenPoe,J
effreyDahmer,TedBundy.ReactiveAttachmentDisorderisacondition
inwhichindividualshavedifficultyforminglovinglastingrelation
ships.Theyoftenhaveanearlycompletelackofabilitytobegenuinely
affectionatewithothers.Theytypicallyfailtodevelopaconscience
anddonotlearntotrust.Theydonotallowpeopletobeincontrolofthem
becauseofthistrustissue.Theycanbesurfacecompliantforweeksifn
olovingrelationshipisinvolved.Withstrangerstheycanbeextremel
ycharmingandappearloving.Uneducatedadultsmisinterpretthisast
hechildtrustingorcaringforthem.Iftheycannottrustandlovetheir
ownfamilythatlovesthem,thentheywillnottrustandloveacasualacq
uaintance!!Theydonotthinkandfeellikeanormalperson.Somefamous
peoplewithRADwhodidnotgethelpintime:Hitler,SadamHussein,Edga
rAllenPoe,JeffreyDahmer,TedBundy>ReactiveAttachmentDisorderi
saconditioninwhichindividualshavedifficultyforminglovinglast
ingrelationships.Theyoftenhaveanearlycompletelackofability to
begenuinelyaffectionatewithothers.Theytypicallyfailtodevelop
aconscienceanddonotlearntotrust.Theydonotallowpeopletobeinco
ntrolofthembecauseofthistrustissue.Theycanbesurfacecompliant
forweeksifnolovingrelationshipisinvolved.Withstrangerstheyca
nbeextremelycharmingandappearloving.Uneducatedadultsmisinter
pretthisasthechildtrustingorcaringforthem.Iftheycannottrusta
ndlovetheirownfamilythatlovesthem,thentheywillnottrustandlov
eacasualacquaintance!!Theydonotthinkandfeellikeanormalperson
.SomefamouspeoplewithRADwhodidnotgethelpintime:Hitler,SadamH
ussein,EdgarAllenPoe,JeffreyDahmer,TedBundy.

Chapter 9

What You See is Not What You Get

Alicia had been gone for a few weeks. I had taken some children in for respite, to give some of the other therapeutic families some rest and relief, during the months after Alicia left us. While dropping one child off in Evergreen, CJ handed me a manila file. I drove home eyeing it before bringing it inside with me. It sat on the kitchen table, prompting me to open it. I wanted to delve into the thick stack of papers inside, but my heart still ached from having lost my little Bottomless Pit, so I procrastinated for most of the day, before sitting down in front of it.

It helped that I had a tiny baby bat that one of the neighbors had found in their garden. It would take me forty-five minutes to feed her every two hours. With a body smaller than the first joint in my thumb, I would suspend a droplet of sweetened milk from an eyedropper as she licked furiously until, after several minutes, it was gone and I'd squeeze out a new drop. Little did I know that God was increasing my patience for a reason. I would need it!

Finally succumbing to my curiosity, I put the wee orphan in my shirt pocket and opened the file. He was a famous child in California. Front-page headlines covered his story of sexual abuse. I looked at the gritty pictures of this child, Willhelm, in the paper as the media hounded his nine-year old body walking into the courtroom. A million dollar trial ensued, pitting young Willhelm against his birth mother and a couple of male family friends. As the proceedings advanced, Willhelm claimed the social worker for his case also made him perform oral sexual acts.

My heart went out to this young boy. His big brown eyes held the same sadness as RB's and with similar colored hair, his looks reminded me of my oldest son. I was moved by his story.

His birth mother, Sheila, had been married for only two weeks before throwing out his dad, Cain, for sleeping around. In that short amount of time, she had become pregnant. Trying to self-medicate her pain and loneliness, Sheila turned to alcohol.

As a result of being marinated in alcohol in the womb, Will's brain was impaired and Fetal Alcohol Syndrome (FAS) resulted. The long term effects of his mother's inability to stay sober would wound Will for the rest of his life.

It took Sheila six months before she was able to show she was straight enough to care for her child. Once he was in her care, the long nights filled with infant wails and inconsolable screams, became too much. Alcohol was cheap and accessible, so she turned to its soothing properties again, and was able to find sleep only when she passed out.

Alcoholism became an integral part of Will's existence. As he grew he became the "little man of the house", taking pride in his ability to care for himself. Although Sheila took great pride in always dressing her son impeccably, Will would care for his drunken or hung-over mother as their relationship became more reversed. That role reversal was hard on his developing psyche.

Sheila had enrolled Will in the finest preschool and private elementary education she could afford. His weekends were spent with his father, Cain, whose anger for his ex-wife flowed from him into Will like hot lava and scorched his already fragile soul.

The trauma of what his mother had done to him during his eight years with her spilled out to the school counselor one morning. He told how Sheila had sold his body for sexual favors to some men for cash. He gave the names of his perpetrators. That afternoon, Social Services took him away from his screaming mother and placed him in foster care. When the newspapers heard of the sex ring involving the child, they published the names of the accused in the paper. One of the men on the list couldn't handle the shame and degradation so he committed suicide during the trial. Even though the accused are supposed to be "innocent until proven guilty" the reaction from the community of condemnation and outrage was unbearable.

Every time Will would testify, his foster family, filled with pity for him, would take him out for ice cream and a movie. The school he had transferred to allowed him to miss assignments and skip tests, giving him special treatment due to the extreme circumstances he had endured. A Social Worker took him to the zoo, museum and other events he might enjoy in an attempt to distract him from his past. That same Social Worker was the one that Will later accused of sexually abusing him. How much bad luck could one child have? First it's his own mother and now a social worker! How much more trauma could this child take?

The defendants were found guilty and sentenced to prison. A photograph of Sheila collapsing into sobs was splashed across the front page of the newspaper the following day. The article said she had tried to reach for her son to say goodbye, but he turned from her and ran to the arms of his foster parents.

I set the thick file down. Closing my eyes, his gaze burned through my mind as I saw his eyes pleading for understanding. His defiant, destructive behavior had caused him to blow out of two other foster homes and a children's residential facility already. Was this his last chance? Had his birth mother broken his heart beyond repair? I began hating Sheila for what she had done. I was sickened by her ability to use her own child's body for financial gain in such a perverted way. I am not a violent person, but if she came to my door I would have punched her in the mouth!

I debated about having him join our family. Jerry and I had decided not to put our children in harm's way or displace them by bringing in a child older than ours. Will was almost a year older than Terena, but he was small for his age. Will was twelve now, and I worried that it may be too late for him. Puberty was going to be hitting soon and I had learned that once those hormones were surging through a child's body, addressing emotional issues was much more difficult. The teen years are a time of separation, not a time of connecting like the early years are. Was it too late for him?

Jerry and I talked about it long into the night. Will had no home to return to, so I hoped if we could turn this boy around, he might be able to become a permanent part of our family and I wouldn't have to ache for him as I did for Alicia. We agreed to give it a try. Calling CJ the next day, I told her we would commit to working with him. He deserved another chance. Will was going to be part of our family. I excitedly awaited the new challenges this boy would bring.

Two weeks of intense therapy had been implemented for all new children joining the program. It was designed after the miracle work that Anne Sullivan did with Helen Keller that opened her heart. Will's caseworker flew with him to Colorado and participated in the daily Attachment therapy. Without the information only a Mom could have, the therapist couldn't be as effective as she needed to be. Without the facts, we couldn't get to the real issues. Working on his basic compliance and the feelings surrounding the information we did have, Will worked hard and applied himself fully to everything we asked.

The poor boy. He had endured so much already that I pitied him. He was strong to have testified for weeks against his mother who had used him. I vowed to love him and care for him as if he were my own. I'd protect him from ever having to deal with such treachery again!

The three weeks of good, thoughtful and compliant behavior from Will caused me to question whether he was really sick. He would eagerly comply, sometimes with the haughtiness and arrogance of adolescence, but he did what I asked. This "honeymoon period" gave me the opportunity to contact his previous families. I learned that the severe entitlement issues he carried caused him to act like the world owed him something. The moms I talked to were filled with sadness that the love and kindness they offered to him was rejected and not enough to help him. They told me how Will looked down at them and their families as if they were his servants.

I didn't see any of the behavior they described. He would often bring me a cup of tea or offer to help with the dishes and cleaning. Not until the first couple of weeks were over did I see behind his mask. The honeymoon was over! It was then that he looked at me like I was the dirt under his feet. A dark cloud followed him that shrouded an arrogant defiant attitude. He refused to do anything. The simple task of bringing his laundry to me on his washday became a fight. He refused to bathe or brush his teeth. When he ate he resembled a starved baboon at its favorite meal. Food splattered from his face and hands as he forced huge amounts into his gaping jaws only to chomp and smack openly for all to see.

In order to participate in fun family activities he only had to make his bed, be dressed with his hair combed, face washed and teeth brushed. He refused to do it. Knots in his beautiful brown hair became mats coated in filth. I had to do something. The whir of the electric clippers drowned out his cussing and complaints as I shaved his head. I didn't want to, but dread locks were the only other option, and with his track record for cleanliness, I imagined the many insects that could inhabit such a hairstyle.

He frequently chose to step directly between people trying to talk so they could no longer see one another. He refused to take responsibility for anything he did or didn't do. When confronted with his behavior, he blamed everyone else. Being passive aggressive, he would show me he was angry by hiding the dishes or acting clueless. With an I.Q. of 130, this child was nowhere near stupid! He interrupted us constantly. When petting the dog, he would call her up onto the couch where he knew she wasn't allowed, so he could tattle and get her in trouble. His behavior was motivated by revenge much of the time, so he would spend hours creating elaborate situations that would cause havoc for his current target.

He was in his room more and more, so while in therapy, I shared my concern with CJ. "I don't feel like a mother here, I feel like a warden", I complained. Addressing Will, the therapist asked, "Will, why do you feel like you need to be in jail?" He mumbled some excuse, but being trained in identifying lies, CJ asked again. Glaring defiantly he said, "It's so bad I can't tell!" With that, he tucked his knees up to his chin and rocked himself. In understanding, CJ responded with gentle compassion, "When you keep secrets, it's like a splinter in your heart. The infection building up behind the spike is the rude behavior you've been showing your family. Until you pull that splinter out of your heart by telling your secrets, you will not get better."

He withheld comment and simply sneered from behind his tucked up legs. Knowing that Will was no longer receptive she addressed me knowing he would get the information he needed that way. "There are five areas that can have secrets that hurt the children: Lies they've told. Things they've stolen. People or animals they've hurt." She tucked a strand of her soft, platinum hair behind her ear and in doing so revealed the dangling earring she wore before she continued, "Things they've broken and sex things they've done. Secrets in these areas will make the child sicker and their behavior will let you know whether they need to come clean about something." Reaching over to gently rub Will's shoulder, she continued, " Will's actions are just that." Will turned his back to us and spurned CJ's attempts at further communication. "Well, I'll tell you what I'm going to do. Since Will doesn't want to work in therapy anymore, I'll have him stay with me until he gets strong enough to spit out this secret. I'm not going to have him go home to continue pushing your family's love away." She stood up and addressed the back of Will's defiant head, "Your family in the mountains is too special for that! Nancy, why don't you give Will a hug and head home so you can get there before dark!"

I sadly gave my new son a hug goodbye. I wasn't sure how long it would be before I would see him again and although he had been rude and belligerent lately, I had already grown fond of him. His narrowed eyes followed me as I walked from the room and I could feel his daggers penetrating my heart.

A week later, the truth came spilling out. I learned that his mother, Sheila, sat in prison because Will had lied repeatedly on the witness stand. The woman I had grown to despise passionately because of what she had done was innocent of everything but alcoholism. Her own son had made false allegations of abuse against her and now she sat incarcerated because of his accusations.

He told how none of the people he had accused had ever touched him inappropriately. Just because Will knew their names, their lives were irreparably damaged. There was no sex ring. There was no pimping of his little body. Molestation and intercourse were only things his father, Cain, had told him about.

Promising him a dollar for every time he accused his mom, Cain was teaching little Will what to say and how to say it. He coached his every word. Training him to look sad, abused and pitiful, he hoped the jury would find the little nine-year old boy convincing. He was mad at Sheila for divorcing him. He was angry at her for taking his son away from him. Years of animosity and hostility caused his brutal revenge to destroy his son in order to send Sheila to prison. Cain promised Will that after Sheila was sent away, that he would remove him from foster care so they could happily live together. It never happened.

Will's lies had hurt more than himself and his mother. He had put two other people behind bars and caused the death of one man. The Social Worker had lost her license and career in the face of great shame. The damage was done. The guilt was immense for Will.

It was this incident that forever changed my outlook on the abusers of the children I cared for. I decided not to jump to conclusions about other parents. I would never again judge or condemn them. I wasn't there. I didn't know what really happened. Even the best parents make mistakes. I had certainly made my share! These parents had given the children life. They could have chosen not to. They had fed them and kept them alive. They had, on some level, wanted them to live or they would be dead.

In an attempt to undo some of the damage and ease Will's conscience, we flew to California for a new trial. He stepped up to the witness stand and bravely recanted his testimony, but the judge wouldn't accept it. He stated that one man was dead, Will had taken an oath of honesty before taking the stand the first time, and had taken the same oath again. The judge concluded he was lying at least once. Not knowing which statement was the lie, the court official decided to leave everything as it was. It was the failure of our justice system that imprisoned three innocent people for seven years after the truth was released.

He had finally told of his deceit, so his heart was able to mend, but not fully. When a child tells the truth we see improvement in their behavior. When they lie we see regression. The guilt of not being able to save his mom hung heavy over him. Will had released the splinter from his heart, but it would take many years for the infection to be conquered.

Will's whole attitude softened after telling. A sparkle filled his eyes and a bounce was in his step. For the first time in three years, the heavy weight of lies was lifted from his soul.

He wrote to his mother asking for forgiveness. I thought, " Could I forgive my own child for doing such harm to me?" Her letter arrived filled with love and understanding. The pecking order in the prison system is very hard on those accused of sexual abuse of a child. She had been beaten by other inmates. They would take her food. I pictured her as I read the letter he shared with me. Her simple cotton dress hung loosely over her thin frame. Her eyes hollow yet still soft as she had smiled at her son when they led her into the courtroom in handcuffs. She forgave him. No, I would never again judge and condemn someone else for their actions!

For six months he worked hard in therapy. Kindness and commitment radiated from the things he did and his chores were completed A+. He was working hard to turn his life around and I was there to cheer him on each step of the way.

Terena was outgrowing her pony, GE. Knowing she would soon be ready for a horse, I searched for months looking for the perfect mount for all of us. I heard about an older mare that needed a loving home. Calling on the nearest horse expert I knew, Joyce our neighbor, and I went to inspect the steed. She was a palomino with a dark golden coat that was patterned with dapples and a flaxen mane and tail that shimmered against the deep green of spring. Her temperament was that of willingness. They agreed to bring Kismet, our new family member, up to our home the following weekend. What an Easter surprise I had for my children!

I planned to take the children to swim at the Hot Springs pool all day Saturday, so that when Kismet arrived, they wouldn't know. Coming home late that night, they trudged off to bed. In the morning I was awakened by Terena's excited yells of: "Mom! MOM! There's a horse in our field!" When she rushed into our room, I lay there in bed with a wide smile on my face. The twinkle in my eye caused her to hesitate just long enough for me to say, "Her name is Kismet. She's 29!" Running around the end of the bed, she threw her arms around my neck with glee. Her life long dream of having a horse was finally real. Although we were amateurs at horsemanship, I knew her immense love for the creatures would drive her to learn what she needed.

That spring, Will and Terena rode the big mare often around our front fields. Bareback and with only a halter to control her, they would both climb on and ride for hours. I would watch as they explored the woods out front, laughing and sharing. They were friends. It was great to see them laughing and having such fun. As their confidence grew, they began to ride up the road towards the National Forest.

I always knew where they were going and when to expect them back, but my heart jumped into my throat when Kismet came trotting home without my children one afternoon. Tying up the loose horse, I jumped into the car, and drove up to where they were supposed to be. Around a bend, walking together, I spotted them with tears streaming down both their faces. I stopped, rolled down my window and asked what had happened. Breaking into laughter, they continued to cry. "Mom, we were giggling so hard, we both fell right off Kismet's back. We tried to catch her afterwards, but we were both laughing so hard she got spooked and ran for home. Is she okay?" Relieved, I offered them a ride and on the way back home I told them she was safely tied to the hitching post. They continued to laugh, but the inside joke was lost on me. I was just glad they were both safe and Will finally had a sibling to have fun with. Watching them laugh in the mountain sunshine was a moment I will always treasure.

Will had been an alter boy with his last foster family. He had been joining us for the weekly sermons at our community church, but apparently he had missed most of the lessons. On one of the many drives to therapy, Will noticed a cross on a hill overlooking a meadow of sheep. "Did someone die there", he asked.   I told him, "Well, we believe that the cross is to remind us that Jesus died for us." Wide eyed with shock he yelled, "Jesus died? When did that happen?" Telling him it was about two thousand years ago, he retorted, "Why didn't someone tell me?" Laughing, I mentioned it may have had something to do with his listening.

><del>米</del>∕∼ ><del>米</del>∕∼ ><del>米</del>∕∼ ><del>米</del>∕∼

Alicia came back from Texas sooner than expected. Elaine had been holding and rocking little Alicia often. The tight structure her daughter needed to feel safe had been in place from the first day Alicia was home. She was learning to love and trust her mom, but six months without attachment therapy had been too long. Without the outlet of the special treatment, her rage had, again, built up to deadly levels that Alicia couldn't control.

A few days later, I drove to the Denver airport to retrieve my Bottomless Pit. She had grown while with her family, but her frail body still looked too young to belong to a seven year old. Knowing her intense rage was about to boil over; we headed straight to Evergreen for therapy.

Meeting CJ at the office, Alicia was given some toys to occupy her in the playroom as we discussed the situation. "I don't understand why she's killing again. Was her mom not tough enough? Was she too tough?" I asked. CJ explained that it wasn't Elaine's fault. The rage had been locked inside her within the first two years of life when Alicia was still with her birth mother. A normal infant is held and loved with soft cooing and gentleness. That handling of the helpless little baby gets internalized by the infant as if it were a cassette tape. As the child grows and sees other baby beings, that tape is replayed over and over. The child reenacts the cooing, softness and gentleness they received as a baby. These Attachment Disorder children internalize a parent tape also, but instead of gentleness and love from a caring parent, it is filled with their own infant rage they were left with when no one answered their cries. They were abused or neglected as babies. Rough handling and mean words fill their "parent tapes", so when they see other beings that are helpless and hopeless like they were, the internalized rage surfaces and can result in a killing rage.

I absorbed every word she said and thought about Terena. She had been loved and cherished as a baby, so her cassette tape reflected that early patterning. As a toddler, she rocked and sang to her stuffed animals and even one quite surprised snake she found in the yard. She would pat them as if she were burping a baby. I realized I had not consciously taught her those behaviors. It was her internalizing my actions that made her so nurturing.

Nodding my head in understanding, I went to call Alicia to join us. Before doing so, I watched from the window separating the two rooms as she held the legs of a doll and repeatedly hit its head on the couch. I saw her mouth the words, "Bad baby! Bad baby!" I made a mental note to rerecord her parent tape with love and gentleness by getting her a baby doll and teaching her the right way to hold and care for it.

Alicia worked hard in her session, but I knew we had a lot of work to 'cure' her of her primal urges to kill. During the therapy she cried in sadness at having to leave her mother again. She raged for along time. Hatred filled her eyes as she screamed 'I want to kill you' over and over. She confessed to having molested another child. While at school, in the girls' bathroom she had cornered a classmate and fondled her. She was being honest, so towards the end of the hour and a half session, her rancor was lifting.

I cuddled and filled her heart with as much love and understanding as I could. Absorbing it faster than a dry sponge in water, a twinkle developed in her beautiful eyes and a peacefulness filled her spirit that I had not seen before. I asked, "How do you feel about attachment therapy?" She answered with, "I don't like having to work so hard. It's really hard work, but I feel better when I get rid of my mad." She softly smiled at me before continuing. "At home I had a lot of mad and my mommy would have me draw pictures to try to let it out. I punched a pillow sometimes, too. She would hold me and rock me and tell me stories. It made me feel a little better, but it didn't take my mad away." She looked away and licked her lips. Giving her a sip of water, I listened, "When CJ works with me she helps me get my big feelings out." I asked her how much mad she had when she stepped off the plane. Knowing she needed help describing it, I offered, "Was it as big as a golf ball, baseball or basketball?" She said, "My mad was as big as from here to the moon!" I was surprised that she visualized her anger as so much bigger than herself while I saw it as taking up a little spot inside of her. It made me sad that this little child had such a burden to carry. Curiously, I asked, "How much mad do you have now after the session?" She thoughtfully paused. "It's as big as this office," she said as she searched my eyes. I smiled.

Seeing tenderness and acceptance shine from my face, her little body relaxed into mine and I rocked her while telling her of the new boy, Will, that had become part of our family. She laughed with me when I told her how the new baby goats jumped and pranced about the mountain. She felt my loss when I told her how Freddy, my old faithful dog, had a stroke and passed away on Christmas morning. As the tears of loss ran down my face, I saw a spark of empathy cross hers.

We drove home and met the school bus as it let off R.B., Chucky, Terena and Will at our driveway. Sneakers, my Corgi dog raced out to greet us. She was very pregnant with purebred pups, and as I backed into my parking place, I realized the situation was a potential disaster. I had to keep them safe! If Alicia were able to hurt one of those puppies, her healing would severely backslide. I also thought about the advantage these tiny pups could have in helping her learn about nurturing and appropriate handling of little, helpless creatures.

Knowing what easy targets the puppies could be, I decided to move Sneakers and the whelping box upstairs into Terena's room. A high hook and latch would be the second barrier of protection. The first was the rule that Alicia was not allowed up those stairs.

Coming inside and sitting at the table while the children ate their after school snack, I asked how their day went. Terena explained how Will had been screaming and hollering on the bus causing the driver to pull over and wait until he settled down. She proceeded to tell me how he had antagonized the smaller children. I knew driving the curvy, often dangerous mountain roads with a busload of children was no easy task, so I thought of an appropriate consequence. Hoping he would learn that riding the bus was a privilege and not a right, Will would walk the eight miles to and from school for the next three days.

The next morning, I met the bus and informed the driver of my plan. With a smile of thanks, Lloyd tipped his brown fedora hat before closing the bus door and driving away with my two boys waving at me from the back seat. I waved back while I thought about my other boy walking the long country road in the morning sunshine to his junior high school.

Alicia stayed home with me during the day, as she had convinced her school in Texas that she was too retarded to do regular schoolwork. Knowing it was an act of rebellion and defiance, I decided to have little Alicia memorize children's poems throughout her summer stay with us. She started the 'chore' by learning one sentence a day and would come in for lunch as soon as she had finished.

The idea for this had been planted in my mind many years before when Iva Lou, Jerry's Grandmother, stayed with us. She was in her mid nineties. Recalling her education in a one-room schoolhouse, she shared the lessons she was required to memorize from the MacGuffy reader some eighty years earlier. Amazing poems would fill our home as her memory retrieved the long stored assignments of her childhood. Thinking how amazing her mental capacities still were, I pondered the practice.

Buying a school desk from a garage sale, I placed it under the big box elder tree out back where I could watch Alicia from the kitchen and dining room windows. I hoped the fresh air, sounds of the creek skipping along, and the peacefulness would be a good healing spot for her. Giving her a bottle of water, I hugged her lovingly and walked her out to her beautiful 'office' surrounded by rustling leaves and wild flowers. The poem was in her hand. Closing the cats in the garage, I waved to her, wished her good luck and disappeared into the house.

It took her three hours that first day. Coming inside to let me know she was finished, I heard her humming. "Okay, Alicia, let's hear how you're doing!" Her chin went up and out rolled: "Roses are red!" I smiled into her eyes and grabbed her up into a bear hug and twirled her around in my arms. "You can be so smart when you want to be!"

On Alicia's third day back, Sneakers gave birth to five beautiful red puppies. Nike, Adidas, Reebok, Converse and High Top joined our family. A few days later, CJ was at our home to do therapy with Alicia. When Sneakers left her puppies for a break, CJ had me pull Alicia up onto my knee and the little red dog onto my other one. I put my hand over Alicia's and guided it as she stroked Sneaker's copper fur. CJ asked how it felt on her hand. "Nice. Kind of tickles!", she giggled nervously. I asked her how she thought Sneakers felt when she was petted nicely. She replied she didn't know, so I told her to look into the gentle brown eyes of the dog. "What do they say? Is she mad, sad, glad or scared?" She watched intently as we continued to stroke the back of the Corgi. "Well mostly glad, because her eyes are half closed." Confirming her observation, I asked how Alicia felt inside. "I feel like killing her," she replied honestly.

We continued to pet Sneakers while I thought about how to handle that. I didn't want to overreact, even though my gut was telling me to grab my little dog and run. "Let's let Sneakers go back to her puppies now", I said as I released my dog. Turning Alicia to me and laying her on my lap, I thanked her for being so honest about her feelings. "Was that hard for you?" CJ asked. When Alicia answered "no," the therapist continued with, "So, those are some pretty big feelings you're having. I'm so glad you're strong enough to talk them out instead of act them out. There are some grownups that aren't that strong. I'm so proud of you!"

Knowing we had to work this through, CJ offered that opportunity to Alicia. "Would you like to let go of those big feelings so you don't have to carry them around anymore?" She looked up at me and replied, "Yes, I do!" I told her that if she let go of her big feelings with a big voice, those big feelings wouldn't hurt her anymore. CJ moved a chair up to the couch and took Alicia's hand as she asked her, "What words go with your big feelings, sweetheart?" Alicia looked down at her hands before answering. "I want to kill the dog!" Affirming her choice, CJ encouraged her to yell the phrase. Louder each time, my little girl screamed repeatedly. I was careful to keep my eyes soft and filled with love even though her powerful hateful emotions were palpable. I knew she couldn't hear me over her own voice, so I spoke to the heart of this wounded child in my arms through my eyes. I wanted her to be able to look up and see acceptance and understanding. I cheered her on as I asked her to look at me while she vented. I felt like a lamaze coach as wave after wave of ear splitting rage brought her closer to releasing her killing feelings. CJ pulled a tissue and wiped the sweat off Alicia's forehead as the child worked hard to let go of her burden of overwhelming feelings of rage. I was so proud of her. The effort she was showing allowed me to see she really did care about healing. A conscience was forming in this little girl, and I loved her all the more for it. When she said she was done, I rocked her and sang to her as I fed her ice cream filled with love. CJ hugged and left me with words of support and hope. "She can make it, she has you." I love CJ for that.

~★~ ~★~ ~★~ ~★~

Week after week, Alicia learned different poems she picked out. She memorized Sally by the Seashore and The Old Woman in the Shoe. At the completion of each poem, we would strategize over lunch about what costumes and props we would use when I filmed the official performance of each poem. Laughing I would set up the video camera and record as she sat and recited them with no cheat sheet each day. Our favorite poem was Old Mother Hubbard because Terena and her German Shepherd, I.Q., were the actresses as Alicia recited the story. Terena was a ham, Alicia was terrific and I.Q. was well trained, so the filming was a hoot. After dinner each evening the film's latest chapter would be proudly shown to Jerry for "Dad's Seal of Approval".

I had always believed television viewing was bad for developing young minds so Jerry and I disconnected the antenna. Children with relationship issues such as Attachment Disorder learned nothing about forming or maintaining closeness from TV, so the lack of constant bombardment from it was fine with me. On most Friday and Saturday evenings, my Cowboy rented a flick from the local store. As a family event, the children who had earned their movie watching privilege were invited to watch. Curled up in our respective blankets, we all packed onto the love seat, beanbags chairs and throw pillows and passed the popcorn around as the plot unfolded. Those that were not ready to watch played nearby.

Alicia had never watched a movie at our house, and as we were the epitome of a western family, my Cowboy rented a John Wayne flick. Having done her chores correctly for a full month, she was finally able to join the family for movie night. At the end of the movie, we all went upstairs to the dinning room for hot cocoa. Discussing the flick, I mentioned to Alicia that she would make a great actress with her talent for charming the camera. Her films of the poetry were proof of that! Her eyes became saucers as she said she wouldn't like to die. Confused, I asked what she meant. "Those guys in that movie were really killed!" I quickly explained that the actors lay down and pretended and someone poured catsup on them for fake blood. "That wasn't pretend! They were really dead! I could tell. I don't ever want to be in movies!" She exclaimed. I tried convincing her that no one really got hurt, but she would have none of it. She was an eight-year old child that couldn't tell reality from fantasy. Later that month I was in a theater and noticed my heart was pounding in terror as I literally jumped in my seat when a dinosaur snapped at me! I was not separating reality from fantasy. How could I expect my already traumatized children to do it? It was this incident that convinced me that no matter what the rating of the movie, or T.V. show; it had the potential to do more harm than good. I would be much more careful about what my family watched!

The next day, as Alicia swept the front porch, I noticed she was whimpering. Moving slowly, she leaned against the broom and wiped the tears from her cheeks. Concerned, I stepped outside to ask what was wrong. Looking up at me, her teary eyes squeezed tightly shut before continuing, "I need to have a shession. Will you call CJ? I really need to have a shession!" I pulled her into my arms, loving that she was finally strong enough to identify and deal with her feelings rather than have them "overtake" her. I knew that when the kids actually asked for therapy, they were near the peak of their healing. I picked up my little Bottomless Pit and carried her into the house where we called CJ together.

>⚘< >⚘< >⚘< >⚘<

Alicia left at the end of the summer, but before she did she was able to recite the preamble to the Constitution of the United States while Chucky waived the American flag. Proudly, Alicia was able to explain what all the words meant. We filmed the grand performance and sent a copy home with the many poems she had memorized over the summer. Her father called to say: "She's not retarded! She is a genius!" I agreed!

Chucky's holding of the Stars and Stripes for that video was a foreshadowing of his acceptance into military school for his upcoming freshman year. Later, he would be honored by being chosen to be the flag bearer for his class. While he was at the last baseball practice of the summer, I called for Terena and Will. Coming up from the root cellar where Will was growing mushrooms, they came running. "I need some help putting Chucky's suitcases in the car. Please work together to carefully put them in the Toyota." With that I sank into a chair on the porch. I was taking my son, Chucky, to military school the next day and I cried in anguish that I was unable to get his stealing and lying under control. I was getting calls almost daily from the junior high about his extreme conduct and the ear piercings he continually inflicted upon himself in class. The thought of the safety pins he poked through his flesh caused me to cringe. Worried sick by his escalating behavior, I allowed the tears to wash my soul of the sadness I felt so I could focus on the hope that this might help him to become honest.

Moping around the house for weeks, my feelings of loss and longing for my son, so far away were lifted when I got a call from Texas. Alicia's parents had called to say they had enrolled her in a private school that didn't know of her supposedly low IQ. I smiled when they told me she had earned being on the honor roll. Acting dumb when she was mad was a thing of the past! She was bonding well with her family, and handling the struggles of childhood with success. Alicia was doing well! She and her family were so happy, my heart soared with theirs!

><del>⁂</del>< ><del>⁂</del>< ><del>⁂</del>< ><del>⁂</del><

Will began to struggle more and more until by fall, he returned to all of his antisocial behavior motivated by revenge. Terena began to avoid him. They no longer rode Kismet together. He had been so helpful and loving for so many months that I felt he was on the road to recovery, but as each day came to a close, I began doubting his ultimate success.

Because he even refused to make his bed, I realized my way of interacting with him was no longer working. I wasn't having fun with this child anymore, he was sucking me dry with his behavior, and I knew that when the fun left, the game might as well be over. So, as a last ditch effort I decided to switch tactics. The old ones were not working. It was time!

While Will was in the bathroom the next morning, I raced to his room with a bag full of jellybeans. I made his bed, tucking the sheets into perfect square corners and pulling the blankets up evenly and smoothly to end perfectly at the pillow. Before finishing, I pulled the top sheet back and sprinkled the whole bag of jellybeans into the bed. Sneaking into the hall outside the bathroom, I urgently called, "Will! Get out here right this minute!" Hearing the sink turn off, I watched as he rushed out. "Yes, Mom?", he asked, surprised. "Will!!! I want an explanation!" In his usual response he claimed he didn't do it, even before he knew what I was asking about. Grabbing his hand, I took him to his room briskly before I demanded another explanation for the neatly made bed. "Mom, I didn't do it really!" he insisted.

Pointing to his bed, I firmly told him, "I don't expect to see this again! I could have a heart attack and die!" His eyes lit up at the chance to kill me off just by making his bed. That night, I heard: "For Pete's sake" as he pulled his sheets back to reveal the sweet, colorful candies I had hidden. The next morning, I turned off his alarm and opened the door. There he stood, in front of his perfectly made bed. I could have bounced a quarter off of it, but instead I pretended to faint and collapse with a coronary about how terrible it was that he had made it. He loved it! I gave him a hug and smiled at my reverse psychology tactic. It had worked and we both won!

Having his bed made so perfectly, only made the rest of his room look like that much more of a pigsty. He usually refused to bring down his laundry and when he did, his basket was mainly filled with the clean clothes from his drawers. The stench from his filthy clothes he stuffed back in the drawers or threw on the floor finally drove me to remove all his clothing from his room. Pulling his dresser from the bedroom, I decided to keep it in the laundry room. I hoped he would find more motivation to put the soiled clothing in front of the washer if it was nearby. It didn't work. After several days, the smell became overpowering and the piles crept into the kitchen. He had clothing strewn from the laundry room, through the house and to his room. I then pulled the bureau into the garage. Maybe if his clothes were out of the house, he would annoy the family less with the stink and mess.

The garage was Jerry's territory so I was ignorant of the disaster Will was making until my Cowboy came storming in one day. "He's got his shit strung from one rafter to the other out there! His shorts are literally hanging from the canoe suspended from the ceiling. I can't get to the animals' grain, it's so messy out there!" I stepped out onto the porch and saw the path of clothing from the door to the garage. From where I stood, I could see the garage was wallpapered with in his stuff as well. Knowing I had to stand strong on my decision, I had to come up with a different plan. I carried his chest of drawers out under the same box elder tree where Alicia's office had been. Again, several weeks later the back of our home was decorated with shirts, socks, pants and underwear. Having fully slimed the house, garage and yard, I decided his clothes should be far, far away. In the field next to us stood a beautiful tree, one that would protect his dresser from the elements. Thinking that if it hassled him enough, he would eventually learn to do it right in the first place, I had him help me drag the bureau under the protection of the huge limbs.

Exasperated, I called CJ when Will's clothes stretched from the back door, through our yard, into the neighbor's field and even up in the old tree. Our house looked as if hillbillies occupied the beautiful property. She explained how I had pushed and pushed and pushed until I had nowhere else to turn. I had created a lose-lose situation for both of us. Describing how I had allowed the focus to be Will's clothing instead of the relationship between us, she made it clear I had hammered a wedge between him and me that was splitting us. CJ recommended that I take total responsibility for Will's clothes and each morning hand him exactly what he needed to wear for the day. Each evening, I was to retrieve his dirty clothes and hand him his pajamas. The problem was solved, and we both were winning again. I hadn't seen his need for help. I had just pushed.

He was getting older, so many of the techniques I used with Alicia weren't working. CJ recommended I get him a journal. It was homework for Will, called his Feelings Book. Each time he was disrespectful or irresponsible he was to write in it. On the inside cover I wrote the specific items he was to address. He was to answer the questions: What happened? How was he feeling? How did he handle it? How can he handle it better next time? His had thirteen entries in one day!

The kids at school began calling him Lurch from the Addams Family because he would stand with his shoulders slumped over, his mouth gaping open and his eyes focused on absolutely nothing, for minutes at a time. I didn't like the nickname, but as his weird posture continued I reflected on our extraordinary family. We were rather odd for taking in all these children. Maybe we WERE like the Addams family!

Driving down the road on our way to town, I instructed all the kids to roll down their windows. In our loudest voices, my children and I began singing the theme song to the Addams family. I watched in the rear view mirror as Will initially refused to join in. But the more we sang, the more I saw him getting into it. At first he just mouthed the words, but as my kids continued adding pizzazz and energy to it, he too ended up hollering out with us. I think back to the few neighbors we had and wonder just what they thought of our weird antics. I can still visualize the Toyota, barreling down the back roads with the wind wildly whipping our hair. Hearing us for miles before actually seeing us, the little tan car would race past the houses with children's heads out the windows while we all sang freely.

I knew how important a child's self-esteem was, so I would search for any gifts or talents each child might have. Will's talent lay in his wonderful writing ability. His poetry was powerful enough to create strong feelings in most people. I found a poem about himself in the laundry, and as I read it, I thought about Edgar Allen Poe. Poe had been put in an orphanage by his mother for months when he was a baby. His pathology is clear in his work. Some say he suffered from Attachment Disorder, and still his writings were famous. I read it again...

I won't clean my room, so fuck you.
I bug Chucky, so fuck you.
I won't do my chores right, so fuck you.
I won't sit right, so fuck you.
I won't take baths, so fuck you.
I steal food, so fuck you.
I get in the fridge, so fuck you.
I put clean clothes in the dirty laundry, so fuck you.
I pee on things, so fuck you.
I boss Alicia around, so fuck you.
I tear up my shoes, so fuck you.
I go 'um' when people are talking, so fuck you.
I poke holes in my wall, so fuck you.
I don't brush my teeth, so fuck you.
I eat like a pig, so fuck you.
I leave food on my face, so fuck you.
I put holes in my blue jeans, so fuck you.
I won't ask for things, so fuck you.
I steal at the store, so fuck you.
I lie, so fuck you.
I mumble, so fuck you.
I don't clean the bathtub with soap, so fuck you.
I argue. I sound arrogant when I talk. I talk to make noise. I finish sentences for people. I interrupt when people are talking. I ask to do things that I can't do. I don't listen to directions. I eye roll. I make rude faces, so.. FUCK YOU!!!

Understanding it was supposed to upset me, I oddly felt proud of my boy to have found such a creative outlet for his anger. I thought it was a very honest and comprehensive list. He had worked hard on it. Calling him to where I stood in front of the washer, I hugged him. Telling him he had great poetic rhythm and potential, I watched as his 'gotcha' attitude changed to confusion. I guess I was supposed to be offended or hurt, but instead I encouraged and loved him more! His plan had backfired.

>ᢍ※ᢍᡕ >ᢍ※ᢍᡕ >ᢍ※ᢍᡕ >ᢍ※ᢍᡕ

Knowing how important respite was for therapeutic parents, I agreed to take Yohanna, a tough little cookie from a family in Denver. She had been out playing baseball with her mom and the church team. Yohanna stood up to bat, but walked back to the bench when her mom informed her it wasn't her turn yet. As her mom practiced swinging, the little eleven year old snuck up behind her and bashed her in the head with a wooden bat. Her mom lay bleeding and unconscious in the bullpen as Yohanna insisted: "It was an accident!"

As her Mom lay in the hospital, Yohanna was being driven up to my house. Snarling as she strutted into my home, I showed her where she would be staying. Telling her I wanted her to remove the backward red baseball hat from her head, I instructed her that in our home, hats were only worn outside. She growled, "Don't ever touch my stuff, bitch or I'll make you pay!" Smiling at her audacity, I replied, "Well, I see why you're here with me. Your parents have definitely earned their rest!" Her cold, black eyes tried to stare me down, but Terena's big dog stood between us and punched the girl with her cold nose. The rage inside this I child was so intense, IQ felt obligated to protect me. Giving Yohanna time to unpack, I activated the alarm on her door and sat to flip through her file.

I read that she had been in nine placements in nine years in foster care. I knew each move was a trauma for a child like this. Each move would put her deeper and deeper into her illness. At five years of age, the little black haired girl downstairs in my home tried to kill her younger foster brother for ripping her coloring book. She had wrapped a shoelace around the neck of her sibling, his face turned purple and his struggling arms went limp before her mom pulled her off. Transferred to a new home, she had used the safety pin from the bow on her Sunday dress to stab the family guinea pig to death. Caught in the act of ripping it open, she smiled wickedly at her power. They moved her out. Left alone to share a bedroom with two other foster children in her new home, the little ones woke up to find her standing over them and peeing. Urine splashed into their faces and soaked through their bedspreads. They packed her stuff in trash bags and moved her again. She had been moved from home to home, until, a year ago; the state placed her in our program in an attempt to keep another potential psychopath out of the criminal system.

Will stood at the wood stove throwing black and orange box elder beetles onto its hot surface. The pop from their exploding little bodies caused a sick smile to curl over his lips. Telling him to stop the carnage as I passed by,

I encouraged him to work on his latch hook craft project. "If you're bored, I have plenty of work that needs to be done!", I said as I went downstairs to where Yohanna was unpacking. Opening the door, I had to resist the automatic urge to hug her. I knew her early years must have been filled with much trauma to have caused the behavior reported in her records. I reminded myself that she was here for respite, not long term, and the techniques were very different for dealing with children in that circumstance. Laying my hand on her shoulder, I instructed her to take a bath and get ready for bed.

In an attempt to help the respite children to reach for their families, no bonding activities were practiced. We didn't want to confuse them as to where they belonged and as I aligned with the tired parents, the child got no hugs or nurturing from me. Their days were usually spent thinking and earning money to repay their debts and in Yohanna's case, the hospital bill for her mom.

I heard Yohanna stomp from the bathroom and slam her door. Knowing she had a long day, I asked if she was hungry. She cussed furiously at me, so I turned the knob and double-checked the alarm before going upstairs to be with the rest of the kids.

Will's bedtime was eight, so he was preparing for bed. Terena woke up much earlier than the other children to do the morning milking and take a shower before school. By eight o'clock at night, she was already sound asleep in her room. My house was quiet with the preparations of nighttime. I followed my Cowboy downstairs into our bedroom so we could talk as he prepared for bed as well. I would soon be the only one awake as I was a night owl. I loved our quiet time alone to talk each night and I eagerly absorbed every word of our conversation.

The next morning, with all my children off to school and my Cowboy at work, I disarmed the alarm on Yohanna's door. She sat, already dressed, on her bed. Seething, she spat venom in my direction. "Where's my mom?" she demanded to know. She had watched the ambulance take her Mom, so she knew where she was. I smiled, "Is there some reason you need to know?" Sneering, she looked away.

Yohanna lived with a Therapeutic Family so I knew she was used to doing strong sitting. I guided her to a "think spot" to sit while I cooked her breakfast. I debated what chores to give Yohanna. My family had been working on cleaning the stalls in the barns, and had about half of the job done. This child had several hundred dollars to earn, so I thought a big project like that would enable her to work off a good chunk of her debt. I also thought that being outside by herself might give her time to think about her behavior. If she was going to dish crap out, what better job than to shovel it? I had found that our horses and goats weren't offended by filthy language. Not once did I ever see a look of surprise cross their faces at the mention of the 'F' word.

Terena had worked and earned $600 to buy a three-year old purebred Arabian Mare named Quest, so I haltered the two horses and led them into the front field. Haltering GE, I led him to the side field where the goats were already grazing. The animals would now be safe from Yohanna, so I handed her a shovel and wheel barrow, a bottle of drinking water and told her if she needed anything to come let me know.

Showering that night, I poured shampoo over my head. It was more runny than normal and as I tried lathering it, a pungent smell filled the air. Yohanna had urinated in my shampoo! Grossed out, I said out loud, "I hate it when this happens!" With urine dripping down my head, I squinted my eyes and held my breath, while rinsing my hair as quickly as possible. Dumping the rest of the bottle down the drain, I found a new bottle under the sink and continued with my bathing. As I scrubbed, I thought about the little girl in the next room. Maybe she had a scientific mind. Was she curious about the chemical reaction between the ammonia from her urine and the synthetic chemicals in the soap? I didn't think so, but I was trying to stay optimistic. That day I decided to never leave my shampoo or conditioner in the bathroom again. Some lessons are hard to forget.

Two weeks later, Yohanna had turned her attitude around. Her Mom was back at home and rested and ready to have her back. Having earned over three hundred dollars, Yohanna was ready to go home. She had written an appropriate apology letter to her mom. Earning the money and buying two bottles of shampoo for me, she handed me a note as she left. My house was sparkling, the animals had fresh straw in their stalls and Yohanna had accomplished a lot. With a smile on her face, she waved good riddance to our family and got in the car with her dad. I opened the note as they pulled away. It read:

Sorry mom Nancy for being rude and snotty. Sorry for peeing in your shampoo. Last week I cleaned the toilet with your toothbrush. sorry! from Yohanna.

Chapter 10

Snatched From the Jaws of Hell

Having used the bedroom downstairs for almost two years, Will had finally earned the privilege of moving to a bedroom upstairs by keeping his room clean. It wasn't too hard for him as I was still handing him his outfits and retrieving the dirty clothes to launder. His new room had plush blue carpet, a large closet, bookshelves and a wall mural of clouds. He earned using the upstairs bathroom which was a big deal demonstrating the trust he had earned. We threw a party for him to celebrate his success. We all laughed and ate happily

Some good friends, Art and Sandy, loaned us an Arabian mare for a year. Her fine, dished face was sweet and her white coat blended in with the spring snow. Troika was her name. We felt like it would be good for Will to have the fun and responsibility of her care. He rode her often and learned to work with her in a gentle way. He and Terena were friends again, but their relationship was never as tight as it had been his first summer with us. They would spend hours in the front field with the horses after their chores were finished.

Quest, Terena's horse was old enough to be saddle trained. I had enjoyed training dogs since 1956. I had taken lots of classes and had trained dogs professionally for years. I loved it! I thought horse training would be very similar. Standing in the round pen, I tried to get the mare to move so I could reward her. I talked to her. I pulled on her halter. I pushed on her rump. Looking at me warily, she snorted, before stomping her foot and glaring at me. I was clueless, so I loaded all the kids into the car and drove to the library. Terena knew where the horse books were, so she quickly ran in and checked out the limit. "It's okay mom! I've already read a bunch of these, so I'll reread them and train her myself. I can do it!" I looked at my sixty pound daughter and wondered what kind of damage a thousand pound horse could inflict but, I didn't dare dampen her enthusiasm.

The next day, I watched from the window, as my little nine year old encouraged the huge horse around the training pen. Walking, trotting and cantering, the steed snorted and bucked. Halting abruptly to rear up in opposition, my heart stopped as I watched Terena run up under the striking beast only to yank on the lead rope and command: "Get down here and knock that off!" The vision of my child underneath the enormous animal rearing up so high over her head took my breath away. She had been an integral part of helping me with the children, and as I watched her handle the horse, I saw the lessons she used with the children were effective with her four-legged friend as well. She demanded respect. When the boundaries were tested, the animal was corrected. Her gentle handling and pain free consequences taught the huge beast to love and trust her. I knew my little daughter didn't have an ordinary childhood, so I was glad she was able to find such happiness.

When the house filled with the screams and rage of an erupting child, Smiles would confirm that I had it under control before dashing to the pasture with a bridle. Throwing her tiny body onto Kismet's bare back, she would disappear up the road at a full gallop in order to keep her sanity. I knew she was strong enough to handle the bizarre upbringing. I also knew she loved every creature that stepped onto our property, no matter how wild they were, and the lessons she was learning would mature her well beyond her years.

Earning money by helping me with the kids, Smiles purchased an old horse trailer and started taking lessons from a seasoned horseman at a private riding facility. Jerry and I would pay for the weekly lessons, but only if she practiced. No matter what the season, my daughter rode for hours each evening after school. Quest was young and unschooled, but Terena's patience taught her to be receptive and gentle. We would all pile in the van to go to the arena to watch the two of them together as they competed in many horse shows.

Her horsemanship was becoming exemplary, and knowing how healing it was for her, I allowed her to give riding lessons to the children. Developing and implementing a therapeutic riding program, Smiles helped build the self-esteem and trust of the kids. Kismet was her first therapy mount because she was old and mellow, but as Quest became reliable, Terena began using her as well. I loved watching this amazing young teen directing the silver mare, mane flying and huge smiling child on top. In amazement, the young horse could sense the emotions of the children. If they were filled with rage, she would chase them out, trying to bite them unless Terena intervened. The same child, after therapy, could enter the pasture and pet or play with her without incident. Quest knew.

That spring, I received another file on a nine-year old Hispanic boy named Jose. The first psychiatric evaluation, conducted in Wyoming, described him as extremely disturbed. I wondered what exactly that meant. Reading further, the Psychiatrist wrote that the boy's violent upbringing had caused him to be hyper-vigilant and hyper-aggressive as a means of defense. That pretty much described most of the children I had taken in so far.

I set the file down as Will entered the room. "Mom! If you don't get enough calcium with your meals, you don't grow. Am I not getting enough calcium?" I tried not to laugh as he sipped from his big glass of milk. "Will, I studied nutrition for years. I feed you well-rounded meals and the supplements you take in the morning give you what I may miss! When you drink milk, you are getting calcium." Seeming satisfied, he returned to the kitchen.

I picked up Jose's file and continued reading. He was physically and sexually abused as an infant and toddler. The long scar he carried down his abdomen, reminded him daily of the abuse he endured early in his life. His grandfather, with whom he lived after his mom left, had tried killing him by driving over his five year old body with the family truck. A neighbor saw this and called an ambulance and the police. When he recovered from his multiple surgeries and broken bones, Jose was introduced into the Social Service system.

He was adopted into a family within months. Ear infections and other strange afflictions plagued his siblings for years, until finally, one of them told his mom what was happening. Apparently Jose was urinating or stuffing his feces into the various orifices of the other children in his home at night. His parents then had him sleep in a sleeping bag outside in a tent in an attempt to protect the other children. He continued to molest and abuse his siblings at night; he just had to wait longer until his parents were sound asleep then would sneak in the back door.

With an I.Q. of 145, he excelled at coming up with new, more appalling ways to traumatize his family. Catching birds and chipmunks, he would impale their writhing bodies on sticks to decorate around his tent. Hearing the screams of pain from the tiny creatures, his mom would run out and try desperately to pull them from their crucifix. Jose watched in delight as they suffered while his Mom attempted to save them. Digging up their rotting corpses, he would stab them back onto sticks to decorate his fort. The family had enough and Jose was removed. A Social Service caseworker packed his belongings into large trash sacks and moved him, like trash, to another home.

Jose was adopted again when he was seven years old. His new parents, Roy and Jean, had another four-year old son, Jessie and not knowing Jose's past, she had allowed the two to share a room. The file indicated Jose had molested Jessie repeatedly, but they hadn't found out until recently. Upon learning this, they immediately sought professional help and separated them. The treatment they were getting was not helping.

The last paper in the file was from the recent psychiatric evaluation. Little Jose suffered from Conduct Disorder, under-socialization and Attachment Disorder. This family needed better therapy, so they turned to the Attachment Center, the agency I worked for.

Jerry came home that night and as I cried into his arms, I asked him how much more horror could children take? Where was our society going? How had such evil and sickness crept into our communities without anyone knowing? I cried for the little boy who needed our help. I sobbed for the children he had hurt. I wailed for the many kids that were out there, needing safety and assurance and that weren't getting the help they needed. The weight of the world came crashing down on me and I decided then, that I had to do more. My gentle husband held me as Will came in and asked for more milk, as he needed protein.

Jerry and I agreed to take Jose and as I waited for him to arrive, I started writing a manual for parenting these tough children. I had to do something! Families were out there struggling, looking for answers while I lived, secluded from the world, finding many of the answers they were so desperately searching for. I felt compelled to share the knowledge.

Will came home from school and as we sat eating ham and cheese on crackers for a snack, he announced haughtily, "Mom! I need protein in my diet!" Drinking from his big glass of goat's milk, he lowered the cup to reveal a milk mustache. Happy that he was learning about nutrition in school, I replied, "Yes, Will you do. What do think the ham and cheese is?" This kind of accusation had dominated much of our conversation lately. He had been questioning everything I fed him lately. Instead of getting annoyed about his barrage of accusations of poor nutrition I decided to get playful about it.

The next morning, as I prepared his lunch for a school field trip, I decided to forego the usual healthy lunch and, allowing the streak of leprechaun inside of me to take over, I made Will a sandwich of chocolate kisses. I placed it lovingly into the sandwich bag. I knew he would be hungry, so I made another. Instead of the usual carrots and string cheese, I stuck licorice sticks and cookies into the brown paper bag. Reaching into the fridge, I passed the 100% organic juice boxes I usually used, and pulled out the one can of soda we had. I was having fun making his lunch! Putting a note with the loving words, "Hope this sweetens you up! Love Mom," into the bag, I rolled down the top and handed it to my son as he raced for the bus. I smiled picturing the look on his face when he opened it!

〜❀〜 〜❀〜 〜❀〜 〜❀〜

Alicia came to spend the summer with us. I was so happy to see her and hug her again! I had been expecting to have Jose to join us first, but his family was having a hard time finding the funding for his treatment. Alicia was a healthy child now. The years of daily chores taught her to be a hard worker, so she no longer needed to have each job carefully checked. Riding the horses with Terena, they laughed often and shared stories of the times they were apart. I loved being able to see my little Bottomless Pit grow into a young lady and as I had reinforced so many years before, she was an excellent cook! Pizza was her favorite. Her father had taught her to toss the handmade crust until it was just right before applying the special sauce and toppings. We all gained some weight that summer!

Chucky also came home from military school. My house was overflowing with children and I loved it; there was never a dull moment. Laughter echoed from the walls when the screaming fits weren't monopolizing the air. The kids played on the slip-n-slide or ran through the sprinklers during the hot days and we all took hikes to the "Indian cave". A campfire dinner or an occasional pillow fight were fun additions to the summer festivities.

Jose joined us in July. Jean, his adoptive mother, flew out with him and stayed during the week of intensive therapy. She found out about his evening activities with Jessie when the little Jessie had come stomping out one morning. With his hand on his hips and eyebrows down, he sharply asked, "Mom, do I have to get sexed anymore? I'm getting pretty sick of this every night!" Needless to say Jean was shocked!

We addressed Jose's inappropriateness with his little brother in the therapy. Learning that he wanted to have sex with his adoptive grandfather, uncles and friends, we realized the sexual outbursts were much more severe than originally thought. He fantasized about them coming into his room at night, in the darkness, to sodomize him. Since it never happened, he started playing the part with his brother. He would sneak into little Jessie's bed to violate his body. Jose had been threatening to kill him if he told so Jessie had suffered silently from his nightly attacks for over a year. Jose believed he could do anything once Mommy and Daddy were asleep.

CJ addressed the issues with impressive skill. Days of intense therapy focused intensely on Jose's early childhood trauma. He told about the things he had done in his previous home, including his desire to kill and maim helpless creatures. Jean was sickened at hearing about his past animal abuse. She had not been told about much of his behavior.

Each night, she would call her husband, Roy, to sob into the phone. The little boy they loved so much was very sick! With each day, her tan skin turned more sallow, the bags under her eyes darkened and her eyes became more bloodshot. She was internalizing the intense feelings Jose was releasing, making them personal. Hearing the woman he loved in so much pain, Roy packed his bags and flew to Colorado with Jessie. As he walked in our front door and reached for her, Jean collapsed into his arms. Heart wrenching sobs filled the room as she tried to tell him how brutally their son had been treated as a baby. They had known it was bad, but as the truth came out, it was more than she could bear. The last year and a half of their life had been a nightmare, but they loved their little boy and wanted him to heal from his past abuse. As they cried together, I held the little Jessie, who Jose had tormented. He was a beautiful child and I was saddened that he had to pay for Jose's past with his innocence.

As the initial therapy phase of treatment came to a close it was time for Roy and Jean to return home with Jessie. The tight family pulled even closer as they said their goodbyes to Jose. They loved him and wanted him to come back home after he was healed. His little brother hugged him goodbye. Still wrapped around Jose's body, Jessie's soft eyes looked up at his big brother, and touched my heart as he said: "I love you, Jose!"

I watched as the family drove off. Jean was so full of love for her son that even after he tormented the family and raped her little son, she wanted him back. She wasn't ready to give up! I wondered if I could be that forgiving.

I grabbed my new ebony haired son and wrapped him in a hug. I think I did it more for myself than for him at that moment. Watching that family disappear around the curve, I knew they had a long battle in front of them. As parents, they carried so much guilt. As victims of this child's wrath, they would all need therapy to heal. Jose wasn't sad that his family was leaving. Why should he be? They were just one of the many he had had.

The children in my home were not allowed to interact with one another unless Terena, Jerry or I were right there overseeing them. After they had stabilized and been trustworthy for several months, the ban was lifted slowly to ensure the mental balance and physical safety of all involved. Jose would not earn that privilege for a very long time!

That first night in our home, the door alarm went off four times. Stumbling out of my room while draping a bathrobe over me, I confronted my new little night owl. Each time, I settled him down and sent him back to bed.

The next morning, after he made his bed and finished in the bathroom, we all sat and ate breakfast together. I shared with Jose that he'd be taking a two-hour nap later that day. "30 minutes for every time the alarm went off last night. That way I can have a rest too because I'm so tired!" I said as I passed the honey to Will.

I needed to get him started on a routine, so after breakfast I gave him a spiral notebook that would be his "Feelings Book". "I want you to write three feelings you felt yesterday and how strong you felt them. Rate them 1-10. One is a tiny bit and ten is tons. Then I want you to write what they were about. Got it?" Mumbling an unhappy, "Got it" he took the pencil and notebook from my hand.

It took Jose several hours to finish his journal entry. Hugging him, I felt his body stiffen. As he dug his chin painfully into my chest, he looked up at me. I decided this child needed some hug lessons. I called for Will. "Okay, Jose, when you're giving a hug, you want your cheek against the other person, that way you don't hurt them with your chin. Your hands should be flat and not touching each other. Here, Will can demonstrate. Come give me a hug!" Jose watched as I embraced my son and he hugged me back. "Okay, now Jose, I'm going to hug you every single minute until you do it right, so the sooner you get strong enough to do it right, the sooner you'll get done!" It took him twenty minutes! What fun I had with that practice! We laughed and laughed as I got lots of hugs that day!

I gave him a caramel to suck on (sugar is an important part of bonding) while I held him and rocked him for a few minutes to tell him a silly story. Handing him the broom, I walked him out to the front porch. I showed him carefully how I wanted him to do the job and told him of the importance of chores to help the family. I left him to finish his chore. Checking on him often, finally, three hours later, I saw he was finished with the ten minute job. The porch looked great until I stepped up to the welcome mat and a stench filled my nose. Looking down, I saw feces on the welcome mat. Surprised I asked him who had done it. He looked thoughtful, shrugged and replied, "I guess I did!" What honesty!

I didn't give consequences for elimination problems and only required that the child clean up after himself. I handed him paper towel, a sack and a bucket with soapy water. Grossed- out, I watched from the window as he picked up the feces with his bare hands and put it in the sack. He scrubbed the spot and when I saw him strong sitting, I had him come inside to wash his hands thoroughly before I gave him a hug! Lunch waited for him as soon as he had completed his five minutes of strong sitting.

He ate with gusto. Food splattered everywhere as he snarfed his meal quickly, without chewing. I told him he was excused from the table; he looked up at me after wiping his face with his shirttail. "Why?" he demanded to know. Knowing that answering that question made the child believe they were in control, I replied, "That's a good question! When you're done eating you can write a paper about why you were excused!" Cursing, he carried his plate into the laundry room where he finished inhaling his meal. "I want more!", he forcefully said. I didn't put up with rudeness. "I want you to strong sit and think about a more respectful way to ask for more. Hop over to your think spot and say "ready" when you have an idea!" Five minutes later he complied and asked, "Can I have some more, please?" Giving him a hug, I then dished out more potato salad and chicken onto his plate.

In his room for the two-hour 'nap time', he wrote a full page about why he was excused. He played quietly and when his time was up, I turned off his alarm and opened the door. "So, Jose, what was it you did that you need to be in your room this afternoon?" I asked. He answered correctly and honestly. I gave him another caramel as I hugged him.

I liked this child already. He had been in my home for less than a day, but his intelligence and strong spirit were appealing. I could see that he was like an apple. If I peeled away the hardened skin, there was a good and genuine core. I had seen children that were more like onions, where the more you peeled, the more you cried and the less you had to work with until finally there was nothing left. I was glad he had a good core.

That night, Jose set off the alarm four more times. The following day, he had a two-hour 'nap' and more exercise. I figured if he wasn't tired, then he must not be exerting himself enough during the day. After lunch, he took his 'nap' and then I had him climb the mountain out front where I could watch. His strong body carried him to the summit quickly and as he descended, I pulled the video camera out. I captured his smile of triumph as his shiny black hair blew in the wind. He was so proud of himself for his successful solo climb.

The alarm only woke me three times that night. I must have been doing something right, so the next day after lunch, he took his hour and a half nap before climbing the front mountain and the back mountain. I pulled my camera out and as he climbed, I took pictures of Will riding Troika, Terena training Quest, and Chucky in his school uniform covered with medals. Jose's climbing achievement was forever immortalized on film. Beads of sweat were on his brow and as a huge smile spread across his face I pressed the shutter. Click!

I was surprised when the singing birds awoke me that next morning. The alarm hadn't been activated once and as I stood, pulling on my bathrobe, I felt thrilled that he had made it one whole night. We had both won!

With that battle conquered, we had many others to deal with. He finger-painted on his walls with his blood, urine and feces. Trying to gross me out, he would lick his filthy, feces covered fingers. Externally, I didn't react to his behavior, but internally, my gut was twisting in revulsion. How could anyone do such a thing just to get a reaction out of another person? I didn't even want to try to understand this child's mind- yuck!!

Picking his scabs or nose until they bled, he would smear artistic creations across the wall. Nearly every morning, I would open his door to find new paintings out of different mediums. He would have breakfast as soon as it was all cleaned off.

No matter how often he scrubbed his room, it still stunk. Then I realized he had been using the small opening between the wall and door to the cellar as a toilet. Unlocking the padlock, I opened it to reveal piles of feces that Jose had shoved through the opening. The stench was overwhelming and it took all my strength to not throw up! He had constant access to the bathroom and I had also given him a 'chamber pot' as a alternative.

Jose clamored up the stairs to get the bucket and scrub brushes. Getting several bags and a few handfuls of newspaper, he returned. It took him hours to clean the mess, and as I knew it would be occurring again until he dealt with the issue, I decided to make cleaning the cellar one of his regular chores.

Jose was not healthy enough to play with the others, so when my kids all went outside to have a mud fight, he and I watched from the porch. Squealing and flinging huge handfuls of muck at one another, the kids laughed and played for hours along the creek. Hearing the dogs bark during one summer mudfest, I walked around the house holding Jose's hand to see who our guest was. An immaculate United States Marine recruiter stepped from a white sedan with R.B. at his side. I welcomed him to my home while giving R.B. a look of confusion. He smiled at me and swelled his chest. I knew he had something up his sleeve and with this man at his side, I didn't have to wonder for too long. We sat on the front porch drinking lemonade, discussing RB's decision to join the military. He was only seventeen, so he needed my permission to dedicate four years of his life after high school graduation.

As we were sitting, waiting for Jerry to return from his office and discussing RB s career, screams, laughs and war whoops could be heard from the back of the house. I tried to pretend I didn't hear them, but when Will tore around the corner with an enormous block of mud flying after him, I knew I couldn't ignore my children any longer. Terena rounded the corner soon after. They were both covered from head to toe with red, sticky mud. Their eyes were the only other color I could see. Terena's hair dripped with clumps of muck. I tried not to laugh as the contrast between my dirt covered children and the spit shined and polished recruiter became terribly apparent.

"Uh...This is my daughter, Terena and my other son, Will", I said in a higher pitch than normal. Terena extended her hand, but when a blob of red mud splattered on the man's shiny shoes, she quickly lowered her arm and offered to clean it. Taking a step back, the officer snapped, "No! That's all right!" Clearly thinking my children were monsters from some lagoon, his orbs flicked from R.B. to the mud children and back. I think he was beginning to think R.B. really belonged in the military and away from this looney bin!

RB cleared his throat as he tried to speak to his sister with his eyes. She picked up his message and escorted Will back to the creek. "Nice to meet you, sir! Sorry about messing up your shined shoe," she said, as they disappeared behind the house. The mood of the sales pitch changed dramatically from then on, but I didn't really need to be sold on the idea. RB had always wanted to be a Marine. I would not stand in his way. I signed the contract. He had to get Jerry's signature as well. R.B. was visibly relieved when the pickup pulled into view. Jerry had hardly closed his door before R.B. and the Marine bombarded him with the paperwork. He signed it on the hood of his truck and before the ink was dry the recruiter was in his car and down the road. Mission accomplished!

At the end of summer, Chucky moved to Denver to live with Lori. His defiant, destructive behavior and continual lying and stealing had told me he was not interested in living at home, so with high hopes, and much sadness I sent my son to live with my best friend, the most skilled therapeutic mom I knew. I prayed she would get through to him what I could not.

It was also time for Alicia to return to her home in Texas. I drove her to the airport and as she walked down to the gate, I told her I would see her again next summer. We both cried as we hugged goodbye. Eight months was a long time to wait to see her again, but I knew her family missed her too, so I waved enthusiastically with my strongest smile in place as she disappeared down the corridor to the plane.

Terena had been out feeding the baby goats with Jose when she came running in. Out of breath she exclaimed, " Jose is out there pushing pebbles into my goats' butts! I couldn't get him to stop, so I tackled him. Now he's really mad." I stepped out the back door where I saw him stalking about the woods. Calling him in, I asked what had happened. Since he was fuming and unable to speak clearly, I had him go to his room until he was calmer. His behavior was so bizarre I decided to save it for therapy the following day.

That week, I also wanted to address some other weird things. I mentioned to CJ that whenever Jose used the restroom, I found dog food floating in the toilet afterward. When CJ asked Jose where the dog food came from, he replied, "When it comes out of my butt, it doesn't flush down." "Why is it in your butt, Jose?", she asked. He explained how he stole it, hid it and then pushed it up his rectum at night after he was in his room. She asked what other things he inserted into his anus. "I had a note book in my room. I tore all the paper out of it and stuck the spiral metal thing that held it together up my butt", he flatly said. I was cringing inside. That had to hurt, but I couldn't even imagine how much. He worked on it in therapy as CJ coached him to scream out the feelings in a safe place. He worked hard in the session as he let out wave after wave of agony filled screams. The pain he had held inside for so many years was unbelievable! I ached all over for him! He said he was done and relaxed afterward. I was able to snuggle and rock him while singing lullabies to him. He soaked up the love I offered and as I held him like an infant, we looked into each other's eyes; he took a deep breath and totally relaxed in my arms. I knew it was the beginning of the trust he needed to heal. I rocked him for a long time as I sang to him.

Later, I asked CJ why he did those things. She told me it was because he no longer had access to others to abuse. "He does it to himself, because he needs to relive his abuse over and over. It's a familiar thing to him. It's insanity, don't try to make sense out of it, Nancy," she explained.

The next morning, I made an appointment with Dr. Kelly, our family doctor to have him checked out for ruptures or damage to his colon. I was concerned about taking him in for an exam. I was relieved when the doctor handled it very professionally and in a matter of fact way. I explained to him that Jose had been abused and was in turn abusing his body. "We are concerned he may have injured himself while inserting various objects into his anus." He looked into Jose's eyes, "Why yes, it sounds very important to check it out." Stepping out of the office, he quickly got the special scope as Jose changed into a gown. "Let me show you the scope," he said as he handed the tool to Jose for inspection. "I'm just going to look up there to see if there are any sores or tears we need to be worried about." Sterilizing it, he asked my son to roll over on his side. I walked over to Jose and held his hand as the doctor finished. Turning the light off on his forehead, Dr. Kelly washed his hands and said, "You're really lucky this time. There are no sores, but there is scarring from where it has been injured in the past. Jose, it's important to not put things in there." He explained that if he continued, his intestines would eventually quit working causing him to need colostomy surgery. I listened while Dr. Kelly described the horrors of wearing a bag to catch bowel movements; I hoped that hearing such things would help him stop.

I never saw dog food in the toilet again. When I asked him about the hobby of inserting things into his butt, he laughed and said, "No mom! I got over that! I don't need to do it anymore, because I let it go in therapy!" Relieved, I hugged him and kissed the top of his head. There was a special place in my heart for this little disturbed boy, and the more he opened up, the more I fell in love with him.

Jose was so sick that he required therapy twice a week. While Will had his session Jose would play in the play room. After each of these sessions, the secretaries had to search the rooms for hidden fecal presents. It always reminded me of some kind of perverse Easter egg hunt as they would turn over couch cushions and dump out toy boxes in search of the elusive turd. I think the turnover rate for the secretaries at ACE must have been very high during that time!

Jose had been with us for over six months, and although some of his behaviors had improved, he was still really struggling. I started focusing more on the positive, so when townsfolk asked how he was doing, I smiled and enthusiastically said, "Jose's getting better!" It was more of a pep talk for me, because I was getting frustrated at his lack of progress. The more I said it, the better he seemed to act, until his healing had hit a plateau, and I began losing hope. Was this child too far gone for me to make a difference?

October was an especially hard month for Jose. The sight of pumpkins and Halloween decorations made him scream in terror. I couldn't even drive into Glenwood Springs with him to get groceries, because he would flip out. That month, I called Jerry often with grocery lists to pick up from work. He would drive in, tired from the long day at work only to find the house in an uproar because of Jose's extreme behavior. Hauling in bags of groceries, my husband would put them in the kitchen, give me a hug and escape as quickly as possible to the barn or garage.

The breakthrough for Jose occurred while I was driving to therapy one cold morning. The road was covered in ice from the storm that had hit the previous night, and I began wondering if making it to therapy was really important that day. As I debated turning around, Jose started talking about his biological grandfather for the first time.

"He thought he was a priest," little Jose said. I asked what that meant. As he replied, the hair on my neck began to rise. "He would pray in a different language and wear a brown bathrobe with a funny hood in the woods. It was always nighttime, so he used lots of candles." He told me there was always a big group of people that would stand in a circle and sing funny songs in a made up language. "He worked at a cemetery, so he would get bodies to use and when he couldn't get dead people, he would find a homeless guy. There would be a lot of people surprised to find out how many caskets are empty." I tried to concentrate on the road while envisioning this scene of horror. "What would happen to the homeless person?" I asked, hesitatingly. "Grandpa would tie them up in the back of the van and take them into the woods with a tractor hitched on the back. He would dig a big hole with it." Telling him I had to pull over for gas, I raced to the pay phone to call CJ. "He's telling me all this stuff about dead people and tied up homeless people for ceremonies! I don't know what to do!" I stammered into the phone. "Listen to what he says, validate his feelings and get here as fast as you can," she replied.

Back on the road, I waited for him to start talking again. The silence was deafening as I began wondering if focusing so intensely on the road for so long had caused me to hallucinate the whole thing. He began speaking again, "My sister, cousin and I would play hide and seek around the dead bodies while Grandpa dug a big hole with the tractor. I think I had a younger sister." He tipped his head in thought and looked out at the snow-covered mountains as we drove. The sharing was over.

That day of therapy stretched into a week as he spilled his guts about his early history. He described how he, his sister and the cousin would participate in the rituals. They would eat the fingers of the dead and drink blood. He was "baptized" in a vat filled with a combination of urine from the group and the blood of a man they killed. Each day the stories got worse. I would wake several times in the night from horrendous nightmares. The pillowcase I was using while staying with CJ, was covered in red rosebuds and after the third night, I ripped it off when I awoke and thought it was splattered with blood. I was so naive! I thought that stuff only happened in the movies! I didn't want to believe any of it!

He told how after each ceremony, an orgy occurred and the occult followers would entertain themselves with each other and the bodies of the children. Jose described how the deceased were buried in the hole in the woods with an upside down cross laid across their dismembered body. He remembered having witnessed at least thirteen murders.

That statement made us want to verify his facts with his biological sister and cousin. We called his older sister first. "Your brother is telling the secrets," CJ stated. There was silence on the other line before she heard a soft whimper. "He's not supposed to tell. They'll sacrifice us, just like they did to all those others!" That's all she said before hanging up. The next day, her family took her to therapy where she told the same horrific stories with identical details. When we contacted the cousin, his family wanted to ask him themselves. Asking them not to feed him information we hung up and waited. When he came home from school that day, they mentioned that his cousin had revealed the family secrets. His eyes widened in horror as he wet himself, and before he said anything, he dove under the kitchen table and curled up in the fetal position. When he was unable to come out of it after two days, the family was forced to admit him to a psychiatric ward. A few weeks later, he opened up and further validated Jose's story.

We called the police department in Wyoming and told them of the murders. An investigator flew out immediately to hear the case. Talking with Jose for over an hour, he came out and told us of his conclusions. "Ma'am without names or dates it's impossible for me to do anything. We have to have evidence," he said before taking in a breath. In a strained voice he finished with, "Of the 200 of these kind of cases we have, not one has ever gone to trial! If I were you I'd change the name of this child and lose his records. I wish I could do more to help you! Good day." He flew back to Wyoming, almost as quickly as he had come.

These people had threatened to kill and dismember Jose had he ever told. He hadn't ever whispered a word of it to anyone. There was no one in his life that he trusted to keep him safe from these murderers, until he joined our program. He felt secure with CJ, Jerry and myself. Believing we were strong enough to protect him if the bad guys came back to take him away, he had finally let go of the secret that kept him sick for so long. He was now free to heal.

He continued to mention that he had a younger sister at one time. In therapy, he again told a gruesome tale. He was five years old and she was two. He told the following story: She had been born and kept in the attic to isolate her from people who might report her existence. She was being harbored up there for use in a ceremony when she was old enough. He was forbidden to go in the attic, but when left alone one afternoon, he became curious and climbed the ladder leading to the upper level. The small area was hot and dark. It stunk terribly and he peeked around the many boxes until he found her. She looked a lot like him.

He went back down to the kitchen and retrieved the butcher's block filled with knives. Struggling to carry the heavy object up the steps he reached the door to the attic, set the block down and swung it open. There, in front of him stood his tiny sister, staring fearfully at him. She didn't have language, and, not having much interaction with others, she screamed and ran away. He closed the door behind him as he set the wooden carrier down and removed as many knives as he could carry in one hand. Sneaking around the many boxes, he spotted her. He took the biggest knife, recoiled his arm and threw. STRIKE! Crying, she looked around in terror. He selected another knife and prepared to throw again. He missed. He only had two more knives, so he tried harder to hit his target. Wham! He had nailed her in the arm. She was really bleeding then and her cries were louder. He walked over to her and stood in front of her squirming body. Trapped by the boxes, she had nowhere to run. He stepped back in order to throw the knife. It sunk deep into the flesh of her stomach. Maddened at the sight of his bleeding, but still living target, he picked up the largest knife. It was the last weapon he had. She lay on the dirty attic floor in a pool of her own blood, with three knives protruding from her little body.

The twitching of her body fascinated Jose, so when his Grandfather returned home, he didn't hear until it was too late. Being dragged by his hair from the attic, Jose cried that he was only trying to impress his grandfather and that's why he did it. It was shortly after the murder that Jose was run over by the truck.

He told the incident as if telling about a day at the park. Showing no compassion, he described the intimate details to us. He had no idea that what he had done was terribly wrong, and maybe, on some level that was his way of coping. I raced to the bathroom and threw up. As I rested my forehead on the cool porcelain I realized the children I had helped before knew their behavior was unacceptable and chose to do it anyway. The little nine year old laying on CJ's lap had no concept of right and wrong. His world had been too evil to learn such rudimentary lessons. He had been taught that evil was right.

I returned to him and cried as I held him after his therapy session. He didn't understand why and I was too over come with emotion to try explaining it. I looked into his dead eyes and understood completely what I saw. The little boy inside of him had died long ago. His innocence was stolen. He was empty now. The vacant hole, where fear, evil and terror once resided was staring back at me. It was my job to fill his heart with love and goodness, so I squeezed him closer and tried telling him a story. The sadness of his life wouldn't allow me to swallow the lump in my throat, so instead of talking, I hummed 'You are my Sunshine' as I rocked him.

I understood now, why October was so difficult for him. Not only did Halloween close out the month, but also the mascot for the Glenwood Springs High School was a demon. The whole town was painted with devils for homecoming, and Jose had taken that much more literally than most anyone else.

At church the next Sunday, the congregation sang an old hymn "Washed in the Blood of the Lamb". I couldn't listen. Grabbing Jose's hand, we raced from the church and sat outside on the stoop, thinking how literal that song could be taken. I was glad we were in the habit of sitting in the last pew because I didn't want to have to explain my reaction to any of the other parishioners. They would definitely not understand!

Jerry joined Jose and me on the step outside. It was cold, so he handed us both our jackets, before sitting between us and wrapping us both in his loving arms. Never saying a thing, the three of us sat, huddled together until the song had long been over.

Jose was beginning to heal. He was earning more playtime and talking about his feelings. He had identified several activities he had wanted to earn the privilege of doing, so when he first came to stay with us, we outlined the requirements needed to earn them. Working towards his goals, he had obtained almost half of them by the time spring arrived.

Loving artwork, he was given a pencil set and drawing paper for his birthday. He spent hours drawing and shading his figures. Drawing a German Shepherd for Terena, he sat and watched I.Q. for hours as she waited for the school bus to deposit her girl. I received a drawing of Sneakers my chubby corgi dog. The resemblance was incredible, and I was sure we had the next Georgia O'Keefe on our hands. I was glad his media had changed from blood to something more appropriate!

>✶< >✶< >✶< >✶<

The summer sun had finally melted all the snow, and the smell of flowers hung in the air. Along with the blooming buds came our little Alicia. Each summer, I was amazed at her growing body, strength and maturity. She was a much more healthy kid now, so she did what normal children do. After her chores she played in the sun, went on sleep-overs, attended Vacation Bible School and rode horses. I no longer feared for the safety of the other children. The animals were not in danger of being tortured or killed and her family was happy with her complete recovery. She was a happy beautiful young girl filled with life!

I assigned chores one morning to all the children, and as Jose walked up the stairs to clean the bathroom, I asked him to keep the door shut until he was finished. There was an alarm on the door, so I knew he wouldn't be getting into the other bedrooms or get distracted by the other workers. Knowing the house was safe and under control, I busied myself with spring-cleaning.

Will was already finished writing in his Feelings Book and Alicia was riding with Terena. Jose was usually a fast worker, so I wondered what was taking him so long. The children's upstairs bathroom was divided into two rooms, so when I went up to check on him, he was in the front room and everything seemed fine. Waiting another ten minutes, I finally called him down. "Jose, that's long enough," I hollered up the stairs. My dog, Sneakers, came trotting down and gave me a really strange look as she passed by. I didn't pay much attention to her, as Jose followed closely on her heals.

After that day, his behavior became more defiant and destructive. He resorted back to urinating and defecating everywhere and I knew something was going on that he wasn't telling about. If there was only one thing that Jose had taught me, it was that his behavior was an excellent barometer to his secrets. As soon as he was honest, his actions reflected his strength. When he was sneaky and feeling like he gotten away with something, his behavior went right down the drain.

Two weeks passed before he finally told the truth in therapy. While he was supposed to have been cleaning the bathroom, he had crawled through the laundry chute down through our laundry room and into the kitchen. Grabbing a large butcher knife, he had climbed back upstairs without me ever knowing. He had lured Sneakers into the washroom earlier. She was a sitting duck. He held the handle of the knife with both hands as he stood over her little furry body, the weapon poised overhead, ready to strike. Her ears were pulled back and her huge brown eyes looked trustingly into his. She didn't waiver her big soft gaze once. Her 'baby seal' face caused him to think about his actions just long enough for him question his motives. Not able to stab her, he turned and looked into the mirror and saw his reflection. Jumping onto the counter, he then carved two big slashes into the surface of the glass. The cuts were even with where his face reflected back at him.

Horror filled my soul knowing that I had left my dog in harm's way. She had come so close to being murdered that guilt flooded into my heart. I then thought about the tremendous power Jose had demonstrated by stopping his murderous actions. He had shown that a conscience was developing.

I lifted him out of CJ's arms. Cradling my son, I wept. This time, instead of crying for his lost innocence or dead soul, I cried at his strength and amazing progress! I was furious at myself for not making sure my beloved dog was safe, but the tremendous effort it had taken to stop himself had kept her alive. He had stopped himself from killing!

After he told the truth about Sneakers his behavior started to become more compliant and respectful again . His elimination problems subsided drastically. He was respectful, responsible and fun to be around the majority of the time. Healing, and becoming more like a healthy child with each week, I enjoyed seeing his progress.

Together, our family drove to Grand Junction where Will was starting an Outward Experience rock climbing adventure. I was hoping that the intense program would encourage him to start accepting responsibility for his actions as well as build his still fragile self-image. We waved at him as his group piled into two big blue vans. He was scared, I could see it in his eyes, but I knew overcoming the fear was part of the journey. Before they closed the van door, Jose pulled from my grasp. "Will, Will, please come back safely," he called. Tears were streaming down his cheeks as he watched the caravan pull away.

"I'm gonna miss him," he cried. I tried comforting him by assuring him Will would be back soon, but to Jose, when someone left, it was usually for good. I couldn't convince him.

The next evening we attended a concert at our church. I was careful not to push my religion onto the defiant children knowing it would backfire. I believed it was important to set an example, the fellowship in the church was good for them, and I needed it, so they often attended services with Jerry and me. I in no way forced them to accept my beliefs, preached at them, nor did I expect their participation in the church activities, yet surprising things happened.

The music was powerful and the message encouraging. We were sitting in the back row, as we regularly did, and as the church quieted down and they ended the sing-spiration by asking if there were any lost souls needing to be saved, Jose asked, "I can't see, are they still up there?" Answering yes, I looked down into his worried face. He asked, "Can I go up front and talk to them?" Nodding my head, he pleaded with me, "Will you come with me?" I told him that what he was about to do was something he needed to do all by himself. Lowering his head, he squeezed past me in the pew and took a few steps towards the front. He rushed back and grabbed my hand before turning to drag me to the front with him. "I want to be saved! I need to be saved!" he cried. The minister asked my ten-year old son, "Are you a sinner?" "Yes!" Jose said. "Will you renounce Satan in your life?" the man asked. With his eyes big and tears streaming down his cheeks Jose sobbed, "Yes, I will!" Accepting Jesus Christ into his heart, he fell to his knees and wept. I kneeled next to him and encircled him with my arms. Crying with him, I thought how strong he was. My son, the Satan worshiper, had just become a Christian!

As we walked from the church he turned and said to me, "I'm a new person now. I have to change my name!" Remembering what the Wyoming investigator had said, I agreed with him. "Why don't you think about it and let me know what name you've chosen." The next day, he flipped through the children's Bible the church had given him. "What do you think of the name Gabriel?" he asked me. Knowing that Gabriel was a powerful angel, I told him that was a fine choice! My son, Jose, was now named Gabriel and his heart was filled with love!

Jean and Jessie came out to visit Gabriel. He was doing so well. I sat in our living room as I began transferring his bond to me over to Jean. "Okay, Gabriel! I want you to jump up and down. Go!" I told him. Smiling, he complied. Having him stop, I turned to his mom. "Okay Jean, now you tell him to do the same thing." She looked, hesitatingly at her son, "Gabriel, I want you to jump up and down." He stood there, struggling, before finally willing his legs to spring from the floor. I gave him another command. "Stick your right finger in your right ear!" Immediately, he shot me a glance of triumph and did it, but when his mother asked him to do the same thing only seconds later, he struggled again. Having to really think about the silly exercises his mom requested, he was forced to fight through the resistance of the past. It was amazing to watch as he could do every activity for me willingly and quickly, without much thought; yet for his mom, it was a constant battle. After an hour of such practice, amid the hugs and giggles, Gabriel was finally able to respond correctly for his mom. We both hugged him, and I knew the transferring would take a full two weeks. They were only visiting for the weekend, so I decided to wait until he was going home for good.

That day of the visit was excellent. Gabriel handled having his Mom and brother sharing us, his therapeutic family. He was respectful, responsible and fun to be around. Since the first day had gone so well, I recommended for the family to go on a picnic. This would be difficult for Gabriel, so I expected him to blow out afterwards, but it was an important step in his growth.

As I had expected, he had handled the morning with Jean and Jessie, but his attitude quickly plummeted into disrespect and defiance later that afternoon. I drove them to the Denver airport the next day and as Gabriel fumed in the back, the three of us chatted and laughed.

On our way home, we stopped in Evergreen for therapy. I learned that while on the picnic, Jean had allowed the children to play horse. I thought about the re-traumatization of Jessie as Gabriel straddled his little body and "rode" him around. His blow out was in response to the overwhelming sexual feelings he had during the playtime. The activity was too sexual and inappropriate for two siblings, with a sexual past, to participate in. For two kids without their history it would have just been a fun game. For them it was sick.

Although Gabriel had come a long way, when Jean found out she was pregnant, she knew he could not go home again. Jean would never be able to trust him with a baby in the house no matter how good he was. It was too dangerous. He was happy that he would have a new sibling, but it was a still a sad, sad day for Gabriel.

That day, he over flowed the toilet by putting the whole roll of toilet paper in the bowl. He tried to flush it down, like the way he felt his family had flushed him away, but when the water started bubbling over, it reflected the anger he felt building inside.

The therapy helped release his building rage, but the sadness of losing yet another family stayed with his healing heart. Knowing he was going to stay with my family helped soften the blow. His feelings of trust and security would end within months because the rug was soon to be pulled out from under my feet.

Mud-fight participants. Looks like
They both won!

Sneakers with her "baby seal"
face that saved her life.

Beth, months after her Mama's death, in a
new loving family but not feeling the joy.
The same expression is evident on her face
that she wore the day her Mama died.

Chapter 11

The Good, The Bad, and The Ugly

Beth: (I continue to share my story with you as it was told to me combined with my own memories)

The minister and his wife were unable to have children. They were astonished and overjoyed when they received the call that two children, a little girl of nineteen months and a little boy of eight months were available for adoption, and would they be interested in having both of them. I later learned, their hearts leapt at the chance to raise two beautiful children as their own. They thought God had surely answered their prayers. My little brother and I moved into their parsonage in April of 1984. Little did they know their dreams of joyfully raising these two young children would soon become a nightmare.

It began the first day, no matter how brightly the sun shone in the sky, feelings of anguish and anxiety clouded my heart. I didn't know these people. I wanted my mama back and in no way could these strangers ever replace her.

When they sat me down at the table for dinner, I wouldn't use a fork or spoon, instead I chucked it across the room and at them, and when I ran out of silverware, the food on my plate became my ammunition. Who were these people? What did they want with me and why was I here? **I wanted to go home!!** *Since I didn't want anything to do with them, there was no way I was going to even eat their food.*

When the anger boiled up inside of me and I was unable to remain in my seat I began to pace around the room, resembling a caged animal. When they tried to gather me in their arms for comfort I'd scream in terror, growl, and arch my back. "Let me go. I want mama! You, let . . . me . . . go!!" When I scrambled out of their arms, I ran in terror from them and continued my pacing and growling through clenched teeth around their living room, keeping a watchful eye on them in case they tried to touch me again. If they tried to approach me I'd stare them down with a hateful look. This man and woman had taken me from my home and the siblings I loved. I was not going to let them comfort me. Where was Cora? Why wasn't she here? I needed my big sister. The poor couple had no idea what was going on and phoned Social Services, begging for answers. Sadly, the only "help" were the words, "Just love her more, or let us come and get her." I smirked. They had to call someone else to try to control me. Two big adults and I had just made them feel useless. The power that seethed within me began to grow like a ravenous, poisonous weed.

That evening at bedtime they were again baffled by the amount of rage that poured from my little nineteen-month old body. The crib they had purchased for me was just another barrier I needed to triumph over. How dare they try to cage me! I knew if I worked hard enough I'd get away from this family. I promptly scrambled over the bars and in the process of jumping from the crib I slammed against a dresser, splitting my head open. Howling in pain and fury I ran from the room and the dreaded crib. The couple came tearing down the hall in dismay. In shock, I ran screaming in the other direction with blood running down my face! See, I knew I wasn't safe here. If they were going to put me in that cage again they had another thing coming! When they caught me and began cleaning my wound I screamed in pain. Inside I thought, I knew you'd hurt me, I just knew it! This just proves it! I needed to get out of there and fast.

They shoved a double bed against the wall and placed me in it. They had expected to put their two little children to sleep quickly and easily but instead they sat for hours attempting to calm each of us. If they left the room I'd howl and carry on until they came back. I quickly learned I could control them with one little screech, because they'd come running. My ranting and raving would become so severe that the minister found the only way to calm me would be to gently lay his body across mine to settle my flailing arms and writhing body, meanwhile his wife stroked my sweat soaked hair. Who was this man and what was he doing? Why was he on top of me . . . What was he going to do? Oh, please. . . please don't hurt me! My screams would turn into tortured sobs until eventually I would fall into a fitful slumber, only to wrench them from their bed in the wee hours by blood-curdling screams.

Each night they would go through the same procedure of trying to lull my brother and me to sleep and then be awakened by screams ridden with agony from horrific nightmares. In terror I would consistently see a man coming toward me as I lay in the dark. I'd back away until my body pressed against the wall and then he would fall on me and hurt me with a part of himself. I'd scream and holler in my dream trying to make him go away. I did not realize the screams were actually out loud until the light would fly on and two strange people would come running into the room. Tears streaming down my cheeks I'd bellow even louder and back against the wall like I had in my dream, throwing pillows and anything I could get my hands on to make them go away.

Taking a bath became another exhausting ritual. I was terrified of the water and the woman trying to wash me. Who did she think she was, my mom or something? Nuh uh! I had a mama and she was coming back, I knew it. And why was she taking my clothes off and putting me in this tub? What was she going to do . . . she could hurt me! So, I'd put my hands on my hips or cross my arms and shout in my best big voice ever, "NO! And ya can't make me!" If she picked me up to put me in the tub I'd scream and kick and hop right back out. Since the tub was slick the more I'd fight her the more I'd fall and then blame it on her. She must be the one hurting me because it was her fault I was in this thing. I would just rather be dirty than do it her way because she'd probably try to put my head under the water or something. I didn't know her and I didn't trust her. Strangers weren't to be trusted. Even people who supposedly loved me hurt me so I was positive she would too. She called the neighbors over and it took four people to hold my little body down to scrub it. My shrieks echoed through the tile as the water cascaded out of the tub and soap went slipping around the bathroom floor. Four people slipping and sliding trying to hold me!! How powerful I must be, I was a tiny child and I needed four strong adults to restrain me. Afterwards, when they'd let me go I'd stand there half clean facing the drenched adults. Through my resistance I smirked inside, watering the poisonous weed.

I wouldn't allow the minister to hold me or let any man near me. Even though I was perfectly capable of speaking, I stopped. I wanted nothing to do with these people so why bother to communicate with them. If I did not get what I wanted I'd go into a rage. My face would take on an incredible shade of purple, fire flew from my eyes as I'd ball my little fists up and stomp my feet. Throwing myself down I'd rant and rave while I pounded the floor. I tore the blinds and ripped the curtain rods down. Satisfied with my destruction I'd stomp around the living room growling. I loved to see the baffled looks on my parents' faces. Their jaws dropping open in disbelief at the mayhem I could cause in a matter of a few minutes. As I ripped their home to pieces I smiled inside. It served them right for taking me away from my family!

While in private I was destroying their home and lives, but in the public eye I was the cutest, sweetest little girl I could pretend to be. The first day of church I fought putting my clothes on. I would rather run around the house naked than have her be boss of me. I ripped my brand new tights and chucked my shoes at the minister's wife while she was trying to dress me. As we walked to the church I fought her each step of the way, desperately trying to wrench my hand from her grasp while she lugged my howling brother on one hip. The moment a person came into view, I straightened up. "Oh aren't you an adorable little girl. I bet you're a great helper with your little brother for your new mommy." I smiled my sweetest smile, nodding enthusiastically; while inside I balked, "new mommy", we'll just see about that! Great helper, huh? Ha! Ha! Oh, if they only knew. As we stepped into the church I gazed at the people. Hmmm, this was my audience, huh? Well I'd better get started. Let the show begin! I flashed a smile, batted my big baby blues and heard the ripple of "how adorable, she's so cute ---- wh-at an a--ngel." as we walked down the aisle. Oh, I was good. Look at this! I looked up into the exhausted eyes of the woman holding my hand. Now, everyone thinks I'm perfect and you'll look dumb and nuts if you say anything. I thought I had the congregation eating out of my hands. It made me feel so strong and big when I could fool everyone. I kept the smile on my face through the whole service until the woman would correct me for anything and it quickly molded into a sneer that I was careful only she would see.

Walking home after church, the moment we were out of sight, I again wrenched my hand from hers and gave her filthy looks. The dumb lady's voice stating "new mommy", was stuck in my head. This woman would pay for that phrase. She was not my mommy and she would never replace my mama. I had realized by now I was not going back to my birth family and decided I needed to take care of myself. I figured I wasn't going back because they didn't want me and my mama died. I must be stronger than her if I am still living. Even though I was mad at her for dying I wouldn't let <u>anyone</u> replace her. Especially this woman. Not happening, lady!

The moment we got home I again threw my food and silverware at the woman and stomped around the living room. "New mommy", hmmph, that'll be the day. I ached for my mama, her sweet scent and the jingle of her laughter. I just wanted to be in her arms again.

A few months later a foster girl came and stayed in the home with us. The minister's wife heard me crying and came into the room. When she saw that my diaper was down she questioned the girl, who stated I'd walked out of it. The woman became suspicious since it was not something I'd done before. The foster girl was removed shortly after.

I could see my little brother had started settling in and the couple began having fun with him. What did he think he was doing? I was supposed to be the center of attention here! I heard him say sounds sometimes that sounded like mama and I got mad. How could he trade Mama in for this woman? They would try to read stories to me and I'd push them away and take the book to look at on my own. My little brother on the other hand would allow them to read him stories. I'd watch as he sat in their laps and laughed with them. Dumb little boy. I hated him!

I kept the feelings inside at first, of him trading in Mama, until I began to throw more screaming fits. My rage continued to build up, then several months later, when I was three, we were at the woman's sister's house and my brother was walking down the stairs in front of me. All the thoughts of him trading in our mama for this woman boiled up inside me, "TRAITOR!" I thought as I shoved him. There that'll teach him. With glee, I watched as he toppled down the rest of the stairs. I felt a pang of guilt and sorrow when he looked up in shock from where he landed and his blue eyes filled with tears, so I looked away quickly and justified it because he'd been trading in our mama. He wailed, "Mommy!" Yeah, that's right cry, you little . . . what?!? Mom -- **Mommy!!** What do you mean Mommy? How could he say that? Since she wasn't there her sister came running, pulled him up in her arms and sent me to the room I was staying in. Oh, great, just great. He gets all the attention and I get sent to my room when all I was doing was trying to teach him a lesson.

The minister and his wife decided they were in for the long run and the adoption was finalized. They hung a huge tie-dyed sign between two trees: "One Boy & One Girl, Just Adopted!!" I realized then that in order to keep the church and the day care we attended believing that I was perfect, I'd better start referring to these people as mommy and daddy. I hated it! But, if I was to keep being an adorable angel to the public then I needed to mold to the world. I submitted, but I decided she'd still never replace my mama in my heart.

We started in day care about six months after we first arrived. The day we walked in I ripped my hand from the woman's and ran to play with the toys. As I sat there amid the pile of playthings I saw other kids crying when their parents dropped them off. I didn't understand. Why are they crying? I overheard one parent tell her kid, "Don't worry, honey, I'll be back later." Oh, I thought, the woman's coming back? Bummer, I wanted to live here among the toys. I didn't want to go home with her again.

We moved to Lexington in June of 1986. I was about to be 4 years old. It was there that I overheard mommy say my mama might have died of complications in childbirth. I didn't know what complications meant but I knew it was something bad if she'd died and I definitely knew what childbirth was. She died not long after my little brother was born so . . . my little brother had killed her? He's the one who took my mama away? If she wasn't taken away then I'd still be with her. We'd all still be together. I watched on as mommy and daddy tickled him. Listening to his three year old laughter made me sick. Anger and venom rose within me. He'd taken everyone I loved from me and now he was taking over this family too. "Oh yeah, isn't he cute," I thought sarcastically. "You just wait little brother, you just wait. You will pay."

I became more and more destructive. I was impressed by my strength. I knew it frightened my parents; therefore I increased my bad behavior. At four years old I had ripped the doorstop from the wall in a rage and punched a large hole in the wall. I had also broken bits of concrete from the back porch and thrown it at the house. When my little brother had a toy that I wanted I would hit him until he gave it to me.

Anything my parents said to do I'd argue with and then destroy something. When I was told to stop running in and out of the house and to stay outside and play one day, I retaliated. Think you can control me? Watch this! I calmly walked over to the car and with all my four and a half year old strength ripped the Toyota emblem from its surface. Not fully satisfied, I grabbed a stick and in my childish scrawl carved my name on the rubber bumper. There! Satisfied, I stepped back and surveyed my work --- yep, see if you can handle that!

When mommy put me in my room I pounded on the door and screamed he was the favorite and no one loved me. Stupid woman, I thought. I caught sight of one of my toys laying on the floor. If I make enough racket she'll come back. I began to throw my toys across the room while howling with anger. My howls were interrupted with laughter as I watched them shattering and making dents in the wall. Just wait 'till they see that. After I'd been in there a bit and she still hadn't come back I decided to turn my energy to tearing up my clothes. I could just picture their faces when they finally laid eyes on what I'd done. Their brows would crease and their lips would pull tight in concern. Oh, just to see the anger shoot from their eyes. That was my favorite part! I didn't have to worry about them loving me if I kept them angry. My Mama had loved me and then she'd died. You just can't trust people.

It wasn't mommy who opened my door later, it was Daddy. What did he want? Oh great, I was probably going to get another whippin'. Fine, whatever. Get it over with. I'd received lots of those before. They never did anything to change my behavior, it just made me get sneakier about it. But this time it wasn't just Daddy's hand, it was a switch. Now that stung! I bit my lip, he wasn't going to get to me. I immediately began to concentrate on other things.

My brother was the reason I'd gotten in trouble anyway. If he'd just given me the toy then it wouldn't have been a problem. I planned my revenge with each smack. Perfect little boy, he never got in trouble. I knew he was the favorite, it was obvious.

I would take the paper from my torn toys and stuff the electrical outlets in my room with it. I tore my bedspread just for something to do. The thoughts that went through my head were just matter-of-fact, well they're not going to like this either. I was bored and it passed the time.

I was still wetting my bed at four years of age, so mommy & daddy decided I was supposed to wear a diaper. A diaper, at four!! What am I a little baby? Well fine, then I wasn't going to go in it. No matter how bad I'd have to go, I wouldn't give them the satisfaction. That made me recall the infamous days of my potty training. I smiled, another time I wouldn't allow them to get their way. Mommy would tell me to sit down just like this, so of course I stood. "No, no Beth, that's how daddy and brother do it. We do it like this." I just looked at her blankly, I know that's how you do it but who says I want to be like you. That's the whole point, woman. Now leave me be so I can go potty, the way I want to. Out in public I'd pee the right way but at home I wouldn't give her the satisfaction. It drove her crazy. I loved it!

In the fall of 1987 I began kindergarten. I was excited. Someone else to control. I had gotten sick of just bossing my brother around. It was getting old. I had still been able to make the congregation and community believe I was an angel and I expected school to be the same.

My behavior had gotten so out of control at home though that it began to spill over in school. I loved school and I enjoyed learning, but I had to be in charge of it. I didn't like this woman telling me how to do things and how she wanted it done and to be a good girl. Be a good girl? Don't you talk to me like you're my Mama. I'll do it my way, not yours teacher. She would say, "Open your books to page two," and I'd open it to page five. Since I never wanted to be read stories by mommy and daddy, I taught myself to read. So it wasn't a matter of not knowing the letters or numbers. I took great pride in being bright but only if I was doing it my way. I always wanted to be smart, because smart people were powerful. At five I'd already learned if you were dumb you couldn't get anywhere. I'd taken it in my hands to teach myself.

After a week of school my parents decided I was old enough to ride the bus. I was to sit in the front seat with the seat belts so of course I sat in the back where there were none. Since I was able to get away with that so easily I wanted to see what else I could get away with. Instead of remaining where I belonged I would scramble over the tops of each seat and when that got boring I'd crawl from the back to the front of the bus under each seat. The yelling of the bus driver would just make me laugh and I'd keep on doing it. What was she going to do slam on the brakes and stop the bus? She had to get those kids home. Again I was unstoppable. Power!

I'd dash off the bus each day with her words, "You'd betta' start keepin' that backside of yours on the seats 'fore I kick it off my bus!" falling on my deaf ears. Chuckling, I'd run inside. Just another adult thinking they could try to control me. Not going to happen!! The weed of power was expanding through my body. Mommy and Daddy would be home about fifteen minutes after I'd get home. I was supposed to go and take a nap while I was home alone but I'd turn on the TV instead. It felt so good to be sneaky. I just felt so much smarter than them. When I'd hear the car pull up into the drive I'd run to my room, hop in bed and fake sleep.

A letter was sent home about my behavior on the bus. It never reached my parents. I took and forged my daddy's initials on the line and handed it in to my teacher. I didn't falter once. She glanced at the note and then called across the classroom, "Beth, doesn't your daddy normally write in cursive?"

"Nuh uh, not when he's signin' his name."

I turned away and began going about my business again. When she yelled at me for trying to cut my eyelashes with a pair of scissors, I in mock innocence, set the scissors down. Batting what was left of my eyelashes and giving her a sickening smile, I drawled, "yes ma'am." and returned to my seat. Oh this was too good. Was she going to blow today? Her face was all purple and she looked like a grape. Ha! Ha!

My face blanched when my daddy walked into the classroom. What was he doing here? Was it because I'd hit that boy the other day? No, I'd told him not to tell or I'd do it again. Was it because I wouldn't take my naps at school and was noisy? No, that was silly. A list of things I'd done ran through my head. When he'd taken me outside, he'd pulled out the letter that had been sent home. "What's this?" he asked calmly.

"I didn't want you and mommy to know." I said, batting my eyes.

"So you lied to us again?"

"Umm . . ." Oh man, now he'd caught me. I'd have to tell the truth and that meant he won. "Umm . . . I . . . uh," I stared at the ground while I twisted my toe in the dirt.

"Look at me when I talk to you, Beth. Why did you lie to us again?" I looked up. Why did I lie, you want to know the real reason why I lied. I'll tell you mister, it's because I hate you and your wife. I hate how you took me from my mama and my family. It's obvious my brother is your favorite and it's obvious you think he's perfect. Each day that goes by I want to wake up and find you gone. Your love hurts me. I've worked really hard to push you away and yet you still try to love me. I don't want you, your wife or your love!

Instead I just mumbled, "I don't know." He brought out the switch again that day. I actually cried that day. All the anger I felt in my heart poured down my cheeks. They weren't tears of shame like he'd hoped for. They hung the paper on the refrigerator to remind me of my dishonesty. I didn't need a reminder, it was my life. Everything I did was dishonest.

We began taking swim lessons at the YMCA. Twice I grabbed my brother and pinched his nose and held him under the water. His flailing arms and legs struck out as he struggled for air, the air I had taken control of and taken from him. The air that if I starved him long enough he would die without. I didn't let go until the arms of adults pried me off him and sent me out of the pool. "He's fine," I said. "See? He's still breathing." Bummer, I thought. Maybe next time. Stupid adults kept getting in my way.

Since I was getting caught hurting my brother, I turned to the animals. The bruises on them wouldn't show and they couldn't tell on me. When I'd get angry at anything occurring in my life or my parents trying to control me I'd take it out on the animals. The golden retriever became my prey. I felt so powerful when I could hurt such a big animal. If she were near me I'd fall and land hard on her or "trip" over her furry body, landing a solid kick to her stomach. When no one answered her cries they'd echo within me and I thought, that's right, that's how I felt. I'd cry and no one would come and if they did they'd scare me or hurt me. I found a ball of needles one day and would stick them in her. Each time I'd approach her she'd sit there looking pitiful and thump her tail on the floor. How pathetic! She doesn't even know to run from me. I felt I succeeded each time she cried. Another being I'd conquered and I was only five.

I had another dream of the man falling on me and hurting me with a part of himself. Once again my bone chilling screams awakened the entire household and I backed my trembling body against the wall. This time I did allow my mommy to hold me as my heart-rending sobs wrenched through my body. "Make it go away," I wailed. "Make him go away!"

It took about an hour and I was finally able to fall back asleep. The next morning when I awoke, I laid in my bed thinking. Why was I the only one who had to suffer through these feelings of pain and dirtiness? No one truly understood how I felt. I hated this feeling. I hated suffering alone. I thought of my little brother. Why'd he have to be so perfect? He was so lucky he didn't have these problems. I decided I wanted my brother to suffer the same way I suffered. I wanted him to understand what I went through each time I went to bed at night, when the nightmares plagued my mind. If he knew what I felt then he wouldn't be so perfect. Mommy and daddy wouldn't love him more.

Early one morning I snuck into his room and climbed onto his bed. When he woke up and saw me looking at him, he sat up fast, his eyes wide. "What are you doing in here, Beffy?" I threatened him that if he told mommy and daddy I'd been here, I'd hurt him really bad. "So you won't tell will you," I questioned. His big eyes filled with tears as he shook his head no. I pulled his pants down then and poked at his privates. "Stop, Beffy . . ." he whispered. No, I wanted him to finally know how I suffered in my dreams. So I pulled his penis hard. When he cried out in pain I looked up startled. I hadn't expected him to make noise. I heard footsteps and quickly moved away from him. Mommy appeared at the doorway. Seeing my brother's pants down she rushed in and grabbed my arm, snapping, "What just happened in here, Beth?" In alarm I looked into her angry eyes. I'd only wanted him to know how I felt.

"I . . . I . . ." I sputtered.

"You what?" she demanded. She looked at my brother searching for an answer but he just stood there with tears streaming down his face. She grabbed me by the shoulders. Each word that came out of her mouth increased in volume and pitch. "What did you do to him, Beth, what did you do?" I'd never seen her this way and I stood there surprised.

"I - I pulled his privates, mommy."

"Didn't he tell you to stop?" she inquired as she dragged me down the hall to my room.

"Yes, Mommy," I whispered.

"Did you stop?", she practically shrieked.

"No, I just kept on."

"Don't you dare move until I come back," she seethed and slammed the door behind her. As I sat on the bed my shock quickly dissolved into anger. There he went again getting all the attention. All I'd wanted to do was show him how I felt and he'd made sure I got in trouble. I had wanted to do things to him to make him feel dirty like I did, but it didn't matter he was still perfect in their eyes.

I heard him sob down the hall as mommy comforted him and my stomach knotted. I'd show him and them. I'd handled the torture of these feelings for five years and he'd had five minutes. I'd teach him to not cry out or tell on me. When I got done with him he wouldn't be their precious little boy anymore. He'd be rejected like I was. I'd make him and them suffer. I was sick of living this torture by myself. If they thought I was bad now, just you wait. The cauldron of hate and evil surged within me and I tore my sheets to pieces. "Just you wait," I promised. "Just you wait!"

I delighted in my strength so I became quite an athletic little girl. I would climb the pine trees next to the house and sit in them. One day as I was climbing I came upon a bird nest. I looked into the nest and saw five little naked birds. How cute. Their eyes were still closed, but they turned their head up expectantly at my shadow. I reached in and touched their beaks, I watched in awe as they opened them and squawked at me. I began to pick each one up and watched as their necks would roll around. So helpless.

I continued to scramble up the tree each day and play with them. After a few days I saw one of the baby birds, shoved to the side and not opening its mouth. I plucked it from the nest and I carried it in one hand as I made my way down the tree. I skipped up to Mommy and asked, "Mommy, is this bird dead?" Her weary eyes looked down at me and then she called for my daddy. She had to get him? What for? Well, whatever it was I'd decided she was pretty weak by now anyway because she always looked at me with such tired eyes. It took two of them to handle me now. Daddy came and glanced at the baby bird. I watched as a look passed between them and he said, "Yes, Beth it is."

After she'd handed the bird to Daddy, Mommy sat down and explained that if I touched the baby birds then their mommy wouldn't come back to them and I should leave them alone.

"Okay, Mommy." I skipped away. What a mean mommy bird I thought. She'd just dump her babies. I scrambled up the tree again and saw the babies all looking at me. How sad I thought, your mommy wouldn't want you like my mommy doesn't want me. So instead of letting you baby birds suffer I'll end it now. I picked each one up and held them in my hand. I closed my hand around each body and felt its warmth. I squeezed them and then dropped each one from the tree. They're so tiny and helpless. Well, at least now if their mommy didn't come back it wouldn't matter, because they wouldn't know. Satisfied with my work, I climbed down from the tree and, without a glance, skipped passed their lifeless bodies on the grass.

Mommy and daddy would go out for church activities and leave me and my brother with a sitter. I soon taught them that was a bad choice. I was a mastermind at torturing baby-sitters. Baby-sitters were in a different category than the community. I was still the adorable angel to the congregation but if any one dared to control me they had another thing coming especially those baby-sitters who had the audacity to try to be my boss. I would tear around the house screaming and ricocheting off the couches. I'd pretend the floor was a huge sea that would swallow me if I touched it and would leap from one piece of furniture to the next. At one point I leapt from a couch to a chair and it slid away. I crashed onto the floor. Shocked I looked at the sitter and screamed, "Now, look what you've made me do." Eventually mommy and daddy stopped going out. With glee, I once again watered the giant weed of power growing inside me.

I was able to turn from sweet to sour in a matter of moments. I could do it with anyone. My brother and I would play with the neighbors. I made friends with the kids that were mean because they were tough like me. One day we'd all been teasing my little brother and he began to cry. I followed him to where he sat crying and put my arm around him. "I'm sorry," I said. "Are you going to be okay? Do you want me to go and get your bike?" He nodded sniffling. I walked back to the kids and snarled, "He wants me to get his bike."

"Make him get his own!" they retorted. "Yeah, make him get it himself." I cruelly joined them in their calls, "Come and get it yourself, you big baby." I saw his crestfallen look as he came back to get his bike. As he walked away with his shoulders slumped I smirked. I won again didn't I little brother. You're not so special with these kids are you?

We moved to another town in North Carolina in June 1998. Why'd they keep making me change my audiences? I'd get the church completely under my thumb and then they'd up and move, so I'd have to work really hard again. Every one in church thought I was the sweet one and gave mommy looks and whispered about her. I enjoyed conning this community. Why couldn't we just stay where we were? Oh well, it gave me good practice.

I was enrolled in the first grade. There was this little girl who was such a wimp. I'd corner her in the bathroom everyday and make her give me a quarter from her lunch money. I never spent it. Why should I? I didn't need the money, I had my lunch. I just enjoyed tormenting her. She was so pitiful it made me sick.

It had accumulated into a nice bag of money that I kept it in my room. My parents found it one day. Oh man, now how was I going to explain this?

When they questioned me I just batted my eyes and said, "I don't kno-o-ow." "Fine, then you can stay in your room until you're ready to tell us." Oooh, these stupid people, they'd let me out eventually. I'll just sit in the corner and count to one thousand. They'll come back. I lost count at about eight hundred something. Maybe they weren't coming back. Oh, fine, my stomach was growling with hunger anyway, I might as well tell them.

They made me go to school with the bag of money and give it back to the little girl. I was made to apologize in front of the teacher so she knew what I'd been doing. I didn't understand why I should lie and say I'm sorry, when I wasn't. Now the teacher's going to really know about me. Well, that's all right. She was a dumb teacher, I could get her again, and I did . . . the very next day. I stole a quarter from the little boy sitting in the desk behind me and then placed it under his chair. I raised my hand and stated he'd stolen my quarter. When she didn't believe me I started crying and said he'd always been mean to me and I knew he'd taken it. I then pointed to the quarter under his desk and remarked, "See there it is. That's my quarter, I told ya he took it, ma'am, I told ya!" She then apologized to me for not believing me and made the flabbergasted little boy say he was sorry for taking "my" quarter and to give it back. I wanted to burst out laughing but I held it in and soaked it all up. I'd just outsmarted a teacher! There you go, another adult marked down on the dumb list.

I was soon relocated to a different school. I had taken over the nap times and would consistently talk during them. I never took a nap. I didn't feel safe enough to. Scary people came in my dreams and I didn't trust this teacher because she was a wimp and the kids were all pretty stupid too. I had to keep a watchful eye on everyone and everything otherwise I didn't feel like I was in control.

It was the same way at home. Instead of taking naps I'd just lay in my bed and stare at the ceiling. This resulted in my missing a wedding ceremony that occurred one evening. The entire family was to attend and in order for me and my brother to go we had to take our naps. Of course, my darling little brother fell right to sleep, but I wouldn't. I knew, they'd take me for sure even if I didn't take a nap. So I thrashed around and laid on my bed for a while and then went to tell them I was done. I was sent back and told to either take a nap or I was to remain in there and would not attend the wedding. Howling, I sat on my bed and threw my covers around. I was surprised when they stuck their heads in an hour or so later and said they'd gotten a baby-sitter and were leaving for the wedding. Wow, they'd actually followed through! I wasn't allowed to go and they really meant it. I was shocked and decided if I wanted to join them next time I guess I should take a nap.

My rage for my brother had increased to an incredible amount by that time. Anything he did or said I despised. I truly believed by he'd killed my mama, he was the favorite and this family loved him more. I would wake up in the early morning and sneak into his room. He'd look so peaceful laying there.

His soft brown hair resting against his forehead. Overcome with feelings of disgust I'd punch him in the stomach. This went on for several months. He would wake up complaining of his stomach hurting, but if he ever mentioned it around me I'd fire him a nasty look and he'd immediately get quiet. Mommy and daddy assumed he must have a food allergy and we went to a special doctor in South Carolina. I loved it!

We were playing in the basement one day when my brother took my toy. In a fury I leaped up from playing with my dollhouse. How dare he? You'd think he'd have learned by now. He got everything in the world, he even had the love of this family and now he wanted my toy! I grabbed him by the neck and began to choke him while slamming his head against the cold cement. "I hate you, I hate you. I hope you die!!" My fingernails dug into his neck and his gasping screams rattled around the basement. Mommy came running down the stairs to pry my six year old fingers from his neck. I turned on her then and began lashing out. "I hate you. Let me go!" I ranted. Sheltering herself from the blows she pulled my body up the stairs and put me in my room. I tore around in there, hollering and screaming. "I hate you! I hope you all die. That way I'd never get in trouble. I hate yo-o-u"

They never quite knew how to punish me for things that I did. I would taunt them each time after they'd spank me, send me to my room or make me lie by apologizing. "Well that didn't work. What are you going to try next?"

Just to prove to them that their punishment meant nothing to me I would remind them of it sometimes. I had hit my little brother on the way home from church one day and mommy had said I was to go to my room when we got home. She never remembered so just to rub it in I reminded her later. Her eyes had begun to turn cold whenever she spoke to me. It was great. The love that used to emit from them was long gone and I'd done that. Since they didn't follow through on their punishments I didn't believe their threats.

I began to believe I was a witch and had special powers. I was able to control so many people. I was smart at school and had been placed in the third grade reading class since I was so far advanced for the first grade. I had conned my Sunday school teacher into believing I was an angel even though all of the children in the class hated me because I was so bossy. I would stand back some days and survey the world I controlled around me. I was good. My parents were wringing their hands trying to get control and my little brother was terrified of me.

One day my brother and I were playing in the basement again when we were distracted by the cat running in the door. Racing up the stairs we shoved the door open and she ran inside. We decided to race on the way down. Off the side of the stairs was an opening with an eight foot drop that I had often jumped from. As we began to run down the steps I saw the opening and shoved my brother. I continued down the steps so I didn't see him land but I heard him. I'd hurt him lots before and he'd hollered and screamed but never like this. I wondered what was different. This kid just never would die, would he?

He came toward me with blood dripping from his chin. My eyes opened in awe. Wow, I'd done that. I stood there in disbelief with him at the bottom of the stairs for a moment. I looked up as the basement door flew open and daddy stood there. "My God, Beth what did you do this time?" I just stood and pointed at my brother's chin. "Oh no, oh no, oh no," he repeated. Picking my brother up he grabbed my hand and dragged me up the stairs. "Go get in the car, now." When I tried to say something he interrupted, "I don't want to hear it. Just go!" He called mommy and we went to the doctor's office. I sat quiet. I was shocked. This was the first time I'd really made him bleed bad enough to have to go to the doctor's. The blood was kind of scary but I the rush of power that pulsed through me when I saw it excited me. My brother came out of the office with five stitches in his chin. Only five I thought, I could've done better. Maybe next time.

On the ride home I overheard mommy and daddy talking and she mentioned grounding me for the summer. I thought, why ground me? What are you going to do, keep me in my room my whole life? There's a plan. I'll just think of my revenge and hurt your precious little boy again. Every time something happens to him you jump to the rescue so I just hurt you when I hurt him. Later, when mommy asked me why I'd done it I just looked at her like she was dumb and simply remarked, "I thought he'd die."

One night I woke up and lay there thinking of mommy. How I hated her! First she took me from my mama and siblings, then she loved my little brother more than me and gave him everything. I decided I didn't want her around anymore. If I killed her then I would truly be more powerful than her. I got out of my bed and tiptoed into her room. I wanted to see how she slept, that's when she was the most powerless. I crept into her and daddy's room. I stood there staring at her and daddy. If I killed them how would I do it? I pondered. I would get a knife and stab them in the heart, because that's where I hurt. I would kill my little brother too. I knew if I killed them and he lived then he'd tell. While I stood there looking at them, mommy woke up. Startled she sat up, pulling the sheets around her, "Beth, what are you doing?" I didn't answer I just smiled, turned and walked back to my room.

They had discovered I was the one who was making my brother's stomach hurt and that I had been waking him. I hid my favorite Halloween costume, a witches dress and hat. I would put it on before dawn and sneak in his room and jump out and scare him. It was great fun, but after my little night escapade to their room they began tying my door shut at night.

They also began looking for places I could go to live. I was too much to handle now and the threat of killing my little brother terrified them and they believed I might follow through. I was excited when we'd go and look at places. I didn't want to stay with them anymore. I was getting bored with torturing them. Same old, same old. I needed something new and refreshing. We looked at several boarding schools but they became aware of a place in Colorado that specialized in working with children like me. When I heard that I thought, "What do you mean like me? I'm just fine. There's nothing wrong with me.

Everyone believes I'm a perfect angel, except for my family but they didn't count."

❧✱❧ ❧✱❧ ❧✱❧ ❧✱❧

In the spring of 1989 I was six years old as we drove the many miles to Colorado. When I wasn't screaming at my brother, (who was now 5), I stared out the window at the scenery. I was amazed as we left the Appalachian Mountains behind, moved into the flatlands in the mid-west and then drove toward the foot of mountains that touched the sky.

We were going to see an Attachment Therapist in a town called Golden. I had been taken to a few adults before to talk about why I was mean to my brother, but I never really knew why those people asked me dumb questions. I remembered looking at a bunch of black splotches on some paper before and I knew all these people were stupid since they believed every word I said. I would always blame my feelings on mommy and daddy and say it was their fault because my brother was the favorite and no one liked me. I told one adult, "I try to get these people to like me but they're just mean and shut me in my room when I don't do nothin' wrong." I would smile sweetly and give the doctors big hugs when I left their offices. It worked like a charm.

I figured this guy would be the same. I had planned what I was going to say to him and I knew exactly how he'd react. Everyone believed me when I said it was my parents' fault. He'd open his eyes really big and go "Oh, really?" Just like the other people did and then I'd go home and make my brother pay for making me talk to one of those people. If he didn't tell on me then I wouldn't get in trouble.

I was training him though. I squeezed his arm one day and left a big bruise, so I told him to tell mommy and daddy his teacher did it. I knew since they believed every thing he said they'd believe that too. I was so proud of myself when the plan worked out. It all went well until they set up a teacher conference and found out it was a lie and made my brother tell them the truth. I got another whippin' for that. I just needed to make him say other kids had done it to him. I knew they'd believe him if he said it right. I'd have to work with him on that. When he was scared of me he'd do anything I told him to.

This new doctor was different. He didn't fall for my cuteness. My plans to con him shattered the moment I walked into his office. At first he sat on the couch asking me questions with my parents in the same room. None of the other doctors had my parents in the same room. It was harder to lie when they were in the room and I didn't like it. When I began to tell him stories, he pulled me up into his arms as if I was a little baby. He'd lay me across his lap and make me look him in the eyes. Then he'd have mommy do it and make me look into her eyes.

I didn't like being held. I was too close to mommy and this man. I'd done a great job in all of my six years keeping mommy and daddy away. The only time I allowed her to touch me was on my terms. I needed to keep myself safe from her love because if she loved me I'd die. I believed I was safer when I was in control. I didn't want Mommy to hold me like this because then I could see the love she had in her eyes and it scared me. He'd ask me what I felt about my brother. When I said, "I hate him," he had me scream it really loud three times. "Good job, Beth! Very good."

The therapist then began to ask me questions about what I felt about being held by mommy. I lied and said, "I like it?" That's probably what he wanted to hear; however, I got busted right away for that response.

"What's the truth on that, Beth?" Shocked, I looked up and told him the truth. "Right, very good telling the truth." This man understood me. He knew when I was lying and when I wasn't. When I'd struggle to get away from my mommy he'd have me scream what I was feeling at her. "Are you mad, sad, glad or scared right now?" "I'm sad?" I said. It didn't matter how angry I got at him I'd never say I was mad, because that meant I had let him be the boss. I hated this man for making me tell the truth. I hated him trying to be boss. I hated to get close to mommy. The rage within me started to intensify and he could see it building as my eyes turned stone cold. "What are you feeling right now, Beth?" "Sad," I stated. "More than that," he replied. "Really, really sad," I seethed between clenched teeth and squeezed my eyes. I could feel the anger rise like bile in my throat and I tightened my jaw. I was going to resist and not show him my mad. My mad was powerful and I wasn't letting it go. It kept me alive. "More than that," he massaged my jaw.

"Don't touch me," I snapped. "Why don't you scream that at me Beth?"

"Don't touch me," I yelled. "Let me have it, Beth, really loud, right in my eyes." I was surprised by the strength behind my words and I shouted in my southern drawl. "DON'T TOUCH ME!!" Fear enveloped my heart. Not fear of him, but fear of my own rage. It was huge. Oh no, I couldn't let him see inside of me and if I keep screaming I don't think I could stop. And if I couldn't stop then he'd see what I was really like and I couldn't let him see that. I couldn't let him or anyone know. This anger inside of me had protected me my whole life. It was my source of power. It had kept people at bay and I could feel the back of my throat begin to tighten. I couldn't let go of my feelings of rage because they kept me alive and if I let them go I thought I would die. I shut my eyes so I wouldn't have to look him in the eyes. "Look at me, Beth. How much do you hate me right now?" he asked.

"A whole lot."

"Then tell me, in my eyes, how you feel." His gentle eyes looked into mine.

"I hate you," I drawled. I looked in his eyes and they were smiling.

"Good, Beth, again." Why are you smiling at me? I just said I hate you and you're smiling at me. Fine I'll really let you have it then. I'll teach you to smile at me. "I HATE YOU!" my words increased in intensity. Between each word I'd see his eyes still smiling at me as he encouraged me along. Stop smiling at me! He wasn't scared by my shouts. Why not? Everyone else was. Dumb man! I'd make him pay. When I got up I was going to kill him. I was going to do him in. Teach him to smile at me, what's he doing laughing at my anger. You asked for it then, it's not my fault, you made me do it. I was really going to give it to him then. "I HATE YOU!!", I thundered. And then it kept coming. The mass of anger that had been rising in my throat came pouring out. My venomous rage exuded from every pore of my body. I couldn't stop screaming. I'd release each scream into the air and fall back exhausted from it. I couldn't hear anything anyone was saying, all I heard were the screams ringing in my ears. His strong arms cradled me. I wanted to fling all of my hate onto this man. As I screamed I could barely feel his hand stroking my head. His, "good jobs" and "there you go, honeys" were barely recognizable as I released each primal scream. Tears streamed down my face. Each yell I released made way for a new one to vault out. I vented and raged until I could do no more. As I lay there exhausted afterwards, I thought, where was my power? He told me I was so strong for letting those screams out but I felt weak and empty.

He lifted me and put me in mommy's arms then. Her eyes were brimming with tears. Did she really care about me? Did she actually understand me? I lay in her arms and gazed into her eyes for a long time. She hummed and stroked my hair. My stomach began to relax the longer she held me. I felt such a strange feeling that I'd never felt before. I had let go some of the anger and now I was afraid. Would I be able to live without my rage? It'd kept me safe these past years. It was my power, what would I do without my power? I was scared this strange feeling could be love. I couldn't fill my emptiness with love because it hurts and it was dangerous. My mama had died and she'd loved me and if this woman loved me and if I loved her then I'd surely die. I was so terrified but I didn't want to move. I just wanted to stay looking in my mommy's eyes. It felt really good. There was a quietness inside me I had never felt before.

When we left that day I walked out in a daze. Later we went to play in the hotel pool and as I sat laughing at my brother splashing, I felt something was different in me and I didn't know what. I wasn't really sure if I liked it. I didn't feel as powerful anymore and I didn't like that. I wasn't really sure about this holding stuff but boy that therapist was the most powerful adult I'd ever met! I was glad when I felt a spark of anger after my brother splashed me. It was still there and I was happy. I hadn't given it all up. I sighed with relief. Tomorrow I'd fight harder. That man didn't know that I needed this rage to stay alive. I had to have this power to keep controlling everyone and everything and if I didn't then I was weak and weak people die. I was not going to die. Yep, tomorrow I'd fight harder.

In the next session I wasn't going to let him win by telling me what to do. Once again the therapist had mommy sit beside the couch as he pulled me up into his arms and had me look into his eyes. He began to ask me how I felt about my brother. When I said, "I don't like him," and smiled he asked how I was feeling. "Happy," I replied. I wanted to fool this therapist. If I got him to believe I was fine then he'd let me continue controlling everyone and every thing in my life. It didn't happen that way though. "Why don't you like your brother, Beth?"

"He always does everything right and I always get in trouble," I stated, looking away. He turned my face to meet his gaze and asked, "What do you feel about that?"

"I hate it," I exploded. Uh oh. It had become easier to get angry and I didn't like that. I knew how to control it, yet I was letting him get ahead of me.

"I mean, I don't like it very much." I drawled to compose myself and most people thought it was so cute. Maybe he would too.

"And why is that?"

"'Cause I always get sent to my room." I flashed my best pitiful look.

"How do you feel about being sent to your room, Beth?" Do you love it or hate it?"

"Love it?" I blinked blankly. I knew it made me hate them but he wasn't going to get the satisfaction of making me tell the truth. That was until he started asking me questions about my brother. In my head I thought, "what if I ask to go to the bathroom? Will he let me up? I know I'll say I can't breathe then he'll let me go or I'll scream he's hurting me. He'll feel sorry for me and let me out of here. That'll work." Before I could say anything the rage that had climbed in my throat burst out and once again I snapped. I had held it off for an hour but this time it was too much and I finally just let go. He had my mommy hold me this time and he had me scream, "I hate you!" over and over at her. As I hollered I looked into her eyes and they were so understanding. Maybe she wasn't afraid of my rage. Maybe she was strong enough to protect me. As I screamed the rage flowed up from deep within me. It was like hot lava flowing to the surface. I didn't want to let it out, it was my survival source. Wave after wave poured out of me anyway. Afterward, I lay sobbing in my mommy's arms and the doctor told me to give her a hug. When I did I felt an overwhelming power of something inside. What was this? I blurted out, "I like you, Mommy." Where did that come from? Once again I felt exhausted and empty. I felt a trickle of something flow within me as I laid in my mommy's arms. I didn't know what it was but I had started to like it. Not a whole lot, because I needed to keep my mad strong, but I still liked the warm feeling that flowed through.

After several mornings of intense sessions the doctor began to ask me about things I'd done to my brother and to the animals. I knew it was useless to lie and play games with this man so I matter-of-factly spoke of the things I'd done and how I wanted to kill my family. He asked how I planned to do it. My reply of "With a knife." made mommy's breath suck in real fast.

He then questioned me about when I'd kill them. "At nighttime," came my reply.

"Why at nighttime?" I looked up, my voice dropping to a whisper and with no expression, passively stated, "So they can't see me do it, but they can feel me do it."

I continued to speak of my hatred toward my brother and how I wanted to kill him. As we continued to speak I felt nothing. It was really no big deal to me. All I was doing was explaining the thoughts I lived with every day. The way

I treated my brother was nothing new to me and the hatred I felt toward my parents was something I experienced daily.

The doctor had a camera man come and film me. He said it would help other children and I would be famous. The film made for television was bought out by HBO. I was told a story was to be made about my family and me and cameramen would continue to film me as I worked on my life. I remained in Golden for therapy for three weeks. Toward the end of that time I overheard a phone conversation the therapist made. "Her mother has discovered there are knives missing and she fears for her other child's life. I need a place for this child to go and fast." I was going to remain, while my family went back to North Carolina?!

Over the past three weeks I had shared stories of traumatic abuse with no emotion and they were worried I would return home and again vent my wrath on my younger brother. They had decided that my pathology was incredibly twisted and the therapist decided three weeks of intensive treatment was not enough. Yes, I had made some steps down the road of recovery but I was still far from the healing point.

It was decided I was to remain in Attachment Therapy and stay with therapeutic foster parents. I was shocked and angry. Who did they think they were telling me where I was going to go? How dare they find another place for me to live away from them! When we'd searched for places in North Carolina, yes I didn't care about staying with them but the feelings inside I have after the therapy are so different. I was starting to want the warm feeling when mommy held me. Tears of anger spilled down my cheeks. I knew it, I knew my brother would eventually take this family away from me too.

Chapter 12

Magnolia Blossom

Beth: *As we made the trip from Golden to Evergreen I sat quietly in my seat. I stared my icy eyes out of the window looking at the dirty snow left along the road from a late spring snowstorm. It was April of 1989 and I'd been in Colorado for over three weeks.*

I was left in the front office of the Attachment Center while my parents were escorted into another room to speak with the director. A teenage girl was sitting at the desk and told me to sit down on the floor beside it with my legs crossed and hands folded. Still numb from discovering I was to remain away from my family I complied. If she'd caught me on a normal day I would have snarled at her and sat in a chair.

Not long after I sat there a beautiful woman stepped into the room. I heard the director lady say they'd been waiting for her. When she looked at me I stared back into her soft emerald eyes. I watched her every move as she briskly crossed in front of the desk and disappeared behind the door into the room with my parents. Who was this lady? Was she the one who was supposed to take care of me? I sat trying to understand what was to occur next in my life. I hated not knowing anything. I needed to know what was happening so I could control the situation and be on top of things. I despised all the secrecy. I strained to hear what was going on in the other room but I could hear nothing.

Nancy: The children were all doing well, and as Jerry and I had very little time to ourselves I planned an adventure for just the two of us. Jerry and I spent a wonderful weekend riding mules to the bottom of the Grand Canyon! We stayed the night at Phantom Ranch down at the bottom where Theodore Roosevelt had once slept. Afterward the long plane ride from Arizona to Denver was a welcome relief to our saddle sore, weary bodies. We landed in Denver and I called the respite provider to let her know we would swing by to pick up the kids.

About a half an hour down the road I mentioned to Jerry that I wanted to stop at the Attachment Center to pick up some papers I needed. He said that'd be fine. As we reached the foothills to the mountains he turned off at the Evergreen exit. When we pulled up in front of the office he said he'd wait in the car with the boys. I hopped out and said I'd just be a minute.

We drove up to Lori's home. I was relieved to see the children looked like they were in pretty good shape, gave Lori a hug and had the boys load their suitcases into the trunk as we all stood in the driveway and chatted about our adventures. We laughed about the fly swatters they'd given us to carry to "encourage the mules". I had not used mine. With the boys seat belted in, Jerry at the wheel, I thanked Lori and hugged her goodbye. We turned the car west, toward the mountains and home.

As I opened the agency's door and stepped inside, the director of the program met me with a big smile and her jangle earrings and said, "Oh hi Nancy, we've been waiting for you. I'm glad you're here." Immediately I wondered why she was waiting for me when I had told no one I was coming. I had just decided to drop by a few minutes ago. She said, "Your new little girl is here." I looked into her bright smiling eyes and thought, "What new little girl? Am I losing my mind? Did we discuss a new case that slipped my mind? Did I fall off a mule and land on my head?"

My eyes scanned the room, I noticed Chastity, one of the sickest kids in our program, sitting behind the secretary's desk looking proud of her usurped authority. She wasn't "new". I searched further. My eyes wandered farther over to another child, a tiny girl, her little face looked up into mine. I saw ocean blue eyes so enormous she looked like a little baby owl. Her flat expression gave no hint of her feelings.

CJ interrupted my thoughts by quickly leading me into her office as she said "The parents are in here waiting to meet you." I again thought, surely I didn't have an appointment I'd forgotten, I've been out of town! Good heavens! I had the kids and my husband in the car! "This is Beth's father, "CJ said. He stood and came around the table to shake my hand warmly. "And this is Beth's mother" said CJ as she indicated a woman sitting across the table who smiled at me apprehensively and said , "Hi."

CJ directed me to a chair next to hers and the father returned to the seat next to his wife. I was given a file with some history, release forms, emergency medical information, etc. They shared with me that she had already had a three-week intensive but was too disturbed to return to her home. She'd been severely abusing her little brother, and the family needed sometime to heal. CJ explained she wanted me to provide tight structure and powerful nurturing for the next three months to see if we could get Beth started on the healing process. My mind was racing, confused with this whole situation. I had no idea how long these people had been sitting there waiting for me and I had a hundred questions I wanted to ask, but didn't want to appear clueless to this obviously distressed family. CJ left us briefly as she stepped out to get Beth.

CJ returned with the little owl in tow, and directed her to stand next to me at the table. From my seated position I turned in the chair to see that I was eye to eye looking into her big owl eyes. As I gazed deep inside there I saw not an owl but a scared bunny, terrified, not knowing what was going to happen to her, not knowing who I was, if she was safe or in danger. She did not know whether she should run or hide. I took her hand and said, "It's nice to meet you, I'm Mom Nancy." CJ said, "Isn't she interesting looking." The mom spoke up, "We have a flight to catch". She and the dad stood up and walked out as I stood there looking at my little owl. Her eyes never left mine as they walked out of the room and out of her life. She was so intensely scrutinizing me she didn't blink as the door closed behind them.

Beth: *I sat next to the desk until the director lady came out to get me. She took my hand and led me into the room where my parents and the pretty woman had disappeared. Closing the door behind us she then led me to the woman sitting at the table. Frightened I listened as she introduced herself as Mom Nancy. I didn't understand why she introduced herself as "Mom" but I just shook her hand. In shock I heard my parents report they had a plane to catch. I glanced quickly at them and then looked back at the woman. Was she strong? Another person to torture, hmmm this could be fun. As I observed this woman I heard my parents leave and the door close behind them. I didn't say goodbye. I didn't care. I had grown to despise this family and I was too busy measuring up this "Mom Nancy".*

Nancy: CJ returned, pulled the little bird up onto her lap, wrapped her arm around her and said, "You're going to be going home with Mom Nancy now. She lives on a farm. Nancy will be taking good care of you. While you are with Mom Nancy your job is to learn to be respectful, responsible and fun to be around. What is your job? The little girl repeated word for word. Pointing toward me CJ asked, "Who is this lady?" Those big eyes blinked, looked in my direction and she said with a toothless grin, "Mom Nancy." CJ said "Right!", put Beth's hand in mine and said, "Okay, see you later." As I walked through the office with my new little charge I was dazed. We walked down the steps and out to the car. Jerry said, "Did you get the paperwork?" I realized I'd forgotten all about it. I answered, "No, I got this little girl instead. Her name is Beth." As I opened the back door to the Toyota Tercel I heard Jerry's surprised, "Ohh!" I had Will step out and I buckled Beth into the middle of the seat before having Will buckle himself in next to her. Getting back into the car, I pulled my visor down to be able to observe this new child sandwiched between my boys for the next three hours as we traveled home.

Beth: *The director returned and pulled me into her lap. She then began to explain to me what I was to do at Mom Nancy's house. I learned they lived on a farm, I had never lived on a farm before and that was exciting. When the lady stated I was to be respectful, responsible and fun to be around and had me repeat it, I thought, what are you dumb and forgot what you just said or something. I smiled as she asked me what the other woman's name was. Were these people weird or what? Mom Nancy took my hand and led me out of the office. I walked quietly with her out the door and down the stairs. So many questions were churning within my head. What would it be like living with her, was she married, did she have any other kids? Some of questions were answered when we arrived at the little orange car where a man sat at the steering wheel and two boys sat in the back seat. She introduced me as their new little girl and had one of the boys get out and buckled me in between them. As we pulled out of the parking lot I looked at the blond headed boy to the right of me with braces and the black haired boy on my left. Both boys looked away and stared out the window when I glanced at them. No one spoke in the car except for Mom Nancy and her husband. Who were these people? What happened to my family? Were they gone? Would I ever see them again? How easily could I control this family? I*

Dandelion on My Pillow, Butcher Knife Beneath   165 *was a cunning little girl and knew how to use my cuteness to my advantage. I plotted how I would work on this family and how I would soon have them under my thumb. I loved a challenge. I began to wonder about the therapy sessions. They said I'd continue them, was that director lady going to do them? Maybe I could act really good and then I wouldn't have to have a session and these people would think my family was dumb! Since the boys didn't talk and I had nothing to say, as the trip grew long I fell asleep and began to dream of how it would be with this family.*

Nancy: As we drove I realized all the preparations that needed to be made for this little one to feel at home had not been done. Where would I have her sleep? What chores could she do at six years old? With her two front teeth missing I would need to remember she couldn't bite apples or whistle. I skimmed through her file and found references to the behaviors she had displayed and the severity of her behavior.

I noticed the checklist of the symptoms of Attachment Disorder under superficially engaging and charming (phoniness) was marked severe. I hadn't seen any charm but with those eyes I betcha she could charm a pig out of a mud puddle. Lack of eye contact was marked as no problem except when her mom got too close. Indiscriminately affectionate with strangers was marked severe. Lack of ability to give and receive affection, not cuddly, I noticed her mother had marked severe; her father had marked occasionally. Extreme control problems were marked severe. Destruction to self and others was marked severe. Cruelty to animals was marked severe. Chronic, crazy lying; another severe one.

Looking down the list, of the twenty two symptoms the only ones that were not marked severe were abnormal speech patterns, abnormal eating patterns and learning lags and disorders. They had marked "never" on false allegations of abuse, I was relieved to see that one after Will's history! Her diagnosis: Reactive Attachment Disorder or what they call RAD.

Of the twenty-two risk factors the list was marked severe on eighteen. With that slight discrepancy of the difference between the mom and dad on not cuddly. I thought about this. Many of the children acted differently for their mother than their father, this little one probably knew how to wrap her daddy around her finger with her big baby blues I would have to watch for that!

I made some plans to quickly prepare a place for her to sleep tonight as we were all so tired. As we pulled up at the house I wearily got out of the car and stretched. I then directed Will and Gabriel to retrieve their bags from the trunk. I latched on to little Beth and felt how warm her tiny hand was in mine as we walked up the porch and into the front door. I made a mental resolution to stand strong for this little girl. I was so tired I wanted to just plop into the rocker with her on my lap and rock her to sleep, but I knew she would be assessing me to see whether I was strong enough to be trustworthy. For her, I needed to make a power move.

Wearily, I led her to our think spot in the living room, directed her to sit on the carpet, fold her legs and showed her how I wanted her hands folded in her lap. I put one hand on her tummy and one on her lower back to help straighten her, directed her chin straight ahead so her spine was in alignment. With her back straight, her little body resembled a darling little elf statue. "Beth, I want you to do strong sitting for a few minutes while I get your room ready. What is it I want you to do?" " You want me to sit here," she spoke in her little mouse voice, appearing timid and angelic. I'd read the file. I knew otherwise. I said, "Right, I want you to sit straight and still and quiet, 'til I come back."

Beth: *I awoke as we drove through a small town. I saw a general store and a gas station and some houses. Was this where they lived? Fifteen minutes later we pulled up in front of a big house out in the middle of nowhere. Mom Nancy held my hand as we walked across the driveway in the dying light. She had me sit in the living room facing the wall with my legs crossed and hands folded in my lap. When I began to slump she ran her hand along my back straightening it out. "If you sit straight and tall it helps you think and breathe better, but I don't know if you're strong enough to do that yet." She turned to her family and explained I was their new little girl and they needed to get the room ready for me. As I sat there briefly I realized I had to go to the bathroom and raised my hand. In my family I'd been taught if I needed something to raise my hand. I sat there with my hand raised until I finally interrupted, "excuse me, excu-use me." Mom Nancy and her husband Jerry were talking in the kitchen. Dad Jerry turned around and addressed me, "Just sit and be quiet and Mom will talk to you when we're through talking." Who was this man and why was he telling me what to do? Bursting with anger I snapped at him, "But I have to go to the bathroom!" I sat there and fumed. I hated it here! I wanted to go home where I was in control. I didn't like depending on other people to take care of me. I wanted to take care of myself.*

Nancy: I trotted down the stairs pulled the sheets off of Gabriel's bed to put clean sheets on and saw that he had yet again shredded the vinyl protector and soaked the mattress with urine. Well I could not have this little girl sleeping on this. I called for Gabriel and Will to come downstairs and give me a hand. Pulling the mattress off the bed tipping it upright, the three of us managed to pull it out of the room. Jerry seeing our heavy, awkward load immediately took over the project with the boys.

Disassembling the bed, I hauled it out. Gabriel and Will returned and stood ready to assist, so I had Will go to the storage closet and get the air mattress and begin to inflate it while Gabriel and I went up to the laundry room. I filled the bucket with hot, soapy water, handed it to him with the instructions to scrub the floor in the little room.

Jerry stopped me in the kitchen, "If you're moving Gabriel out of the little room, where are you going to put him?" As I turned to answer him I saw my little elfin statue with her hand raised and I thought, "What is she doing? This is not a school. Surely she doesn't raise her hand in her family to ask a

Dandelion on My Pillow, Butcher Knife Beneath

question!" Jerry turned as she interrupted in a snotty voice, "excuse me, excu-use me." Jerry told her she needed to wait a minute and I turned back to his tired eyes and shared my plan of temporarily moving Gabriel upstairs. He was not thrilled and questioned the wisdom of moving this child with a severe urine problem into one of the carpeted bedrooms. He envisioned it as a disaster. I told him it was only temporary and that I was hoping it might be really good for Gabriel to feel like a normal child in what Gabriel called a "normal room" instead of what the kids had dubbed, "the new kid room" with its washable tile and alarm that could jolt me from my sleep to be there in an instant.

As I headed downstairs I noticed Jerry had brought her suitcase in. I rummaged through to find pjs and toothbrush and directed her to the master bathroom off of my room. I put the sheets and blankets on her air mattress while keeping a watchful eye out for her return. As she walked toward me I noted how cute her brown hair was cut in a short pixie cut and thought maybe someday she'll be cute on the inside too. I resolved to give her that chance. I reached to give her a hug; she glazed over. I don't even think she felt the hug. I let her know we have alarms on all the doors and then said, "Good night. I'll turn your alarm off in the morning and let you know when it's time for you to come out."

Beth: *I was sent to the bathroom and later put to bed in a little room. There was a big window, a dresser and an air mattress. Where was my bed? I was used to sleeping in a nice big double bed. Mom Nancy explained there was an alarm on my door so I was safe and she knew no one was getting into my room and I wasn't getting myself into trouble. That was nothing new, my parents had been tying my door shut for several months now. "Good night," she stated as she hugged me and shut the door behind her. Crawling onto the bed I decided tomorrow, I would show her I'm perfect and I don't belong here. Yep, tomorrow.*

Nancy: Closing the door and arming it, I went upstairs to where the boys were already in their rooms, hugged them and set their alarms. I settled on the couch to finish reading Beth's file. At midnight I turned the lights out, rechecked the alarms and crawled into bed next to my warm cowboy. It felt great being home.

The next morning I got up and used the bathroom, got dressed, went upstairs and turned off Jose's alarm so he could use the upstairs bathroom, my older daughter, Terena, had already let Will out so they could go to school.

I went back downstairs, turned off Beth's alarm and found her already dressed with her bed made, her blankets smoothed, her things unpacked. I was impressed and said good morning and pulled her in for a hug. It was a very stiff hug and so I showed her how to do it right and hugged her again. Hug's are essential to help children heal, so I playfully told her I was going to hug her so much I was going to turn her into a huggy Beth Bear. Her face almost broke into a smile.

I led her to the bathroom and told her she could use the toilet and I closed the door and waited outside. When she finished we brushed our teeth, washed our faces and combed our hair together before heading upstairs.

I directed her to sit in the think spot while I prepared breakfast. Gabriel came down and joined us. I gave him a big hug and told him how handsome he was with his hair combed so nice and his teeth all nice and shiny. Since his usual think spot was occupied I had him sit just on the other side of the wall five feet away where I could clearly see them both while I prepared breakfast. Beth wasn't used to the sitting exercise so I thought I'd start her with just a few minutes before I built her up to the expected six minutes (since she was six years old).

I observed her excellent sitting, straight back, quiet and still for three minutes. Then I went to her, told her she was done and gave her a big hug. Her hug was better than the last one, but it still needed some work. After all she didn't really know me yet. "Beth, I want you to set the table. The silverware's in this drawer." I got the plates down and set them on the table and showed her where the napkins were so she could fold them and put them under the forks. She did an excellent job, forks were in the right spot with the plates in the perfect position. I directed her to her place at the table and told Gabriel he was done with his 10 minutes of strong sitting and gave him a hug.

We all shared breakfast together. I noticed little Miss Magnolia Blossom had impeccable manners, a real southern lady. Gabriel finished quickly and asked politely to be excused. Little Beth with her Magnolia blossom accent echoed what he had said. I thought, "Well she's a fast learner and trying very hard to impress me". I smiled and said "Yes, you may". She followed Gabriel in clearing her dishes and setting them next to the sink.

It was a beautiful spring day so I decided Beth needed some fresh air. Her chore would be raking. I carefully marked off a five by five foot square area, handed her the rake and said "I want you to rake this into a pile. When you're finished I want to see you do strong sitting right here in front of your job, so you can see if you got all the leaves up. What is it I want you to do?" She said, "You want me to rake every single leaf and every single stick and do strong sitting." What a good listener you are!"

I noted her somewhat startled expression and felt my enthusiastic parenting might be little overwhelming for this little one. Then I decided she'd just have to get used to me the way I am, because I parent with gusto.

Headed toward the house I found Gabriel focused on vacuuming the living room intently. I noted the time and decided to check on Beth in ten minutes. I quickly glanced out the window to see how she was doing. There she was leaning on the rake staring off into the distance with tears streaming down her face. I was hoping the tears were because she missed her family. I was hoping the tears were the sadness and loss she should have been feeling. I was hoping wrong.

Beth: *That first morning Mom Nancy retrieved me from the room. She pulled me into her arms for a hug, correcting me when I tried to hug her incorrectly. I had put my arms around her and tried to lock my fingers. Pulling my hands apart she placed them flat on her back. "Like this," she said. "There you go, good job." "Now hop off to your think spot. "Okay," I replied. "Yes mom," she corrected. I smiled my toothless grin, "Yes mom!" and hopped off to the spot I'd sat at the night before. I was going to be just perfect for this lady and then they'd send me home. If I acted normal then they'd believe my parents were lying and I was just fine. After I'd finished my sit and eaten breakfast Mom Nancy took me outside to do a chore. She gave me a rake and with her heel scraped an area for me to rake in. "When you're done sit like I have you do in your spot, facing your chore. What do I want you to do?"*

"Sit facing my chore when I'm done," I repeated.

"Right, good listening."

The moment she walked away I looked at the area she'd marked off for me and burst into tears. I hated this and I hated this woman. I tried to be perfect for her and she saw right through me. I wanted to go home where I was in control and didn't have to do anything because they were to busy chasing me around. Well fine if she wanted me to rake I wasn't going to, I'd just stand here. I never cried tears of sad, they were always mad. I didn't understand sadness because all I'd carried inside of me was mad. I started to howl while leaning against the rake. If she wanted me to rake this thing she had another thing coming. She came outside then and said, "I'm so glad you're right here howling and leaning on the rake, that way I always know where you are." Shocked I closed my mouth. I then squeezed my eyes up and howled even louder. Ooooh! Mean woman. What do you mean "so glad you're here", well I'm not glad I'm here, lady. I want to go home and I hate you!

Nancy: The time passed and I went out to check on Beth. She hadn't moved the rake yet; I saw that she had been doing some deep thinking, which is good. I gave her a big hug, and said I loved knowing right where she was so I could get a hug whenever I wanted one and to take her time, no rush. I went back in and decided to check on her in another ten minutes. I sat down and made a grocery list. Ten minutes later I went out and noted the rake still hadn't moved. She was still leaning on it. I gave her a big hug with gusto and went back inside. I remembered how frustrated I used to get when a child wouldn't do their job and was pleased to not feel that way anymore. It seemed the more happy I got the more motivated the children got, so I decided to be very happy about the slow raking. I checked on and hugged her many times in the next few hours and noted the rake had been moved several times and some leaves and sticks had been moved closer to the pile.

After three hours and twenty minutes she came joyfully in the door and announced she was done. I was happy for her pulled her into my arms and said, "What are you supposed to do when you get done with your chore?" Her over-dramatic clueless reply let me know she was playing another game, no problem, so I said, "Hop back outside till you figure it out." The glare I got as she stepped outside the door was impressive but, I had seen better. I thought well, I guess the honeymoon's over. My little prim and proper Southern Belle just got real. I was glad. I didn't like to waste time with the fakey honeymoon behavior I wanted to cut right to the chase.

I peaked out the window, saw her doing strong sitting, and dashed out to lift her off the ground in a huge hug, twirling her around as told her how smart she was for remembering what she needed to do. I checked the yard and praised her for a job well done.

Beth: *I leaned on the rake for what seemed like forever. Mom Nancy came out and continued to check on me, giving me a hug or patting my shoulder. I hated her and I wasn't going to do her stupid chore. After I stood there for a long time I stared at the spot and decided fine I might as well get it over with, it's getting hot out here. I wasn't going to do it fast though. I'd do it slow and make her suffer. I would drag the rake behind me and then stop to stare at the sky or mountains. After finally finishing my job I went in and blubbered, "I'm done."*

"Oh good," Mom Nancy replied as she gave me a hug, "what was it you were supposed to do after you finished your job?"

"I don't kno-ow."

"Well, hop back out there until you figure it out." she smiled at me while patting my back. Hop back out there until you figure it out? If looks could kill she'd be long dead. Hop back out there . . . why I outta. I walked down to my chore and stared at it. Oooh, I really did not like this woman, I thought as I plopped down. I sat up strong and faced my job.

Nancy: We went inside and I had her go over to her think spot, "Do your strong sitting while I make lunch." Gabriel was long done with his chore by then and had been working at the table doing some artwork and reading, so I had him put his things away and head over to his think spot as well. I made soup and sandwiches for the three of us and then had them wash up. We sat around the table, held hands and said grace before eating. After they had both asked to be excused and cleared their places it was playtime for Beth. I told her she could go out in the front yard and play and asked "Do you want to take a ball or something with you? She replied, "Uh huh." I said, "When you speak to me you say, "Yes mom. Got it?"

"Yes mom!" "Got it!" I was beginning to feel a little like a drill sergeant but I was afraid she would slip back into honeymoon mode. She needed tight structure to give her little opportunities to resist so we could stay on real terms rather than having her putting up the fake southern belle act again. It had been clear from the file that this little one despised her mother. Beth needed to show honest feelings to heal.

I handed her the colorful nine inch ball and watched as she went out the front door into the front field. I stood in the living room and watched from the window. It was one of the saddest things I had ever seen. This tiny little girl in this beautiful farm yard with bald eagles that flew overhead and thousands of things to do but she was standing like a robot throwing the ball up about a foot high and catching it over and over and over with this blank expression. After about fifteen minutes she came inside. With kind of a glazed over expression she said, "I'm done." I just cocked my head and looked at her and asked, "Did you have fun?" "Uh huh." Her mouth was hanging open and the noise uh huh fell from it. She was in kind of a stupor. How sad. That was her idea of fun?

Beth: *After lunch Mom Nancy asked me if I wanted a ball to play with outside. When I said "Uh, huh," she corrected me and made me say, "Yes Mom" and "Got it"! This lady was so bossy. Grabbing the blue and white ball I wandered outside and stood in the yard. "What the heck should I do with this," I thought. I stared at if for awhile and began to toss it in the air. I hadn't even realized what I was doing, I'd stared off into space thinking. Why was I here? This woman was very different than anyone I'd ever met. Each test I'd thrown at her she overcame. I stopped thinking and glazed over. It was something I'd begun to do often. When things got tough or I didn't want to focus on life I'd zone out. It was almost an out of body thing but I wouldn't know what was happening. Time would pass and I'd still be standing there. It was a lot like sleeping with my eyes open. After a bit I went back inside.*

Nancy: The next day's playtime was even stranger. I asked "Do you want to take a ball with you?" She said "no." I said "Say: no thank you, mom". She echoed "No thank you, mom", and walked out in the front field and wandered around and around looking down. Then I noticed she stooped down and lifted something. She brought it up to the porch and started chattering away to it. I thought she had found a little baby animal or a grasshopper or something so I stepped out to see what it was. She had an absolutely lovely, silver-gray, nine-inch, round rock. I questioned, "Umm what have you got there?" She said, "This is my new friend." I thought "Whoa! Fruitcake!"

When she finished with her playtime and came back inside, she asked "Can I bring in my friend to sleep with me tonight?" I thought of the teddy bears most children slept with, and then visualized her snuggling up to this rock. Yes, she was odd. She looked pretty serious about it and I thought it would be pretty safe with the alarm on the door, so I said," Sure you can, honey." We rinsed the rock off with the hose, and she went to put it in her room before she went to the bathroom. I thought how sad it was that this little girl didn't even know how to play. At least she has an imagination, a really weird one but she has one. Nothing wrong with being unique. Sadly, it actually was an improvement from the day before.

Beth: *The next day when I went to play I found a nice rock. It was my special friend and would be a terrific listener. As I sat on the front porch speaking to it, Mom Nancy appeared. "Umm, whatcha got there?" she asked.*

"It's my new friend, I named her Rock and Roll."

Nancy: The next morning it was raining, so rather than have her rake, I gave her a little whisk broom and directed her to sweep the eight stairs going up from the entry way to the upstairs bedrooms. "We sure get a lot of dog hair and stuff I'm really glad we have you to help. It will be so nice to have these stairs all clean! I want all the dirt off." I gave her a big hug and went to go do snuggle time with Jose.

I held and rocked Jose. We shared stories and laughed together. I fed him ice cream even though it was right after breakfast. He needed sweetening up. After a bit I settled him in to play with Legos. I went to check on Beth and there she sat in the exact spot where I'd left her thirty minutes before with a look of defiance across her face. I knew it was not physically possible to force her to sweep the stairs, so I gave her a happy smile, picked her up and gave her a big hug. I said, "I love it when you take a long time to do the stairs, I can just come by and give you a hug", and walked away.

Off and on throughout the day I went by and gave Beth a hug and a smile. Lunchtime came and went. She hadn't moved yet! I didn't think she could bond if she was starving so I made her a peanut butter and jelly sandwich. As I brought it to her with a big glass of goat's milk, I told her I was glad she was doing our stairs, and happy that she'd found something she liked so much. There was no rush, take your time sweetheart. The rest of the family enjoyed our dinner together, with the usual conversation and laughter. I took her some food. The other kids seemed oblivious as they came and went walking past Beth with no interaction. After supper we played scrabble, laughed and had a lovely evening.

As bedtime approached she finally asked to use the bathroom. I was amazed at the bladder control of this child. At that point she had been sitting on my stairs since 8:30 in the morning. It was now seven o'clock at night. It had been a very easy day for me and I'd gotten a lot of hugs. I was aware this was same intense resistance that she had given to her poor mother in North Carolina. I was glad she's getting real because then she could heal. I took her hand and led her downstairs to the bathroom. While she was in there I went and got her pjs and toothbrush and handed them to her to change. When she was all set I gave her a big hug and tucked her in, "Good night Beth!" When she smiled victoriously; I wondered what she thought she'd won. She had lost a whole day of her little life. She had set her brakes and they were stuck. She was the only one who could unstick herself. I was willing to wait her out, no matter how long it took. Tomorrow I would up the motivation. Yep, tomorrow!

Beth: *The following day began like the others, Mom Nancy came and got me out of my room and I did my sit and had breakfast. Since it was raining outside she decided to not have me rake. Yes!! Maybe she wouldn't have anything for me. Wrong! She handed me a little broom and took me to the carpeted stairs. "I want you to sweep the stairs and sit facing your job when you're done, got it." She grabbed me into a hug. Gosh, this woman would not stop hugging me. For Pete's sakes lady, stop! I turned toward the dreaded stairs. I didn't want to sweep the stairs. She went in the other room and was holding Gabriel. Oh he gets held and I get to sweep, what fun! I sat down on the stairs and picked at a dog hair. I don't want to do this. This is dumb. I wonder what she'll do if I just sit here. Before if I leaned on the rake I wasn't right in her face, but this time I was. So I sat there, staring off into space.*

She returned a little while later and saw I hadn't moved an inch. Instead of the ranting I expected she just smiled and gave me another hug. "I just love it when you take a long time, I know right where you are so I can give you a hug anytime." I shot my best hate look at her. She didn't even notice! Boy, this woman was weird. Well, I still wasn't going to do it her way. I lay down on the steps. She wouldn't make me stay here all day would she? Why didn't she understand I didn't want to do her stupid job and I wasn't going to do it?! So I sat there and stared at the ceiling and the pictures on the wall. A little spider walked across the floor and I watched it until it became boring and I stepped on it. I stayed strong and refused to do it her way. She wasn't winning this time, stupid bitch!

After I heard them eating she brought me some food. Will and Terena came home from school and only gave me a fleeting glance as they rushed up the stairs to their rooms. There you go, grind in the dirt, I don't care. I'm not doing it. I sat looking out the diamond shaped windows in the door and hummed. Dinner came and went and in one of Mom Nancy's many trips by to give me a hug she brought me another sandwich and milk. After eating I heard them all playing a game. A part of me longed to join in their fun but I needed to be strong so I sat flicking the dog hair and dirt around on the stairs. Bedtime came and with a smile of victory I stepped into my room. I had won. I had out lasted her. I was so proud of myself.

Nancy: The next morning, bright and early, I got Beth up. She used the bathroom and we went through our usual getting cleaned up for the day together. She seemed to be eying me during the morning time, almost confused that I was so happy. I do love a challenge and this child was a challenge. She did a good job of strong sitting then we all ate breakfast together. She actually looked quite surprised when I handed her the whiskbroom and took her back to the stairs and told her to take her time, it didn't matter when she got done whatever day it was, no problem. I gave her a big hug.

Again throughout the day I stopped by the stairs and gave her more hugs, quite content to have such an easy child to care for. At lunchtime I made her a sandwich, brought it to her on her perch with a big glass of milk and a hug. I wanted her to feel like she was missing out on some fun so I put on some lively music and Gabriel and I danced and got silly in the living room and then went into the kitchen to bake chocolate chip cookies loudly with laughter. I stopped by, off and on, throughout the afternoon to give her hugs. She was stuck. She needed to work through this and I needed to love her and support her while she did. I stayed joyful and loving, not pushing or prodding just accepting her actions or lack there of.

Off and on she would actually move the broom some along the carpet, sometimes she would shift from one step to another. Occasionally I'd find her actually looking at the dog hair and picking at the fuzz, but most of the time she just glared at me or stared into space. She wasn't hurting anyone; she was just stuck taking her time. About three thirty I noticed a lot of furious movement in the direction of the stairs, I stepped around the corner to find Beth digging at the stairs with the whiskbroom like a badger tunneling. With the dog hair and debris flying everywhere around the entryway as it was flung off the stairs. I decided not to interrupt her. At four o'clock she was sitting at the base of the steps straight back, chin high, chest out. I wondered, "Is that pride in her work or was it defiance?

I looked at the stairs. They were immaculate. I looked at the child. She was grinning. I picked her up, twirled her around in my arms, shouted "Whoohoo!" I looked her in the eye and said, "You know what? You now hold the record for the slowest stair sweeping in the house, eighteen hours! Maybe tomorrow you can break your own record and go for 19 hours or even twenty, it's okay with me as long as you're happy sweetheart, you can sweep my stairs as long as you want to!" I was impressed with her determination to not do it and the determination she finally showed to do it. This was my kind of girl!

Beth: *In the morning I expected a lecture of some sort about the stairs. When none came and we went about our normal ablutions I figured it had been forgotten. I smirked as I passed the infamous stairs. I won I thought, I actually conquered this stupid woman.*

After breakfast I was dumbfounded when Mom Nancy handed me the little broom and brought me to the base of the stairs again. You're joking, right? You're just playing a game on me, I know you are. With a hug she smiled and walked away. You're not joking. I slumped onto the bottom stair. I banged the broom against the stair. Dumb stairs, I thought. Well, I did it yesterday and I can do it today too. I'll outlast her, just you watch, I'll do it. I didn't understand why her smile got bigger and bigger each time she came by to give me a hug. Every once in a while I'd throw some hair around but just because I was bored. I was not going to do it her way, I couldn't let her win. Once again lunch came and went and I didn't care. I was winning again and I delighted in the strength I was displaying.

Later I overheard Mom Nancy talking to Gabriel. "It makes her weak when she lets her mad take over. I bet she can be strong when she wants to be but she just lets that mad get in the way and it makes her so weak she can't even sweep the stairs. Aren't you glad you're working on your life?" "Yes Mom," he said. What do you mean I'm weak when I don't do it her way? I thought I was strong! I didn't understand. With my family in North Carolina when I wouldn't do something the whole family got agitated and I won, but here it was different. But if I submitted would I lose my power? I began to sweep at the stair. As I worked harder and faster I enjoyed the way my heart beat faster and the speed in which I could get my hands and arms to move. I beat the hair from each step and watched as the dirt flew from the stairs. Breathless I stepped back to survey my work. It had felt so good to move! Wow, I looked at my job, it was beautiful and I actually did feel stronger. As I sat inspecting my chore, I heard Mom Nancy approach behind me and puffed my chest out. She scooped me up in her arms, whooping. I giggled in response. She said something about a record of eighteen hours!! She twirled me around. This woman was so vivacious, it was

Dandelion on My Pillow, Butcher Knife Beneath

almost overwhelming. I had almost forgotten what it was like to laugh. It felt good and I wanted to soak it up.

I had my first therapy session that week with CJ. Oh boy, I had thought the therapist in Golden was the most powerful adult I'd ever met. Well not anymore, these two women had just beaten him hands down. CJ could see through everything and she always seemed to know what I'd done that week. I began to wonder if she was psychic or something. She asked me how I felt about my parents leaving. I told her I was mad at them for leaving me and I felt they loved my little brother more than me. She had me scream "I'm mad" over and over and I actually felt such a relief afterward. When she asked me about the stairs I told her how I wanted to feel stronger and more powerful than Mom Nancy. "And did that work for you?" she asked.

"No, I sat on the stairs for two days," I reported.

"Right and you didn't get to enjoy the sunshine and the mountains did you?"

"No ma'am."

"So do you miss your family, Beth."

"Yes, ma'am."

"What do you miss about your family?" I missed being boss of them that's what I missed. I missed torturing my little brother and seeing my parents faces get red and their eyes bulge with anger. There was no anger toward me in this home and I didn't know how to act in a home like that. I was used to controlling everything and I wasn't able to here. "I don't kno-ow." I said.

"You miss being boss of your family don't you, Beth?" Whoa, this woman was good! Was she reading my thoughts? I nodded. "And was that good for you or bad for you?"

"Bad." I looked into her eyes and saw an awareness of my behavior. CJ said "I want you to yell: 'I like being boss of my family'. Go." I just laid there looking at her. I wasn't going to say it and she couldn't make me. When she noticed I'd clammed up she calmly replied. "That's all right, you can just kick until you're ready. Just say 'ready' when you're ready!" I began kicking my legs, lifting and dropping them on the couch. In my head I thought, I hate you and I hate this. You people are always trying to be boss of me and I hate it. Can't you see I'm boss of myself and I do a great job of it. Finally I was sick of kicking and my legs were getting tired. "Ready." I called out. "Good, stop kicking. Go ahead."

I softly said, "I like being boss of my family."

"Again."

"I like being boss of my family."

"Again." My voice began to increase in volume. "I like being boss of my family."

"Louder," she called.

"I like being boss of my family," I yelled.

"Yes, you do and that's not good for your little heart is it?" I shook my head. "No, it's not." she answered. "How do you feel about your brother going home and you staying here?"

"Fine." I lied.

"What's the truth on that, Beth? You're mad your little brother got to go home and you had to stay aren't you? Tell me how mad you are at your brother. One being a tiny bit and ten being a whole lot." I thought for a minute. I was shocked because it was exactly how I felt. Had she read my mind again? I thought about how much I hated my brother. I won't tell her how mad I really am so I'll say I'm just a six. Before I answered she spoke as if looking into my thoughts, "If you don't let the truth out then it eats you up inside and you become really weak." I paused before my answer.

"I'm a ten," I said softly. "Very good. That was hard for you wasn't it."

"Yes," I said and burst into tears. Rocking me she spoke, "That's good, Beth, let it out. Underneath all that mad are some scared and sad feelings, aren't there?" I didn't even hear her anymore I just sobbed and sobbed. I was shocked that my own anger had actually scared me. I loved my anger but something was different. I didn't realize how much I had inside of me. CJ stroked my hair, continuing to encourage me and letting me know she was still there for me.

Afterward she put me in my Mom Nancy's arms and she just held me. Rocking me back and forth she told me funny stories and made me laugh. It felt so good to lay there in her arms and soak it up. I was still scared of it though and was afraid to let it all in because I still believed I'd die if I allowed all of my mad out and let love in.

Nancy: Stair sweeping became Beth's daily chore. She started out with the all time longest record of 18 hours and quickly became one of our fastest most efficient stair sweepers after her first therapy session. In that first therapy session with CJ she worked so hard. I watched in amazement as her tiny body released wave after wave of seething rage. As she peeled away layer after layer getting closer to her inner sweet core, tears flowed down my face for all the pain this child had suffered. For the strength that she had to again face her early trauma and overcome it in a healthy way. When she opened her mouth wider and wider with each scream my ears rang at the intense volume, my heart rang with joy that she wouldn't have to carry such a burden any longer. When she was finished, emotionally drained and limp, I rocked her little sweat soaked body and held her close to me. I did everything I could to fill her up with my love. For the first time I saw her laugh, freely laugh. A little spark of joy flitted through her eyes. I had hope and I believed with the strong will that God had given this little one she had the strength and the courage to overcome the abuse she had suffered and the abuser she had become.

The next morning after her therapy she triumphed over the chore with a final time of 11 minutes before graduating to a more advanced chore of bringing in firewood. Beth was not having any problems with urine and Gabriel was flooding the place with it upstairs. I had them switch rooms. Gabriel scrubbed his mattress that we had taken out to the garage and left it out in the sun to air out and dry before we put his bed back together in his room. I replaced the vinyl cover on the mattress upstairs and Beth and I put clean sheets on it together. I told her she had graduated to the normal kid room because she was working so hard. She proudly moved into her new space.

Beth: *Since I was not allowed to be around the other children, I was not able to act out my anger on any of them, so I began to inflict the pain I felt inside on myself. I would stand at the top of the stairs and throw myself down hard enough to ricochet against the wall across the room. At the store I'd stick my foot under the grocery cart over and over. I loved seeing the concern cross Mom Nancy's face each time she ran over my foot. She'd get so upset thinking it was her fault. I felt I succeeded each time! This happened until she caught on and would have me do jumping jacks, later at home. Since I couldn't get a rise out of her anymore I stopped.*

Physically I couldn't feel anything. I had shut myself down so much from my inner pain that I'd also destroyed my outer feeling. I was bringing in firewood one day. I hadn't finished the chore right the first time and was angry. I was swinging my arms and had not realized I'd touched the burning wood stove. I stood there for several moments until I smelled something burning and saw it was me. Yanking my arm back I stared at the rising blister on the back of my hand. I stood there in disbelief. I hadn't even felt it.

One night at dinner after I'd been with Mom Nancy and Dad Jerry for several months I sat steaming mad at Will. He'd told on me for something I'd done earlier that day. Staring at my plate I contemplated a way I could get back at him. Will sat next to me at the table and when we went to say grace I dumped his milk. I watched with glee as it splashed into his plate and overflowed into his lap. Yes!! I had gotten him back. Mom Nancy had me clean it up though. I hated that part but I enjoyed seeing Will's face as the milk dumped down his clothes.

The next night Gabriel had done something that I was angry about. I sat in my chair again contemplating how I'd dump his milk from across the table and then my time came. "Mom, may I please have some more corn." I reached rudely across the table before anyone could hand it to me and in the process of grabbing the bowl I hit his glass of milk. I again watched with glee as the milk dumped in his food and splattered on his clothes. Gotcha!! But once again Mom Nancy had me clean it up. It wasn't fun if I had to clean it up. Man, this woman was too good and could read right through me. For lack of fun, I stopped spilling milk after that.

Nancy: It had been several weeks since Beth had had access to her usual outlet for her frustration. She was no longer able to abuse her brother or anyone in our home because she was so closely monitored. I was in the living room working at the desk the first time I heard her body rebound off the stairs and slam into the wall across the entryway. I rushed to her, "Oh my gosh! Are you all right?" Picking up her body searching for wounds. She replied, "It was an accident." I was horrified this little body had crashed into the brick floor and the wall with such force, I was sure there must be broken bones. As I checked her all over I was stunned to see no expression on her little face. There was no fear, no pain; there was no surprise, just blank emptiness. As I helped her up she replied, 'I'm fine. It was an accident." I hugged her and, shaken, returned to my work at the desk.

Several hours later she had asked to use the bathroom and gone upstairs. When she returned I heard the same sickening thud as her body tumbled and bounced against the wall. I again rushed to her to comfort and soothe. She was getting up as I came around the corner, "Oh my gosh! Are you all right?" "I'm fine." And she went back outside to play with her rock. Later that evening while I was cooking dinner I heard a loud thud and came around the corner to find that Beth had once again fallen down the stairs. Did she have a balance problem? Was there an equilibrium difficulty here? Should I get cushions and place them along the floor and the wall? What was causing this strange occurrence?

The next day, after several more of Beth's crashes down the same steps into the same wall, I called CJ. She asked what I had done each time Beth had fallen. I assured her I had rushed to her aid and comforted her and held her to me as any mother would do. She surprised me by saying, "Well that's the problem." I thought: "Comforting a wounded child is the problem?" How could I not rush to comfort a wounded child?! Certainly she doesn't expect me to do nothing when my child has fallen so dramatically. It's against my nature! Sure enough she said, "Children with attachment disorder crave excitement. She's creating the excitement and you are feeding it with your response. Children with this disorder actually prefer negative attention to positive attention. So even though you're giving her pizzazz and attention over doing things right her sickness causes her to prefer excitement over doing things wrong." CJ was the expert. She had over twenty years experience working with troubled children. Who was I to argue or disagree with someone who I had seen repeatedly being so amazingly right?

I thought about Beth's little body. I had found no bruises. She had not needed ice or bandages after her connections with the floor and wall. So I agreed to follow the therapist's direction and not respond to any further body surfing down the stairs. Only an hour later I was faced with trying out this new technique when I heard the now familiar sound of Beth's body hitting the wall. My stomach ached for her. I wanted so much to rush to her again, but I stopped myself and waited. She marched through the living room after picking herself up and returned to setting the dinner table with no reaction or comment. The following day there were fewer crashes and within a week her focus had been changed to burning herself on our wood stove rather than hurting herself on the steps.

It took weeks of rage releasing therapy sessions before she could stop bashing, cutting, burning, and bruising herself intentionally. I found that children with Attachment Disorder don't feel their bodies and can do unbelievable torture to themselves. They also think very differently from a normal person. If normal children are not comforted when they're wounded they feel abandoned and neglected. Comforting makes them feel loved and cared for. When a child with Attachment Disorder is self-inflicting wounds, adult attention escalates the behavior. Their whole purpose is to manipulate the adults. When they can manipulate or con an adult they don't feel safe. The less safety they feel the more frustration and anger they feel and the more they abuse themselves. It's a huge catch 22. Beth and I had been caught in it.

One of the most powerful sessions, that was a turning point to Beth's healing, came after Mother's Day. Over the years I had seen that Christmas was the most difficult time for emotionally disturbed children. Mother's day came in second and the mom's birthday is third. These were usually days decorated with violence. This particular Mother's Day had been torturous for me, with nonstop acting out from Gabriel, Will and Beth. The Three Stooges caused less havoc than my crew of three had done.

Beth's therapy session had begun by dealing with her dastardly deeds over Mother's Day and then quickly shifted when she defiantly stated, "I have special powers. I'm not like the other kids. I'm a lot more powerful than they are." CJ lovingly pulled her over into her arms smiled and said, "Well sweetheart if you have special powers then just use those special powers to get up. Go ahead. Let me see your special powers." Beth's little body began to writhe. She bit, she pinched, she clawed, she kicked, she hissed, she growled, she spit, she cursed and then she fought some more. CJ stayed calm and smiling as she said, "Come on show me your special powers, where are they?" I was flabbergasted at the amount of energy and fury flying in all directions from such a small child! She was like a wild animal.

The struggle continued for a good forty-five minutes before the little bundle of fury wound down. Her body relaxed, she unclenched her jaw and looked up confused and expectantly. CJ asked gently, "So where are you special powers? How come you couldn't get up?" The realization that she had lied to herself and actually believed it became clear. Beth revealed that she now believed the love that CJ had and the love that I had was more powerful than the hate she had. Beth had an insatiable thirst for power, and in the following weeks I saw her seeking the power of love much more than the power of hate, revenge, destruction and defiance that she had sought in the past.

Beth: *After several weeks of staying with the Thomases I had a session that would be forever ingrained in my mind. I told CJ I believed I was a witch. I truly believed I was one. I raged and raged for a long time until I was so worn out I didn't even want to speak anymore, I just wanted to fall asleep in her arms. She carried me to lay in my Mom Nancy's lap. Why was I not as powerful as them? What did they have that I didn't? As I looked at the love emitting from her eyes, I knew. "Your love," I said softly, "Your love is more powerful than my hate." I realized something then. My hate had gotten me no where. I wasn't with my family in North Carolina because I just wanted to be boss. The need for power in the wrong way had cost me years of my life. As I lay there gazing into Mom Nancy's eyes, I felt a warmth that started down in my toes and flowed through* *every part of my body. I felt like I could explode when I was done I was so filled with this feeling. This feeling of love that I had never wanted to experience before. It was beautiful. I felt like I could fly high above everything but I didn't want to leave this spot for fear that it would disappear if anything changed. Love had healed me and brought me from my depths of rage. Once I felt it, I didn't want to turn back ever. I began to work on my life a lot harder. I wanted more of that feeling!*

Nancy: I believe each child is given a special gift from God. I had been searching Beth's activities, trying to discern what her gift was, in order to nurture it and help her to build her self-esteem. As she reached daily for the power of love she began to ask to climb the mountain after she completed her chore. I watched each day, as she would climb part way up and perch on a huge monolith in the sun. The sound from that mountain echoed through the valley. She would sit up there and chatter to herself; then she began to sing. Not too well at first, but, as day after day she spent hours with her little voice echoing songs throughout our valley it became clearer and softer. The beautiful music she began to create filled my heart with joy. Beth had found her special gift!

Beth: *I had given up having rocks as pets. I began to climb the mountain and earned playing with the other children. Mud fights became one of my favorite activities. I loved being able to go outside and get completely covered in muck and throw the mud around. Although Gabriel had been baptized as a Christian and changed his name to Gabriel he still wasn't healthy enough to join us in our playtime. He would play next to mom. The rest of us would tear around down by the creek chasing each other with mud. All of the children that were healthy were able to go out and play with plastic farm animals down by the creek and ride horses.*

When I climbed the mountain I found a big rock that I'd sit on for hours on end. The Little Mermaid movie had just come out and I began singing the songs from it. I enjoyed singing and listening to it echo across the mountains back to me. I would finish my chore quickly each day and ask to climb the mountain so I could sing.

Nancy: Beth had been with us about six months and her progress had been astounding. Her once cold heart filled with a killing rage had softened day after day and now overflowed with song. CJ felt she was ready for a visit, so she set one up with the minister and his wife to come to our home to celebrate Beth's seventh birthday. I assumed that the mother knew what my job was as a therapeutic mom. I looked forward to the visit. It often stirred up deeply buried emotions in the children and gave us more opportunities to heal different areas of their wounded psyche. We did not tell the children when a visit was impending. They had found through years of working with these disturbed children that rather than giving them time to prepare and something to look forward to, it escalated their anxiety level to outrageous proportions and caused major acting out.

CJ arrived that morning and helped Beth process her feelings in her arms as she had done many, many times over the months. After Beth released enough rage to be able to relax and allow me to rock her, CJ said, "Let's go out to the back across the creek to your campfire circle." I said, "That sounds like fun." Earlier Jerry had carried the birthday cake up, Terena had made punch and snuck it out and had met our guests in the driveway and directed them to the designated spot. Will, Alicia, and Gabriel were on their best party behavior. We shared cake and laughter.

Beth: *I had fallen in love with Mom Nancy's birth daughter, Terena. I would follow her around and copy everything she did. I thought she was so perfect and beautiful and I wanted to grow up to be just like her. All of the children looked up to her and she'd watch us when Mom Nancy and Dad Jerry would go out. She taught me how to ride and I began to help her practice for her horse shows. I had to do my chores fast and snappy and right the first time for a week to be able to ride, so I quickly earned that privilege so I could ride all over the pasture and mountains with her. I adored her then and I still do.*

After I had proven I wasn't going to hurt animals and was honest about my feelings and hadn't acted out in crazy behavior for several months, I got to move into the same room with Terena, her dog, IQ, and two love birds. This was an incredible experience and I was so happy. I would enjoy feeding the birds and holding them on my shoulders. I was able to see the beauty in creatures now. I could see the helplessness and not get a surge of rage, I would marvel in it and began to fall in love with the animals. In the beginning when I would go out to the horse corral with Terena, her horse could feel my rage and would literally chase me around the arena. I'd run screaming in terror before climbing out of the pen. I was able to ride her horse now and the horse would come up to nuzzle me and let me pet her.

My seventh birthday was rounding the corner and I was excited. After a session one day CJ decided we were to go for a walk across the creek. When we got there Mom Nancy told me to run ahead, I was shocked. She did not allow us children to run ahead of her because it was not respectful. I obeyed and ran ahead up the hill. I stopped in disbelief at the top. There was my family from North Carolina shouting, "Surprise, Happy Birthday!" I ran into their arms, this was exactly how I pictured it. I was filled with unsurpassable joy. When I reached to give my brother a hug he hid behind my mommy and daddy. Heartbroken I shoved it aside and figured it was what I deserved for being so mean to him.

Nancy: Terena saddled up the old mare for Beth and invited Beth's six-year old brother to ride double on her gray mare. They laughed in the sunshine as they rode around the fields together. The minister, his wife and I, together with CJ and Jerry watched every move they made from the front porch.

I noticed that Beth's adopted mother spoke very little to me. I was busy with the children most of the time, but I was concerned because the moms I had worked with in the past had been eager to asked me questions about how their child was doing, about how I handled things. They had wanted to assure themselves that their child was okay and were anxious to learn things to help their child. She asked nothing and seemed to keep a wary eye on me.

After the horses were put up we all went inside to visit. Terena made lemonade and ice tea for everyone while Beth served. I was surprised and confused by the insistence of the little brother to go out in the back yard and play with Beth. I couldn't imagine why this child kept trying to get with Beth unsupervised. That, of course, was not going to happen. He then tried to convince Beth to take him upstairs to show him her room. What was this child thinking? Why would he want to be alone with a little girl who had so horribly abused him? He jumped on her repeatedly. He grabbed her hands and at one point , when she was sitting on the floor, he actually tackled her and laid on her! It got more and more disconcerting as the day went on. Beth's mother did not correct him or intercede. I wondered if she was suffering from Depression.

Later in the afternoon CJ took me aside to share Beth's mother's concern that Beth had been abusing the horse. She had told CJ that every time I turned my back, Beth would be yanking on the bit with great force. I couldn't imagine how that could have happened with the five adults watching from the porch and Terena observing from horseback and none of the others had seen anything. Why had she not said anything at the first occurrence? I had video taped much of the horseback riding activities and determined to review that film closely later that night. I knew that it was a very common thing for these children to do things behind closed doors to their mother that others never saw. Beth was not stupid and to be so blatant in broad daylight with so many adults was hard to believe. I had to assume that it was possible and give this wounded woman the benefit of the doubt.

Beth: *We went riding and I got to ride big ole' Kismet. My brother sat behind Terena on her horse Quest and we rode around the field laughing and sharing the time together. I was so happy to have my family there. What a perfect birthday surprise. My little heart just wanted to burst I was so filled with joy. I wanted them to see how much better I was getting. I wasn't perfect but I wanted them to see I was working hard.*

Nancy: That evening they returned to their hotel with plans to meet us in the morning. One of the advantages of living in this unique community was the Hot Springs Pool. The mineral water was the same temperature and had similar properties to the fluid around the unborn child in-utero. Having the moms hold their child while they floated in this magical mineral water connected them on a deeper level. As they were held afloat by their mom in the body temperature liquid, they heard their mothers voice through it. I believe the sound, in-utero, of the mother's voice through the amniotic fluid would be very similar.

I wanted Beth's adopted mother to experience the peaceful gentle water connecting them. It didn't happen. Instead she spent the time visiting with the therapist. The minister and I were kept very busy playing with Beth and her younger brother. At one point the little hyperactive overindulged brother jumped on Beth's back, wrapping his hands around her throat. I insisted he immediately get off. He glared at me and didn't move. I pried his hands from her neck and escorted him back to his father. Beth assured me she was fine. When we got out of the pool to sun ourselves on our towels, next to CJ and the adoptive mom, I was shown a large scratch down her brother's arm and was told that Beth had attacked him in the pool while two adults were totally focused on the two children! I had spent most of the time standing between Beth and her brother except for the one time he had jumped on her and I had pried him off. I didn't believe there was anyway that Beth could have injured him. He certainly had never cried out or indicated he needed any assistance, but there was evidence on his arm that he was scratched. So what was I to believe? They insisted that Beth apologize, I did not believe in forcing children to lie and say they were sorry when they didn't mean it or when they were not even admitting they had done it. I felt it was premature. Beth willingly apologized and on the surface the subject was dropped. The goals for the visit had been to reassure Beth's family that she was healing and to help reconnect them. It wasn't happening.

Beth: *The next day at the Hot Springs Pool I played with my family and Mom Nancy. I was told to stay away from my brother and I obeyed because I didn't want to get in trouble. At one point, when we were all playing, my brother jumped on me and started choking me. Oh great, what was I supposed to do now? If I touched him I'd get in trouble, if I say anything, I'll get in trouble. I was so relieved when Mom Nancy took over and told him to get off of me; he didn't. I had never seen someone stand up to Mom Nancy and win so I wasn't surprised when she pulled him off and took him away.*

When we got out of the pool, I was blamed for a scratch on my little brother. Had I scratched him when he jumped on me? I couldn't remember but he did have a scratch. I knew I hadn't done it on purpose but Mom Nancy didn't believe in accidents so if it was there I must have done it. I quickly apologized for the scratch; I could tell Mommy wasn't very happy with me. I wanted her and Daddy to see me being good but it didn't work. Maybe I'd never be a good girl. I was discouraged but Mom Nancy helped me to keep working on my life. I wanted to get better and live with my family in North Carolina happily ever after.

Nancy: I was beginning to have serious concerns about this mother. I noticed throughout the visit how caring the minister was, how gently he hugged Beth, how fond he was of his son, and how supportive he was, often putting his arm around his wife throughout the day. He imitated Donald Duck's voice to delight all of us, causing ripples of laughter and hysterical giggles throughout all of the children and adults. I liked this man and I was sorry his family had been torn apart by mental illness. I was glad I could be a small part of helping them to rejoin and be happy together. I hoped that the loving support he was clearly giving to his wife would help heal the obvious emotional pain that she was suffering; before Beth would be ready to return home. Beth hugged her family and we headed home as they drove to Denver to fly home.

Dr. Ken, the psychologist that had done the original work with Beth, called and asked to come out and do a some follow up filming for a documentary he was creating on Attachment Disorder. I thought about the huge leaps in healing that Beth had done. I thought about the strong will that she had, and how hard she had fought to conquer the deep emotional pathology that she had carried.

I trusted Beth now. She had proven herself and now shared a room with Terena and slept there at night with no alarm. I had no concerns that she would harm my biological daughter. It usually takes a year to earn having the alarm off their door. Beth had done it in record time. Our two lovebirds shared a room with the two girls. It had been an extremely difficult battle that Beth had undertaken to heal herself and she was winning. She trusted me and had internalized me. It showed in that her once beautiful magnolia blossom accent had faded and she had taken on my Colorado accent. Her hand gestures were the same as mine, her voice inflection echoed my own. We were bonding well. It would be a good time for Dr. Ken to come and film.

Even though it usually took several years for a child this sick to heal, Beth's incredible determination had sped the process up. The film crew came out with their huge professional cameras. I was concerned that the Hollywood air would bring out the facade in each of my children (great actors and actresses). They loved to perform. My every waking moment was spent helping them to be real, honest about their feelings, sincere and we had this whole Hollywood thing going on that could disrupt that. I was relieved when the film crew left that there had been no hamming performances by my little charges. Beth had been honest, sincere, and very real. I was proud of her.

Beth: *I started the second grade and was enthusiastic about school. Since I didn't feel I needed to control everyone I could let myself learn and enjoy it. I had an excellent teacher who didn't put up with misbehaving. She was tough but loved all of us children. I didn't have to worry about being in charge of the classroom. I had stopped being bossy with the other children and was able to make friends easily. I met Jessie that year. She was really popular. All the kids liked her because she was so beautiful and sweet and I decided one day we would be the best of friends. I wasn't fully healed yet but I was sure working hard on it.*

Nancy: Not too long after that, in church one Sunday I noticed Beth being particularly attentive to the sermon Pastor Eddie was preaching. When he invited those who wanted to give their lives to the Lord to come forward, I felt a little poke on my elbow. Looking down I saw very soulful eyes looking up pleadingly, "May I please go up there?" The expression on her face gave me all the information I needed. I told her that ,yes, she could go. After services, Beth told me she wanted to be baptized. I was so proud of her and I just wanted to race to the phone to share with her father that his daughter who had admitted to worshiping Satan had turned her life to the Lord. I just knew he would be overjoyed. I felt that the baptism could be helpful in bringing Beth together with her family.

As I shared the exciting news there was silence on the other end of the line and he said, "Beth has already been baptized." I said, "Yes, but she was worshiping Satan then. I don't know if that counts. She's really motivated now and she's asking to be baptized." He said, " In our religion we do not believe in re-baptizing people, they are only to be baptized once." I was discouraged and disappointed. The vision I had of this moment pulling Beth and her family closer together had been shattered. What was I going to tell Beth? How could I let her know she was not allowed to be baptized? I was saddened and confused by his reaction.

Beth: *We would attend church every Sunday, which was nothing new to me since I was a minister's daughter. In the beginning I despised it. I didn't want to sing the songs and learn about Jesus. I despised my daddy and mommy and anything they loved and I wasn't going to love their God. After many months of therapy and Mom Nancy's structure I stood in church with a different feeling. When I looked at the preacher up there talking I thought he was talking to me. I felt a tingle within me and something told me I needed to go up there and talk to him. I didn't understand the feeling but I had just felt love for the first time not long before and that was pretty weird too, but . . . oh the feeling afterward was amazing. So I listened to my heart and when the minister did an altar call after church, I turned to my mom and said, "Mom, may I please go up there?" "Sure, Beth," she replied. I walked past my whole family and marched up to the front and asked the preacher what I needed to do to love Jesus. He prayed with me and I told him and my mom I wanted to be baptized. The feeling that flowed through me was powerful. I sat on the mountain that day and thought of my life. Before I had come here I was an angry little girl that only wanted to be in control for the power. That was a different power though because with the love from my mom and the love from God I felt like I could soar. I'd never felt this way before. This was a deep kind of happiness and I wanted to bask in it forever. I dreamed of my family in North Carolina and me laughing and growing up happy with them like I had been growing up happy here. I loved it here but I still wanted my family to come and get me.*

Nancy: The months flew by with Beth continuing to make outstanding progress, the few incidents of resistance that she gave me she quickly overcame and went on. Her conscience development was very apparent as she would sometimes cry in my arms about the pain she had caused her brother, her parents and their pets.

One night Beth came out of her room about ten thirty. She had been crying and was very agitated. I pulled her up in my arms and asked her what was going on. She said she'd been lying in bed tossing and turning. " What I did to my brother was so mean, I was awful to him. I don't think he can ever forgive me for what I did." With tears streaming down her face, between deep sobs, she shared with me incidents that had been eating away at her newly forming conscience. I rocked her, shared her sadness and her pain and was so proud of my little girl, whose heart was healing. I hoped one day she and her brother could reconnect in a loving way.

Beth: *In October of 1989 Dr. Ken came out to do some more filming. He was impressed by all the hard work I had done and was proud that I had earned sharing Terena's room and my animal privilege. I still had jealous feelings* *toward my brother that I needed to work on and my relationship with my adoptive mom but he said he could see I had made incredible progress.*

    Another boy came to stay with us at this time. His name was Teddy. We never knew anything about each other's past, Mom made sure of that. I got jealous. I realized later why I was becoming jealous of the tiniest thing. I was worried this new boy was going to take my mom's love away. I was used to sharing her with the other kids but I couldn't believe that with one more she could still have enough love for all of us. I had a therapy session with CJ and told of my fears. Mom assured me she had more than enough love for all and quenched my concern.

Nancy: Beth's newfound Christianity was a giant boost in her healing. She had been with us eight months. It was almost Christmas and Dr. Ken wanted to do some more filming. With no reservations, I quickly agreed. We met him in Evergreen at the therapist's home and Beth was again open, honest and truly beautiful on the inside, but on the outside her chapped lips were cracking, and the dark circles around her eyes were evidence of the internal conflict she now struggled with day and night. The nightmares about what she had done to her brother, to her parents, to the animals haunted her ceaselessly. It was a difficult thing to watch Beth go through it.

Beth: *The last filming for HBO was done in December of 1989. Dr. Ken and my mom and I gathered at CJ's house. Dr. Ken asked me questions about my life and my killing feelings for my brother. I had worked on these issues for months now and it hurt me to remember them in vivid detail. Dr. Ken asked me who I had hurt the most. I answered, " my brother." My Mom Nancy piped up and said, "Who did it hurt the most, Beth?" "Me," I stated honestly.*

    "And how did it hurt you the most, Beth?" Tears filled my eyes as I replied, "Because when I hurt other people I hurt myself." It was really hard to talk about my feelings of rage toward my brother and adoptive parents. I hurt for all the pain and torture I'd put them through. Mom Nancy pulled me into her arms and held me while I wept tears of sorrow and shame about the pain I'd caused.

Nancy: There was no way I could ease her suffering. She needed to sort through the shame, the sadness and the guilt she now felt for what she had done, in order to completely heal. In the final film footage with the shadow of pain around her eyes and her lips, the burden, her shame so evident in her eyes came through clearly. It was heart breaking to see.

    I was hoping that the upcoming Christmas visit would lighten her load some as she spent time in her home in North Carolina. Her adoptive mother called me several weeks before the visit asking for suggestions for a gift for Beth. She had never asked for my input before, so I leapt at the chance to be helpful. I shared with her that Jerry and I had purchased a cute winter coat and a huge teddy bear. I let her know how much Beth loved singing and I felt Beth would really treasure a little cassette player with maybe a few sing along tapes. She thanked me for my suggestions.

Beth: *The best Christmas present I could ever receive was given to me that year. I got to go home to my adoptive family's house for a visit! It was such a joyous time, but I wish I could have just had time with my family.*

Nancy: The afternoon before Beth was to fly out, I shared the news that her family wanted her to come home for a Christmas visit and we needed to pack for it. She was overjoyed and giggled and laughed while we packed her things. The next morning we left early for the four hour drive to the airport. I hugged my little magnolia blossom and entrusted her to the stewardess for safekeeping during the flight. I took the rest of the children to therapy from there. CJ shared with me that she had prepared Beth's adoptive mother for the visit with clear directions and guidelines and that Beth was to call me each evening while she was gone and that it was vital that I be near the phone and available so that Beth could do really well during her visit. I was glad that I'd be able to hear from her. I knew I'd miss the little one.

 I waited near the phone as I had been instructed to do each night. I never received a phone call during the entire visit. I was gravely concerned.

 At the appointed date and time, I returned to the airport to retrieve Beth. She got off the plane chattering a mile a minute. I wondered if she was excited or nervous. I asked why she hadn't called me, she said, "Oh we were very busy, we went to parties every night and sometimes two or three in one day."

 I was appalled! These people had been instructed that Beth, at this point, had had what was akin to heart transplant surgery and was to be treated physically and emotionally as if she were healing from such surgery. She was to be kept very quiet, close to her mother at all times, nurtured and not to be around other people. They had done exactly the opposite! They had been told to have her call nightly so that she had an emotional outlet and connection in order to give her the best chance for a successful visit. She was absolutely not to be left alone with her brother.

 When we got home, I helped Beth unpack and asked to see her gifts. The final straw was when she showed me a new coat and teddy bear that the minister and his wife had given her for Christmas! I thought that maybe I hadn't been clear on the phone and maybe she had misunderstood. Then Beth shared with me that they had given her a tape player. I said "Oh how wonderful! Then you can sing along with it. Let me see it!" Sadly she told me that it was only half hers. The other half belonged to her brother and he was to keep it.

 I was amazed at the fuel they had added to the fire I had been working so hard to put out in this child; The fire of hate and jealousy toward her brother. And here they had given her a gift and taken it away and given it to her brother so she again felt betrayed, felt less important than him and felt unloved. Were the coat and teddy bear, a test?... some sick evaluation where Beth would have to choose which bear she would like better? Was she supposed to choose between her adopted mother and me? Each time she selected between each coat and each bear was she selecting between each mother that she loved? What was this sick game?! Furious, I called CJ.

I assured the therapist that I had no intention of playing a game of tug-of-war with a child's heart between two moms. It was sick and twisted and I would have none of it. I questioned, "Didn't this mother understand what I was doing? I was giving my heart to her child so that her child's heart could heal and then connect to her." Did she think I was trying to steal her child? I loved this child with my whole heart, willing to give her up to the family that I felt she belonged to, the family that I thought loved her and wanted her home. Didn't she, herself, have two sets of grandparents that she loved? CJ was greatly concerned. She assured me she would call the parents and straighten it out.

Beth: *Then April rolled around and I realized I'd been with this family for a year now. So much had happened in the past year. I loved this family more than anything. Terena was the best big sister a little girl could ever have and I loved having mud fights and riding with the other kids. A few weeks before Easter my mom told me I was to go home for another visit. I was so happy., My family did want me! We went the night before I was to leave and stayed at Mom Nancy's mom's house.*

Nancy: Months later Beth was scheduled to return to North Carolina for an Easter visit. We shopped together for a cute Easter dress. Because she was so healthy I told her several weeks before, that she was going home for an Easter visit. We purchased her ticket and laughed together while we packed. Beth and I drove to my mother's to spend the night as she had an early flight. While we were having dinner, I got a phone call from Dr. Ken. He told me the family had called. The mother, nearly hysterical, had said that Beth's brother had just revealed that Beth had molested him over the Christmas visit. They did not want her to come for Easter and they did not want her home ever again. He told me I needed to tell her. I refused and assured him he needed to tell her.

Beth: *After we'd been there a short time Dr. Ken arrived. We all went for a walk and Dr. Ken relayed the terrible news. "Beth, your brother has told your parents of some things you did to him over Christmas and I'm sorry, Honey, but they don't think it's a good idea that you go and visit them right now." My eyes filled with tears as he spoke these words. What had I done? I'd fought with him over some toys. Was that it? My parents didn't want me back because I'd fought over some toys? Heartbroken, I put my bags back into the car to return back to our home in the Rockies. Why didn't they want me? What had I done that was so horrible they couldn't have me home for Easter? All of my joys and dreams of sharing a wonderful Easter with my family in North Carolina crumbled.*

Nancy: Dr Ken didn't feel that sharing that they didn't ever want her again was appropriate as he hoped the mother might change her mind. We stayed overnight at my mom's. I drove home the next day with a very sad little girl sitting beside me.

Beth: *The next day CJ came up to do a session and told me what my parents had told her. "Beth, your brother stated you molested him behind some sheds over*

Christmas break and pushed him down on some rocks." I lay there in disbelief. I hadn't touched my brother in any way like that. When CJ asked if I'd done it I shook my head violently and said, "No ma'am, I didn't do that! The only thing I did was fight with him over the toys and Daddy made me sit. I didn't do that to my brother, ma'am."

Mom Nancy pulled me into her arms and said, "Now Beth you know if you tell a lie it eats you up inside?" "Yes Mom," I replied, "but I'm not lying, I didn't hurt my brother." I didn't want to hurt my brother anymore. I just wanted to go home and grow up together with him. I sobbed as my mom held me. I just wanted everything to be normal. I wanted to be sharing a wonderful Easter with my family.

Nancy: The information that CJ shared was that Beth and her brother had been left alone in the church parking lot to ride their bikes. One of the parents was supposed to be checking on them periodically through a window. I wondered why exactly the child waited four months to reveal this. Why had Beth been doing so well when she came back from Christmas? If something had happened, Beth's behavior would have taken a serious downward spiral. There had been none.

Beth repeatedly denied hurting her brother. The more she cried in sadness at the loss of her visit the more I thought about her profoundly disturbed little brother. He had gotten to be an only child for a year now. Because they felt guilty about his abuse in their care he had been doted upon and clearly overindulged by the parents. He may very well have taken the opportunity to seek revenge on Beth who had abused him so much in the past. In my mind I saw him laughing while he skipped between Easter eggs on the hunt, while I saw Beth crying as she gathered ours. We would never know the truth of what had happened over that Christmas visit when the parents had betrayed Beth by putting her in harm's way.

The film that Dr. Ken had compiled from his therapy before I met Beth and from the follow up footage had been sold to HBO and was to be shown nationwide. We didn't have television but friends told us when it was scheduled to air. I worried about how people would talk about it in our small town, and what the fallout might be after it hit prime time.

Beth: *The HBO special, <u>Child of Rage,</u> aired that May of 1990. Since we didn't have TV, I never saw it when it aired but I knew it was showing around the country. A lot of people wrote letters. One that I received from Dr. Ken was of a twenty-three year old woman whose father had been abusing her for years as a child and after seeing my film she acquired the courage to leave her abusive father and get help. My story did that? I was happy I could have been helpful to someone but it still surprised me that I was able to help someone so much older than me.*

Nancy: The day after the filming we were in the grocery store. The lady at the checkout counter looked quizzically at Beth. I cringed when she said, "Honey you look like a little girl that was on TV last night." I was so worried she might say something to hurt Beth. She smiled and said, "Yes ma'am that was me."

The woman looked compassionately at my daughter and said "God Bless you sweetheart, I'll keep you in my prayers." I was worried that mothers would grab their children and run screaming at Beth's approach, not allowing their children to play with her. Or they might treat her like an alien, but I found our community compassionate , understanding and supportive of Beth. There was no fallout. Dr. Ken received bags full of mail and faxes from people who saw Beth's courage and had gained strength and understanding. It was healing for Beth to know that her story warmed people's hearts and helped them to understand and maybe to stop hurting their children. Little did I know that Beth had more pain to endure.

Beth's family decided her brother could not heal with Beth in their home and that she should not return to live with them. Because we knew that the success rate for birth siblings who both have Reactive Attachment Disorder in the same home was very poor I agreed with their decision. Her adoptive mother asked me what the chances were of having Beth remain with us. I assured her that I loved Beth very much and we'd be delighted to have her remain in our home. I needed talk to my husband and family about adoption and would call her back the next day. My family all agreed that Beth fit in our family and that we loved her very much and that it seemed to be in her best interest to stay with us and grow up. I called Beth's mother and gave her the news. She said she wanted to call back that evening and tell Beth their decision. I quickly called CJ to have her available to help Beth handle the heart break of being separated from her family permanently. I shared with CJ that I did not want to tell Beth she was going to live with us. I believed it was essential at Beth's age of seven and a half that she be given some control in the decision making process that was going to affect the rest of her life. My heart was so heavy all day knowing a bomb was about to be dropped on my little girl.

Beth: *CJ came up to our house one afternoon, I hadn't seen her in awhile and it was nice to see her. I had been doing so well lately that I hadn't had Holding Therapy and now I just had talk sessions once a week. CJ told me about the phone call I would be receiving from my parents that evening and then began to ask me question about my behavior. "Are you stronger than you were before?"*

"Yes ma'am!" I smiled.

"You've been doing really well lately, working on your life and doing your chores fast and snappy and right the first time, right? So what would you do if something happened and you got really upset, would you go hit Ted or yell at your mom or have to hurt yourself again?" she jokingly said.

I shook my head, "No ma'am, I would go and tell my mom and she would help me."

"Right, because you've worked really hard on your life. We're very proud of you, Beth." She smiled her loving smile and gave me a big hug.

My parents called a few minutes later and told me they had something to tell me that was going to be difficult. I felt a lump begin to build in my throat. "Honey, Daddy and I love you very much but we believe it would better for you and us if you did not come home anymore. After this Christmas we just feel that in order for your brother to heal we can't allow you to come home to us. We're sorry it had to come to this and we love you very much and this is the hardest thing we've ever had to do." I nodded with the tears freely flowing down my face, when I realized they couldn't see me nod, I answered, "Yes Mommy, yes Daddy, I understand." After I hung the phone up Mom Nancy pulled me into her arms and rocked me. "Let it out sweetheart, it's all right, let it out." I ached. Every part of me ached, but especially my heart. I was unwanted and unloved. I didn't care how much they said I love you I didn't feel loved. I had just lost my will to fight. Where would I go? What would I do now? Who would take an unwanted child? I looked into my mom's eyes and saw they were wet from tears and I knew she felt my pain. She always had, she'd always been there and held on strong even when I'd wanted to kill her. She was still there.

I spoke, "Where will I live?" I pictured myself moving into an institution and being left to grow up alone and unwanted. She then asked me, "Where do you want to live?" I wanted to live with my family in North Carolina but that wasn't possible. The only other place I wanted to live was here. I loved it here and I loved them. I wanted to ask her but I was so scared. What if she said no? What if they don't want me? I quietly asked barely above a whisper, "Can I live here?" She pulled me up into her arms and said, "Yes, I'd love for you to be my little girl and stay here forever!" In relief I sighed. I was wanted! I was loved and I would love living here. Tears continued to fall over my cheeks as I ached for my family but rejoiced with my new one. She brought over Dad Jerry and Terena and had me ask them if I could stay there and grow up. Dad smiled at me with his knowing smile and the crinkle in his eyes and ruffling my hair he stated, "Well of course you can kiddo." I smiled at him, "Thanks Dad." I was filled with relief, even Dad wanted me to stay. Tears began to spill from my eyes again so I quickly turned to Terena and asked her the same question, her reply was, "Of course you can baby sister!" I felt so loved by this family. This family knew me at my worst and loved me then and they knew me at my best and loved me then. I knew in my heart they'd never give up on me.

ReactiveAttachmentDisorderisaconditioninwhichindividualshave
difficultyforminglovinglastingrelationships.Theyoftenhaveane
arlycompletelackofabilitytobegenuinelyaffectionatewithothers
.Theytypicallyfailtodevelopaconscienceanddonotlearntotrust.T
heydonotallowpeopletobeincontrolofthembecauseofthistrustissu
e.Theycanbesurfacecompliantforweeksifnolovingrelationshipisi
nvolved.Withstrangerstheycanbeextremelycharmingandappearlovi
ng.Uneducatedadultsmisinterpretthisasthechildtrustingorcarin
gforthem.Iftheycannottrustandlovetheirownfamilythatlovesthem
,thentheywillnottrustandloveacasualacquaintance!!Theydonotth
inkandfeellikeanormalperson.SomefamouspeoplewithRADwhodidnot
gethelpintime:Hitler,SadamHussein,EdgarAllenPoe,JeffreyDahme
r,TedBundy.ReactiveAttachmentDisorderisaconditioninwhichindi
vidualshavedifficultyforminglovinglastingrelationships.Theyo
ftenhaveanearlycompletelackofabilitytobegenuinelyaffectionat
ewithothers.Theytypicallyfailtodevelopaconscienceanddonotlea
rntotrust.Theydonotallowpeopletobeincontrolofthembecauseofth
istrustissue.Theycanbesurfacecompliantforweeksifnolovingrela
tionshipisinvolved.Withstrangerstheycanbeextremelycharmingan
dappearloving.Uneducatedadultsmisinterpretthisasthechildtrus
tingorcaringforthem.Iftheycannottrustandlovetheirownfamilyth
atlovesthem,thentheywillnottrustandloveacasualacquaintance!!
Theydonotthinkandfeellikeanormalperson.SomefamouspeoplewithR
ADwhodidnotgethelpintime:Hitler,SadamHussein,EdgarAllenPoe,J
effreyDahmer,TedBundy.ReactiveAttachmentDisorderisacondition
inwhichindividualshavedifficultyforminglovinglastingrelation
ships.Theyoftenhaveanearlycompletelackofabilitytobegenuinely
affectionatewithothers.Theytypicallyfailtodevelopaconscience
anddonotlearntotrust.Theydonotallowpeopletobeincontrolofthem
becauseofthistrustissue.Theycanbesurfacecompliantforweeksifn
olovingrelationshipisinvolved.Withstrangerstheycanbeextremel
ycharmingandappearloving.Uneducatedadultsmisinterpretthisast
hechildtrustingorcaringforthem.Iftheycannottrustandlovetheir
ownfamilythatlovesthem,thentheywillnottrustandloveacasualacq
uaintance!!Theydonotthinkandfeellikeanormalperson.Somefamous
peoplewithRADwhodidnotgethelpintime:Hitler,SadamHussein,Edga
rAllenPoe,JeffreyDahmer,TedBundy>ReactiveAttachmentDisorderi
saconditioninwhichindividualshavedifficultyforminglovinglast
ingrelationships.Theyoftenhaveanearlycompletelackofabilityto
begenuinelyaffectionatewithothers.Theytypicallyfailtodevelop
aconscienceanddonotlearntotrust.Theydonotallowpeopletobeinco
ntrolofthembecauseofthistrustissue.Theycanbesurfacecompliant
forweeksifnolovingrelationshipisinvolved.Withstrangerstheyca
nbeextremelycharmingandappearloving.Uneducatedadultsmisinter
pretthisasthechildtrustingorcaringforthem.Iftheycannottrusta
ndlovetheirownfamilythatlovesthem,thentheywillnottrustandlov
eacasualacquaintance!!Theydonotthinkandfeellikeanormalperson
.SomefamouspeoplewithRADwhodidnotgethelpintime:Hitler,SadamH
ussein,EdgarAllenPoe,JeffreyDahmer,TedBundy.

Chapter 13
Doctor Marvel

Our home was full of laughter and joy the majority of the time as Beth, Gabriel and Will were going to stay with us permanently. Everyone felt wanted and settled. After completing their schoolwork, entering their various feelings in their journal and finishing about thirty minutes of family chores, playtime often followed. We had campfires in the woods where we cooked dinner and marshmallows and sang old Girl Scout songs. Together, the children and I would hike the trail to our private cave while pretending we were Native Americans tracking game. Silently we would sneak across the mountain pantomiming and gesturing to each other. Finding alternative ways of communicating was a great way to preserve the stillness of the woods and keep from scaring off the wildlife so we could see it

Pandemonium was still a common occurrence within the walls of our house as the children overcame their inner demons, but for the most part, the family was peaceful and happy. Each child was in a different stage of healing, so when CJ dropped another manila envelope into my hand, I eagerly tore at the seal to see what my next 'mission' was.

Pulling the whole pile of papers from the file caused the photo of a Korean boy to float to the floor. Theodore's extremely cute nine year old smile charmed me and as I flipped through the rest of the pages in the file, I imagined seeing his little form already a part of my family. I wasn't surprised when I found out a modeling scout had seen him in the grocery store and had hounded his mother for a contract. With reservations she had agreed only because his therapy costs were increasing so dramatically that the family had begun to feel its financial burden. Teddy was an instant hit as he charmed the camera with his warm complexion, dimples and engaging smile, but little did the viewing public know of the rage filled child behind the facade.

As a three year old Ted had been found in Korea in a dank alley, eating garbage. Frostbite had nearly claimed the tips of his ears and the frozen fingers he used to pull scraps of cabbage and meat from the cans. He had nearly succumbed to the cold before the police found him. They searched for weeks to locate his family, not knowing whether he was abandoned or lost. They were unsuccessful, so little Ted was sent to a Korean orphanage. He had become one of the many 'children of the ashes' because in the society of third world poverty, that's all they considered orphaned children were worth.

His distended belly was framed by emaciated ribs and hip bones. Parasites crawled from his feces. Ted's fingers and toes were saved from amputation, as were his ears, but their slight discoloration would forever remind him of the bitter Korean winter. Green mucous was coughed up from his lungs as pneumonia had infiltrated his tiny weak body. Thinking this little boy was destined for the morgue anyway, the orphanage staff passed his frail body around for sex. They sold his body to anyone willing to give them money. Even after he had physically healed from living on the streets, his body was used as a sex tool by the adults of the facility.

When Laura and Jeff had seen his little picture at the adoption agency, they booked a flight right away to go see him in Asia. They had five biological children who were nearly all grown and gone off to college or careers. Tess, who was thirteen, was the last one still at home. Knowing they were capable, loving parents and dreading the empty quietness of their large house, they turned to adoption. Three years previously, they had successfully adopted Angelica from Korea and were ecstatic at her gentle, loving manner, so they were eager to find her a brother. Adoption, so far, had worked well for them.

Teddy was four when he stepped off the plane at Logan Airport in Boston, Massachusetts holding the hand of his new mommy. Jeff was excitedly waiting with Tess, and three year old Angelica at the gate to greet them. Teddy was a wild child right from the start, but they reasoned it was due to the life changing events he now had to deal with: a new country, a new language, a new family and new social customs.

Within a year, his behavior had worsened. He was beating up his younger sister and had been called home numerous times from kindergarten for fighting and bullying the other kids so Laura had turned to her local therapist for help. The therapist told the desperate parents that Ted was going through a normal developmental or adjustment phase and to start using a star chart to point out the good behavior. In time he would surely grow out of his aggression. Six months later, after weekly therapy visits, his behavior was worse. This time the therapist stated that Laura and Jeff were the reason because they were doing the star chart improperly and needed to be shown again how to do it. When the next six months went by without any improvement with weekly visits and the chart system, Laura began to search for a new therapist. She had raised five children and had never seen this 'developmental phase', so she began to suspect other things were going on that behavior modification techniques were not able to reach.

While between therapists, Ted began masturbating at the dinner table, in church or while in the presence of other family members. Thinking he didn't know any better, Jeff tried talking to Ted about his inappropriate behavior but found that by doing so, it escalated the problem. Laura took him in to the doctor to be sure there wasn't a physical problem, but they found no allergies or problems. The parents tried sending him to time-out. They grounded him. They tried spanking him when he fondled himself at inappropriate times. They tried motivating him with candy and toys for behaving properly. Their efforts were to no avail as the problem persisted.

As I read this family's struggle with Ted's sexual acting out a red flag went up my mind. I knew from all the children I had worked with, that when a child fondles himself excessively with no medical cause, he has often been a victim of sexual abuse and as Ted's file confirmed that, I also knew that the other children in his home were likely to be his sexual targets. I worried for their other little adopted child. Was she a victim now too?

For three more years the family tried different therapists. Each time, Ted would be led into a separate room without Laura or Jeff where he would proceed to make up lavish tales. At the end of each session, the therapist would call in the parent and explain how Ted was a sweet boy that was misunderstood. He just needed to be loved more. Afterwards on the way home, Ted would sneer at his mom, "Do you know I told that guy that you only feed me once a day and that you make me work all day. I told him you love Tess and Angelica more than me and that you don't let me do fun stuff because you don't love me." Smiling confidently he would finish with, "He believed everything I told him. He's so stupid! Why do you keep making me waste my time with these dumb people?" Typically, he spit hatred at his mom anytime they were alone, but while in the presence of others he poured on the charm and sweetness. His diagnosis: Attachment Disorder.

Luckily, she found our program through a workshop she attended for parenting tough kids and had called right away. I accepted the case, preparing for Ted to join us. Three weeks later, Jeff, Laura and Teddy were on their way to our home to start two weeks of intensive therapy with CJ and myself.

The first day of therapy was focused on building trust and gaining compliance. CJ cradled the tiny nine year old in her arms as he lay on her lap. Laura sat across from CJ holding Ted's hand while Jeff sat at Laura's side to comfort and support her. Ted tried his usual tactic of lying and conniving his way through the session, but with his parents sitting right there, his lies were directly confronted. He was busted! His manipulation tactics, which had worked on so many other therapists, weren't working. It made Ted mad!

The first session was long as Ted was stubborn and tenacious, but these same qualities were those that I knew had kept him alive in Korea and would help him in his healing. It ended when he allowed his mom to kiss his cheek and hug him without flinching away in horror and disgust. He was learning to trust that we wouldn't hurt him, nor would we accept lies and manipulation as the past therapists had. He was going to have to work hard in therapy if he was to get over his issues of abandonment and sexual abuse to live a happy and fulfilled life.

That night, while Ted slept in our 'new kid' room, Laura, Jeff and I sat around the living room table talking. I learned how successful their biological children were and how happy they were that they had decided to adopt. Their younger daughter was a happy and loving child while giving back to the family and Tess was willing, loving and helpful. Laughing and loving was an integral part of the family. They played well together and tried hard in school. Ted, on the other hand didn't show even slight interest in being part of the family. He acted as if schoolwork was beneath him. Interacting with the other kids quickly became a battle. He drained Laura of all her energy with frequent power struggles. She was constantly correcting him and refereeing when he was around the others. He started fights and getting him to help around the house was more hassle than it was worth so she had stopped asking him even to make his bed. He would howl and scream for three to four hours anytime she asked him to do things. At one point it got so bad the neighbors knocked on the door to ask what was happening. As soon as Ted heard a new voice in the house, his tone quickly changed from screams of rage to wail of sadness. Pitiful moans escaped his lips while he heard his mother being told to be nicer to him and love him more.

Aside from his academy award winning performances that would suck people in, what really hurt the most was that when they'd be out he'd be helpful and kind to people he didn't even know while refusing to do anything, even hold hands with his mom. Everyone would tell her how lucky she was to have such a good boy, while she was enduring the hateful looks he threw at her and his blatant defiance when no one was looking. Smiling sweetly, he would open doors for others while slamming it shut for his mother and siblings. He even happily played with the cousins so when Laura mentioned any of his odd behaviors to her relatives, they started thinking the problem was with her. She must just be playing favorites or expecting too much. Her own mother, who had supported and watched her raise all the others, even believed the problems were because of Laura. She was heart broken to know her own family didn't believe her. Her community criticized her when she tried disciplining him and her confidence was dwindling down to zero.

I listened as this woman sat sobbing at my table. I knew where she was coming from and I knew how hard this was for her. Her huge heart and loving ways had brought this little needy boy into her life and now he was destroying her. But, I could support her, help her and give her hope that her son, whom she loved so much, would someday learn to love her back.

As we were preparing to turn in for the night, she grabbed my arm and started shedding fresh tears. "I want you to help my son. I don't care what it takes, if we have to sell our home and live in a small apartment to afford his treatment we'll do it. Just please help my son!" She had given nearly all of herself to this child and as she stood in front of me shaking, I grabbed her in a hug of support before responding. "He can learn to open his heart to love. It's a hard, long road, but you love him enough for both of you right now. When you get home, fill up your other two and trust that God will heal your son!" That night, I was glad that Jeff was there to comfort Laura as she grieved.

The more therapy Ted had, the more he learned to trust, and the more he was willing to share about his heinous activities back home. We learned that he used to carry a special shoelace in his pocket that he would use to strangle Angelica. Nobody would question why he carried it as little boys often have strings and things in their pants. At night he would sneak into the room where Angelica and Tess slept to rape his younger sister, and whisper to her that if she told he would kill her and mommy. This explained the nightmares Tess often had of someone being in the room with them. When she found out about the trauma Angelica endured while she slept only a few feet away, Tess was overwhelmed with guilt and shame. She was heartbroken she had not protected her little sister. More tears flowed.

Five days into the intensive, as we all sat eating the lunch that Terena had made she screamed in pain as her hand hit the red-hot burner. We rushed over to help. One person ran to the sink to turn on the cold water while another ran over to the Aloe Vera plant to cut off a chunk. We hugged Terena and made a big deal out of the blister forming on her hand.

The next week, I saw that Ted had a similar burn on his hand and asked him about it. "I burned it on the stove. When Terena burned her hand, she got lots of attention, but when I turned the stove on and burned my hand nobody paid any attention to me!" I explained how we need to know that he was injured in order to help him. His response of, "Oh" was neither surprised nor confused. I asked him if it hurt. A look of contemplation came over his face. "No. It didn't hurt when I did it and it doesn't hurt now." I realized then that he had no feeling in his body. The abuse of his infancy had been so traumatic that he had tuned out his body in order to survive the pain he had endured. He didn't know when he was hungry nor hurt. I was sad that he didn't know it was supposed to hurt when he cut himself or tickle when touched with a feather. He literally had no sense of feeling.

Little Ted had poured much of his soul out to us during the therapy, but the heaviest burden was yet to come. With only three more days left of his intensive daily therapy sessions, he finally told how he had tried to drown his sibling. He explained how he had held his younger sister under the water in their pool several times and the last time his mom had to jump in to pry his hands off the little girl. She was gasping for air as Ted watched in disgust from the side. He wasn't allowed in the pool anymore after that.

He said he didn't kill her only because he needed her alive to do 'sex stuff' and if she were dead, someone would find out. The child never told what was going on because Ted threatened to kill her or mommy if she did.

He told us that nightly he visited the younger sister and at least six neighbor houses while everyone slept. After Jeff and Laura read the evening story to the children they would get down on their knees for prayer before tucking each child in for bed. A few hours later Laura would peak her head into each room to confirm that all was well and quiet before heading off to bed herself. Ted would lie awake awaiting the last loving check, pretending to be asleep, before starting the countdown. Thirty to forty-five minutes later he knew he could sneak from his room in the cover of darkness.

The children would be startled awake by his icy fingers clasped to their mouth or as the shoelace was meticulously wound around their neck. As they gasped for air, he would mount them and physically show them his power and dominance by penetrating any orifice his penis could find. Their cries were muffled by a pillow.

When one was amply convinced of his dominance he would remove himself and whisper into each terrified ear, "If you tell, I will kill your mommy first and then come for you!" On to the next victim he would go, trailing the length of cotton in his hand.

When his helpless sister was thoroughly worked over, he began hunting his rural neighborhood for victims. Climbing up their back steps, he would find back doors left unlocked. There were many young children in the neighborhood and as the community was small, they were all playmates. Ted knew exactly where to go to find his next victim.

I wondered why none of the victims had bruises or physical signs of being choked. I asked Laura and Jeff if they had ever seen any evidence. Numbly they shook their heads, no. I was amazed this little kid could do so much damage! Where were all the parents?!

As he told us of his deeds his chest puffed out and his eyes narrowed in triumph. The corners of his mouth turned slightly upward as if an evil grin was preparing to spread across his face. He had conquered at least six neighbor children and his arrogant manner told us he was not remorseful at all.

His nightly activities were darker than any moonless night could be. The clock in his room often read three or four in the morning before he slid back between his sheets. Some nights he ran home so that he could sneak back into the house before his parents alarm went off; those nights he didn't sleep at all. He averaged 3 to 4 hours of sleep.

Tip toeing into his room, Laura would gently kiss his cheek to wake him for the day. "Good morning, Sweetie. Did you sleep well?" Yawning and stretching he would smile brightly before answering, "Yes, mommy. I had a good night."

Ted looked over at his mom as a glimpse of victory flashed across his face. "You didn't know, did you Mommy?" She didn't answer him, but instead asked to use the bathroom. The truth and emotions were too much for her to bear and as soon as she stepped from the therapy room I heard her collapse onto the floor. Beyond overwhelmed she sobbed for the third time that day.

CJ and Jeff continued to help Ted cope with telling the truth as I slipped out into the hallway. She couldn't meet my gaze as she reflected on the horrors that had just be revealed. I sat down next to her and rubbed her trembling back.

"He has seen five therapists since I brought him home from Korea. Why didn't any of them find any of this out?" The tears stopped flowing as if someone had run the well dry and I saw anger beginning to build. "They talked to him or they played with him. They did games and sand tray therapy. We spent thousands of dollars and hundreds of hours on therapy that allowed this... this..." She paused and began to weep again. Refusing the tissue I offered she whispered, "I allowed it to happen. This is my fault. How am I supposed to go home and tell all my neighbors that my son, little sweet Teddy, raped and tried to kill their children?" Shame and guilt crept into Laura's voice as she spoke. "How can I tell them? How can I face them? All those beautiful, innocent children!" Sobs wracked her slight frame again.

Ted was in the therapy room giving the names of his victims with no expression whatsoever on his face. He was having no reaction to telling what he had done. His mom, who wanted only to share her home and love with her children, was carrying the full burden of his misdeeds. She was cracking under the pressure.

"I knew within the first year that something was different with Ted." She sniffed and wiped the caked salt from her thick lashes that lined her swollen eyelids. "I took him to all the specialists and did all the things they told me to do. It wasn't easy and he fought me tooth and nail every step of the way. I had no idea. I was so naive. I am so stupid! I trusted these people, who were nice enough, to help my son and all they did was give him more time to hurt more people! Why couldn't they be honest with me? Why didn't they just say they couldn't help him or that they thought there was more going on than Ted was telling?" She sat up and allowed the grief to escape from her soul. Hugging her knees to her chest, she began to rock herself and stare off into space. Sadness weighed heavily on her spirit, and occasionally another tear would slip from her cheek to fall silently.

Jeff stepped from the other room and asked that I join CJ. As I stood up and went to join CJ, I could see his loving embrace envelope Laura as he too began to cry. The door clicked shut behind me as I stepped back into the confession hall with Teddy, a serial rapist and attempted murderer at age nine.

He would definitely not be going back home with his parents for a long time and would definitely need a therapeutic environment. I began thinking of the preparations we'd have to make. He was already in the new kid room. I had no children younger than him, but the animals would be potential targets for sure. Sneakers, the dog had long been spayed so we wouldn't have any baby companion animals, but the goats were due to kid any day. He would have to be closely monitored anytime he was outside as hurting another being would be devastating to not only the creature, but also to Teddy's long term healing. I would be sure that the alarm on his door had fresh batteries and was placed well above his reach. He wasn't the sickest child I had ever had, but certainly was the sneakiest and the most sexually active.

Laura and Jeff searched for a hotel room, as staying in our home while Teddy was there, was becoming too traumatic for them. With two evenings left and only two therapy sessions to go, they were more than ready to go home. After Ted's morning therapy, I would take him and begin teaching him the rules of the house. He was learning to strong sit while I prepared the meals. He resisted this often, not because he didn't like it but because he despised giving up control to someone else. I knew it was a task he needed to practice because it was important.

Researchers were beginning to find amazing information about the brains of children who'd suffered abuse. The temporal lobes of the brain, which are responsible for memory, were showing big black holes where there was no neural activity. The brain stem in control of fight or flight responses was hyper aroused. These children were using the most primitive parts of their brain the most! That's why we were seeing so much defiance and arguing. It was the overdeveloped fight or flight part of the brain! These children were in a constant state of vigilance. Studies had shown that when the brain was functioning from the brain stem, the limbic system, (the emotion and love department) wasn't working right. Their brains would often get "stuck" in one part of the mind. The strong sitting helped the child to develop the part of the brain that shifted gears. It was an exercise to help their brain get unstuck so they could develop the logical or the loving part of the their mind. If anybody needed their brain to shift gears, it was Ted! Helping him to develop the ability to strong sit for five minutes became my mission.

When he had worked up to a whole minute of strong sitting correctly, we celebrated by going for a walk in the woods. Gabriel still hadn't been able to handle public school, so he was the only other child I had home that fall afternoon. As I held his hand on the left, I held Ted's hand in my right; Sneakers and Terena's German Shepherd trotted happily along in front of us.

The dry bronze, oranges and greens of the fall foliage were in sharp contrast to the deep blue sky with only two white puffy clouds in the distance. The black and white magpies played tag in the cooling air above our heads as the mountain chickadees chirped their greetings. Hummingbirds raced past whirring on a quest for nectar. The fields were full of cows grazing as their adolescent calves raced up and down the fence with their thin tails held high in the air and their young legs carrying them confidently about.

As we walked and soaked it all in, I asked Gabriel what he wanted to be when he grew up. Walking five or six steps, he thoughtfully contemplated his options. "I think I want to be a detective like the cop that came from Wyoming to talk to me last year. I would be good at getting clues and finding answers anyways, I wanna wear the cool suit and hat!" He smiled up at me, something many of my kids do to see if I approved. He had internalized me so well up to this point that he was able to read my expression and moods with a quick glance and this was no exception. The smile from my eyes told him his decision was acceptable and he returned to kicking the pebble on the trail in front of him.

"Ted, what would you like to be when you grow up?" Thinking he, too, would want to be a police officer or fireman, I was startled by his response. Without much thought or hesitation he grinned and stated, "I want to be a rapist!" I sadly looked down at the beautiful child on my right. He didn't know that being a rapist wasn't a profession, and I didn't dare respond to his decision. I decided right then that we didn't need anymore rapists in the world and that I'd do my best to change his mind. Luckily the school bus came roaring past with my other three children pressed to the windows waving frantically. I knew after the bus turned around a half mile up the road, that my home would be full of excited children with papers and homework. The subject of future professions was dropped as we tried to race the bus home.

Terena, Will and Beth rushed from the bus. As I listened to their tales of school activities, we all sat around the table and ate celery with peanut butter for a snack. Will, as was becoming typical, was in a sullen and withdrawn mood so he asked for his chore immediately in order to avoid the family situation. Hugging him, I assigned him to laundry folding in the living room where he could still participate if he wanted. He had been doing fairly well, so we had cut back his therapy sessions to twice a month, but in light of his recent sullen attitude, I decided to increase to weekly meetings with CJ. Will had been having a hard time acting responsible so I hired Beth, for a quarter a day to make his lunch and give it to him on the bus. I knew that if I made it for him, he would reject it just as he had been doing with my love lately. She was seven years younger than he was and yet, she was much more responsible.

Ted's therapy the next day focused on the feelings and understanding of Jeff and Laura's leaving without him. Ted wailed when he heard he wouldn't be going with them and I felt a tug at my heart for the sadness and abandonment he must be feeling. They each hugged him and kissed him and cried on him as he screamed and begged, "Please Mommy take me home! I'll be good! I promise I'll be good! Don't leave me here!" I held onto his hand as he tugged toward them while they got in their car. Wrenching and pulling, he stretched his free arm out to them and begged. Laura had to avert her eyes in order to keep the guilt from flooding from her soul as the tears were now doing. The rental car pulled out of our driveway and started its three-hour drive to the airport.

Sorrowfully, I watched as Ted cried out one more time. This poor child's heart was breaking because he couldn't go home and I was the one holding him back, but just as I was getting ready to apologize to him for his parents leaving, he quickly straightened his posture, narrowed his eyes and stomped his foot. "Fine. Leave you stupid people. I hate you anyway!" And with that, he ripped his arm from my hand and stood up to me. "I hope that my screaming will give her nightmares for leaving me here. She deserves it!"

I had been sucked in again. This little boy was such a master at conning and that he had convinced three adults that he was truly devastated by his parents departure when really, he was angry that he didn't get his way. It was clear he didn't love them. He couldn't love them. He was so caught up in himself that focusing on anything but him was unnatural, but understandable. He had kept himself alive as a toddler on the streets when he was betrayed by those who were supposed to love him.

It took a full week of gradually building on time before Ted could strong sit for five minutes. When he had succeeded, I made pizza (his favorite). We celebrated. The following day, after breakfast and entering his feelings in his feeling book, I started him on his first family chore. The bathroom was a safe place where I could monitor his activities and be sure all the animals were safe. I had long ago built cabinets around the laundry chute in order to keep kids from crawling through it, so I no longer worried about that potential hazard. I directed him to scrub the sink.

I gave him the cleaning tools, showed him how to use each and told him I'd be back to check on him in fifteen minutes. I had thought his mom was exaggerating when she said he would throw three and four hour long fits in order to get out of doing stuff, so when I heard him start up, I looked at the clock; nine- thirty. I started Gabriel on his home school assignments and fifteen minutes later, I opened the door to find Ted sitting against the wall with the most pitiful face. "I can't do it! It's too hard." He wailed. Giving him a hug and a word of encouragement, I told him I'd be back to check on him.

Loud wailing and howling filled my home. Complaints of inadequacy and weakness reverberated from the walls. Again, when I checked on him thirty minutes later, he was still sitting against the wall. "I really can't do it! I can't." I grabbed him up in a big hug before telling him, "That's okay if you'd rather sit and fuss first. The sink will always be here and your lunch will be ready when you're finished. Take your time and let go of whatever fussing you need to." I closed the door and listened as he wailed further. My heart was pulling for him and I was really having to resist the urge to run to him, scoop him up into my arms and rock his troubles away. I wanted to tell him he didn't have to do the bathroom sink. It wasn't very dirty anyway. I wanted to tell him it would all be okay, but I knew, that this was a test. If I gave in, and allowed his performance to manipulate me, he would not be able to trust me. I bit my lip, swallowed the lump in my throat and went downstairs.

Knowing what she would tell me, I called CJ anyway. I wanted to reach out to this poor, poor little child. This broken kid that had so much hardship already was up there upset by himself. What difference did it make if I cleaned the sink or he did?

She told me again, for the hundredth time that his early upbringing created a child who could not trust. Without the trust he had not formed a conscience thus he was able to kill and maim without feeling remorse. Without the foundation of trust, he could never truly open up the shell of isolation he had been forced to create in order to survive. Without breaking down that wall he could never learn to let love in.

"But CJ, why would going to him now break that trust? Wouldn't he see that I care for him and want to ease his pain?" I asked. I could visualize her resting her forehead on her palm as she shook her head in disbelief that after all these years, I still didn't really understand.

She explained how children without a conscience don't think or feel like healthy individuals. If they did, they wouldn't be able to do the things they do. Slowly, she laid it out as if I were a child. "Sadness is a feeling of weakness to them. These children have learned early on to believe that weakness means death. If they are weak, then they can't survive the hardships life is going to throw at them. The only feeling of strength they have, which is really a cover up feeling, is anger." She asked if I was following along so far before continuing. "The sadness you think you see and hear is only Ted trying to get you to give in. If you give in, then not only does he not have to scrub the sink, but he also sees himself as more powerful than you. Do you trust people who you see as weak? Would you trust Pee Wee Herman with your life or would you rather trust Arnold Schwarzenegger?" I was starting to see her point. I had to be Arnold and in order to do that, I had to show him I was worthy of trust and not easily manipulated by fussing and whining. Thanking CJ, I hung up the phone feeling more confident.

I walked back upstairs and opened the bathroom door. He still hadn't moved and continued insisting that scrubbing the sink was too difficult. I hugged him, gave him a warm encouraging smile and told him that if he truly was sad, we would deal with it after the sink was finished. Still embracing him, I shared with him that I had all day and was willing to play music if he'd rather howl to something with rhythm. Scowling, he furrowed his brow, stopped the noise and sent a poisoned hate look aimed right at my soul. I was convinced that anger was overflowing from his heart and that there was little room for any sadness.

At noon, Gabriel and I started making homemade bread. The dough was rising when I checked on Ted at half past the hour and the pleads of inability continued to flood from the bathroom as I hugged him and closed the door. By one o'clock, the smell of fresh baking filled the air and I hoped the scent would encourage him to finally pick up the scrub brush, but when I opened the door to check on him, I found that he still hadn't moved from the floor. Again, I hugged him and assured him that I'd save some bread for him when he was through. He spat on me when I left and closed the door and as I wiped the slime from my arm, I heard him mumble 'I hate you, you fucky face!"

When one-thirty rolled around, I ascended the stairway and stood outside the bathroom door. Pressing my ear against the wood, I strained to hear. Silence. To my amazement, when I opened the door, Teddy was strong sitting proudly. He had finally scrubbed the sink clean and was ready for me to check to make sure he did it correctly. I grabbed him up into a hug and told him the sink was the cleanest it had been all day. I checked his biceps and with a surprised look announced, "Oh my gosh! Look at how strong you are now! Your muscles are getting bigger since you got strong enough to do your chore! That's so awesome!" Laughing, we both went downstairs to eat. He had tested me. I had stood strong. We had both won.

The following day, after breakfast and the feeling book entry, I again handed Ted the cleaning supplies and directed him to clean the sink. Three hours and thirty minutes later, the howling had stopped and his chore was finished. Each day, as I gave him the same chore, the fussing and fits decreased in length. Within three weeks, I could ask him to do a simple task without much balking.

Ted's day could be decided from the manner in which he made his bed. If it was made nicely, I knew he would have a good day. When the sheet was still bunched and crooked while the comforter was smoothed over it to hide the mess, the day would be full of sneaky behaviors. The trap door of defiance was tripped when I awoke him and came back ten minutes later to find his sheets still in a wad and his comforter on the floor. I appreciated the heads up as it gave me time to prepare special activities for good days, be on extra guard for when he was sly, or cancel all my appointments to stay home while he raged.

On one of his good days, I asked him as he finished vacuuming the living room, "On a scale of one to ten, one being mad a tiny bit and ten being mad enough to kill, how mad are you right now?" Wrapping up the cord neatly, he stopped long enough to answer. "I'm a ten." Looking at him, I saw that his face was soft. He didn't have any sign of a killer, yet the rage he held inside was strong enough to seek death. I learned a valuable lesson that day-what you see may definitely NOT be what you get when looking at a child with Attachment Disorder. I thanked him for telling me the truth, gave him a hug and immediately called CJ to set up a therapy session.

Teddy had a urine problem that was more than just bedwetting. Every morning I would open his door to the stench of ammonia, and when asked if he had wet in the night, he boldly and consistently denied doing so. My nose told me otherwise. Morning after morning I was overwhelmed with the smell and as fall was nearing, the closed windows were making the aroma much more rank. Dealing with it on a daily basis, I wanted to have a better understanding.

One morning after having confirmed that Teddy had soaked the bed yet again, I asked him about it. "Just help me understand this. Does it happen at night when you're starting to fall asleep and you relax? Does it just leak out then or is it more in the morning when you're bladder is full?" His lips pouted as he shook his head with his eyes darting about. "No. I just stand up in the middle of the night and pee and then lay back down." I just dumbfoundedly replied "Oh". I didn't learn the truth about the reasons for his urination until a few weeks later.

Ted had confessed in therapy that he urinated in his bed because he knew I would have to smell it, so I decided to hire one of the more healthy children to do the sniff test for me. Will had an excellent nose and he jumped at the chance to make some extra cash. He was hired to do morning sniff patrol for twenty-five cents. He got a fifty-cent bonus for every room he found saturated in urine. Flabbergasted, Ted exclaimed, "You mean if I pee in my room he gets a bonus?" Not looking through those lenses before now, I replied, "Yeah...I guess so." In his typically defiant manner Ted shot back, "Well then I'm not going to pee anymore!" Smiling to myself I told him that sounded like a good idea. He graduated to moving from the new kid room to upstairs when he stayed true to his word for a whole month. Good thing, as Gabriel still needed the easily cleanable surfaces of the downstairs room as his elimination issues were still surfacing occasionally.

The leaves were starting to turn orange and yellow as fall closed in around our home. The chilly nights warranted a fire in the wood stove, so s-mores were an occasional treat we all savored. The children who had made good decisions throughout the week were allowed to roast their own marshmallow while those that hadn't, but were making good decisions for the day prepared their graham crackers and chocolate slab awaiting for me to toast their mallow. Gooey fingers were licked clean and the evening story or movie followed for those who had earned the privilege, the rest headed off to their rooms for the night.

Finding a baby-sitter was an impossible task, as they had to be highly trained and strong spirited to handle my difficult crew. Jerry and I hadn't been out together, alone, since our Grand Canyon adventure so when Terena was in eighth grade, I started having her watch the children when I had errands or appointments to run. The healthy children could decide whether to stay home with her of come out with me.

She was a great help and I realized how rare it was for someone of her age to be responsible and mature enough to handle such a task. She had been helping me with the children for over five years and had often attended training seminars with me. Her patient, loving, yet strong, character allowed her to be an authority figure to the children. They had learned to trust and respect her. She knew which child had which privilege and she knew the family rules. I knew I could trust her one hundred percent.

After returning from a movie, Jerry and I found Terena awake and waiting for us. I was worried at first, especially when I saw red all over the dining room tablecloth, but when I saw her amused expression, I relaxed. That night, she had prepared spaghetti and as one of the children had thrown a fit, dinner had gotten cold. The tenseness of the house was obvious, so Ted, being the charmer, took it upon himself to entertain them all. He pretended to fall asleep and landed head first right in his plate. Unsure as to whether he had injured himself or not, Terena had tentatively waited for him to raise his head and as he did so, noodles and sauce were plastered onto every conceivable crack and crevice. The table was dead silent until he smiled his cherub like grin and then laughter and giggles filled the room. He had succeeded in lightening the mood and in the process sprayed red sauce from one end of the tablecloth to the other when he shook the pasta off like a dog!

Our first snow landed before Halloween. October was always a hard month, especially for Gabriel, so the fresh powder helped cleanse the mood and change the atmosphere briefly. It was only a few inches, but the novelty of it intrigued all the children. The three of us built a snowman while the other three were in school.

Therapy and high structure was helping Teddy to be compliant enough to begin home schooling and as a tutor came twice a week, he was beginning to learn to treat all adults with respect. He was a smart kid but was far behind in his academics, as he had never really applied himself before. As a ten year old, his math skills were two years behind while reading was at a second grade level. He had a lot of catching up to do and as winter was fast approaching, he would have many hours stuck indoors to do it.

Terena had started noticing that some of her panties were missing. It started out with just one pair, which was hardly noticeable, but after a few months, she had only two pairs left. Frustrated, she began a search. Beth was sharing her room, so we started searching first within the tight confines of their quarters. None were found. Each of the boys' rooms were searched with no success. Thinking the dryer had eaten them for dessert after its normal helping of socks, I went out and simply purchased more. For the time being the problem was solved.

As I did most nights, I went into Ted's room to say goodnight and turning on his alarm. As I bent down to kiss his forehead a glint of metal from under his pillow caught my eye. Lifting the pillow, I found the same knife Gabriel had used to slice the mirror. I was shocked at the sight and I fumbled to grab a hold of it. "Ted, what is this doing here?" I stammered, holding its handle in my hand as the light reflected from its massive steel blade. His weak response of "I don't know" didn't convince me. "Ted, I want you to go to your think spot. Strong sit there and when you're ready to tell me the truth about what's going on I want you to say ready. Got it?" "Got it," he said as he trudged upstairs and sat in his spot.

Pacing in the other room, still holding the weapon, my mind raced. We used this knife to carve the holiday turkey, but twice now it had been stolen. A few minutes later I heard Ted call out, "ready!" Setting the large knife down next to the couch, I pulled him up into my lap. "So what happened?" I asked. In a weak voice he told me that he had stolen it when putting his supper dishes in the sink. He had slipped it under his shirt and then asked to use the bathroom. He had hid it under his pillow two days ago and was planning to kill Jerry and me while we slept.

I thanked him for the truth, gave him a hug and told him to hop off to bed. As he skipped down the stairs, I again thanked God for keeping the knife from drawing blood. We would deal with it further in his next therapy session. Knowing I couldn't hide all the knives because it would give him the message I was afraid of him, I decided to take an evening inventory of the knife drawer. I knew there were more weapons in any home than one could hide. Rocks, pencils, shovels, hammers, chairs etc. had all been used as weapons. I couldn't hide everything!

A few weeks later, as Terena, Will and Beth prepared for school, I turned the alarms off and let everyone else out for the day. I noticed Ted was walking in an unusual manner to the bathroom, but assuming it was morning cramps or a full bladder, I thought nothing more about it and went upstairs to start breakfast for everyone.

With eggs sizzling on the skillet, I poured out milk and added freshly sliced melon to the plates. Gabriel, Will, Beth and Ted were strong sitting already. Calling them all to the table, I noticed Ted gingerly walking to his spot. Even if he had been out riding the horses the previous day, the typical after effects would be a bow-legged walk, yet he hadn't been out riding and his movement was much more exaggerated.

I watched, analyzing as he pulled out his chair and very carefully sat down. While Terena and I handed out each breakfast plate, I asked if he was all right. "Last night I couldn't sleep, so I was messing around. And I have this sack with two, like, grape things down, between my legs. I tried and tried to pop one, but it was real slippery! I never could pop it, so I just went to sleep. Now it's sore when I walk!" He took his first bite and started chewing before noticing the rest of the table had not only stopped eating but also were all staring, in disbelief, at him. I was glad he wasn't in school, as I would have had a difficult time explaining why I had to pull him out to go see dear old Dr. Kelly. I don't think they would have understood.

As we drove to Glenwood for the appointment to get Ted looked at, I couldn't help but wonder what this wonderful, dedicated doctor thought when I called in for an appointment. If it wasn't Terena with a broken bone or Jerry with a concussion, it was a child coming for an HIV test or rectal impalement. He had checked out so many bizarre things while serving my family that he never knew what to expect when I came through his doors. He seldom even raised an eyebrow at the odd health concerns of my children.

Luckily Ted was fine, a bit swollen and bruised, but Dr. Kelly didn't think any long-term damage had been inflicted. I breathed a sigh of relief, paid the bill, and left. Ted would be walking carefully for a few more days, so I made a mental note to be sure to take that into consideration when he was doing chores or playing. My life was never boring!

As the snow fell and Thanksgiving neared, the festivities of the holiday season were well underway. Ted was well again and as energetic as ever. Some of the community were very supportive of our work with the children. Some looked at us as weird. There were more good folks than others. Art and Elaine, a family for whom I had trained two large golden retrievers, sent us a large ham to have for the special dinner. We greatly appreciated their gesture of caring and love, so each child worked on a thank you card for them. Earlier that fall, before ski season had started in Vail, these kind folks had invited my large family up to Vail for a picnic and gondola ride up Lion's Head Mountain.

The experience was one of wonder and excitement for the children as they had never been in such a contraption before. We were well above timberline after the large swinging gondola lifted us quickly and effortlessly to the peak summit. It was cool and windy, but the scenery was spectacular on top of the world as the rugged Rocky Mountains fell away in every direction. Surrounded by delicate wild flowers and the powerful majesty of the mountains, it was awesome! The generosity of Art and Elaine was much appreciated and my children were given that special day as a memory that will remain with them as a priceless gift. The support and acceptance of good people in the community is an important part of the healing process. They still talk about that adventure.

When Christmas neared, I found an envelope with an invitation and ten tickets to the Bolshoi Ballet at the Betty Ford Theater in Vail. It read:
I hope you and the children will come and enjoy the show! We will meet you at the box office.
Love, Art, Elaine and the Bears (dogs)
We did enjoy the show and seeing such wonder and beauty allowed the children to grow further in their healing. They saw a family give them an

evening of joy and entertainment while receiving nothing in return. The children had to drop their usual self-centered mind frame in order to understand. The dancers had spent years in training and hard work to create such power and grace and then had traveled from Russia to share it! As I was bombarded with questions after the show, my sons were in awe at how masculine the men were even as they danced in tights. The preconceived notion, that men dancing ballet was taboo, had been shattered that evening. The girls twirled and fluttered about the house for weeks afterwards. This family from Vail had again touched my family with love.

Ted was still having rough days about a third of the time, but the majority of his sick behaviors had dissipated. His feeling book showed a tremendous progression. In the beginning most of the entries were the feelings of jealousy, resentment and rage. As I parented him using strong boundaries and limits and even stronger affection and unconditional love, his daily entries changed to much more happiness and appreciation as well as anticipation of reaching his goals. The weekly therapy was giving us the foundation on which my and Jerry's parenting was able to build a secure attachment.

Hurting animals was still a concern, but as he was talking about his feelings instead of acting them out, I was giving him more and more freedom. I was still hypervigalant about keeping him separated from our animals. He had been handling things rather well, so when I sent him out to sweep the dusting of snow off the back porch, I thought he could handle it.

P.J., an orphaned adolescent raccoon, had been entrusted to us by the Division of Wildlife to raise until he was old enough to be set free. In an attempt to keep his wild instincts he had been raised outdoors and would only come near the house occasionally for food and usually at night. He occasionally came out of his semi-hibernation looking for food; this was one such day.

Teddy was humming as he swept and because I still checked on him frequently from the window, I saw P.J. coming out from the woods. Curious to see what would happen, I stepped back from the glass far enough to be out of Ted's view. The shiny gray animal sauntered up the steps and stood staring at Ted, asking for food. I tensed ready to rescue the coon. Thinking no one was watching and noticing the animal was small, he swatted the raccoon with his broom. Rushing to intervene, I stopped abruptly when I saw P.J.Coon chasing Teddy through the back yard toward the woods. P.J was a wild animal, but he had been raised by us, so he was usually quite gentle, but now he jumped and nipped at Ted's fleeing tush. Screaming while he ran, Ted did the only thing that came to mind; he scrambled up one of the many limbs of our box elder tree. Way up high, Ted now sat, watching the enraged beast below climbing toward him. I had to rescue them from each other until they both cooled down.

Knowing how important natural consequences were, I pulled up a chair and watched as Ted finished his snow removal. Ten minutes later P.J. started sauntering slowly back to the porch while Teddy worked. Watching the raccoon warily he continued his sweeping with one eye on the corner where the black masked face stared back at him. Ted had learned to respect the creature, even if it was fifty pounds lighter than he was and later that evening, I had him set out a dish of hamburger and dog food as restitution for his rudeness.

When the children would be rude or take from the family, it was vital to their healing that restitution be made. Ted was inappropriate with P.J., so he fed the raccoon to give back to the animal. Because these children were so used to taking from the family and never giving anything back, it was part of the program to teach them reciprocal giving and taking. When I smiled at them, they learned to smile back. When they did family chores they participated in the fun family activities. When they drained the family of energy they needed to give energy back. It was a real world lesson that was taught early on and as Ted was still having a hard time occasionally, he earned about thirty minutes of 'give-back' time a week. One of the many tasks I could have them do was to make hot chocolate for everyone or do the family chore of whomever he hassled.

He was talking about his feelings more spontaneously as well as handling his consequences really well, and "Heart Man" was another reason I believed he was getting healthier. He had been drawing pictures of knives, weapons and people with claws when he first came. Now, when he drew, he made loving cards or pictures with Heart Man as the main theme. The figure was composed of nothing but hearts. A heart for his upper body and another, inverted heart for his lower body. Each limb contained two long skinny hearts and his head was a fat smaller heart. His eyes and smile were the only lines that weren't shaped into a heart, and even they sometimes were.

He had started drawing the figure about ten months after he had arrived and as months passed, he began leaving them for me. I'd find them at my place at the dinner table or on my pillow at night. He would watch carefully as I picked it up and looked it over. He'd wait to respond until I looked into his eyes and smiled. He would smile back ! That reciprocal smile was a significant sign that he was internalizing me and was becoming attached to me.

He was also finding joy in doing things that made me smile, including his chores. He went out of his way to help out around the house. Instead of arguing with me regarding his responsibilities and completion of chores, he'd happily hop off with a good attitude and finish whatever needed done.

Nicknames that reflected a unique and positive talent were something I loved to give the children. As a giveback chore, Ted occasionally rubbed my shoulders. I gave him the name "Doctor Marvel" because he was a gifted masseuse and could find tight spots by just gliding his hand along my upper back. He was so skillful that he'd work out the knots quickly in a caring way. It was a tender way that he could pay back and he was excellent at it! When he got himself in "hot water" he could get out of it quickly by saying" Can I rub your back to make it up to you?" I was always happy to oblige! It made us both happy.

The winter was growing colder and the snow had accumulated to over two feet. Ted was working hard, daily, on his books in front of the wood stove to catch up in school so I decided to enroll him for a half day. Before doing so, CJ and I met with the elementary school principal and his teacher to discuss his behavior and how to respond appropriately to testing and outbursts. Our education system was excellent, here in our little town, and as most of the teachers had seen the drastic turn around my kids did, they were willing to follow through with what the therapist and I asked. They learned what strong sitting was and how to do the "take a hike program" and when to use it. They learned not to tolerate any rudeness, not to dole out second chances, and most importantly, they knew to call me to come get my child immediately if they were blatantly defiant. Teachers were an important part of the team. They could make or break the future of a child by allowing manipulation or stopping it quickly. I had to trust them tremendously before I would give them my child.

We shared with them that Ted's history included molestation and that he needed to be closely monitored. Terena was in Junior High in the same building and had volunteered to help. Everyone understood what precautions were necessary to avoid a destructive situation. A plan was made and it was agreed Ted would attend after spring break.

The first few weeks were difficult for Dr. Marvel and I had to go often to pick him up early, but as the teacher held him accountable quickly rather than giving him warnings when he tested, he soon learned to trust them and began fitting in. He was placed in the fourth grade and excelled at his lessons. The tutor still supplemented his education, so by the time school let out in the spring, he was ready for full days the following year.

As school was over until fall, the yearly 4-H club projects went into full speed. Terena, Beth and Will each had a horse project so, along with the weekly therapy trips to Evergreen, we hauled various horses to the fairgrounds for meetings. They were also enrolled in the dairy goat project and Terena was the junior leader for her dog 4-H group.

Knowing that Gabriel and Ted weren't ready for an animal project, I decided to lead a leather-working group in order to make them feel included. 4-H had so many learning possibilities that I wanted everyone to benefit from it. Record books were kept throughout the summer, which taught math skills, record keeping, responsibility and organization. The weekly meetings also gave the children a sense of order and routine and friendships.

Alicia was still joining us for summers and as she became more and more healthy, her time with us was spent in play and fun rather than emotional healing and intense therapy. Along with 4-H, which Alicia couldn't actively participate in because she missed the sign up deadline, we had art lessons in the teepee on the other side of the creek. Using techniques, which stimulate right brain activity, we did drawings of our hands and feet, the dogs, and whatever we could find. Each day, we had a different project; one day we'd draw without looking at the page, the next we'd all draw an image that was upside down. Gabriel excelled, and I quickly found that he had an exact eye and could reproduce most anything put in front of him. I had found Gabriel's special gift!

>✷< >✷< >✷< >✷<

Terena's panties were still coming up missing. I had purchased more for her before school let out and she was down to only two again. The mystery was perplexing. We did room searches and came up empty handed each time. Knowing she needed underwear, I went out and purchased more. This time though, she decided to hand wash them and hide them securely in her room.

Will had been participating in weekly therapy sessions, but his attitude was still bad. He struggled to finish eighth grade and rarely did his chores right anymore. His room was so deep that I hadn't seen the carpet for weeks and in a last ditch effort, I gave him three days to pick his things up. When seventy-two hours lapsed and he hadn't attempted to straighten his room, I paid Beth two dollars to go in and sack up everything on the floor. An hour later and four large sacks removed, his floor was uncluttered. Angry beyond words, he stomped around glaring at everyone and spat obscenities in my direction.

I informed him that when I saw the remaining items in his room picked up neatly for a week he could earn one bag back and for each week thereafter that his room was tidy he would get another sack. His offset jaw, sneering lips and slits for eyes told me he was not happy with the arrangement. He was sixteen now so I didn't think I was expecting too much. I may have been wrong because after he earned the first bag back, the other three were left in the garage gathering dust awaiting the time that Will would keep his room clean for a whole week. The time never came.

In an attempt to teach Will responsibility, I signed him up with a wilderness group designed to help tough kids. He was to leave at the beginning of July for the rock climbing adventure where strength, endurance, self-motivation and responsibility were the focus. It was a four-week course and I hoped that it would help him pull out of the slump he had been in for so many months. The end of June was spent shopping for the various items on the long list the group had sent. Will was ready when July ninth came.

We drove to Marble, Colorado where the rendezvous point was established with the staff. There were a dozen other kids with large backpacks and lots of gear. Will was worried, but I reassured him, gave him a hug and waved as the group hiked away.

Ted's family had left him with us nearly a year ago and were eager to see him. They had talked with him frequently over the phone and often sent letters. Dr. Marvel was doing so well, that we decided he had earned a visit back home. The family had been forced to move. After informing the community of Ted's brutal crimes, amid shame and glaring faces, they packed up and left. Still living in Massachusetts, they purchased a round trip ticket from Denver to Boston for their son. He would be with them for a week. They had been studying how to interact therapeutically with their son as he was still in the healing process. A door alarm was installed in preparation and the children were prepped for his arrival.

As I drove him to the airport we had three hours to talk. In my usual manner I asked, "On a scale of one to ten, one being mad a tiny bit and ten being mad enough to kill, how mad are you right now?" Thoughtfully and with his eyebrows pulled down, he slowly said, "I am a zero." Trying to keep my eyes on the road while giving Ted glances of encouraging eye contact, I questioned, "What does that feel like, Ted?" Looking down at his folded hands he quickly glanced at me before placing one hand over his heart subconsciously. "It's a little scary, but it feels kind of warm." Wanting him to explain further, I implored, "Does it feel like sunshine on your skin?" Excitedly he responded, "Yeah, like sunshine!" Glancing over at him, I stated, "That's what love feels like!" Quizzically he tipped his head and asked, "This is love?" Smiling at him I shook my head and emphasized, "Yes, that's love."

Proud of him and wanting to have a moment of silence to absorb this triumphant moment, I handed him a fig Newton cookie. He put the cookie to his mouth and held it up with a bite removed. "This is the smile on my heart", he said as the crescent became clear in my view. I smiled at him, rubbed his shoulder and knew that moment would forever be a smile on my heart too!

In celebration, I directed Ted and the other children to roll down their windows, as we sped up the mountain highway at seventy-five miles an hour. I began the traditional "hoity-toity" song. This ritual was called a freeze out as the cool mountain air whipped through the car sending goose bumps down the arms of everyone. It was always a blast. The Tercel tore around the curves as Ted, Gabriel, Terena, Beth and I sang at the top of our lungs, holding the first syllable the longest. "Hoity-toity, hoity-toity, hoity-toity!"

Rolling the windows back up, we laughed as all of our hair was in a rats nest and our cheeks were flushed from the exhilarated singing. Smiles adorned everyone's face. As we settled back in, I began thinking back to when I had asked Ted about his future profession. "Teddy, what do you want to be when you grow up?" I asked, praying silently that he had decided on something other than a rapist. He sat still for a moment before replying. "I think I wanna be a doctor or a chiropractor 'cause I'm good with helping people with sore backs." I felt sunshine warm my heart that shined from this boy.

I knew Ted was on the right path when, in the middle of his visit, I received a call from Laura. "Ted's having sexual feelings for Angelica and asked to talk to CJ. I left a message for her but, I don't know how I'm supposed to handle this!" I assured her that when he was talking about it, he was less likely to do it and to snuggle him up and thank him for being strong enough to tell the truth. I also encouraged her to call CJ back and have Ted talk with her. I knew that even though he was having these feelings, he was doing what he had been taught to do. We still had a long way to go with Teddy, but he got an A+ in my book for being strong enough to trust his mother by sharing his true feelings. He was healing and I was proud of him.

Beth and I at the top of the world in Vail.

Beth blowing a dandelion at Lions Head, Vail.

Chapter 14
She Loves Me, She Loves Me Not

Nancy: I felt it was vitally important for Beth to know that she had been accepted by the entire family rather than just by me. So I had her ask her new dad and sister if she could stay. As I held her I felt her body relax with each answer of "Yes, we love you! Yes, you're accepted, and yes, we want you to be part of our family." I saw how crucial it was that a child never be left dangling not knowing where they would go and who they would live with. I vowed, in the future, anytime I was involved with a child who had to be moved that he/she would be told and moved very quickly in order to not extend their time in terror. I had seen the powerful trauma rock this little girl. I vowed to make it as painless as possible for any child I worked with in the future. I smiled inside and outside day after day as I watched Beth putting her roots down deep into the mountains, riding horses, playing in the sunshine, and laughing. The music that poured from inside of her and echoed from her mermaid ledge on the mountain became more and more beautiful as it filled with joy and spilled out of her.

Beth: *I could live here, and just be, now. I didn't have to worry about anything. I could ride horses and laugh and settle. Will had lost the privilege of owning his own horse for the summer so the rest of us shared her. Since I was healthy and worked hard on my life I was able to ride the beautiful white Arabian mare. Troika was on loan for the summer but she was my friend I loved her. Will had become irresponsible and Mom began paying me a quarter to make him his lunch. I always worked really hard to make him yummy sandwiches. It made me feel important and responsible that I was seven and he was fourteen and he needed my help.*

I still climbed the mountain and sang everyday. Singing was my passion and I continued to let my voice echo across the valley. I missed my family in North Carolina but I loved my family here. I was glad I was going to grow up in this house. I loved Mom, Terena and Dad. Chucky had moved to Denver to live and RB had just gotten married, but I was so excited I had two big older brothers and a new sister-in-law. She was very beautiful and they were so much in love. It was like a fairy tale.

As the months passed I melded even more with my family. I made a card for Mom Nancy at the end of July that said "I love you", "Love is true." I then walked out in the field looking for the just the perfect addition to the card. Bending down, I saw it. It was just what I needed. Plucking it gently, I carried it inside. Sneaking down into my mom's room I laid the card on her pillow. I then placed the beautiful, bright yellow dandelion I had just picked beside it. With utmost joy and a smile stretched across my face I raced from the room in satisfaction that she would find her surprise that night when she pulled her covers back.

Nancy: Often during the days Beth would say, "Mom can I talk to you?" We'd step into my room so she could speak freely without so many ears, about her latest concern about something. It had been so long since I had to correct Beth for any misbehavior it was clearly a problem of the past. She had made gargantuan leaps as she marched from severe mental illness up the huge mountain to mental health. She was honest about her feelings and her actions. She was fair in her work and her play. She was dedicated and devoted to being the best that she could be as a human being as a loving daughter, as a Christian, as a student, and as a sister.

Beth had healed more quickly than any child I had ever seen or heard of. She had been on solid ground for many months when CJ called and let me know her ex-family wanted to come out and spend the weekend with her for her birthday and as a farewell visit. I had no doubt in my mind that Beth was strong enough to handle anything that was thrown at her. She had been through hell in her little life and come up victorious. She hadn't been hardened and calloused by the pain she'd endured. She had become like gold, refined through the fire.

The year I had spent focusing her on her ex-mother's love had not turned out the way it had been originally planned. I felt that the strange behavior I had seen from this woman and her rejection of Beth had been due to her own emotional pain. I wondered if she was emotionally disturbed before Beth came to live with her or if Beth's bizarre behavior and the chaos created by it had forced this woman over the edge. I did believe that she loved Beth and had Beth's best interest at heart. I had no idea I had been chosen to play the part of Judas to my beloved daughter.

Beth: *I was told my family from North Carolina was coming to visit me to say goodbye in person and I was looking forward to their visit with mixed feelings. I was ready to say goodbye but it would be difficult since I had spent many years with them and had worked really hard to love them. I dreaded the day as it got closer and closer. This would be really hard for me and I was scared. I already ached from their rejection and seeing them would reinforce it. Mom helped me to be strong and when I got scared she'd hold me and rock me and let me sob as I would remember the rejection. I loved this woman so much and I was so thankful God had brought us together.*

Nancy: I loved all my children whether they were biological or placed in my care by other parents. I loved them the same. Beth was as deeply embedded in my heart as my own children. I cheerfully helped Beth pack for the weekend visit with her ex-family, and drove her to Evergreen. I noted some stiffness when we met the minister and his wife and chalked it up to their concern about the impending farewell they would have to go through. I noted they had come without the younger brother and was glad Beth would have them all to herself for a fun weekend. I hugged her, waved goodbye and drove to CJ's home to spend the night and await Beth's return so we could all go home.

That night CJ got a call from Dr. Ken. I saw her body stiffen and I felt something was wrong. I saw her eyes fill concern and fear. She began to argue with him and they set an appointment for the following morning at his office. She hung up the phone, slowly turned to me and said, "I can't believe it, those people have no intention of bringing Beth back. They have a ticket to take her back to North Carolina and put her in an institution!" My heart stopped, I just stood there hoping I'd heard wrong. Surely they wouldn't rip her little heart to shreds! Surely they wouldn't hurt her again! They knew she was healthy, that she loved us and was doing so well in our care. What was happening to Beth? Had they told her and left her in limbo? Was she suffering in agony? Did she think I didn't love her? Did she think our family had betrayed her?! I had told her forever. They were making me a liar to the little girl I had taught to be brutally honest no matter how hard it was. CJ said, "I insisted they let you meet Beth tomorrow morning with the psychiatrist at Dr. Ken's office." I was somewhat relieved I would at least get to say goodbye and explain things. But, Beth wouldn't get to say goodbye to her dad! She wouldn't get to say goodbye to her sister! I then realized the heartache this would cause my family as their little sister was ripped from their hearts!

CJ and I sat up all night and talked. We were both angry. We had been betrayed and they were hurting the little girl we both loved very much. We could find no reason, no sense to their plan. I knew how vital it was to transfer the bond to keep from causing tremendous regression in the progress she had made. She was doing so well in the last few months. How could she learn to trust anyone ever again? The psychiatrist and I drove together. I carried a videotape of The Little Mermaid movie and several papers to help these people understand the trauma of moving a child from one placement to another and hopefully make it less painful. I gave Beth a big hug and was glad to see she looked okay although somewhat pale. Whenever she was stressed shadows would circle her eyes like a little raccoon. I saw those shadows. As I pulled her to me and gave her a hug I wanted to just release my sobs, but held them back feeling that it would add to her pain to see mine. I bit my lip, and went into the meeting. In the meeting the mental health professionals reiterated repeatedly the vital importance of transferring the bond carefully by maintaining daily phone contact with me for a week or two and then every other day and then less and less until it was just a few times a year. The Minister and his wife wholeheartedly nodded in agreement saying they were 100% committed to doing what ever it took to help Beth. They lied.

Beth: *July 25, 1990 was the last time I saw my Mom Nancy, Dad Jerry, Terena and the rest of the family. I didn't realize it would be several years before I saw them again. The true meaning behind the visit was soon revealed. They were to take me back to North Carolina. I didn't understand. I wanted to stay with my family in Colorado now. My heart was a mass ball of confusion. I had been told I was going to be able to remain with my new family and grow up with them as their little girl forever and now so suddenly this plan had changed. Was it something I'd done? I didn't understand and I really didn't know what to think. I felt trapped between a rock and a hard place. Discovering I was to return to North Carolina with my original adopted family bewildered me. A few months* ago they didn't even want me as their daughter let alone let me live with them and now I was to be taken back. I was so excited and so scared, I had wanted them to finally accept me. I had worked so hard to renew their trust in me, but I didn't want to leave the people I had grown to love so much. What was happening?

Nancy: I got to spend a little bit of time with Beth while the mental health professionals continued to meet with these people. I told Beth that I wanted her to have the movie that she loved so much. I told her we would be just like in the song's words "Somewhere out there someone's thinking of me and loving me tonight." I wanted her to know my love would be there as long as there were stars in the sky. I couldn't tell her she had been betrayed and her worst nightmare was about to begin. I couldn't tell her that the people had said she would never cross their door again, she was not going home ever, they had found a place for her in a program for the most violent, mentally ill children in the state of North Carolina. They were preparing a "special place" for this one, was what I had been told. They were going to have her stay with someone else while the preparations were being finalized. I saw at least two more moves, two more major traumas for this little one to endure. How much could she take I wondered, how much more suffering would this child have to endure? She had already had much more than her share. I wanted to take her and run away, catch a bus to Mexico, protect her from all of this. I decided to get an attorney and fight for her right to be a little girl and climb mountains and ride horses and have a family and a home. Hugging her goodbye I released her into the care of these two people that I now saw as self-serving and cruel, playing a game with my daughter's heart on a string like a yo-yo. It was beyond a doubt far and above the most painful moment of my life.

Beth: *Mom Nancy and I went for a walk down the streets of Golden, CO. At that time, Golden was one of those towns that even though it was growing rapidly, it was straining to keep its small town feeling. We passed the historic homes and the many trees that had been aging along the walk. I thought of how those trees had seen the lives and memories that were made in that town for years. They hadn't been ripped out and replanted, they'd been able to settle and that's what I wished for, to settle. I was just a little girl, my eighth birthday was literally days around the corner but I wanted to settle. I'd been moved enough, why did I have to go through this again. I thought I had finally come home and now once again I wasn't. I wanted to stay with Mom Nancy and Dad Jerry. Why was I being abandoned again?*

When Mom Nancy wrapped her arms around my little, lean body, made strong from working on the farm, doing chores and climbing mountains, I felt empty. The butterflies in my stomach threatened to take over and tears washed down my tanned face. The coldness in my eyes and the ice on my heart that had once been there was long gone and it was all because of the love this woman had helped me feel. I hurt and I just wanted to go home. Home to Dad Jerry, Terena, the animals and the mountains. Why wasn't I waking from this terrible dream? I hadn't even said goodbye to Terena because I thought I was coming right back. Will was in Outward Bound so I'd been unable to see him and Dad Jerry had been at work. As they drove to the airport I let the tears stream down my face. I didn't care anymore. I just wanted to be loved and cared for and all I felt at this point was confusion and more rejection. I didn't know what to think. I sat numb as we went to catch our flight.

Nancy: I drove home the hundreds of miles over the mountains just wanting to be held and comforted by my cowboy. I knew I would soon have to share with him the heart-breaking news that he had lost his daughter and face Terena with the same news. It would break her heart. I hated the minister and his wife. I despised what they did to Beth. I detested what they were doing to my family. I loathed them for ripping my heart open!

I prayed hard for God to keep Beth's little heart safe. Terena threw herself in my arms when I got home and told her. We sobbed together, trying to make sense out of any of it. Gabriel ran to his room screaming, "That's not right! She worked harder on her life than any of us! She was the best one! Why are they hurting her?" Ted sat numb with fear.

Jerry held me for hours as we grieved together and I sobbed myself to sleep. I had nightmares of my little girl in a dark dungeon with no food, no love, calling my name begging me to save her. I was chained to a wall, helpless to protect her, helpless to rescue her. I envisioned them visiting Beth in her cell on the weekend and then returning home with her brother after each visit, fueling the jealousy I had worked so hard to help Beth dissipate. They were twisting her gentle caring heart into the heart of a monster. I saw the petals of the magnolia blossom dropping off one by one as if Beth were saying, "She loves me, she loves me not, she loves me, she loves not."

Chapter 15
Ripple Effect

The dandelion Beth had placed on my pillow only a few days before was wilting and sad in the vase near my bed, but I couldn't bring myself to throw it out. The red heart card, that she had lovingly made, still sat on my windowsill. Each morning, after having a restless night, my eyes would open to see the sun shining on her message of love. Although it made me happy, I was also reminded of the horrible truth. Beth was gone.

I prayed and prayed and prayed, that her little heart would be kept safe; and that God would surround her with good and loving people. I asked him to keep her safe from the violent children she was to be raised with. I received one phone call from Beth the day after she was "kidnapped" and didn't hear from her again. I wrote letters telling her how much I loved her and that we really did want to keep her. I wrote that we were so sorry, telling her how much we missed her and were hoping she was all right and happy. I sent them to the minister and his wife. I never knew if she ever received them. I didn't know where she was.

 I called everyone I knew, even our state Senator, begging for help. Some friends, Art and Elaine, who had been so generous with the children, heard the news that Beth had been ripped from us and offered the services of their attorney. I worked for weeks to get the reports together from all the professionals involved in the case. I had a glimmer of hope that I could save my child. It took what seemed an eternity to get all the people to write their reports. The whole family held their breaths while we awaited the report from the attorney about what we could do to bring our daughter home. He called to let me know that as licensed therapeutic foster parents we had no legal rights. We had no leg to stand on to fight for Beth's right to be in a family where she was loved.

The minister and his wife had their attorney contact our agency to forbid any transfer of records to the agency that Beth had been placed with, but gave no names or addresses that could be followed up to find her. I found out these cold-blooded liars had not only betrayed Beth, they had not paid a dime for her fifteen months of therapy and care.

I still had no idea why they had done this. I finally got a clue when they sent a scathing, rambling letter. They claimed that I had misused the 'clothing allowance' they sent as evident by Beth's wearing of clothes that were too big. They didn't bother to find out that Beth preferred to wear Terena's hand-me-downs because they were filled with love. Her closets were full of new stuff, but not because of any money they supposedly sent.

In the same report they stated how insulted they were that Beth was forced to call me 'mom' and Jerry 'dad', even after they said they were relinquishing rights and we could adopt her. In the last paragraph, it became obvious what this was all about. They claimed to have every right to have normal parental feelings of jealousy. Was that why they were tearing Beth to pieces, because they were jealous? Did they not understand our job, as therapeutic parents, was to build the skeleton of a relationship so that they could add the body? I knew it had been clearly explained. I was in the room with them as CJ laid out the process. She had told how it was my job to teach Beth to love me and then transfer the bond to the minister's wife. It was a sick game these people were playing and Beth was a pawn. To me, they were lower than the sludge in the bottom of a septic tank.

Will was still rock climbing and had no idea his home was falling to pieces. Ted was terrified that his adopted family would do the same thing, so for a week he returned to his old behaviors of howling, urinating everywhere, acting defiant and refusing to do anything. When CJ called him to assure him his family wouldn't tear him away she said she would have his parents phone. Laura and Jeff called later and consoled Teddy by telling him they would not take him home until he was ready. Convinced, he relaxed and became respectful, responsible and fun to be around once again.

As my heart was aching in pain, Gabriel was more in need of me than ever, but I was in so much emotional agony myself, I couldn't give him what he needed. Although I hugged, rocked and tried to keep the daily routine the same, his behavior deteriorated day by day and the elimination problems came back in full force. Even if I had been there as I was before, Gabe would never be able to trust me like he once did. With his history it was essential that he feel safe. If I couldn't protect Beth, then how could I protect him?

Week by week his behavior became more defiant. His sullen attitude was magnified by his withdrawal from me; even his hugs became cold and stiff. He stopped talking about his feelings, and, when I attempted to have him enter them in his journal, he became violent. He was slipping further and further from me. Feeling his introversion made my already broken heart bleed more profusely. I was losing him and I could do nothing about it. The damage was done the moment he saw I couldn't save Beth.

CJ decided to move Gabriel. His inability to feel safe with me anymore was just too strong to assume I could regain the lost ground to save him. One month after Beth was taken, Gabriel packed up his belongings and moved to Lori's home in Denver. I grieved now for three lost children, Chucky, Beth and Gabriel.

By August, when the County Fair started, almost everyone had a project entered, but the festive time was dampened by the fact that our family was no longer complete. Beth's record book still sat, open and only half finished, on Terena's desk where she had last worked on it. She was technically too young to have a 4-H project, but the leaders had seen her deep desire to participate and had allowed her to start a mini- project.

Gabriel's drawings hung in the exhibit hall with blue ribbons attached; but he wasn't there to see them. Alicia was preparing to go home. She had received a second place for her drawing, and was the only one who was able to escape the oppression of the heavy gloom that had settled in. Her joy was only momentary. The weight of our misery was crushing the children's spirits.

To make matters worse, the Persian Gulf War was underway and R.B. was deployed. With the constant fear of RB's death hanging over us all, Kymm, his young and very beautiful wife, came to live with us. While he was fighting she was creating our first grandchild. The miracle of the expected new life was wonderful and Kymm was a Godsend. She helped out a great deal aroung the house, even preparing meals and was only affected by the loss of Beth through our mourning. Her gentle and optimistic attitude lifted the heaviness of the house. It was great to have her with us.

Before school started, I picked up Will from his adventure camp. His grinning bronze face quickly reflected the concern and depression in my expression. Crying softly in the back seat he mourned the loss of Beth as we drove home. He chose to stay in his room much of the time once he got back to the house. I rarely saw him except at meals. Everyone was devastated.

I cried until I had nothing left to cry. I was sad and afraid. Being so empty, I had little left to give to the family that so desperately needed me. I tried to function as best as I could. Jerry was a great help. He was quieter than normal, but he was able to cope in a more productive manner. Supporting me, he was not only my shoulder to lean on and confidant, but he made sure the daily tasks of survival were still completed. The chores were finished, the animals fed and dinner was cooked by my cowboy. He was angry at the minister and his wife, not only for what they did to Beth, but because his family was in such ruins. His logical and rational demeanor gave him strength that helped us all.

Terena was no help. She was so broken by losing Beth that she was lost. Becoming snotty and defiant, she was livid with CJ and myself for allowing such a tragedy to occur. She couldn't understand that we had no way of stopping it. Knowing she was drinking alcohol and failing the first quarter of her freshman year only hammered one more nail into my coffin. I understood that she was numbing the pain by drowning it with booze. She wrote to Beth as frequently as I did; and, although we didn't know where to send the notes, we kept writing.

I fought through her resistance and showed her that I wouldn't lose another daughter right now. Understanding, she forgave me, and pulled closer to me instead of farther away. Her drinking stopped and her grades came back up. She still had a hard time dealing with the intense feelings of loss and grief that crept into her heart, but she started reaching out to me for help.

In September, Terena and I were given the privilege of being at Kymm's side as she gave birth to my first grandchild. Kayla was a beauty and having a new tiny baby in the house helped distract everyone from their sorrow. I watched as bonding between mother and infant occurred right in front of my eyes. Kymm was an awesome mom with natural instincts to do the right things. She did an amazing job with the loving eye contact between her and her child. The loving smiles that passed between them helped ease her fears of losing her husband in the war so far away. She snuggled and rocked that baby almost non-stop and the touch the two shared sealed the bond. They were very close.

Kymm was an excellent, responsive mother. She instinctively knew when her baby was over stimulated, wet or hungry. Breastfeeding allowed her to make loving eye contact with my grand daughter many times a day and she used touch and her voice to help soothe her baby. She would spend hours rocking, talking, playing and reading to the tiny one.

When she had to go places, Kayla was placed in a safety seat, but was removed and carried her in her arms when not in the car. I was glad I didn't have to encourage her in this. I have a problem with mothers who would rather carry the hard plastic carrier than the soft cuddly baby. I still call those carriers "leprosy seats" because to me it felt like the mom's carried them like that so they wouldn't get germs or something. They separate the mother from the baby. Kymm had read lots on parenting and came to me with a dilemma. She wondered if she would spoil her new born by picking her up right away when she cried; or, should she let her cry sometimes. She did not want to spoil her, but it broke her heart to not pick her up when she cried. I answered her question by explaining how the cycle of bonding occurs in infancy.

Thousands of times within the first two years of life a cycle occurs which builds trust and develops the conscience. When an infant cries it is because they have a need. Sometimes they are wet, other times they are hungry or lonely. As language has not yet developed, the best communication an infant has is cooing and crying. When a mother can identify the need and satisfy the baby by changing, feeding or cuddling, the baby becomes gratified and stops the crying. The baby learns that when they have a need, mom will come to take care of that need and in turn the baby learns to trust mom. When the infant learns to trust, they learn to attach or internalize (or take in) the caregiver and form a conscience.

There is little research indicating the number of times this cycle has to be broken in order to create attachment problems, but studies by Mary Ainsworth in the sixties and seventies showed that almost forty percent of babies have attachment difficulties. When attachment issues come up, conscience development is affected. A child with no attachment can have no conscience. Without a conscience they can lie, steal or kill with no remorse. Trust issues, respect problems, control dilemmas, aggression, defiance and lack of normal brain activity can result as the infant grows into a toddler and then a child and on into adulthood.

Kymm's eyes widened in horror as she listened. "You mean that the theory of leaving your infant to cry could actually damage their brain development?" Nodding my head, I sadly agreed. "New moms that are reading those books and implementing those ideas could be creating more children like the ones I work with." Snuggling her daughter closer to her, Kymm leaned forward in interest. "Sure, they probably won't be as sick as the children I care for, but they will have big problems. Someone said that RAD is a time bomb set in the first two years of life to blow at fifteen years of age. It is set by breaking their heart.

She asked me what she should do so she wouldn't have a spoiled child. Smiling, I told her when her baby was around one year old, limits should be set and rules laid out. The first year of life is the time of enthroning; they peep, we serve. The second year of life is the time of dethroning; they peep, we say no. At that point, crying for a short while until she fell asleep was okay sometimes.

Knowing there were many different philosophies to parenting, I told Kymm that after having a helping hand in re-parenting other people's children, I had learned what I thought worked best. I raised Terena that way and although she was having a hard time right now, she was a good person with a giving soul. I had trained many young moms with troubled infants or toddlers to parent and many who practiced what I had learned were enjoying parenthood with respectful, giving, obedient children.

Kymm learned from me and I learned from her. One day little Kayla said "EEP", Kymm said, " Oh she needs to burp." A while later Kayla said " EEP". Kymm said, " Oh, she's hungry." I asked, "How can you tell 'EEP' from 'EEP.' Kymm said, "I just know". And she did! I was fascinated watching the two of them communicate with no language!

Watching the two of them interact gave me hope for the world. I had seen so much damage from bad parenting, that it was an inspiration to see it done with love and gentleness. Kymm was totally devoted to her baby and it was a refreshing breath of air.

While R.B. was sitting in the desert of Saudi Arabia with his troops awaiting the beginning of the war against Sadam Hussein, I was home praying that he would be kept safe. With the holidays approaching, the thought of my son eating canned food with sand in it while we had roast turkey saddened my heart. One of his many letters arrived and in between all of the exclamation points he shared the news that from over one thousand marines he had been selected to eat Thanksgiving dinner with the President of the United States and the first lady. I was so excited and proud; I called the newspaper in our little town to share the news. The headline read: " New Castle Man Selected to Have Thanksgiving with Bush". A week after the big day the mail arrived with the news from the front. R. B. wrote that although only certain troops had been selected for the honor of dining with President and Mrs. Bush, hundreds had shown up for the event. It was a huge gathering outside the wall of sand bags. There was not enough food for my son to even have one bite. He sat on the top of the wall at a distance from the President. I was so sad thinking of my son so far from home, lonely, hungry, and feeling rejected on Thanksgiving Day. I read on, "Mom," it said, " Mrs. Barbara Bush looked up from her table. She looked right at me and she smiled and waved!" No family, no food, but a smile from a very special lady to remember forever. Another mom had lifted my son with a mere wave of her hand to make his Thanksgiving a special one. I decided I would love Barbara Bush forever.

When R. B. was a little boy, I refused to allow him to have toy guns or even to play violent games like cops and robbers. I wouldn't even let him make a gun shape with his hands. He is a US Marine now. He uses huge guns that can do real damage. He drives an amphibious tank, a.k.a. AMTRAK with a sixteen-inch cannon on the top. I also would not allow my children to eat sugary breakfast cereals. During Boot Camp he proudly showed me his locker. Inside there was a box of Lucky Charms cereal. It's ironic how the things I tried so hard to pull away from my children were the things they became most strongly drawn to. Unfortunately what I had pulled away from Chucky was his desire to steal. He was now totally focused on it and it was destroying him. I would learn to use the tactic of pulling away what I wanted them to reach for later on to help oppositional children.

Spending hours watching Kymm nurture and fill up the new little heart of my grand daughter warmed my aching heart. Kayla's tiny little face broke into a huge grin just at the sight of her mother. The coos, giggling and bubbles of laughter echoed throughout our home filling my soul with delight. Each developmental milestone became an Olympic gold medal achievement. One of my fondest memories of that time was of the baby watching her own reflection dance and laugh in the bathroom mirror. Picking her toes up as elegant as any ballet dancer, her muscles would vibrate with excitement as her eyes widened in wonderment at the reflection of the baby dancing with her. Kymm and I would laugh with joy at the simplicity of finding happiness in just being alive and moving.

Desert Storm started and no amount of cute baby antics could comfort Kymm or me. We were terrified that RB, my oldest son and the man she loved would never get to come home to us or see his beautiful baby girl. Facing the very real possibility of his death was frightening and exhausting. There was nothing we could physically do to help him. We prayed and comforted each other during that dark time.

Kymm was a wonderful mother and when her child was sleeping, she often helped with my children. Will was struggling with even the most minor tasks. His bed was not made, his clothes didn't make it to the washer on laundry day and he seldom bathed. He had fallen back into the pit he had worked so hard to climb from.

In an attempt to help him, I thought I would re-teach him to make his bed. We pulled the sheets from the top mattress and began with the bottom sheet. As I lifted up the corner of the mattress to tuck in the sheet, I noticed some articles of clothing tucked between the box spring and mattress. Reaching in and pulling them out, I saw there were at least a dozen pairs of girls' panties. The culprit who had stolen Terena's underwear had been found and I quickly realized why Will's attitude had been bad for so long! I called CJ and she started the long drive to my home.

In the session, we found that Will was stealing them from Terena's dirty laundry basket and sniffing them as he masturbated. I was thoroughly grossed out. We sent him outside to take a long walk.

Already raw from the loss of Beth, Terena blew up when she found out. Feeling victimized, perpetrated on and her most intimate space invaded, she demanded I choose between Will and her. She could no longer live with him. Talking to CJ, I asked what alternative I had and what options were available for Will. Being born an only child, CJ thought that maybe he would do better in an environment where he was the only one, so I began searching for a home close to me, where I could still visit and keep alive whatever attachment Will and I had created.

The next day, my friends, Arthur and Sandy agreed to take him. They were only ten minutes away, had a horse-breeding farm where Will could nurture his love of horses and all their children were grown and gone. He had spent time with them, so they wouldn't be strangers and they had already applied for their foster care license. I was relieved.

Within one week, CJ had him transferred. He had packed his bags, hugged the family goodbye and began settling in quickly. Checking in on him, I found his mood improved and his behavior acceptable. School was still a struggle, but at least two out of three had been restored.

Having to clean out Will's room after he left, I found another poem tucked behind the bed. Wondering what this one would say, I unfolded the yellow lined paper and began reading.

When I do something bad
and get caught,
I act ever so more
like a snot.

I always seem to know
when the time is right,
to do everything wrong
when mom's not in sight.

Sometimes I really swear,
that I wish
my stupid mom
would disappear.

As surely as I go
to sleep in a bed,
All is true
that I have said.

And since I realize
I love you very much,

from now on I will give
an extra loving touch.

And since I have so
much that I should mend,
I think this poem
has come to an end. by Will

Smiling, I folded the paper back up and put it in my pocket. Gladly, I breathed a sigh of relief as I compared this poem with the last I had found. At least some progress had been made during the years he had been with us.

It had been months since we had last heard from Beth. The highlight of my day was when the mail would arrive and with it the possibility of a letter from her, but each day, as I sorted it, my heart would sink again. Feeling my little daughter needed her belongings, no matter where she was, Terena, Kymm and I began the tedious and difficult task of packing her things into shipping boxes.

We wrote over thirty tiny notes and hid them in various pockets, shoes, nooks and crannies. Each memo emphasized our love, support and encouragement. I stuck a family photo in her wallet and other pictures of her animals and family in her books and papers. I hoped that if we saturated her boxes with enough love, she would feel it. I shipped them to the home of the minister.

The intense longing I felt was compounded by sending away her things. Feeling empty, I began filling up with food. I would gain sixty pounds within a year because no matter how much I ate, I still felt empty. Jerry was wonderful as he hugged, kissed and consoled me, but no matter how much he gave, I ate it up and needed more. I had become inconsolable and although I was beginning to pick up where I had left off, the tremendous feeling of loss shadowed me everywhere.

Falling ever deeper into depression, I hardly noticed when the holiday season approached. As if waking from a daze, I realized a few months of my life had disappeared without my recalling any of it. With Will, Gabriel and Beth gone, I only had Ted to worry about and as he was getting stronger and healthier, my job was becoming easier.

Knowing that I had to prepare for Christmas in a hurry, I pulled Terena aside and asked her what she wanted as a gift. My heart ached for her when I realized she was still broken too. "Mom, all I want for Christmas is a plane ticket to North Carolina so I can find my little sister and bring her back!" Seeing her eyes fill with tears, I hugged her for a long time. Neither one of us would be healing anytime soon.

I wouldn't get Terena a plane ticket because I knew she would find Beth and steal her back. She would either be in jail or running to Mexico and that would mean that I would have lost two daughters. As much as I wanted Beth back, I knew there was a better way of doing it, we just had to have faith that God would take care of it. I made Smiles purple leather chaps and a purple satin shirt to wear to horse shows. Sewing and shopping for everyone kept me busy. Christmas was quiet that year.

Feeling a little like my old self, I decided to help another family by taking their child to give them a rest. I got two for the price of one. Chastity, who had come to stay with us a few times before, came for a few weeks because her family was going out of town. She was nearly sixteen and had some sexual issues. I knew I would have to be careful when she was around Ted or Scott, the other boy staying with us for respite (relief).

Scott was eight years old and adopted from Russia. As an infant, he also was used for sex at the orphanage so he had similar problems to Ted's but had no history of trying to kill. Moving constantly like a wild animal, he slurred his words and talked incessantly. His hyperactivity was unbelievable, so when I found out he didn't know his alphabet, I wasn't surprised. How could this child sit still long enough to soak up any information? In one therapy session with CJ he memorized all twenty six letters in the proper order. His mother, the principal of a school and special education teacher, was ecstatic.

Scott's behavior had worn down his mom. She was exhausted and needed a break. As he rejected her and her love, he rejected everything that was important to her. Education was very important to her so he refused to learn. When she discovered he had urinated in all her houseplants, she decided she had had enough and called for respite care. I agreed to take him. Scott wasn't really a dangerous kid, but he had worn out a lot of people with his fit throwing. Smiling, he told CJ, "At least I can do something right!"

He was so skilled at throwing fits that he would let out repeated blood curdling screams while playing or thrashing about. It depended on whether anyone was there to see him or not. Because I worried the neighbors might suspect foul play, I decided to have him throw his fits out in the front field where all could clearly see the child was not being harmed. When he would start up, I would send him out and immediately go call the neighbors to let them know what was going on. They were used to the strange things happening at my home, so they usually just thanked me for the heads up and went about their business. We had extraordinarily understanding neighbors.

Their biggest show of understanding occurred when I left Terena in charge of Scott while Jerry and I took Ted to a parent teacher conference. Thinking she could control the little eight year old since she had handled kids much older and larger, I left with no worries.

They were both out cleaning the garage and as Terena became absorbed in her work, she realized she hadn't seen or heard from Scott for a few minutes. Looking up, she saw him in the distance coming out of the neighbor's garage and heading into their barn. Dropping her broom, she ran towards him. He had been in their tack room where he had smashed a bottle of black gooey antiseptic and spread it everywhere; he had also found a long lunging whip. As she neared him, he flicked the whip at her and caught her across the cheek. Blood rushed to the welt. Taunting her, he challenged her to come get him and as she did so, he whipped her again. This time though, she grabbed the long whip and pulled it from his hands.

Knowing Terena was livid, he ran into the back woods and disappeared while laughing. Thinking he'd walk it off while hiking the mountain, she took a few deep breaths to calm herself, she returned the whip to their barn, found some paper and a pen in the tack room and wrote a quick note of explanation and apology and tacked it to the door. Heading up their driveway towards the road to home, she found the boy, coming from Jack and Linda's, the other neighbors' driveway. In his little arms he carried a box of cereal.

"Where did you steal that cereal, Scott?" she demanded. Smiling slyly, he cockily retorted, "I didn't steal it, I just told the lady up there that I was starving and she handed it right to me. I didn't even have to say please!" With that he proceeded to throw little pieces at Terena, taunting her some more. With as much restraint as she could muster, Terena got a hold of the child's arm and began pulling him back to our house. He screamed and attacked her, but Terena simply used a restraint technique learned at the Crisis Prevention Intervention class to pick him up safely and carry him home. Once there, she put him in his room and turned on his alarm.

When I got home and heard the news, I immediately called both neighbors to smooth things over and find out if anything else had been damaged. Both ladies nicely confirmed that all was well and assured me they were not upset and that they understood. Breathing a sigh of relief, I thanked God that I had such kind hearted, compassionate and understanding neighbors. I knew that if it had been me, I would have been angry to find some kid had broken in and wrecked my property; yet here they were, forgiving.

The next day, Scott was to return to his home. I felt guilty for sending him home when he hadn't earned it, but I was ready for my relief and happy that he was out of our hair. Living with that child was like living with five wild raccoons! We were wiped out from just a few days with him and his destruction. As I was joyously waving to him and his mom as they left, Joyce, our neighbor called. She had found the big chest freezer in her garage had been unplugged, but luckily she had caught it before any food had spoiled. Wiping my brow, I was glad Scott wasn't a longterm child of mine. I said a prayer for his poor mother!

Two years later, I received a phone call from Scott's mom. He had been in treatment for three years and his progress was tremendous. Brain scans taken before starting therapy and specialized parenting showed many areas where his brain wasn't working. Three years later, when he was respectful, responsible and fun to be around most of the time another brain scan was taken; his brain had healed and was functioning normally!

Even the toughest kids could make it in this program if they wanted to change, but the desire had to be there. Ted wanted to be healthy. By March he was making really good decisions, sharing his feelings the majority of the time and was fun to be around. He had been handling full days at school since Christmas. He was ready to go home.

As we prepared Ted for going home permanently, although he didn't know that's what we were doing, Kymm and the baby moved down in to Denver. The long drives and limited opportunities in our rural community were becoming a strain on her. Thanking us for all our help, she packed up her little car and hit the road to her father's home in the city. She had been like an angel sent from God when she was with us. The help and joy she and my grand baby provided helped my family and myself come out of the darkness of Beth's departure. I was sad to see her go.

In the beginning of April, I started editing the hundreds of hours of videotape I had taken of Ted while he was with us. Knowing how important continuity was for these kids, I liked to send a video home filled with memories of being with us. Powerful music with uplifting messages was played while clips of them doing their chores, riding the horses, climbing the mountain and living in our home played out. On a beautiful sunny day in April, we took our canoe to Harvey Gap reservoir and shot a few more hours of video. Swimming, laughing, paddling and singing filled the viewfinder as I watched Ted for the last time. His mom, Laura, would be coming that night to start the two weeks of transferring the bond before taking him home with her. I cherished our last day together.

Knowing that if I had told Ted of his mom's arrival he would spend a lot of time worrying, I kept it a secret. That night a knock on the door caused all the dogs to jump and bark. I asked Ted to answer it. As he rounded the corner his mom stood in the entryway. He ran to her, melted into her arms and smiled in her embrace. Grinning, with tears of joy spilling from his eyes, he looked up at Laura and locked into her gaze; they held each other lovingly for a long while.

Throughout the next weeks, I transferred the intense bond Ted had created with me to his mom. She rocked him in the rocking chair, sang lullabies and told stories to him. She had him do chores and fed him ice cream. They spent a lot of time connecting, not reconnecting because they'd never connected before. A dozen days we spent transferring his attachment from my heart to her heart.

I loved watching them together. Laura was a good mom and the bonding activities came naturally to her. Ted, for the first time, was allowing his mom's love into his heart, willingly. He molded against her while she held him and rocked this now large boy. I watched, first actively participating and then gradually stepping further from them each day. I was proud of Ted. He had come so far and worked so hard that I knew he would succeed in his home. He had a good heart now and a full conscience to keep him out of trouble.

As they bonded, one last piece had to be put in place before Ted could go home. He had terrorized his younger sister so badly, that she had been undergoing therapy. In order for her to continue healing, she needed to know that Ted had changed. Calling her on the phone, Ted asked if she would please tell on him if she saw him doing something he wasn't supposed to be doing. Hesitantly, Little Angelica promised to tell right away. Then, Ted had to ask for forgiveness and permission to come back home. It was hard for him, because he knew that if she said no, he wouldn't be allowed back home except for visits. With the acceptance of his homecoming, his smile grew bigger. The last 'yes' caused Ted to jump excitedly and twirl around. "She has forgiven me and said I can come home!" he squealed. Wanting to reach out and hug him, I held back as Laura filled the position of mom.

As they drove away, Ted smiled and waved at Jerry and me. We had spent valuable time transferring his bond from me to Laura, but my bond was still firmly connected. The cord of attachment stretched and finally broke as they drove down the mountain. Crying, I sank into Jerry's arms and cried for one more child I had lost. Ted was healed and my mind knew that his going home was the ultimate goal, but my heart, which was firmly connected to the little boy, knew only that he was gone.

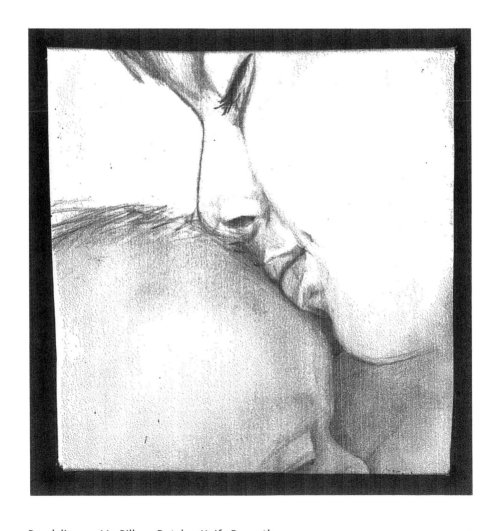

Dandelion on My Pillow, Butcher Knife Beneath

Chapter 16
Tsunami

Beth: *I slept most of the way to North Carolina after I said goodbye to Mom Nancy. When we arrived, we went to eat at what had been one of my favorite restaurants. There, I learned the whole truth of what was going to happen next in my life. I discovered I was never allowed back into their home again. Confused, I asked, "Where then, will I be staying?" I was told I would stay with a relative in West Virginia until the place they were preparing for me in North Carolina was finished. I sat there in utter disbelief. Why had they brought me back? What purpose did it serve for me to be here, if I was never to be allowed to live with them? The beautiful concoction brought for my early birthday celebration had lost its flavor, the rich chocolate didn't seem appealing anymore and everything around me seemed to grow dim. Inside I hurt. I ached for my family in Colorado and I ached for the happiness I had found there. If I closed my eyes, I could still smell the sweat of the horses after a ride, hear the creek as it gurgled along, Gabriel and Ted's laughter and each family member's voice. We left and I was silent on the drive to West Virginia. So many questions churning in me but I just kept them to myself.*

Uncle George and Aunt Marie welcomed me and showed me my room. As I lay curled in a ball in the huge bed that night I finally let the tears go. I let loose all the anguish, confusion, pain, anger and fear I had within me. My seven-year old body was wracked with sobs. What was happening to me, why was I here, and why wasn't my family in Colorado coming to get me? They had said they wanted me as their little girl so why couldn't I have stayed with them? Why was it that everything I loved got taken from me? What was wrong with me? Was I just doomed to live an unhappy life? I felt pitiful and decided I needed to stop feeling sorry for myself. Pity was weak. I had to be strong. This was how it was going to be and I needed to get used to it. I'd handled everything else in my life right? So, I was going to get over this. I wasn't sure how yet, but it was going to work out okay. I made a decision that day that I needed to take care of myself and trust only me. Once again I'd trusted someone and was betrayed. I began to see crying as a weakness and I vowed to stop it. It would be over a year until I finally allowed tears to fall.

My aunt had a birthday party for me and invited my adopted Grandparents. I hadn't seen them for two years. It was a cheerful day, at least as much as could be expected. I felt a tug at my heart when I thought of my family in Colorado, but I stuffed the feelings back inside and tried to enjoy the day. Every time I'd speak of my Colorado family, no one seemed to understand or they got stiff so I began to just not talk about them anymore.

My aunt did a wonderful job of taking care of me. She was sweet and loving. She'd bring me a piece of chocolate at night before I'd go to bed and made me copies of music tapes to listen to. I had a love for horses after having lived on the ranch in the Rockies and longed to ride again. She found a stable nearby and took me riding. Aunt Marie taught me fun crafts to make. I remember making potholders together. I still have one that I'd made those twelve years ago.

My cousin, a handsome, athletic teenager of 14, was a great swimmer and could do amazing back flips off the diving board. I knew he got sick of having me tag along but he'd still let me come with him to the pool. He had really cute friends for lifeguards. Since I was just a little girl they'd let me ride around on their shoulders and make me feel special.

I was getting in line to go down the water slide on one day when I noticed three teenage boys standing by the fence talking and pointing at me. I ignored them until they came and stood by me on the opposite side of the fence. One of them asked me if I was the girl in the movie "Child of Rage". Since, I'd only received positive feedback from it I was not ashamed and answered "Yes". The boys' eyes filled with hatred as one of them spat out that if I was his sister he would have killed me and I was lucky I was standing on the other side of the fence. In terror I ran and hid in the locker room until my cousin called that it was time for me to go home.

That evening I told my aunt what the boys had said. She told me next time to run and tell someone and my cousin would take care of me. When I saw him nod in agreement I realized that on some things maybe I wasn't strong enough to take care of myself and I could use a little help. It seemed an odd way to learn a lesson but I thanked God that night for keeping me safe.

After having settled in for a month or so, I started playing mean games with the family. It became a sadistic game for me to jump out from behind things and frighten my poor aunt. Television became my escape. I would sit in front of the tube and just zone out for hours. I felt empty inside my heart so, I tried to fill the void with food. That and the lack of exercise resulted in my gaining weight.

I had no contact with my family in Colorado at this time, except for a little note I found tucked in the fold of one of my socks. I never received any letters or calls, so feeling disowned and unloved, I pushed them out of my mind and heart. I did question the little note however. Why was there only one? I had gone home to visit my family in North Carolina for Christmas about a year before and I'd found notes tucked in every pair of socks and folded in each shirt from my mom, Nancy. It meant she was thinking of me and I loved each note. I knew she must have packed more. Digging through all of my things I found none, so I cherished the one I did find and kept it close to me.

I didn't realize how much the West Virginia family gave when they opened their home and their hearts to me, until later. They didn't have to take care of me, they could have said no, but they didn't. They lovingly allowed me to stay with them until the place in North Carolina was ready. Someday I hope to locate them and thank them from the bottom of my heart for being so caring.

It was a sad day for me when I left the pretty, green state of West Virginia and the kind family. Who knows, the family might have been sighing in relief! My adoptive mom came to pick me up. It seemed whenever she arrived my life was , once again, going to make an abrupt change. As we drove to Greensboro, NC my heart raced with anticipation and anxiety. What would the place be like that I was to live in? Would there be other children? In my mind I was tortured with visions of a padded room or something of the sort. My pounding heart rattled in my chest as these thoughts churned in my head.

We stopped by the school I was to attend first and I pondered the name, Cone Elementary. Who would name their school after a seed of a tree? I didn't realize it was actually the last name of the founder of the mills nearby. I then realized I was filling my head with nonsense to hide from my thoughts of impending doom. While Mommy watched me at the playground, I noticed the pine trees swaying with the warm North Carolina breeze. The power that moved the limbs stirred something within me and I knew I was going to be okay. I knew God was right there with me. Hearing Mommy call my name, I looked up and took a deep breath. It was now time for me to see the new place I would start my life in.

Mill House was a one story brick home in a quiet neighborhood; though I soon discovered the place brimmed with children and interesting neighbors. I walked into the house and stood in a small, comfortable living room. Wow, this was nothing like the pictures I had been drawing in my mind. We first had a tour of the house. Down a hallway was my room. I was relieved to see it wasn't padded! It was a normal room that a normal child would have. There was another room next to mine that stood empty. I was later told the Willie. M. Program spent a million dollars to prepare this home and have it staffed 24 hours a day just for me and my therapy. There were no other children because they had been told that I was incredibly dangerous! My previous therapist was forbidden to send my treatment records, so these people had no idea I had healed. They thought I was still the sick little girl I was at six years old in the HBO documentary.

We returned to the living room, where Mommy, content I'd settled in, announced her departure and with a quick hug and a promise to call, was out the door. It was getting late and she needed to return to the rest of her family.

I turned to the three young women sitting on the brown couch and quietly sat down. With a smile they all introduced themselves and then began to ask me questions about my life. As I answered I studied each one carefully. Since I'd made the decision to take care of myself I needed to figure out who these women were and if they were strong enough for me to trust. Theresa was the wisest of the three. An African-American woman, she had deep soft brown eyes that emitted understanding and knowledge and I soon realized I couldn't fool her. Throughout the months we spent together we butted heads sometimes. I hated it because she always won; however she was the one I grew to love. Toni had short hair that always seemed to change colors. She stayed the shortest time of the three but definitely made an impact. Marie, fair skinned with pretty strawberry-blonde hair, was studying for her Master's degree.

As I told them my story, I spoke of Colorado with contempt even though, inside I yearned for it and wished and dreamed of returning home some day. I had loved being with my family there. It had been the happiest times of my life, but since I felt rejected, I covered my pain by throwing it scornfully on my Colorado family. After we visited a bit, they got down to business. Rules and bedtime were established, a schedule was written for the day and chores were assigned. A menu was drawn up. I unpacked my things and made my nest. It would do.

In the beginning, under the watchful eye of the staff, I wasn't allowed to roam far but, as time went on, I proved I was responsible enough and they lightened up. I loved to play with the neighborhood children and became best friends with Moesha, a beautiful African American girl, who lived next door.

My first day of school came much too quickly. The other children had already been going to classes for a few weeks and I was worried I'd be so far behind and was terrified of their possible rejection. As I stepped into Mrs. Womack's third grade classroom I could feel every eye focus on me, the new girl. I didn't realize I was shaking until I pulled my crayons from my bag and in horror watched them dump and scatter across the floor. I quickly dropped to my knees to pick them up, my face flushed beet red in embarrassment. Too busy berating myself for being so clumsy, (and in front of everyone else, no less), I hadn't even realized someone was helping me until I heard a voice. "Here's some, should I put them in the box for you?" I looked up into the pretty blue eyes of the little blonde girl helping me. My heart leapt. I was startled that she looked so much like my best friend I'd left behind in Colorado. "Umm, sure... thank you," I stammered out. "You're welcome. My name's Maki, what's yours?" Rocking back on my heels I softly replied, "Beth." At her questioning look, I spoke again, louder, "My name's Beth and thank you again for helping me." Smiling she sat down and pointed at the empty desk next to her.

School went well that first day. I realized I wasn't behind and the things I didn't understand I decided to just spend extra time to learn. I loved the challenge of learning new things. My teacher was an elderly woman with a strict system that helped keep each child on track. Since I constantly looked for leadership in each adult that crossed my path, I was glad I didn't need to worry about her. She was tough enough to keep 30 children in their seats, but loving enough so each child was still comfortable.

I didn't see Moesha until that afternoon on the bus, since she was a grade ahead of me our paths didn't cross during the day. I was so excited about my first day that she laughed and clapped her hands with amusement as I told her my stories from the day. When I got to Mill House I rushed in to tell my staff how my day went. I was so exuberant, I felt like I was jumping out of my skin. After my afternoon snack I was sent to do my homework, then my chores and finally I was able to go play.

After having lived in the neighborhood for a while the questions started flowing. Why don't you have any parents? Who are those people who watch you? I would avoid them as much as possible. I was embarrassed for people to know my family lived in another city and wouldn't let me live with them. So I kept my home life to myself. If they made stories up I didn't care. The less I said the less they knew and I wouldn't have to worry about being teased. Since the boys had taunted me in West Virginia, I made sure no one knew about Child of Rage. It was difficult at times since I was still young enough to easily be recognized. After several months someone dubbed the staff, "my baby-sitters" and it stuck. Theresa, Toni and Marie laughed when I told them.

Time went by and Christmas was coming soon. Silently, I wondered what type of a Christmas I would have and decided I'd make the most of it. Toni surprised me by inviting me to spend it with her and her family in Winston-Salem. I was overjoyed at being with a family-any family! It was a wonderful Christmas and I had a great time.

Mill House helped me to learn the basics of surviving life independently. I learned to do my own laundry, to cook, and to keep the house and my room clean. The staff taught me well.

Because they had been told I was "super sick" I began to see a local therapist. After several sessions of playing with toys in a sand tray I became bored. She would then show me a picture of people doing an activity and have me make up a story about the people in the picture. After watching her write word for word what I said and then never asking me what I felt or explain what it meant, I would leave feeling as if I'd accomplished nothing. I was used to feeling better after my therapy sessions, yet when I left her office I felt nothing. I needed a safe place to unload my feelings. I thought this therapy was a waste of time. I believed she was stupid and what she did was dumb. Thankfully, the agency stopped my sessions with her and assigned me to a different psychiatrist; therefore I began to make the long trips to the University of North Carolina in Chapel Hill for therapy. My adoptive mother or staff members would drive me.

Since I had already had attachment therapy and had been able to connect securely with Mom Nancy, I could now work successfully with a talk therapist. Talk therapy is all about establishing a relationship with the clients so they will trust the therapist and talk about their feelings. I thought back to the years before when I had Attachment Disorder. I did not want a relationship with anyone then so talk therapy had not helped me. Back then, I would manipulate and con the therapist; which made me sicker (You can't trust an idiot!). This kind and gentle woman would have been an easy target to control. But, I had already discovered, after a year of intensive Attachment Therapy in Evergreen, how good it felt to talk about my feelings so I didn't want to manipulate and con her. I needed someone I could easily talk to and trust. She was that person. I felt comfortable with her and enjoyed being able to finally share my feelings and emotions. I appreciated her help but I knew she didn't truly understand me or what I'd been through. Talking with her helped me but, since she had not been with me when I was deeply disturbed, she could not fully understand me. I appreciated her support and her ability to listen but I still felt isolated because no one there really knew who I was or what I'd been through.

For the year and ten months I remained at Mill House I had at least ten different staff members care for me. As the time went by I knew which ones were tough and which ones I could easily manipulate. With so many different people in and out of my life it was very confusing. There were special ones like Joan who invited me to her home for family potlucks, birthday parties and would make beautiful clothes for me. Wendy was another one who would take me home with her to share family dinners. These women made me feel like I was a normal person who they cared about as a human and not just their "job".

The staff member who left the most footprints on my heart will always be Theresa. She remained the entire time I lived at Mill House. Most of the other people only came because I was their job. I didn't understand, I wasn't someone's job. I was a little girl. I needed to feel special and loved but they didn't really care. After a time I began to believe there must be better opportunities out there than taking care of some little kid. Would I ever be special to someone again?

Theresa was there in a different way than the other staff members. She didn't dump me and abandon me like the other staff members who came and went. She treated me like I was her own daughter. Theresa reminded me of my Mom Nancy. I connected with Theresa because she was powerful enough to stand strong. Boy, was she tough! She wouldn't stand for my manipulation. When I tried to manipulate other staff I would worry about how Theresa would feel and I would feel bad for letting her down. I could picture her expression of disappointment in me. There was no way I could pull the wool over her eyes because she knew me. I'd immersed get so mad at her sometimes. I'd give her a look and she'd match me with the look of "You'd better get yourself in that room and don't you come out until you've cleaned up your attitude." I respected her enough to do as I was told. She expected my chores done right and my room clean. She never raised her voice at me, she had a quiet meaningful presence. Since she was powerful and smart enough to not be conned by me, I felt safe with her. I trusted her and began to love her.

I thought if I worked hard enough my adoptive family would change their minds and take me home. I was consistently on the honor roll. I yearned to go home and be a regular kid. I would see families playing at the park together and would turn away. It hurt to see them so happy and I myself not being able to share in their joy because in my life a family wasn't possible.

Television was an addiction. I would numb out and escape my life. I couldn't even remember what I watched, it was just a way to keep my mind from wandering to painful memories that haunted me.

Even though I played in the neighborhood with my friends, I still put on weight. We began to walk more and eat healthier foods but it didn't help. I didn't realize the weight I had gained wasn't moving until I overcame my losses. I just plain felt empty and tried to fill that emptiness with food. I became excessively hyperactive while I stayed there. I figured if I was constantly a bubbly, cheerful little girl then people would stop dumping me. I felt I had to continually look over my shoulder to make sure no one was coming to take me away again. I just wanted to settle and live my life.

Mommy and Daddy phoned often and would come to visit; sometimes they even brought my little brother. It was during one of the visits that my life changed forever. My brother came one day and we played in the play room where he got to meet some of my friends. I remember a wave of jealousy passed over me and I asked to speak with my mom and dad alone. I had been taught at Mom Nancy's house to always share my feelings or they would eat me up inside. So, I shared with them the feelings of jealousy I had because I knew after he was done here he'd get to go home but I would stay behind. I shared how that made me want to hurt him. I also shared how it scared me because I really didn't want to hurt him so I needed to tell them about it so I could let go of the feelings by talking them out. I knew if I talked them out I wouldn't act them out. Instead of the hugs of acceptance and support I expected, (and needed for being strong, and talking about my feelings rather than acting them out), Mommy gave me a look of horror and rushed out of the room. She was clearly appalled at my honesty. They quickly prepared to leave. Talking about my feelings had always made me feel better, but this time, I wondered if I'd just made the biggest mistake of my life.

As they were leaving, my little brother gave me a big hug and said, "Good-bye Bethy, I love you," and ran to get in the car. As they pulled away we waved to each other until the car disappeared around the corner. I didn't realize it at the time, but it was the last time I would ever lay eyes on my little brother. I received a letter not long after that. I was at the psychiatrist's office when I opened it. I recognized the handwriting of my adoptive mother:

Dear Beth,   Aug. 1, 19

This is the hardest thing we have ever had to do, but yet we know after several years of trying that we have come now to the point where we have to say good-bye. This may be difficult to understand, but to hang on to you is hurting you more than it's helping.

We realize now that expecting you to be able to live in our hom and control your feelings is asking you to do more than you are able. You are such a bright and talented person that we have high hopes th someday in the future with hard work you'll be able to deal with the past and live with less anger and pain.

In our minds, you will always be our daughter, because we hav always loved you. There hasn't been a day that goes by that we haven wished we could have had you before your birth parents. By hurting you, they've hurt us all.
While not in our home, you are in our hearts.

Love always,
Mama
Daddy

I bit down hard on my lip to stop the tears that threatened to spill over my cheeks but as I looked up into the doctor's compassionate eyes I finally let them fall. Confused and numb I just sat and stared at the letter. I wondered if it was because I'd shared my feelings of jealousy with them. I thought that the way to control them was to talk about it. I'd always been taught in Colorado it was the right thing to do but if it made me lose my family then I would not do it again. Foolishly I made the decision to keep my feelings inside after that. After I'd sat there for some time, my psychiatrist had me write some questions down to ask my parents when they would come on September 6, 1991 to say goodbye to me.

It started out as a sunny day and, since my meeting with them wasn't until later that morning, I was still required to go to school. My heart sank when I noticed they had not brought my brother. I asked if I would ever see him again and was told they would not allow me to contact him until he was 18 years old. A sob caught in my throat as I counted the years. "Will I ever see you again?" "Probably not." came the heavy reply that echoed through my heart slamming the doors behind it.

I felt utterly and hopelessly alone. The dark clouds that now covered the sky matched my mood. I cried for hours after they left. I just laid on my bed drowning in my grief. My stomach twisted into a knot. My heart was breaking again! I cried until no more tears could come. This had been the final blow. All I wanted to do was just fall asleep and never wake up. I was an orphan. I had no family and no one who loved me. I was unwanted and unloved.

I cursed God, "I've had it! I thought You were there for me, even if no one else was, I thought for sure You were. Why did You do this to me? Why must You take everything from me and make me suffer? I hate You and I don't want anything to do with You!" All the pain I felt from the rejection exploded out and I hurled at Him. Several hours later my body limp and exhausted from the sobs and tortured thoughts, I fell into a restless sleep.

When I awoke later I sat in deep thought for several hours and wrote in my journal my feelings for the day. Looking back I realized how robotic my handwriting was. It was like I wasn't even human which was exactly how I felt:

I was not given time to grieve or mourn. I was expected to just go on like nothing happened. My life had been shattered and I went to school the next day. My eyes were still swollen from crying. "Would they know?" I wondered. I didn't want them to know what had happened. I was ashamed. I shoved what I'd experienced inside and told none of my friends. I wanted to seem and look like a normal kid, not some wacko whose parents didn't want her, even though inside that's exactly how I felt.

A month later another girl was brought to share Mill House with me. She was constantly flaunting her preteen status and at least once a week in the beginning she would call the staff filthy names and run around the house screaming bloody murder with the staff hot on her heels. Having seen children restrained quickly and easily in Colorado it shocked me to see her run so out of control like a rabid hyena. She would scramble up to the backs of couches barking nasty words from atop her perch. She could easily hurtle chairs in her way and slammed doors behind her to evade the staff. Any object not nailed down became her ammunition. It was impressive to see how adept the staff became at dodging the objects she'd hurl. In terror I would watch it shatter and slide down the walls behind them. Each time she'd flip out my heart would catch in my throat and every nerve in my body would tense. I would watch in astonishment as the staff would finally wrestle her flailing body to the carpet. She would strike her arms out throwing punches and slaps and when her arms were restrained she'd use her legs or her teeth to do damage. All I wanted to do was run screaming from the room but instead my body would freeze and I would just sit in disbelief or pull my knees to my chest and rock myself on my bed as I listened to her ranting rattle through the air and the sound of furniture crashing.

One time we were making crafts and she caught me completely off guard with one of her ear splitting screams. I burst into tears. It was as if the floodgate had been opened, all of her screams bubbled up within me and my nerves finally shrieked, "ENOUGH!" Between my sputtered sobs, and my roommate hissing, a staff member tried to explain it wasn't my fault and that my housemate was just upset and confused. This was her odd way of handling it. As Theresa gathered me in her arms my speeding heart began to settle. I was learning to understand they were powerful enough to take care of me and control my wild housemate. I grew strong enough to not allow my housemate's behavior to affect me. (She gave me lots of practice!) I had been through hell and back and I was letting some twelve year old's rages bother me? How pathetic was that! I wouldn't let her craziness affect me anymore. I was stronger than that!

The time came that she stopped acting wacko and earned the privilege to return home to her family. With mixed feelings I watched her pack. I couldn't understand how she'd earned the right to go home. How was this even possible? Although I was happy for her that she'd be able to go home, it hurt me to see her dreams come true while mine were destroyed. It wasn't fair that she got to be with her family while I stayed at Mill House. I thought I behaved better than her and worked even harder at being a good kid. I never had to be restrained and therefore it was hard for me to comprehend how she'd earned going home and I'd earned being dumped. As the date for her departure got closer and closer I grew more and more angry.

The only way I could cope with my pain was to dream of going to a family who would love me and welcome me in their home. I would surround myself with these visions until the knot in my stomach softened enough to allow my exhausted body and mind a few hours of sleep. Each morning I'd drag myself out of bed, plaster a smile on my face and ask my housemate if she needed any help with her packing.

I thought I'd done a fine job of masking my troubles until things at school started going wrong. When I burst into tears because a teacher corrected me for interrupting, I realized things were getting out of hand. Every little thing affected me. I would look at each of the children in my class and ache inside. I was different from them. No matter how hard I tried, I would always be different. Even my whacked out housemate was able to now lead a normal life and I was stuck forever in this unending limbo. I felt defeated and I began to just look at each day as another trial to overcome.

The different staff that came and went through out the months became a blur. I don't even remember some of their names because it just didn't matter anymore. Theresa became the motherly figure I needed. She was there when I first moved in, my first day of school, when my best friend moved away, the day I lost my family and the day I moved out. She gave me a safe place in her loving arms to release my pain and sadness. Because of her strength and devotion during the time I spent there I grew to love her deeply. She was my rock through the relinquishment and, when my housemate was able to go home, she was the only one who understood my defeat. As the walls of my life seemed to crumble, Theresa would help me build them back up again. When I would question why bad things happened to me, she'd reply without a pause, "God has a plan." She instilled in me that my life had a reason. I didn't know what it was yet but,... God had a plan.

Later I received a letter forwarded through my ex-adoptive parents. It was from my family in Colorado! This was the first contact I'd received since I was ripped from their home fourteen months before. Excitement enveloped me as I ran around the house announcing its arrival. In my reply I wrote of all that had occurred in my life in the past year, and I told them I wanted to come home. I was so scared I'd be rejected and they wouldn't want me anymore. Maybe they had never wanted me in the first place. I'd walk to the mailbox each day in a panic their letter would be in there and in a panic that it wouldn't.

I went for a walk not long after I got that 1st letter and stumbled upon a small patch of dandelions. It reminded me of the little dandelion I had placed on my Mom Nancy's pillow several days before I'd been taken from her home. The memories of all the fun times we shared came flooding back as I sat down to surround myself with the delicate, sweet smell. Those simple yellow blossoms seen as a nuisance weed to some and a small treasure to others filled me with hope and reassurance that somewhere out there someone loved me. Plucking one that had already gone to seed I closed my eyes and made a wish that one day I could go home to the family I loved. I pursed my lips together, inhaled deeply, and with a blast of breath sent the seeds scattering into the wind.

Chapter 17
The Eye Of The Storm

My home wasn't without that "Old Woman and the Shoe" feeling for long. I continued to take in children for respite care and agreed to work long term with another two girls and a boy. Arriving within a few months of each other, they all had varying degrees of psychosis and even more variable histories. As one child graduated out of the "new kid" room, I would be placed with another new child. The last child, a boy, was called Damon.

The photo showed a rail thin child. His pale complexion emphasized unusual facial features, evidence of his cocaine addiction at birth. The file was thick with his story. Olivia, the caring nurse who had held Damon's tiny, newly born body through his blood transfusion, and withstood his tremors and high pitched screams caused by the pain of his withdrawals immediately connected with the infant. Knowing his biological mother had a year to clean up her act and prove competency before the infant could be adopted, Olivia applied for a Colorado Foster Care License and took the baby home.

I remembered reading about babies addicted to cocaine like Damon. Their nerve endings were raw, so each loving contact, a gentle touch, a kind word, caused a feeling like electrical shocks to emanate throughout their tiny bodies. It caused severe pain. I recalled reading about the destruction of the limbic system of the brain (the love and attachment department). I wonder how much damage he had endured. I read on and sadly understood. Hugging, snuggling and rocking weren't comforting to tiny Damon, and because every interaction with people resulted in agony, he resisted the only way a tiny baby could. He pulled deep within himself.

Each time Olivia would talk to him or touch him to feed or comfort him, his wails overcame her quiet suburban home. Even just turning on a light at night to check him resulted in ear splitting screams. Her love persevered. She took a hiatus from her nursing position at the hospital to care for the baby. Although she had taught many new mothers the required feeding and care requirements for a newborn, it was very different with a baby suffering from cocaine damage. He cried most of the time and when he wasn't wailing he was limp and unresponsive.

As Damon grew, his body had overcome some of the many effects of the cocaine which had saturated every cell in his little body. His high risk status and exhausting care needs caused so much stress on Olivia that she became extremely ill and asked to have Damon removed temporarily while she recuperated and regained her strength. She knew that with his compromised health, her viral infection could kill him, so she sadly handed over her six month old foster child to another family. Loving him so much, she called and explained to the temporary foster mom how to use his respirator when he had difficulty breathing and to be extra cautious on chilly mornings or if the pollution was high. Packing his little bag with enough clothing for two weeks (and the specialized formula along with his supplements and organic baby food), her heart was weary and sad as she stood across the room and blew a kiss to Damon in order not to infect him.

A few weeks later, Olivia was feeling as exuberant as ever and called to arrange to pick up her son, but her request was refused. Their excuse was that he had just settled in, and another move would be too hard on him. Knowing how important every day of his young life was to the foundation of personality and conscience, she begged and pleaded with the family to hand over Damon. She was met with resistance. Turning to the social system which had licensed her to keep the special needs infant, she exhausted every avenue until finally, after five months had lapsed since she had last seen Damon, a woman in management finally listened to her pleas. A month later, Damon was returned to her and her husband, Rob's, joyous arms, but their little boy pushed them away.

Since a year had passed since his birth and his biological mother failed to meet even the minimum requirements for his return to her, Damon became available for adoption. Rob and Olivia jumped at the chance for him to be a permanent part of their family. He had already been absent for half of that time, and the couple knew that they didn't want to miss one more day of Damon's life.

His odd behaviors and lack of self-control were readily apparent, but since Damon's parents knew his cocaine laden history, they wrote it off as either a growth phase or a result of the drugs. Their worries of brain damage were laid to rest when he excelled in preschool and kindergarten, but their concerns over his behavior began to deepen. Every teacher he had said variations of the same thing. "Damon has excessive energy, picks on weaker kids and seems to have a total lack of self-control." Concerned, his parents sought help.

Having worked at the hospital, Olivia first went to the pediatrician that she had worked under. No insights were gained by their meeting, so she went to a neurologist to see if Damon's behavior was the result of his in-utero environment. Again, she left his office with little information or help. Setting up an appointment with a psychiatrist, she explained her unsuccessful attempts for help in controlling Damon's escalating behavior. As she was leaving the receptionist's desk, she noticed an announcement hanging on the bulletin board. There was to be a seminar on a medication for hyperactive children. She made a mental note to call and sign-up for the workshop.

The psychiatrist offered her behavioral modification techniques to implement, and told her to reinforce his positive behavior more than consequencing his negative actions. Olivia was given a star chart to use and left feeling like she finally received some helpful advice.

The following week, she attended the seminar and became convinced that she should try Ritalin with Damon. It claimed to help reduce excessive energy levels and seemed like the miracle drug that would help solve her son's problems. She called the psychiatrist's office and setup another appointment.

She had been using the parenting techniques the psychiatrist had recommended to encourage more positive behavior. Olivia knew it wasn't working when he began flunking first grade and beating up other children on the playground. She prayed that the Ritalin would be her answer since the behavior modification star chart was failing.

After a year and a half on the new fad drug, she had seen some improvements in his ability to focus and stay on task. His rude and obstinate manner persisted as did his frequent violent outbursts. When, in third grade, he burned down the storage building in their back yard after burning down the neighbor's garage only a few days previously, she knew something else had to be done.

Having taken Damon to frequent therapy sessions since the first visit with the psychiatrist, she had spent many hours in the waiting room. On one such occasion, as the worry about her son's future loomed over her heart, she saw another announcement on the bulletin board. It was titled, "Parenting the Disturbed Child." Thinking she might possibly have a severely troubled child on her hands, she read further. Dr. Foster Cline was teaching a two day seminar on Reactive Attachment Disorder and bonding. This disorder was new to her, so she read the list of symptoms and realized her son might be suffering from RAD.

With renewed enthusiasm, she rushed home after Damon's therapy and opened up her library of books on child development. Sure enough, there, hidden in an obscure passage of her college text was a paragraph on the Ainsworth study that broke attachment issues down into four categories, along with a list of possible causes. As if Damon's picture were next to the heading of in-utero trauma, Olivia's eyes jumped to that exact spot. Her texts were old so they gave no current information, but now that she had a lead, she became determined to find more. She laughed through out the intense workshop on RAD. She laughed, not only because Dr. Cline was humorous, but because she finally had hope for her child. It felt so good after seven years with such grief and worry.

Even though the original research was done by Dr. John Bowlby fifty years ago, because the disorder was not yet in the manual psychiatrists used for diagnosing disorders,(the Diagnostic and Statistical Manual-DSM), the psychiatrist had no knowledge of the diagnosis and could offer no help. Olivia searched the library and found a book Dr. Foster Cline had written on the subject. Understanding and Treating the Severely Disturbed Child offered her insights into the symptoms, causes and therapies for children with Attachment Disorder. Luckily, she thought, The Attachment Center at Evergreen that the great doctor had started in 1972 was right in Colorado and was one of the few centers in the US that offered treatment for these children.

Obtaining the phone number for the agency, she called them right away to setup a consultation with Rob, Damon and herself. At eight years old,

Damon was admitted into the specialized therapeutic program. At long last they had finally found help for their son.

During the two weeks of intensive therapy at the start of Damon's treatment Rob and Olivia learned that the abuse of the smaller school children was much more severe than they thought. They knew that Damon showed no remorse for the bad things that he did, but during therapy, they learned just how little empathy their son really had.

As the treatment day after day uncovered the depth of his mental illness, the professionals involved started discussing long term options for Damon. He was much more disturbed than Olivia and Rob had known and since the eight year old boy held a deep seated anger towards his mother, all involved thought that placement in a therapeutic home was best for Damon's ultimate success. She was exhausted! A schedule of visits was created in order to ease the pain Rob and Olivia would inevitably feel at leaving their son's care to others. They left their boy, with heavy hearts but hopeful expectations.

Damon had been placed with another family in the agency, but his severe defiance and minimal progress after 6 months caused his therapist to consider other alternatives. That's when I was called. They felt that my rural environment, tenacity, and experience with tough kids could bring Damon around if he truly wanted to heal.

I already had two girls that had each already earned moving from the "new kid room" to rooms upstairs, so knowing I had room in my heart and room in my home, I agreed to take this troubled child. He had flunked out of one therapeutic family, so I prepared for a hellish child that even professional parents had a hard time with. Imagine my surprise when he walked politely through my door, with his suitcase and bottle of Ritalin, and smiled at me.

His fifty-five pound frame was frail and his presently quiet demeanor matched his build. Shaking my hand firmly, I noted that his blue eyes held sadness as he looked straight into my eyes and said "nice to meet you." When I sent him off to his room to unpack, he replied with a firm, "Yes, Mom Nancy!" before trotting off to put his things away. My image of this child as a monster was changing quickly. His freckle faced grin touched me.

The next day, I started Damon on the normal routine of breakfast, feelings book entry and chores before playtime. He strong sat before meals and completed his chores quickly and right the first time. I was impressed with how hard he was trying to please.

Terena liked having him around because he quickly earned his horseback riding privilege and the two of them spent days in the summer sun absorbing the movement of the steeds they rode. She taught him how to sit on a horse bareback and how to ask them for a back or side step. Damon excelled with horses. We had found his special talent!

Damon helped Terena prepare for the rodeo queen competition by brushing Quest's coat until the sheen was nearly blinding. He helped wrap the horse's legs and pick out her hooves while Terena changed into the purple outfit I had made as her gift the previous Christmas. He eagerly dusted her boots when she finally mounted and smiled at her as we all watched her enter the ring for the competition. We all cheered each contestant from the stands. Knowing a tack change was coming up, as she finished her last flying lead change and stopped, he raced to the gate to meet her. As I watched, I saw his eyes alight with joy while he worked with my daughter and her gray mare. I knew that had Beth been there, she too would have been excitedly helping Terena.

He helped hold her horse as she dismounted and as Jerry and I rounded the arena corner to greet them, I saw Damon wrap his arms around his older sister and exclaim, "That was perfect! You looked awesome out there!" Jerry hugged her and took Quest's reins as I embraced my daughter. With a huge smile and shining eyes she lovingly told how proud she was of her horse; Damon patted Quest in admiration as Terena turned to take her horse back to the trailer for a drink and some grain.

We all anxiously awaited the results along with the parents of the other 17 participants. The Rodeo Royalty from the previous year was there to crown the winners. As we waited the tension increased. Terena had worked for three years and competed twice unsuccessfully. This was a huge goal for her.

Finally, the score sheets were tallied and the judges had made their selection. When Terena's name was announced over the loud speakers, the whoops and hollers that erupted from the stands were so enthusiastic it startled some of the horses waiting nearby. She had many friends in the competition and even though they were competitors they congratulated her profusely. I watched from the stands as they pinned the tiara on her cowboy hat and wrapped a rosette of roses around Quest's neck. She had done it!

As her tear stained cheeks sparkled over her big bright smile, she looked at me and with a glimpse of sadness whispered, "Beth should be here!" Her only sister, who had helped her get to where she currently was had to miss the biggest honor Terena had yet achieved. Her crown was beautiful and sparkling, but to her, it had lost its luster since she couldn't share it with Beth. I flashed back in my mind to the vision of Beth carrying the American flag around the arena as Terena trained her horse to carry it with honor.

Terena was the rodeo queen. Beth was still missing. Chucky had served his time in jail and was now working hard on an Alaskan fishing boat. The danger and adrenaline rush of working so strenuously and for such a large sum of money was teaching him some valuable lessons. He wrote of the beauty he was seeing and the intense will it took to work so hard. I laughed when I received a huge salmon in the mail with the ice melting; the mail carrier didn't find it quite so amusing. That fish was full of love! It felt good to feel proud of my son.

As the prayers for my children were answered I was relieved and overjoyed. Chucky was off on his Alaskan adventure, my oldest son, R.B., was returning home from the Persian Gulf. He would be with his family again soon, and with the war over he was safe from enemy fire and the threat of capture. Ted was excelling at school and in his family life as was Alicia. She was now in high school and handling the challenges of life. Will was still struggling in school, so his family decided to apply for a program which taught occupational skills while at the same time finishing high school. He was preparing to leave for Utah to begin. Gabriel was working on his life and preparing to go to school full time while living with Lori. He was back on track and I was pleased to hear of his progress. He had worked hard while living with us and I was relieved to see my many prayers for him had been answered. He was building new relationships and trust with Lori's family.

The children who had once resided under our roof still filled my heart. I ached for them. With each bit of news I received about their successes and accomplishments, I felt a combination of nostalgia for when they were living with me and pride at how hard each had worked to become a loving part of their families.

The periodic letter or phone call I received throughout the year from the families and children I had helped was like having Christmas all year long. Each call or card was a treasured gift. Terena wrote to her little sister who had been gone for over a year. The knowledge that Beth might never receive the offerings of hope and love didn't quench our thirst to contact her so we kept writing. I had nearly given up, yet Terena persevered.

One September day, returning home, I pulled into the driveway to find Terena jumping up and down and shrieking. As a teenager, I hadn't seen her act so childish and as I stepped from the van, she nearly bowled me over. As if I had just learned that the Red Sox had finally won the World Series, I was overcome with emotion as I deciphered Terena's excited chatter. "Mom! Mom, Mom! I got a letter. I got a letter Mom. It's right here!" Handing me a crumpled purple envelope, I had hardly pulled the parchment from it when Terena tackled me in a hug. "Let's go get her Mom. Let's go!" Knowing who the letter was from long before I actually saw Beth's signature at the bottom, I stood in the driveway and absorbed every word she had written to Terena. There was no information about where she was in the content of the message, but the return address was clearly visible and I knew we now had a chance to reach out to her.

There was one thing I needed to know right away. My heart was full to overflowing with hope that my daughter would now be able to come home. Did Jerry feel the same? I was terrified that he might say we have had enough children, we didn't need one more. My heart would forever have this gaping hole in it reserved only for my Magnolia Blossom. I rushed to the construction area beside the house. My cowboy was putting the foundation in for our new barn. He was in a trench five feet deep. When I rushed to him calling his name he stood up with only his head above ground. In this comical position I asked him the question that was burning within me. Can we bring Beth home and adopt her? He looked up at me from the trench, squinting into the sun he quickly stated, "Well, of course!" I love that man! I sighed with relief and rushed inside with Terena.

Immediately, Terena and I put pen to paper and bled our hearts out into two separate letters. We had found her and now, we had to convince her to come home where she belonged. I stayed awake all night to edit the many hours of video tape I had recorded when she was with us. As dawn broke, I had limited it to forty minutes filled with visions of laughter, love and the life we shared with Beth. The music I over laid on the video added extra emphasis. Placing excess postage onto the thick manila envelope, we excitedly placed the letter gingerly into the mailbox the following day. With a prayer, Terena and I watched as the postman collected and carried it off on its long journey across the country.

As we awaited Beth's reply, Damon finally got real with his emotions and I began to see the child that had blown out of his previous therapeutic family. For five months he had been compliant, respectful and helpful; the honeymoon was apparently over as he stomped through the house shooting hate-filled looks at those he once got along with and cursing anyone and anything in his path.

On one such day, he caused $175 worth of damage to my van when I asked him to take the trash out. Angry at the world, he took his aggression out on the rear windshield wiper, bending it back and forth until it broke off into his hands. Later the same afternoon, he tried stealing some of the baklava I was making so I had him go to his room and come out when he could think of a better way to get the dessert. His rage boiled over as he walked toward his room. He grabbed the video camera from the table and threw it across the room. A spray of pieces rained down as it came crashing down onto the floor. Looking into his defiant face, I smiled sadly as I said, "Well Sweetie, now you have two things to think about while you're in your room." The repair costs were well over $1000, and as I used natural consequences to teach each child, it was now Damon's job to earn the money for the damages. He would have to earn $5 each day until he paid it off. An expensive hobby!

While Damon worked on his life and earned the repair money, Terena and I eagerly checked the mail daily. Sure enough, two weeks after we had sent a reply to Beth's new address, an envelope arrived from North Carolina. I thought it strange how our address was typed, but I figured Beth must be learning keyboarding skills. I tore open the letter. It was typed as well.

The opening line of "Dear Mrs. Thomas" didn't fill my heart with hope and as I read on, I learned that Beth hadn't written this letter. Her caseworker had. Fear overcame me as I read its message.

"You have no right to get this child's hopes up. Your statement telling this child that she is coming back to live with you when there is no evidence to back it up is irresponsible and reckless. If you ever write anything like that again, we will stop all communication with you!" I took a deep breath when I realized these people didn't understand the immense magnitude of our love for Beth and how she truly belonged with us. How could they? Still paralyzed with panic at the thought of losing Beth again, I started carefully composing a letter to the case worker explaining my history with Beth, our intentions, and sincere apologies for causing any difficulty.

After that, whenever I wrote to my dear daughter who was two thousand miles away, I talked about the weather, the animals and similar fluff subjects in order to keep the boat afloat. How desperately I wanted to open my heart to little Beth, who I thought, must be wondering if we still loved her or if we ever had.

I learned through several more letters from the agency that the minister or his wife had told them that Beth had been removed from our house because she had tried, on several occasions, to kill me. She supposedly tried to push me down the stairs. It never happened and I quickly set the record straight. I also learned that a multi million dollar project was started for Beth and other severely disturbed children, and that the whole project was forced to move faster in order to accommodate Beth when her family placed her there. She had special therapists, around the clock staff and an entire home all set aside just for her, because she was 'so dangerous'. As I learned about the huge expense the state of North Carolina had incurred that could have been used to help many needy children I was furious. Why had these people not contacted us to find out the truth? When Beth left us she was well on the way to full recovery!

Once we started communicating I was relieved to learn that the agency now caring for Beth, was not surprised to find out the truth regarding Beth's behavior and healing. They had seen no violent tendencies or signs of emotional disturbance since they'd had her.

Knowing that I had to prove my worthiness as a parent to the social workers in North Carolina, I began a campaign to obtain letters from anyone willing to write regarding my relationship with Beth to help us bring her home. Our minister, Beth's teachers, the school principal, the psychiatrist, other therapeutic families and the 4-H leaders all poured their hearts into the cause with beautiful letters.

In the meantime, as I was fighting for Beth to be returned, Damon was fighting his own battles. He pushed everyone away by refusing to brush his teeth or bathe. Some days the stench was pretty wicked. I made the mistake of having the orthodontist put on braces to straighten his very crooked teeth. As I gave him his morning hug and sent off him to the bathroom to get ready for the day I noticed a piece of spinach dangling from the thin wire as if it were Spanish moss dangling from a tree. We hadn't had spinach in four days.

Having worn braces myself as a kid, I understood the importance of cleaning one's mouth after every meal in order to avoid tooth decay. I thought that maybe he had never been taught the proper care for his new mouth jewelry, so I set aside special time to teach him how to brush and floss properly around the wires.

Several days passed and I saw that he still refused to maintain proper oral hygiene. I broke down and finally started to brush his teeth for him daily, not realizing that in doing so, I was taking all the concern from him and putting it on myself. I was actually empowering him to not care! As he became more insolent I realized my mistake and stopped.

Not sure what to do next, I decided to hire the dental hygienist to clean his teeth weekly. Damon earned twenty dollars every week to pay for the service and as he gradually got more and more into debt, I realized I had set up a situation that neither one of us could win. His heart was more important to me than his teeth, so I stopped worrying about his brushing routine altogether and decided to allow nature to take its course. I could love him even if he had putrid breath and he may have to lose a tooth before he would learn the importance of the simple brushing.

Damon had been with us for about nine months and his lack of bathing was becoming a problem. He had cleaned himself regularly for the first five months he was with us, so I knew he could do it, but he chose to make a power struggle out of it instead. Initially, I would tell him, "Damon, please go take a bath". Filling the tub full of water, he'd sprinkle a little water on the floor and in his hair, he'd come grinning out of the bathroom minutes later. (The dirt still firmly in place!) I would tell him to go take another one, this time to wash with soap. Again, the tub would be filled, water sprinkled and instead of just a little water on his hair, he'd rub some shampoo into it and walk out without rinsing it.

Weeks went by and I realized my trying to get him to bathe was just a way he was manipulating our relationship, so I quit. Hugging him one afternoon, I told him, "I love my horse and I love my dog and they don't smell very good. So you don't have to smell good for me to love you either. Whenever you're ready, just ask and you can take a bath."

Eight weeks went by and as his stench became so overwhelming that the family drove with the van windows opened and the fan on high. Fungus had infected his feet to the point where they were purple and cracked clear up to his ankles. When I asked him about his condition he insisted it wasn't fungus from dirt but a 'weathering' problem. Thinking to myself I wondered if that was like the weathering old barn boards get from being out in the elements for years on end. As the skin inflammation was getting worse from the filth, I knew I had to take action.

I felt that if left to Damon's own accord, he'd never take a bath again, no matter what body parts of his rotted and fell off so I came up with a plan. Filling up the tub with warm water and bubble bath, I called for Damon to put on his swimming trunks. A snotty demanding, "Why?" was the first thing out of his mouth. Looking straight into his eyes, I asked, "What did I just ask you to do, Damon?" He told me he was going to his room to change. As he did so, I found a washcloth and some liquid bath soap.

He stood in the bathroom door watching me as I swirled the bubbles about the warm water. I had him get in. "I never had a chance to wash you as a baby, so this will be fun! You'll be all clean and shiny when we're done!" I scrubbed his arms and legs, lifted his arms up and washed his pits. Scrubbing his back, I watched as the layers of dirt, sweat and grime mixed with the bubbly water to make a homogeneous muddy foam. "Rubber ducky, you're the one. Rubber Ducky, you're so fun!" I sang as I scrubbed. Pouring shampoo into the palm of my hand, I built the song to a higher pitch with more enthusiasm as I made a frothy mound out of his hair. His mumbling grumblings stopped and his glare almost broke into a smile as he looked at his reflection in the faucet when I made several spikes out if his hair to make him look like the Statue of Liberty. His blonde hair, which had been hidden under a dark layer of slime, made great spikes when supported by the soap. As I finished rinsing his hair, I handed him the washcloth and started to leave the room. With my hand on the doorknob, I turned and said, "If you want to keep what's under those trunks you might want to wash it." With that, I went out and closed it behind me.

The next night, I watched as his eyes narrowed into angry slits when I asked him to put his swimming trunks on again. Steam just about blew from his ears as he stomped off to his room. Again, I filled up the tub with warm water and bubble bath and I scrubbed him while singing the Rubber Ducky song. I did a great job! Twenty minutes later, I handed him the wash cloth and gave him the same instructions about washing under his suit as I left.

On the third day, as I was filling up the tub, I told Damon to go put his bathing suit on. He stood, defiantly and stared at me. "I think I can do it myself, Mom," his nostrils flared as he haughtily tilted his head up. Smiling at him as I poured in the bubble bath, I said, "No Sweetie, really, I don't mind. I don't think you're ready yet and besides, I didn't get to do it when you were little and I really enjoy singing to you while I scrub!" Still standing squarely he insisted again, "Mom, really, I can do it myself!" I playfully resisted one more time. "Damon, I don't think you're ready yet!" "Mom! Please! let me do it myself!" Smiling I gave him a hug and said, "Oh all right, but if you need some help just holler. I'm not so sure you're ready, but I suppose you can try it."

Closing the door behind me, I turned back and pressed my ear to the wood. Splash! Ker-plunk!" I listened as he stepped into the water and began washing himself. Ever so quietly, I heard him sing, "Rubber ducky, you're the one. Rubber ducky, you're so fun!" Giggling under my breath, I turned away knowing that he had done some valuable imprinting over the past two days. I smiled harder when I visualized him fifteen years older, washing his own baby son, singing "Rubber ducky, you're the one!"

From then on, whenever he went more than three days between baths, I would start filling the tub. That was his cue to race into the bathroom and ask, "Mom, can I please take a bath now?" Smiling, I'd give him a hug and say, "Yes, Damon, the tub is ready for you!"

Damon was small for his age at ten, and people believed he was several years younger. I had read about his ability to smile or cry at will when reading his intake report and how his instant, ready smile had caused many adults to say, "You're so cute! I could take you home with me!" I thought about how undermining this was to Olivia as she struggled to keep her son under control while he pushed her love away. Each time that was said, Olivia had shared how it sabotaged her attempts to get her son to love her and want to be part of the family. It made her feel even more like a failure. I had read that he could go from pitiful sobs to a charming grin in about two seconds flat, but had yet to see this behavior.

Sure enough, when he had been with me for year, I got my chance. We were at Vacation Bible School and as I signed the other children in, he tugged at my shirt and whined, "I wanna be in Vacation Bible School!" The day before I had shared with him that since he had not yet earned the privilege to be with other smaller kids he and I would spend the time together doing something fun. Knowing full well that tugging on my clothing and whining would get him nowhere, I looked at him and softly said, "Well Sweetie, since you're not strong enough to ask correctly, I guess you'll stay home with me this week." I watched as he stared at the bright light bulbs in the sanctuary before squeezing his eyes shut, tears streaming down his cheeks. Sobbing and stomping about, he screamed, "I wanna go! You're so mean! Everybody else gets to go! You just don't like me!" Throwing himself on to the rug, he bucked and rolled around as he screamed and kicked. I watched in amusement as he threw a complete temper tantrum in the middle of our church. Fortunately my fellow parishioners knew I worked with sick children, so they simply stepped around him and continued on with their business.

The usual response to those around Damon when he threw such a fit was to feel sorry for him and blame Olivia for the outburst. He received none of the typical, "Oh, don't be so hard on him!" or "Oh, let the poor boy go if he wants to so badly." His tears and fit throwing used to allow him to manipulate the adults surrounding him; with me, it only emphasized his inability to handle Vacation Bible School.

When his whines had softened a bit, I clearly stated, "Damon, you'll have to figure out a better way to get what you want than that." I just pictured him in 10 years trying to get a raise from his boss with that whopper of a fit! And with that, I hugged the other kids and left with Damon in tow.

During the week of Vacation Bible School, Terena turned sixteen. Her boyfriend, Leon, had driven up from Denver with another one of his friends, Adam, and as they prepared the horses for a trail ride I heard Damon screaming outside. Rushing out the front door I called them all to the house and demanded to know what had happened from the three teens. Terena started. "Damon and Adam were bickering when all of a sudden Damon grabbed a shovel and smashed it into the back of Adams head!" Leon, having known Adam for several years quipped, "Damon's really lucky to even be alive after a stunt like that!" I agreed and thanked the adolescent for his self-control.

Returning to the house, I asked Damon to give me his version of the story, not because I didn't trust Terena, but because it was important for Damon to tell the truth. I was proud of him when he admitted to losing it and using the shovel in an attack. Hugging him, I informed him that he had to do a restitution chore for Adam before he left. As his anger swelled up, I saw him control his feelings and process through the rage. For the first time, he had controlled his emotions and allowed his mind to think first instead of just acting on the feelings. I hugged him again and felt that, although the previous episode didn't support it, he was getting stronger.

It was when Damon was almost healthy that I received a letter from North Carolina social services. Beth's caseworker, Mary Jo was finally convinced that it was acceptable for Beth to see us. When we got word of our visit approval, I booked two airline tickets to North Carolina and Terena and I began packing.

The cold October weather had settled in over Colorado and as we drove to the airport construction had closed the only highway to the airport. Sitting in traffic for hours, we watched as our departure time approached and finally passed. We had missed our flight! After hours of sitting still on the highway, the traffic began to creep forward as the state patrol rerouted the miles of backed up vehicles. Our tires were moving, but our spirits were so low that I'm sure the van had trouble dragging us along. What could we do now? Had we blown our one chance to hold onto Beth and convince the state that we were her family?

Arriving at the Denver airport two hours after our flight had departed, we were left with few options. Not willing to quit, we convinced the airline to work with us. We flew all night changing planes many times. We arrived frazzled, tired and worried, then rented a car and tore through the city until we arrived at the hotel where we were supposed to meet Beth. It was 9:30 am.; we were an hour late and we both prayed that she'd still be there.

They were preparing to leave and as we walked into the hotel lobby, our little Beth, who wasn't so little anymore, saw us and ran into my arms. Terena waited patiently to hug her long lost sister and as tears streamed down our three faces, I saw Beth's case worker, Mary Jo, and her current foster mom Nanette, watching from across the room. They were crying too. The image of the little eight year old, strong, healthy girl that had left my arms two years previously was replaced by the ten year old young girl standing in front of us, four inches taller, sixty pounds heavier!

I hugged her again, not really believing that I was there, in North Carolina, holding my sweet, wonderful Magnolia Blossom. I cried into her hair and kissed her chubby cheeks. I had waited so long to see her again, to hold her and talk with her and here she was, very real, excitedly talking a mile a minute.

Taking Beth's hand we walked to the couch and surrounding chairs where we sat and talked for a few hours. All the while, too excited to sit, Beth and Terena talked and explored the hotel lobby. They giggled and laughed, skipped through the hallways hand in hand and shared ideas they both had for the future. My heart was dancing on clouds as I watched the two of them together again.

Feeling like I was trustworthy and honest, Mary Jo left Beth with us overnight. The girls and I shared the afternoon shopping, eating and talking.

Before we knew it, it was time to head to Beth's foster family's home for dinner. I learned then that Beth's excessive weight gain was exactly the same amount of weight, to the pound, that I had gained and as our plump bodies meshed into a hug, I didn't care what her outside looked like. I loved what was inside.

That night, Terena and I had been awake for 36 hours. We crashed but, Beth didn't sleep a wink. She bounced around our hotel room jabbering and giggling the entire night while Terena and I slept. She continued to feel the excitement and couldn't find rest, so the television kept her occupied until we awoke the next morning.

Sharing breakfast, the three of us discussed Jerry's barn project and how someday, when Beth was able to come home, she and Terena would move into the loft of the barn for the summer. They planned the decor and a big rope to swing downstairs in a hurry when supper was ready. I watched as I thought how different our little Beth was from when she left. Physically she had changed. Emotionally she had changed. Mentally she had changed. I wondered if we'd ever find the Beth all of us had so deeply fallen in love with.

As we drove to the airport, Mary Jo was following behind to take Beth back to her foster family. I yearned to just steal her away and take her home with us, but we had come so close to getting her back into our care using the legal avenues that, of course, I wouldn't mess it up now. Terena's urging to kidnap Beth didn't help, but I knew God was watching and he'd correct the situation before too long.

I kissed my daughter goodbye and watched as Terena and Beth embraced one final time before we boarded our plane. I turned around once, when through the gate, to see her waving and smiling, gritting her teeth to hold back tears. I was doing the same and I blew her a kiss before entering the plane. The visit was over and I didn't know what would happen next.

When we arrived in Denver, I picked the children up from their various respite places and began the long drive back into the mountains. We stopped in Evergreen for some therapy and since Damon was becoming healthier the therapy was getting less intense and less frequent for him. Thinking he had been on Ritalin for long enough, CJ called the prescribing psychiatrist and asked if we could start pulling him off the drug. It was agreed that for the next month, his dosage would be reduced until he no longer was taking any. We also addressed Damon's stealing. He was still craftier than a wagon full of monkeys, so CJ told him his therapy homework was to be sneaky in loving ways.

I'd find little loving notes hidden in my bathroom washcloths or a pretty picture hidden between my pillow and blankets. Tucked into my shoes I'd find flowers with poems and pretty rocks hidden in my dinner napkin. He was able to sneak into my car, my dresser, my closet and the bookshelf. I found tiny notes tucked in various places for years after that assignment, each time, a smile would spread across my face and a warm glow would fill my heart. The activity had worked. Damon could use his sneakiness to do loving things.

While Damon was busy finding ways he could fulfill his therapy homework, I was talking to Beth and writing to her regularly. Within a month of our visit, the state of North Carolina decided she could come home to us. My family would be complete again and I was ecstatic! I tried to stay grounded those few weeks we waited. The feeling of lightness that had so long ago disappeared returned with such force that I felt if I wasn't holding on to something, I'd float away. So much happiness filled my being that it counteracted the force of gravity. Try to figure that out Sir Isaac Newton! Beth was coming home!

The household was jittery in anticipation as we awaited Beth's return; it was almost as if we were expecting a new baby. As the time ticked by, the children continued going to school. Terena was a junior in high school, so she was applying for scholarships and starting her college selection process. Damon was excelling in school, exhibiting self-control and responsibility.

Damon had never had many friends before, so when he came home from school one day beaming at me, I asked what he was so happy about. "I have a friend!" he exclaimed enthusiastically. Curious, I offered to pick him up from school the following day to meet his new buddy. The next afternoon, the two boys came strutting over to the car with their arms around each other's shoulders. "This is my friend Johnny!" Damon explained. I shook the little boy's hand and looked in amazement at the two boys. They both had the same facial features indicating their shared cocaine addiction at birth. Like is, indeed, attracted to like.

Damon, who had been off all medications for several weeks, was making such good decisions that I began entrusting the care of Troika, an older Arabian brood mare to him. Twice a day he would remember to ask to apply her ointment to her various cuts and scrapes. In a gentle and caring manner, he would cautiously apply the salve while talking quietly to her. When she stomped her foot or walked away from him, his patience was obvious by his ability to wait for her to return and stand still. He had developed compassion and empathy for not only the horse, but for other beings as well.

My good friend Jo had seen Damon work gently, diligently and carefully around the horses during some of the shows Terena had participated in during the summer. Knowing the children in my care came from rough homes and even tougher beginnings, she wanted to do something for Damon to encourage his work with horses. As she was an amazing seamstress, she carefully cut out a pattern of a duster on the heavy canvas in her shop. Working for hours, she sewed the many pieces of the long, cowboy coat together before the next show and presented it to him after first asking for my approval. He beamed with pride as he tried it on and proudly wore it throughout the entire day. He knew that she had thought so much of him that she had made him a gift that made him look on the outside what he felt on the inside. He was warm, practical and most of all, he was a cowboy.

The community support I received from my little rural town was a tremendous help. They accepted the kids and loved them for what they were just as my family did. They often asked what they could do to help or offered their prayers and resources for my family. The police were used to receiving odd calls from me regarding runaways or thefts and would occasionally refer troubled youth in our community to me for help and guidance. Without their help, I don't believe I could have had the success that I had working with these children.

I could see that Damon was doing well, but the acceptance from the community allowed him to believe he had truly changed for the better. The duster jacket he had received taught him that others saw him for who he was and what he did, and could identify that he was a hard working part of society. It helped him to see that good deeds don't go unnoticed and that if he wanted something bad enough, in his case to be a cowboy, he'd eventually get there. He wore that duster everywhere!

Terena with Quest,

happy Rodeo Queen!

Terena watching Beth during visit in North Carolina.

Beth's first day back home in Colorado. Dark circles reveal her stress.

Chapter 18
Mountain Mermaid

Beth: *My heart pounded with anxiety the day I finally held the letter they wrote back to me in my hands. Not wanting to face the pain of rejection I was too terrified to open it. What would it hold? Had they moved on easily in their lives without me? Did I even mean anything to them or was I just some little kid they'd worked with? I set it aside only to keep returning to it until the suspense became too much. I couldn't stand it anymore and I ripped it open. I hadn't realized I'd been holding my breath until it rushed out of me in relief as I read the words, "We love you and want you to come home!" I was ecstatic!! I wasn't just some little kid everyone had a forgotten about. My dreams of one day being in a family that loved me were possible.*

They explained they'd sent numerous letters and they were so happy to hear from me. Wait a second, I thought. They had sent letters before this one? Why hadn't I received any? My face flushed with anger as I thought of my ex-adoptive parents. Why would they do that to me? Didn't they realize how important this family was to me? Didn't they realize I thought I'd been forgotten, unloved and tossed out like yesterday's news? Those letters would have made me feel like I was special. I was so confused as the questions circled in my head.

I tried to put them aside as I read and reread each word from the letter. I still had feelings of rejection screaming within me that told me to be cautious, but I didn't want to be cautious anymore. I just wanted to believe I was someday going home and actually be a normal kid. I imagined myself climbing the mountains, riding horses and having mud fights with the other kids there. I had so many questions about every thing. How was everyone? What were they doing these days?

I would soak each letter up when it arrived. Each one would become dog-eared from being read over and over. I discovered Ted and Alicia were able to return home to their families and were doing terrific. Will had moved in with a family that wanted a son. I never learned very much about Gabriel and I wondered what happened to him. Terena had been selected as Rodeo Queen! I was so proud of my big sister. The letters filled me with hope.

After a while I began to question why I wasn't returning home to them. They had said they wanted me but why was I still at Mill House. I knew there must be something wrong. I didn't say anything but I would lay awake at night wondering what was taking so long.

It was at this time my life became blessed with Mary Jo. I was terrified the first day I met her. I had no idea what she would be like and I wondered why I needed this woman in my life. I had so many people coming and going that I'd just given up trying to remember them all. Mary Jo brought me a stuffed animal and explained to me she was to be my caseworker. I was amazed a grown up was actually taking the time to explain things that were about to happen in my life. Her grandmotherly appearance did little to hide the strong willed woman inside. When Mary Jo wanted something done she got it done. I was filled with relief when I saw she wasn't going to just breeze in and out of my life like so many others had. She was in for the long haul.

The plan of relocating me to a foster family was revealed. I then realized Mary Jo's true purpose was to find me a foster family and help me settle in. My heart dropped at the thought of moving. Why did I have to move again? I enjoyed Mill House. Yes, it wasn't a real home but I felt safe. I had grown to love Theresa, Joan and Evelyn. Now, again, I was to leave behind people I cared about and the friends I'd made. Since my parents had relinquished rights I figured I was to remain in Mill House until I was eighteen and then move out on my own.

This was supposed to be a joyful time. A time of "graduation", but I did not feel any joy. I was filled with apprehension at the upcoming change I would be making.

Mary Jo took me to three different foster homes. I was lucky I was actually being allowed to choose who I wanted to live with. After meeting the first two families I felt sick to my stomach. I didn't want to move, especially if I had to go to one of these homes. I tried to open my mind but I didn't want to. I just wanted to run back to Theresa and Mill House. The knot in my stomach that had slowly begun to unwind with the letters from Colorado returned. The families were nice enough but I knew I'd be just another foster kid. The other children in the homes seemed happy but I felt uncomfortable the moment I walked in. I tried to put up a good front but my heart was heavy. Couldn't I just go home to Colorado? Why did I have to live in a foster home?

The third foster home we arrived at surprised me. For starters the woman's name was Nanette which means "Nancy" just like my mom in Colorado. She, her husband, and 16 year son lived on a seven acre farm with animals and small garden. The smell of a cake baking in the oven wafted to my nostrils as she opened the door. I felt something inside me tug and I began to ask questions about her and her family and what kind of rules she had. I startled myself when the words, "What would I call you if I lived here?" tumbled out of my mouth. "Mom," came her gentle reply. I knew then I'd made my decision.

During my last days at Mill House I carried a heavy heart. A going away party was thrown in my honor on June 29, 1992. It made me feel special to see neighbors, my friends from school and staff at my party to give me hugs and words of encouragement. Tears filled my eyes as I listened to each of them describe special memories we'd shared. Theresa enveloped me in a hug and promised she'd think of me often and I'd be missed.

My new foster mom arrived then, the time had come to leave. I can still remember the neighbor children shouting their good byes as we pulled away. I was quiet most of the way to Nanette's home. I would truly miss Mill House and the people who helped make it what it was.

My nostalgia quickly turned to fear when I realized I had no idea who this woman really was. Would she take care of me and feed me? Would she allow me to remain in contact with my family in Colorado? As I began to unpack I became confused. Should I fully unpack my stuff or leave it in boxes? Was I supposed to grow up here? Could I ever return to the Thomases? Once again the questions were churning within me and once again I suppressed them. I never got anywhere when I asked questions. I was always on a need to know basis and I guess I just wasn't important enough to need to know.

A month went by and I celebrated my tenth birthday with my new foster family. It was the first birthday I would celebrate without my ex-adoptive parents. Even while I had been in Colorado they had come to visit me. Ten years old . . . So much had happened in my life already. Just in the past two years I had had eleven different caretakers! Eleven? No way. I counted in my head again. Yep, at least eleven. That wasn't even including my uncle or foster dad. I sat for a moment looking at all the candles on the cake. "Make a wish!" What for? They never seemed to come true. You know, I wonder if it's possible to wish on someone else's star. Besides I didn't believe in all that mumbo-jumbo anyway. Aaah! For ten years old I could be such a cynic. Might as well give it a whirl. Halfheartedly I sucked in my air and wished to one day return to the Thomases. A smile crossed my face when after a blast of air each candle ceased to burn. Maybe, just maybe . . .

With my foster family I didn't have near the amount of structure I had at Mill House. It wasn't expected. Mill House was a residential facility and this was a real home. I was still given chores to do every day and my room had to remain clean but it was much more lax. I didn't have the same schedule to follow and therefore I'd get it done when I wanted to. This soon proved to be a problem. Although, it was a regular home I had major trust issues and still needed that structure to feel safe, at least for the first few months until I was able to fully settle in. I would watch TV for many hours daily. It was still my self-medication. I still would zone out.

I didn't realize how rough I'd gotten over the months I'd been there. I began to wrestle with their German Shepherd and flip the poor cat upside down. I would get into "play hitting wars" with my foster brother. We were constantly terrorizing each other. It just seemed the normal thing to do. I wanted to seem tough because tough people could take care of themselves. I delighted in listening to the teachers tell me if I wasn't careful while playing football with the boys I could get hurt. Nah, I thought, I would be just fine.

The NBC movie version of Child of Rage aired one evening on TV. I sat in disgust as I watched. This was not the HBO documentary I had been in, this was a Hollywood version with actors and actresses. It sickened me to see them illustrate my birth sister as a prostitute when she was nOwhere near that. She was a beautiful young woman, with a family, studying toward her degree. When my mama had gotten too sick she had also become my protector. I was heartbroken. It portrayed some of the problems I had but many of them were exaggerated. Dumbfounded I watched as the little girl who played me would cast her wrath on any unsuspecting victim. Was I really like that? They showed a holding session. It was not even close to how it really was. When I saw her run from a therapy session I thought, "No way, she has complete control of those adults." I told my foster mother how I'd never been allowed to run from a therapy session and I was glad I hadn't. If they'd let me do that I would have never trusted them after that. When the going gets tough and the feelings are too much then they let me go?!? That's what everyone in my life had done, except for them. That's why they had been the only one's I'd ever trusted!

After the movie my foster mom, Nanette pulled me in her arms and held me as I sobbed and sobbed. I had been such a sick little girl. I grieved. I called my Mom Nancy in Colorado and told to her about the film. Since they did not have television in their home I was certain she hadn't seen it. All I wanted to do was crawl in a hole and not come out. What if someone from school had seen it? Would they hate me and threaten me like the guys at the pool? I was so ashamed of my past and of myself. I never wanted to go out in public again. I felt like trash and it had just been reinforced by the film.

In October of 1992 part of my birthday wish came true. Mom Nancy and Terena flew to North Carolina to visit me. (I waited at the hotel with Mary Jo until their arrival.) I was practically jumping out of my skin. I felt my heart stopped beating when I heard they'd missed their flight because of construction and were doing their best to get there. They had flown all night and had no sleep. An hour later they pulled up in front of the hotel.

All of a sudden a streak of fear ran through me. Would they still love me? Their letters professed it but ,would it be the same in person? Would I be good enough for them? I hadn't seen them in two years would they still even recognize me?

The fear was replaced with the warmest feeling of joy when they both rushed out of the car and gathered me in their arms. The hotel management must have thought a bunch of fruitcakes had invaded the lobby. We were laughing and crying and jumping around. We couldn't hug enough. My mouth was running about a mile a minute and I was bouncing up and down with excitement. This was my family whom I loved and they loved me back! It was one of the most beautiful and memorable moments of my entire life.

Excitement filled every pore in my body and bubbled out! At the mall I buzzed around like a honeybee to each shop. I was so nervous I just chattered nonstop. I was so full of energy I didn't sleep that night. I stayed awake the entire night watching movies. When they left I was exhausted. Had I impressed them? What if they didn't want me? What would I do?

A few weeks later I learned of the Thomases' decision to adopt me. Adopt me?!? **Really?!?** They wanted me . . . They really wanted me! My heart felt like it would explode with joy!

I got down on my knees that night. It had been over a year since I'd wholeheartedly prayed. I was too mad at God before. I thought He had deserted me. All the pain I'd been through I blamed Him for it. Theresa said He had a plan for me, and she was right. "Thank you," I said softly. "Thank you for letting me finally go home. You really didn't forget me. I don't understand why I've been through what I've been through, Lord, but maybe that too will be explained one day. Until then, thank you for still loving me and answering my *prayer. In Jesus name, Amen." I crawled into bed and slept the best I had in over two years.*

The time came when I had to say goodbye to my friends again. I was constantly saying good-bye. I was so glad I eventually wouldn't have to do that anymore. My fifth grade class gave me a going away banner they'd all signed. I would miss that little town. I'd lived there for four months but had made some nice friends and memories. Saying good bye to my foster family was difficult. They had opened their home and their hearts and loved me as their own daughter. God had truly blessed me with the loving people he'd placed in my life in the past 28 months.

Nancy: The drive over the mountains to the airport was filled with echoes in my mind. Could I help her? Would she ever trust me again? Would she ever recover from the betrayal that she must feel I was responsible for? I knew that Beth's ability to recover hinged completely on her ability to trust me. I pictured in my mind the little toothless girl that had arrived in our home several years earlier, that had latched so powerfully onto my heart, that I ached being separated from. I knew the nightmare was almost over, each turn of the tires brought me closer to my daughter, my child. Each passing mile brought me closer to holding her in my arms and the beginning of squelching her fears and pain. My own fears crept up in the back of my mind. I pushed them back down. This was going to work!

I arrived at the airport and impatiently awaited the opening of the jet way doors. The throng of people forging toward the gate blocked my view. Moving to the side I held my breath as I searched the faces for my daughter. At long last I saw her face! My focus moved from the smile on her mouth to the look in her eyes. I saw fear encircled with dark rings of stress and pain. She bounced into my arms for a brief flash before rebounding around the area as I spoke to the wizened, experienced caseworker that had brought Beth home to me. We chatted about the flight as I observed Beth's agitated antics. Reaching for Beth's hand to connect and to calm her I felt her warmth and filled with joy at having my little girl so close. I decided to help her to feel safe so she could calm, and to help her to ease the stress and lighten the raccoon mask around her beautiful eyes. I held her hand tightly and determined she would never again be taken from us.

Beth: *Mary Jo, my social worker, accompanied me to Colorado. Stepping off the plane in Denver I felt a wave of nausea. I can do this, I thought. What's the matter with you? Snap out of it, you're home. For good though? What if I screw up and make them mad. Would they get rid of me? With my thoughts of distress in the back of my mind, I melted into Mom Nancy's arms. I was home. I was finally home!*

The entire drive home from the airport I couldn't stop talking. I was so nervous and so excited and really scared. Two years was a long time. Would everything be the same or? My stomach was twirling itself into a knot but I tried to forget about it and continued chatting. I was actually back in Colorado! Snow had already begun to fall and the mountains were breathtaking with their powdered sugared tops. As we pulled away from the city and drove past the little mountain towns I rolled down my window. What a smell! The sweet scent of Aspen and Blue Spruce filled my senses. As we pulled into the drive I couldn't even wait until Mom stopped the car before I dashed out and into the arms of my Dad and Sister. Home sweet home. I couldn't stop the tears that freely streamed down my face. Laughter bubbled from within me. How I loved being home. This was where I was supposed to be, this was where I belonged.

Nancy: We all chatted as we drove the three hours home. As I was about to stop the car at the end of our long gravel driveway Beth lunged from the car shrieking with joy to jump into Terena's arms and then in a flash she jumped into Jerry's. Hugs and tears of joy were shared by all as our family, once again, became whole.

I found myself becoming increasingly worried over the next few days, as the caseworker, Mary Jo, stayed with us. Fearful that she would change her mind and take Beth back I found myself being phony to impress her. All of the years I had spent teaching children to be open and honest about their feelings, to use their words to express how they felt, failed me. This woman wielded tremendous power. If she changed her mind and took Beth from us the horrible heartbreak would have devastated us all again.

While Mary Jo was with us I was as patient as a saint. I was calm and reserved rather than doing my usual silliness and playful antics with the children. I observed Beth being disrespectful and wild; I didn't correct her when she needed discipline. I didn't give consequences. I just let her run wild, for fear Beth would reject me and Mary Jo would do the same. I let my fear of heartbreak control my decisions and did not intervene to help Beth as she struggled. When Beth tested me and asked with her behavior; "Are you strong enough to keep me safe? Can I trust you?" Rather than stand strong I avoided it. Emotionally I ran. When I could catch her round little body I would embrace her for the brief moment that she would allow before she flitted away. I knew her nonstop talking was harmful for her and was a smoke screen she was using to avoid feeling her feelings. I had missed her little voice so much that even though it was destructive to allow her to jabber incessantly, I let her.

Beth: I talked nonstop to keep anyone from asking me questions about what I was feeling. I was ashamed to admit I was scared to be home. Yes, this was my haven but this was where I'd been taken away. Even though the good memories outweighed the bad by millions, I was still worried. Would they get rid of me again? What if I was awful, would they drop me? Mary Jo left after a little bit and I was sorry to see her go. We'd shared a lot and I would miss her.

Nancy: After the caseworker left I became determined to knuckle down and set things right, but I couldn't bring myself to do it. I felt guilty that Beth had been hurt. I had said she'd be our little girl forever and she had been taken away and I had been unable to stop it. I had allowed people to harm my child by taking her. Part of me felt that I needed to win Beth's love back, that I needed to pay my penance for my failure, and that I needed to protect her heart. So I began our second chance on the wrong foot. We gave her an allowance which I feel strongly is a great way to teach a child how to prepare for welfare checks later in life. It was guilt money. We gave her her own baby goat. She was not responsible with the little doeling. She played rough and she teased it. Knowing better I would say "Beth don't do that. . . Beth, stop . . . Beth, that's not nice. . . Beth, we don't tease animals here. . . If you do that one more time. . ." I didn't take action. I should have given the goat to a new home the first time she was not kind to it, but I didn't.

Beth: I was happy to learn I didn't have to go to school for 8 weeks. Being home was enough for now I didn't want to have to face another big step at this point. I began sledding nonstop and riding horses through the snow. I lost the weight I'd gained in North Carolina. I held back whenever I hugged my mom. I was too afraid to fully let go yet. I felt I needed to be reserved. Pictures painted a happy girl but when you looked into my eyes you could see the fear that threatened to tear me apart. That is if I held still long enough. Each day seemed a battle to me. A battle to remain good enough to be their daughter. I had to win this one because if I didn't I would be lost forever. This was my second chance I couldn't let it go.

I didn't have any chores and I was ecstatic. I didn't fully understand why, since I'd always had chores before but none were given to me. I was given a little white and black doeling with a pink nose. She was so adorable. I trained the little goat to do things that I knew would be trouble but I thought it was fun. Mom, Dad and Terena told me not to do some of the stuff I did but I just shrugged them off. This was my goat, I could take care of her how I wanted to. I laughed when she would chase anyone that came in her pen but go out of her way to love on me. It made me feel special. I didn't see how her butting at other people was a problem. I thought it was funny and I didn't care what others thought.

Nancy: Beth's frame had filled out from quite slender to sixty pounds overweight. She had attempted to fill up the emptiness inside of her with food just as I had. My frame had also filled out sixty pounds extra as I tried to fill up the gaping wound of hollowness with food. I had seen Beth's foster mother, a loving, caring lady meaning well, criticizing Beth's body, saying "tuck your tummy in sweetheart, you can't wear a two piece with your chubby tummy." I wanted Beth to accept her body and love herself. I was concerned about future anorexia and bulimia problems that come from a child's twisted vision in their mind of the shape of their body. My plan of action was to fill up Beth's heart by holding her, loving her, feeding her three nutritious meals a day, offering her all the dessert she could hold after dinner until she would refuse it, and making sure she got plenty of exercise. This worked amazingly well in three short months. Sledding, building snowmen, romping through the snow with the horses and still eating desserts, Beth's beautiful body became healthy and slender once again.

Beth: I liked being able to get away with things I would never have gotten away with when I was little. I questioned it and wondered if this was because I was a "regular kid" now. I didn't even bother to notice I was being just as rude, if not more, than some of the other kids there. I got along rather well with the other children. The only problems I had were with Damon. We were continually bickering. He always started it according to me and I always started it according to him. Since we were the same age, the same size and strength Mom put us outside and said, "Don't come back in, until you work it out." It took us two hours of yelling, screaming and almost a fist fight until we finally promised to be nicer to each other.

CJ came and I had my first therapy session and that's when everything changed in the house. Mom became strict again and I got my goat and allowance taken away. I wasn't even allowed to go visit her. I was hopping mad. Sadly not just because my goat was taken away but because things weren't going to be the same anymore. The way I had set it up I was not getting as close to Mom which I figured kept me safe. That way if they got rid of me again then it wouldn't hurt so bad. Then Mom told me they would love me no matter how I was. That they were not going to give me up. So I had to test that. I pushed and I pulled. Well what if I teach my goat to jump up? Will you get rid of me? What if I don't do my chores right? Will you get rid of me? What if I try to get between you and Terena, how about that, then will you get rid of me? What if I turn you and Dad against one another? Yet, they never did.

I did see that it hurt them when I did mean things. I was pushing away the family I loved. Even if they were going to keep me forever it didn't mean they were always going to be happy with me. But if I chilled out and let it happen, things would work out just fine. I couldn't help it though, no matter how much I loved this mom and this family I couldn't trust them yet. I was hurt, no matter who's fault it, was I was hurt. I blamed my mom because I always thought of her as my protector. It was going to take some work to get me to soften up and just be myself.

Nancy: We set up two holding sessions with CJ to give Beth the opportunities to release some of her pain and reconnect and to begin building the trust that was so essential. Beth clearly wanted to be apart of our family and remembered what she needed to do to heal. At the first session, CJ walked into the room, she saw the dark circles around Beth's eyes and she saw the dark circles around my eyes. She asked what had been happening and I shared with her that Beth was being unkind to her goat, jabbered nonstop, was pushing me away, that her allowance money was coming out of her pockets every week in the laundry as she threw it away and that I was at a loss as to how to handle things to help her. CJ lifted one eyebrow looked at me sideways and said, "What are you doing? You're giving her an allowance?! You gave her a pet when she's not ready? Do you have her put her hand over her mouth when she's jabbering?" Sheepishly I replied, "No, I didn't want to hurt her feelings."

"You're letting her drown in her sickness because you don't want to hurt her feelings?! She needs you to stand strong. She needs you to be powerful enough to keep her safe. She's testing you and you are failing. Do you want her to get better?" CJ inquired as she stepped over to me and wrapped a loving arm around my shoulders.

"Well yes," I stammered. "But I can love her just the way she is. I can tolerate her jabbering, but I worry about it getting her in trouble in school." Looking down at my feet I said, "I just want her to be happy."

CJ looked at me with her wise expression, reached for a Kleenex and handed it to me before asking, "So, is she happy?" I burst into tears and buried my face in the Kleenex before admitting, "No, she's miserable and so am I." Gently she replied, "You know how to do it right. You know Beth needs boundaries before she can fill herself up. You're smothering her by giving, giving, giving and expecting nothing in return, not even respect. For Beth to heal she needs to be in balance, she needs to give and take. You're not letting her give. Is she doing chores to give back?"

I was ashamed to admit we were just having her do a few little minor things like take out the trash or set the table and she wasn't even doing those well. CJ walked me through writing up a list of thirty minute chores for Beth to do each day. I agreed to eliminate the allowance. Beth had been teaching her goat to jump like she was a horse and she had been jumping the fence even though we had all told her to stop repeatedly. Beth had to be told if her goat jumped the fence one more time she would lose custody. Beth agreed to fix the fence and do a better job. I agreed to consequence Beth's disrespectful behavior more quickly in order to help her stop.

The next day her goat was out and I had to follow through with the plan. Snowbird was no longer Beth's. Beth appeared to be upset about it but not concerned enough to fix the fence. I felt awful. I thought she'd hate me. She was angry, but she got over it and her trust level began to rise each time she tested me and I stood strong. She worked very hard in the therapy sessions with CJ and released her rage and feelings of betrayal and abandonment.

Beth had been working hard on her relationship with Terena and had been pushing me away. I had allowed it, wanting her to fit in; even though I knew it was a sick triangulation that shouldn't be allowed. When Beth opened up during the session and told how angry she was at me for letting her be taken I wanted to scream, "it wasn't my fault, it wasn't my fault I didn't do it, I didn't let this happen." I knew it was important to work with Beth's feelings rather than my own so I allowed the tears to run freely down my face as I said over and over, "I'm sorry, I'm so sorry!"

We had a local caseworker, Mrs. Blythe, who had to interview Beth privately once a month for a year and fill out a report before our adoption would be final. As the day approached trepidation would fill me and my heart would pound. I would remember the horror stories I'd heard of case workers misinterpreting stories and ripping a child from their home. I thought of the tales of many families destroyed by an angry child lying, distorting the truth, or making false allegations of abuse.

I would drive Beth to our little town on the appointed day, and wait in front of the park in my Toyota, silently praying that each interview would go well and we would be safe. Not wanting to scare Beth by telling her to be careful about what she said and that this woman had the power to yank her from our home, I kept the conversation light as we waited each time.

Mrs. Blythe would pull up and park in front of us. I would step out to greet her she would blandly say, "Well, how is everything?" I thought to myself that there was no way I'd ever tell this woman anything. If she thought I wasn't a good mom she could take my child and break my heart. So I couldn't let her know Beth's acting up. I would smile and cheerfully say, "Everything's fine." I never admitted we were having problems or needed help. After replying, "Well, that's good to hear." She would invite Beth to sit in her car, leaving me standing in the road. Filled with fear, my palms sweating and my heart pounding, I would turn away and return to my car to sit and pray that the interview would go well and we would be all right. I was never told what went on in their conversations. If Mrs. Blythe had concerns or problems I never knew. I never saw any reports. I wondered how many other parents in the process of adoption were terrified to the point that they didn't open up to their caseworkers about problems and concerns with their child.

Beth's forgiveness of me was total and complete during the second session. Her trust began to rebuild, her healing heart made giant leaps forward. My heart made leaps as I watched her. It was working. Most days I saw progress. There were more good days than bad.

The teacher's reports of her behavior and schoolwork validated our belief that Beth was doing well. The other students at school accepted Beth back into the fold and she also made new friends. They were nice kids. She'd have them over and we'd all make pizza together. They'd ride horses, hike, giggle and laugh. At Christmas time Beth's music teacher selected her to sing the solo of Little Drummer. Sitting in the audience I was so proud as my beautiful daughter shared her gift of music and warmed people's hearts with her song. The spotlight that shown on her that night was not as bright as the light shining from the inside of her. After the performance neighbor after neighbor came up to congratulate Beth on her exceptional voice. She was loved and accepted not only by us but by the community as well.

Beth: I had a second therapy session with CJ. This session was my turning point. I told Mom how angry I was at her for letting me get taken away. I poured out the pain and fear I had. I opened up and told her I was so scared to fully love them again for fear they'd leave me. I was trying to push them away because I just felt safer that way. Mom held me and sobbed as I sobbed and we just clicked. I felt a lightness come over me and my heart I had not felt in a long time. This was my mom, the woman I loved and this was my family. I could actually be myself now. I didn't have to be fake. I didn't need to be rude and roll my eyes. Matter of fact I didn't even want to and I couldn't imagine doing it anymore. The relationship I had with my mom at that point was more powerful than any relationship I'd ever had. She had taught me how to love and also shared her love with me. She had softened my heart twice now. She had helped me become the person I was supposed to be. Things were just different from that point on. It felt as if I had been given roots and given wings at the same time. I couldn't imagine ever being separated from my family and the idea was not even an option.

I was eleven years old when I received a letter in the mail from my birth sister Cora. It was a wedding invitation. Thanks to Mary Jo I was able to get back in contact with my birth siblings when I was nine years old and lived at Mill House. It was incredible since I had not seen them since I was two. I was so excited when I received the letter. Mom booked us tickets and we prepared to fly back to North Carolina. We decided to visit my foster family, see some old friends of mine, and get in touch with Theresa as well. I was so nervous. I had changed quite a bit since I'd lived there. Not only was I thinner but I had a healthier attitude and outlook on life. The day of the wedding was a beautiful day. As we walked into the church I heard ripples of whispers pass from pew to pew. She's here! Beth's here. That's the missing sister! The moment during that day that imprinted my heart was when I met my grandfather (my mama's dad). I was guided to a heavyset older gentleman sitting in the church. Looking into his eyes was like looking in a mirror. So that's where I get my eyes, I thought. He was told I was his granddaughter Beth. Nodding his head he quietly stated, "I know who you are." Tears filled his big blue eyes as he opened his big arms and pulled me in. "We were so worried about you when we saw the HBO film but I'm glad you're all right now," he whispered. "The last time I saw you was when you were just a little girl." I couldn't help it, as I sat there my eyes overflowed with tears. This was my birth family. This was the father of the woman who had given me life.

I saw my sister Cora for the first time in years when she began walking down the aisle; she was breathtaking. She made a beautiful bride. At the reception, after an excited and emotional reunion punctuated with hugs, we took pictures of all of us six sisters together. The only ones of us missing were my two brothers. It was an incredible healing experience and I thanked God for giving me such a wonderful gift.

When we returned home to the mountains I scrambled up to my perch on Mermaid rock. I took a deep breath as I looked down on the valley I loved. "Well, Lord, I'm not really sure why my life went the way it did but I'm sure You have a reason. Thank You for bringing me home. Thank You for giving me my family back and thank You for giving me my spirit back." I sat there in peace,

*looking on as Dad fed the horses and goats. Mom was probably starting dinner.
I guess I'd better see if she needs any help I thought. With that, I hopped off the
rock, raced the dog down the driveway and slipped into the house laughing. The
smell of homemade bread and roast beef met my nostrils. "Hello, it's me," I
called.*

*"Hi Smee, we're in the kitchen," replied my mom. As she squeezed me
into a big hug I breathed a deep sigh of contentment. Home sweet home, I
thought. Home sweet home.*

Nancy: I embraced the joy I felt at hearing Beth's little girl giggle back in my
home and listening to her amazing voice fill the valley with song from her
perch on Mermaid rock. Sometimes I would remember the days when, with
sadness, I would look up to that rock outcropping and see she wasn't there, but
now, there she was, my beautiful mountain mermaid, my Magnolia Blossom,
with the sun glistening off her hair sending out clear notes filled with life, filled
with love. As her voice was lifted in song, my pain was lifted with it and floated
away with the notes as they disappeared down the valley.

The deep shadows that once encircled Beth's eyes took months to
disappear, but once she felt safe again, she sparkled from the inside out. She
was calm, relaxed and yet when she walked into a room, she lit it up with her
sunshine. To see how happy she was, I relaxed and enjoyed my daughter
without having to be a therapeutic parent, without having to correct
constantly, just laughing and loving, watching her grow. The nightmare had
turned back into a wonderful dream. All of my prayers had been answered, my
beloved daughter had been kept safe and had been returned to where she
belonged- with us!

Chapter 19
Where Two are Joined...

Beth was emotionally healthy and happiness beamed from her. Damon was making good decisions and the professionals working with him considered him emotionally stable. Both children showered the family with loving surprises such as cleaning the entire house while the other children and I worked in the garden. They were both trustworthy and had long ago earned being with the animals or in the house with no supervision.

In the evening, when the sun had set I'd put silly music on in the living room where we'd all dance around or sing loudly. Old classics such as "There's a Dead Skunk in the Middle of the Road", "Home Grown Tomatoes" or "You are My Sunshine" were always musical favorites. We'd teach the children the two step, country swing, jig, waltz or just to keep rhythm while twirling or moving. In exhaustion, we'd all crumple to the couch laughing trying to catch our breath.

That summer, each child worked on a performance. One learned to make balloon animals while another worked on a dog act. Terena and I.Q. also prepared a skit. Hula hoops, jump ropes, and the theme song to "2001" were some of the many props required by my traveling circus. Loading everyone into the van, my crew and I drove into Glenwood Springs where we visited the local retirement community and nursing homes. Baby goats amused the crowd by jumping about and following anyone with a milk filled bottle. Dogs jumped through hoops and rolled over while others retrieved items from the audience or rocked a basket with a teddy bear inside. Balloons were twisted into animal forms and occasionally popped to keep even the groggiest of watchers awake. It was a well organized, enthusiastic combination of an amateur Cirque de Solei and Ringling Brothers. My hope in creating such a performance was to entertain the lonely Seniors and create a sense of community involvement in my children. I think both goals were achieved!

Our friends, Art and Elaine, took my children white water rafting through the Glenwood Canyon where class IV rapids could be encountered. With wild screams of vivid vitality, the children learned to paddle together at the request of the leader while enduring the occasional saturation of icy snowmelt water. It was an awakening experience!

I tried hard to build the self image of my children. Each child in my care graduated from my home with a special video of their accomplishments, but along with that, I sent glamour-type photos with them looking their very best. My best helpers, usually Terena, Damon and Beth, would help me set up the lighting, backdrops and different camera lenses while I assisted the children in outfit selection and hair styles. With an audience, I'd click the shutter over and over as the child in the spotlight reacted to those standing behind me making jokes and faces. Costume changes, prop changes- usually the dogs- and lenses would create different effects. When one child was finished, they switched places with an 'audience' member and the whole thing would happen again.

A week later, when the ten to fifteen rolls of film would come back developed, I'd hunt through them quickly and pick out the inevitable pictures that weren't appealing or might make the child feel bad about his self-image. After the initial sort, I'd pull all the children together into a big group where we'd oh and ah at the remaining visual display, each time, filling the child in the pictures with a greater sense of their specialness.

All the children could vote for their favorite picture of each child, and the winners were either enlarged or put into their photo album. The remaining lot was distributed between the therapist, the refrigerator door, the adoptive parents and anyone else in the child's life. Not only was the process a blast, but it fed the child's self-esteem.

With the warm nights numbering fewer and fewer as Fall closed in around us, I found many of the children had earned going to school. Terena was a senior in high school now, and the fear of sending my daughter into the big old world was crushing down on me with more intensity as everyday passed. Beth was starting junior high, so the typical emotional roller coaster about every little thing set in with her.

If her hair wasn't perfect, she'd mope around. When she'd come home from school, I could tell if one of her friends had said something mean or hurtful by the dragging of her feet and the dip in her mood. She was also extreme in being happy. When a boy asked her to go steady, she floated on the breeze or when her friends had apologized she was ecstatic. Luckily, she had learned to talk about her feelings, so when her vacillating moods surrounded her when she walked through the door each afternoon, she would look me in the eyes and pour her heart out to me. Although the many things that either made or broke her day seemed trivial to me, I knew, after watching Terena grow through that phase, that it was important to validate her feelings and encourage her to find her own answers. I smiled at how quickly she thought of solutions and knew that skill would come in handy as an adult.

Damon was the same age as Beth, but since he had been removed from school for about a year when he was working on his life, he was only in the sixth grade. It frustrated him sometimes to know that Beth was his same age and yet he was a year behind, but overall, he accepted it and worked hard in his studies.

His adoptive parents were a three hour drive from my home and although the highway was sometimes closed because of severe weather or terrible wrecks, we often handed Damon off from one family to the next as if he were a baton in a relay race. He had been with me for over three years then, and both CJ and myself knew he should be ready to return home. But to our dismay, each time we tried it, he would go home to Rob and Olivia and become rude, snotty and defiant within hours.

It was CJ's policy to assume problems were caused by the child and not the parents, but after having such a disastrous experience with Beth's first adoptive parents, CJ began doubting Damon's parents more and more. I did as well. Because Damon was well behaved and respectful with me and my family, I wondered if maybe his lack of success in their home was because Olivia was doing something wrong. I should have known better!

To solve the dilemma, CJ asked Olivia and Rob to hide her in a closet of their home so she could listen to what went on when they brought Damon home. He wasn't there for more than a minute before she heard his disrespectful belligerence. Walking through the door, he threw his red jacket onto the floor where Olivia nearly tripped over it. Gently asking him to come back to pick up his coat and hang it on the hook, he turned around snarling and said, "No! You pick it up!" With a firmer voice, Olivia asked again for her son to be responsible with his belongings and to hang it up properly. His voice crackled as he hissed, "What are you gonna do about it, you can't make me pick it up, bitch! Do it yourself!" And with that he started stomping off to his room, but just as he neared the closet where CJ hid, she opened the door to face the startled boy. His arrogant stance changed sharply when he realized he had been busted. CJ saw for herself that Damon *did* act differently for his mom than he did for me. It wasn't Olivia! It was divide and conquer!

Knowing that more therapy was needed to address the Doctor Jekyl/Mr. Hyde game he was playing to torture his mom, weekly therapy was scheduled. He had been doing so well, that he had graduated to having less therapy. Now, he was demoted back to weekly sessions which often involved his adoptive family. He continued to do well with my family, but his struggle to be respectful, responsible and fun to be around with Rob and Olivia persisted.

His constant battle with his adoptive family mirrored my own inner struggle with sending Terena off to college when she graduated. Not only was she stepping into the adult world, but she was engaged to be married to her high school sweetheart after she accepted her diploma. Her plan to jump into marriage added to the pain and fear I already harbored.

My baby was strong and capable of making decisions, but I feared for her none the less. She was so gentle and sweet that I feared the American mentality of dog-eat-dog might destroy the gentleness of her heart. I worried about whether I had taught her all the life skills she would need to make it on her own and with a husband to boot. He was a good kid, I loved him like a son, but he was so young. Not even twenty years old, he had much growing up to do as well. They loved each other immensely, I knew that, and having similar upbringings as biological children in a therapeutic foster home, they related well, but I didn't understand their sense of urgency, except that he had joined the Army and was going to be stationed in Tacoma, Washington. She was planning on moving to the west coast to be with him, but that meant she'd be fifteen hundred miles away from me.

The nightmares of one daughter being chained in a dungeon were replaced with night terrors of my other daughter jumping from a diving board, not into the pool of life, but into an empty cement pit. Sometimes the vision was of the pool filled with blood that her pale body was diving into. It was gross! I rarely woke up feeling rested. I didn't want to even close my eyes!

Terena was so important to me. We had a close bond that had caused us to be not only mother and daughter, but teacher and student, confidantes and friends. Her mature nature allowed for adult conversation. As she grew mentally and emotionally throughout high school, I entrusted her with more responsibility of caring for the children. She was my right arm, and although Jerry was my husband and best friend, Terena was a close second. We thought the same way and worked well side by side.

I knew she was struggling with how to handle the transition as well, and we stayed up many late nights discussing the options. Internally, I was dying, but externally I stayed composed and coherent. Jerry, as a logical engineer, didn't understand my intense emotions. I often teased him by calling him Spock from Star Trek because his overall lack of emotion and total logic was clearly evident as I tried explaining my feelings over the matter. He would listen, but his lack of understanding caused my ache to deepen.

As was customary, Grandma Bobbie (Jerry's mom) came for Thanksgiving and made her soothing pumpkin pie. It was one of the few treats that appeased the growing anguish that I felt. Each bite, with its hint of nutmeg and cinnamon was like a salve being applied to the sore, rawness in my heart. Watching the wise lady accept every child in my home as her own kin, I realized that she might understand the heartache I was enduring. She had sent Jerry off to college, although years ago, I was sure she would understand.

Pulling her aside, I asked her how she coped with sending her son off to college. Smiling in her knowing way, she looked at me directly and said, "Find strength in the Lord, Nancy. He can handle anything." It wasn't the response I had anticipated, but it was welcomed and cherished. I thanked her for advice and found solace in her words.

Prayer helped me to survive Christmas, knowing it could possibly be the last time I spent the holiday with Terena for several years. Knowing that she had a hope chest that was still in need of items, I purchased the remaining things and left them under the tree for her. Enthusiastically, she cheered our selection of blankets, towels and kitchen appliances.

I was careful to get equally awesome presents for the rest of the children. I was so proud of them. Each had earned money to purchase gifts for the rest of the family or had spent their own time making lasting gifts.

That winter, the agency held a conference on a different type of holding therapy. As I was required to attain at least fifty hours of training yearly, I eagerly signed up. Hungry for knowledge to help the children, I usually attended well over the necessary number of classes. That particular seminar was held by Martha Welch, MD, on couple holdings and mother holdings. The goal was to provide a safe 'place' for the people involved to release and process feelings.

CJ asked if Jerry and I would be volunteers for the couple holding. Knowing that I still had trust issues from my first marriage, I kindly declined. I didn't want to share those intimate feelings with a group of several hundred observers. I, did however, eagerly anticipate attending. Dr. Welch was one of the pioneers of one style of the powerful intervention, so I was excited to see what insights she had.

The hotel conference room had a padded platform where mothers held children in their laps and husbands held their wives. Simultaneously, four to eight holdings were occurring at one time and the emotional energy within the room was charged. I watched as the waiters and hotel personnel nearly dropped the trays of food and beverages as their eyes bugged out of their head in confusion and fear as the people on the platform screamed and yelled as they released their feelings.

The mother holdings were astounding as moms held babies and let them rage in their loving and safe embrace. After the initial release of pent up negative emotion, I watched as a peacefulness overcame each child and their mom looked lovingly into their eyes and told them that no matter what they said or did, they would love them.

Watching the mother holdings was comfortable territory and as I sat in the audience observing, I realized I was strongly avoiding the couple holdings. I felt quite strange sitting there, watching two adults discussing or screaming about private happenings. It was weird.

A few months later, the agency set up a couples retreat at a five star dude ranch for the heads of eight of their therapeutic families. We were a close knit group and as we sat around the fireplace talking I saw one husband and wife holding hands, looking lovingly at each other and sharing little secrets. As I watched them I was reminded of honeymooners.

The retreat facilitator asked a question and requested that each couple take turns in replying. Sitting next to Jerry, I watched as the firelight danced on each person's face as they thought about their answer. The wife of the first couple spoke up, then the female half of the next and again, the woman of the third couple spoke. As each woman finished, the question came to the couple who had been holding hands and giggling with each other. Instead of the wife leaning forward to reply, I saw her look lovingly up to her husband with expectation; he took his cue and answered with wisdom and authority.

Amazed, I reflected on the difference between this couple and the rest of us. Working with high-risk children in our program requires a high level of structure and control. All of us women, as we were the primary caregivers to the children had accepted that and allowed it to bleed over into out marriages. We had all become the control element in our marriages. I wondered why this couple was immune to that. I had spent much time with them before and had wondered what had drawn them together as I saw the husband as immature and disrespectful of his wife. Now, their entire relationship was different.

The question soon came around to Jerry and me, and as usual, I didn't even bother to consult Jerry and instead spoke for both of us. I continued to ponder the change well after the group had finished talking and had dispersed.

Throughout the entire weekend, I watched the couple. She looked up at him with love and adoration anytime he spoke, whether it was to her or not. The admiration I saw them both give each other was astounding. They treated each other with dignity, honor and respect in everything I saw them do. Walking hand in hand wherever they went, I saw him reaching out to her or exchange knowing glances.

Out of total curiosity, I had to know what they were doing differently. "All right, you two, what are you doing that makes such a difference?" I asked. Her reply shocked me. "We've been doing couple holdings and they have been really great!" Confused, I asked, "You mean you let him hold you down?" Nodding her head, she reached for his hand and the two of them smiled into each other's eyes.

In my mind I had decided I would never do that. There was no way I would let Jerry hold me down. No way- never! I decided they were weird when she told me she loved it!

For a few weeks after, I thought about the couple I had seen transformed. Jerry and I were great business partners. We didn't fight, we discussed the budget and made decisions with each other in mind. We had a good marriage, but after seeing this couple, I knew there was something missing; the passion, the closeness of a connection had long been over. I realized I missed that and I wanted it again. Jerry and I hugged and respected each other, but the feeling of being madly in love like honeymooners was gone. I began thinking about why I wouldn't allow Jerry to hold me like I had seen at the seminar. My heart sank when I did a soul search and realized I wouldn't allow it because I didn't trust him. Had Butch squeezed out every ounce of trust I had? I couldn't accept that. Jerry had never raised a hand to me. He had never betrayed me or been dishonest. It wasn't right or fair to allow my past baggage to interfere with my current marriage and in doing so, I was robbing my relationship with Jerry.

I knew that I needed something different. With Terena leaving, I needed to find support and understanding from Jerry, so I built up the courage to move against my fear in order to conquer it. I asked Jerry to do a holding with me so I could let go of whatever came up. I knew it didn't make any sense to him; it didn't make much sense to me either, but I had seen it work! I also knew I needed to trust my husband and in order to do that, I had to let go of some past feelings that were deep inside of the core to my being.

After much discussion and convincing, Jerry agreed to hold me if CJ were there to facilitate and supervise the session. In his words, he wanted her there 'in case you go crazy'.

A week later, CJ drove up to the house and helped prepare the floor with pillows. The longer they prepared, the more fear crept from my heart into my throat. With nausea and trepidation, we got into the couple holding.

My fear level was intense. Jerry's face was only inches away from mine, and I couldn't force myself to make eye contact with him. I made every attempt to avoid the feelings that were beginning to surge through my system. Just like I had seen the children do so many times, I tried changing the subject. "Eew, you're breath is bad. You should have shaved. You're breathing on me!" I tried everything to take control, where I was comfortable and secure, but I couldn't.

I was really afraid to make eye contact with my husband because I knew if I did, I couldn't hide anymore. I knew the whole point of the holding was to deal with the emotions I carried with me that held me back in order to learn to trust Jerry, but I had to get emotionally and mentally close to Jerry in order to do that and I was terrified.

Jerry and I have been close. We have children for Pete's sake, but this was different. It was *very* different.

As I wiggled and squirmed I told him he was hurting me, I locked eyes with him in defiance and in doing so, the floodgates burst open. Trivial things he had done years before that I had thought I'd forgiven him for came to the surface with such force that I exploded. My temper boiled over as I ranted and raved about past things he had said or forgotten to do and with intense violence, I tried to over power him. In fact, I tried throwing him through the ceiling. I surprised myself at the level of anger I held over such petty things that had occurred so long ago. As I breathed and processed, I realized what was really motivating my anger. It wasn't Jerry or what he said or did or didn't do; I was so upset over the little things because they were tied into bigger feelings from earlier on, before Jerry was even in my life.

As I rested I began thinking of Terena's eminent departure and addressed his lack of support for me. I let out all the feelings of loss and abandonment her absence would create, I watched as tears welled up in Jerry's soft eyes. I had never seen him cry, even at his father's funeral, but here was my cowboy, " Spock" with tears running down.

The first thing that came into my mind was that I must be physically hurting him. "What is it? What's wrong? Am I hurting you?" I begged for him to answer. He looked deep into me and said, "I'm going to miss her too."

I had been so wrapped up in my own pain, that I had neglected to notice that he would be losing his daughter as well. We had the same pain!

We both laid there, and shared our fear and grief of sending Terena into the world. It was the first connection I had made with Jerry in a very long time and I savored every moment of it. Although it was painful to face each other's heartache, I never wanted the moment to end. As we laid there talking, I realized I understood him on a deeper level than I had before but even more incredible was the fact that he understood me. He knew my pain! I felt safer, more loved and more understood than I had ever before in my life. I never wanted the feeling to end. I wanted him to hold me forever.

While in my husband's loving embrace, I relaxed into the moment and allowed the ocean of peace to soothe my soul. I thought of how comforting it was to know the man holding me loved me, even after I had screamed and raged at him. Thinking about how wonderful the feeling was that was washing over me, I was glad that the children who had been so terribly traumatized earlier in life were able to access such intense tranquility and love by being held by their mothers. I was pleased to know the feeling could be created so easily by releasing old feelings within the enfold of another's arms.

I had bonded so deeply with Jerry, that even after only one holding, I ached for him when we were apart. I wasn't complete until we were together. We were closer than ever before and, more passionate than we had ever been as newlyweds.

Several weeks later, because the first holding had been so powerful, we engaged in another, only this time, CJ wasn't present. As I processed and released more pent up emotions from the past, Jerry was right there to validate my emotions and comfort me through my cleansing. Only after first having escalated into a full blown rage was I then able to reach that sanctuary of safety and peace.

Again, as I laid in Jerry's arms, I thought back to an article on how Bald Eagles court. Flying together, the male and female soar high into the sky before the male sweeps the female from her independence to lock talons with her. Wrapping his wings around her, they drop from the sky, bound together. Just above the treetops, the male releases his mate and they return to the top of the sky. The female eagle then grabs onto the male while she wraps her wings about him and, as one, they free fall towards earth. At the last minute she releases him and they both fly back up into the sky. On the third run, they equally clasp each other and mate as they seal their life long commitment.

I treasured Jerry even more after the second session. We were more than business partners now, and knowing that I could count on him to lean on emotionally, I was freed from the burden of carrying all the pain as Terena's graduation neared. He was raised high on a pedestal, above any other person I had ever met or any possession that I ever had. I had been married to him for over nineteen years and only now was I able to realize he was everything to me. I not only trust him now, I love that cowboy with all my heart!!

Chapter 20
Where There's Smoke...

The cold Colorado winter soon blossomed into a magnificent spring. Beth's adoption became finalized and the monthly interviews with the social worker ended, much to my delight. Terena had been accepted to Puget Sound University and although she had only received a few thousand dollars in scholarships, we were happy and hopeful for her future. Terena, Beth and Damon, along with the other children in my care who had earned the privilege, spent many hours astride the horses after school. After climbing the steep mountains around our home, they would bring the horses in at feeding time usually very hot and sweaty from the intense workout. As I watched them walk their steeds around the front field to cool them off, I reflected on how happy the children appeared as they laughed and joked about.

I had been under a tremendous amount of stress and as the date for Terena's wedding neared my level of anxiety increased. Instead of sleeping, I spent much of the night pacing, worrying about everything. When I could bring myself to lie down for a rest, I stared at the ceiling feeling like I had a mouse trapped in my mind that wanted to run on its wheel forever. I couldn't shut my mind off to get any sleep. In the morning, I'd drag my unrested body from the bed and begin the anxious, memory impaired task of making sure the family ran smoothly while at the same time, preparing the garden for Terena's wedding.

Six days before the intended union, my responsible, hard working, selfless daughter decided that getting married wasn't such a good idea at her age and with her decision came an incredible sense of relief. She wasn't going off to Puget Sound. She wasn't going to be a teenage bride, and maybe I'd get to have her at home a little while longer.

Terena was planning to attend a local community college since it was too late to apply anywhere else, so I happily accepted her decision to stay nearby. After competing in the fair, she packed up her things and moved into the dorms. I tried my best to function on the level I previously was able to, and although I was thoroughly convinced I could 'fix it myself', I knew that I still had problems because I found myself overcompensating. I thought my sudden onset of memory difficulty, paranoia and sleeplessness would go away then. I didn't realize that I suffered from depression and medical intervention would provide the only help for me.

The children I worked with didn't handle change or transitions well, so I continued to trudge through each day, giving them all I could. I believed God never gave you more than you could handle, so I kept my chin up and motivated myself by convincing myself that I had to keep going for the kids. I had to keep going for Jerry. I had to get keep going for the dogs. I had no problem finding things that needed me to keep going, so before long, the gradual decline from my happy, bouncy former self into a sullen, frustrated exhausted mom came over me. It attacked so slyly that months went by before anyone noticed. I had gotten so used to being forgetful and worried that I hardly realized it was abnormal for me. My sense of humor was gone.

To me, the world was stable. My children were healing, my marriage was successful and I was enjoying speaking publicly. What did I have to be depressed about? I had been able to subconsciously compromise so well for my reduced abilities, that most people close to me had no idea I was falling deeper and deeper into a state of hopelessness. I didn't even recognize it myself.

My once jovial spirit lay dormant throughout the entire winter of 1995. In between semesters, as the snow fell, Terena moved from the dorms where she couldn't keep her dog into a two bedroom home on a quarter acre lot. Knowing her hope chest was still sitting unused in her room, Jerry and I moved all of her household things into her new abode. She was only fifteen minutes away, so she often came up for dinner or to ride the horses with Beth and Damon.

Winter soon melted into spring and spring blossomed into summer. Knowing Terena would be finished with college for a few months, I asked her to move back to the house in order to save money. Resisting at first, she eventually decided that moving back home would be a good idea and, she packed up her things and came home. My heart wildly celebrated her return, but outwardly, I stayed happily reserved. After seeing so many of my children leave, it was really nice to see one step back through the door.

I thought everything was going really well until I received a phone call from my best friend as summer turned into fall. Her two and a half year old son, Daniel, who had been potty trained for about four months, had altogether stopped wiping and would cry heavily anytime he had a bowel movement. He had also suddenly started to wet the bed. As she laid out the situation for me, she concluded with, "As I helped him wipe tonight he blurted out that he missed Damon, and I thought that was a weird thing to say at the time I was cleaning his bottom." Agreeing with her, I told her I'd check it out and get back to her.

Pulling Damon aside later that evening, I told him he hadn't written a list of sneaky things he had done lately, and that I wanted him to have a clean slate. "I want you to get strong by getting rid of your secrets, because keeping them inside is bad for your heart. Hop off to your room and work on it, and when you're done come back downstairs."

Ten minutes later, he trotted down the stairs and handed me the list. He had stolen some batteries, lied about finishing his chores twice, and about brushing his teeth. Knowing the list had to be longer than that, I sent him off to work on the list again.

After twenty minutes, he slowly descended the stairway and hesitantly handed me the paper. Three more things were added, as well as a note at the bottom of the page that read, "I didn't do anything to Daniel!" He had trapped himself. Consciously making sure I never mentioned Daniel, I had given him very loose guidelines for writing his list. Knowing now that he did indeed do something to Daniel, I pulled him into a hug and looked down at his scared green eyes before saying, "If you're going to get strong, you need to get all the secrets out. You need to tell the truth Damon." I sent him back to his room to further work on the list.

A short time later, he came down from his room and had added the new line: "I did sex things with Daniel." After giving Damon a hug and telling him how proud of him I was for being strong enough to tell the truth, I sent him off to the bathroom to prepare for bed. My hands were shaking with grief and pain as I held the paper holding his confession, I immediately picked up the telephone and began dialing CJ's home number. We set up a therapy appointment for two days later and as our state required, CJ called social services and the police to report the findings.

Since Daniel wasn't in immediate danger, the authorities agreed that CJ should find out as much information as possible before making any further claims. When CJ was getting ready to leave for our home, Olivia called her.

Damon's mom was concerned about a newspaper article she had just read focusing on a teacher who had molested and sodomized his students. She was concerned because Damon had had this same teacher when he was in the second grade. She asked, with growing fear in her voice, if CJ thought there could be any connection between Damon's behavior and this teacher, because when he was in the second grade his behavior had severely worsened. Knowing that it was probable, CJ simply said, "Olivia, we'll find out. I'm on my way up there now and will let you know about everything as soon as I know."

On her way out of town, CJ picked up a newspaper and found a picture of the teacher on the front page. Tucking it into her purse, she focused on the long drive ahead of her and the devastating deeds she would soon learn more about.

It didn't take CJ long to change from driving mode to therapist. With one glance at the man's mug shot, Damon's face pinched into a painful grimace. Knowing the picture was the catalyst for truth telling, he recounted the story from the beginning.

The teacher would find ways of making Damon stay in for recess or to come in after school. Once there, alone with the big man, he was told he was the teacher's 'special friend' and they had a 'special game' to play. Leading the eight year old by the hand, the teacher would take him into the storage closet, where he gradually went from fondling the boy to full blown sodomization. Damon wasn't the teacher's only 'special friend'. His best friend at that time was also the teacher's 'pet', so after having learned the 'game', the two boys would play it together.

As he told the story of how he and his friend had taken turns having sex with each other in the doghouse, I thought back to the one time I had met the friend. As I sat talking with the boy's mother, I noticed the young child holding the end of his penis through his pants. Thinking that behavior was odd, I mentioned it to CJ before dismissing it. The realization of what that little boy was trying to tell us through his body language hit me like a boxer's punch.

The music teacher had sodomized both boys repeatedly throughout the second grade. As a result, Damon's already fragile psyche had shattered and pyromania had taken seed in his mind. He began tearing up his clothes and toys, and destroying anything he held dear. His mind decided that not only did love hurt, but his family couldn't keep him safe, so he emotionally pulled further into himself, and attacked at anyone who tried to pry him free. His behavior was much like a moray eel protecting its home. With any encroachment to his being, he would strike out with hateful language and mean spirited tantrums. To him, he was protecting the only place he knew was safe- his lonely heart that had built a wall around it to keep others out.

Just as he had been sodomized, he began molesting and victimizing his cousins. Pulling his wagon around at a family gathering, he would drag the little vehicle around to the back of the shed where he would play 'teacher and student' before pulling the child back around where the adults were expecting to see them. Around and around he went, each time with a different child and each time, his sickness infected the other children in his family.

Listening to my boy who had lived with me for nearly four years, I had a hard time believing that this was the first time he had ever told the story. Damon had no history of sexual abuse or sexual predation in his file. I had never seen any of the tell tale signs of sexual inappropriateness such as his hands on his crotch or excessive masturbation. He did have a history of setting fires, and I knew that *could* be an indication. But how had he lived with a therapeutic family for so many years and had so many therapy sessions, and never trusted any of us enough to tell?

While Damon was on a pilgrimage releasing secrets, CJ encouraged him to tell about his 'sex stuff' with my friend's son, Daniel. My friend had visited my house regularly, but on the tragic day it happened Terena, my friend, her husband and myself all sat on the front porch sipping lemonade while the children rode big wheels and bikes around the driveway and front field. Damon was pushing Daniel's tricycle through the tall field grass and as they made the rounds, both children happily waved at the on looking adults. I remembered the day clearly. Apparently, as we all watched Damon push the little toddler in another circle, he would stop pushing at the far end of the field where the grass was tall enough to cover them, and briefly sodomize the little boy. Just as he had done to his cousins, the duration of each encounter was short, and within a few minutes, we'd see their smiling, laughing faces round the corner and heading back towards us. Nothing seemed out of the ordinary.

Guilt filled my mind and heart as I listened to Damon's graphic confession. The goal for me in all those years was to *stop* the cycle of abuse, and here it had occurred with four adults watching. It had happened right under my nose! Daniel was a beautiful child with a bubbling personality and a vivacious nature; I couldn't believe that he had been victimized by one of the children I had viewed as healthy. Daniel's innocence had been stolen from him by a child I considered to be my own son!

Knowing that Daniel's mom would need to know what happened, I sadly phoned her after CJ finished with the police. An investigator was scheduled to question Damon two days later. I slowly dialed the number. Her perky voice answered the phone and as I started speaking, I feared that would be the last time I ever heard her voice so carefree. "The day we were out talking on the porch, Damon was pushing your son around on the big wheel. Do you remember?" Hearing a sudden chill come through the phone I heard a tense, "Yes" before continuing. Not knowing any softer way to state it, I sadly told her. "Damon just told us that when he and Daniel were far into the field where no one could see, he pulled your son's pants down and raped him. It didn't happen just once, but nearly every time he pushed the little tricycle into that back area."

Hearing soft crying, I apologized profusely before telling her that Damon would be moved from my home as soon as possible. Not knowing whether that would help console her, I told her that I loved her and her friendship, but would clearly understand if she could no longer continue our relationship. I knew that in order for my friends to heal, she needed to know he was gone and that I wouldn't accept what he had done even though the little boy owned a piece of my heart. Hanging up the phone, I called the boys ranch where Damon would be going.

Five months earlier, little Damon had been told that he'd blown out in Rob and Olivia's home too many times to expect them to mend the relationship. They had given their entire hearts and exhausted much of their financial resources and couldn't continue doing it. Their son sat in limbo, feeling rejected and unwanted for months, even though he had been stable in my home. His parents had put him on the waiting list to get into the boys ranch, because they knew of his passion for horses and thought that maybe he could possibly be happy there. The urgency of our situation forced his name to the top of the list and we expected less than two weeks to lapse before his ultimate move.

My heart was broken. Thinking back to my relationship with Damon, I realized I had thought we had a good relationship, but I was wrong. I loved him so much that I thought it was enough for both of us. I had connected to him, but the feeling was not mutual. He didn't love me. He was compliant and respectful, but he had never internalized my love and learned to love back. I should have known by his constant battle with Rob and Olivia. He couldn't love, and in the end, his inability to give and receive affection in a healthy manner caused him to seek it in an unhealthy way. He did what he had been taught, but that was still no excuse.

My guilt soon melted into anger. I felt betrayed by Damon since he'd been with me for so long. I had given him ample opportunities to talk about it and instead, he chose to act it out. He had worked so hard in other areas of his life that I felt like he had done it all in vain. I felt like I had failed as well, and indeed I had.

The news hit me hard and I racked my brain trying to find reasons. I had been right there that afternoon and I hadn't seen a thing! It wasn't like I wasn't watching the children; it was second nature to me to keep an eye on the children that I kept under my wing. I knew how much trouble they could find when not supervised for even a minute. Had I been so out of it lately that I had let down my guard? Maybe, I thought, but what about the other three adults. They hadn't witnessed anything and they were watching as well! No matter how I wrestled with it, I felt totally and utterly responsible for what happened.

Knowing that a little toddler, who was once happy and healthy, would have to live with that wound for the rest of his life because I didn't pick up on the few signs available to me, caused me to begin doubting myself and my abilities to parent these tough children. What else had I missed lately? Were there other signs that went past me unnoticed? What about the other children, what were they able to get away with?

That night, as I watched CJ pull out of our driveway, Jerry pulled in from a long day at the office. Coming into the house, I ran to him and collapsed into his arms. "Pa, so much has happened today. I really, *really* need to talk to you, but it'll have to wait until after I put all of the kids to bed." Jerry's embrace filled me with the little bit of strength I needed to finish the evening, and as I hugged and tucked in each child for the night, I closed their doors and activated the alarms. I had survived the day, but I had no idea how.

After recreating for Jerry the chain of events leading to the therapy session with Damon, I confided in my husband. "Pa, I feel so responsible. I should have known. I should have seen it. I know he had no history of sexual abuse, but the few signs he did give, I should have seen. The fact that he blew out each and every time he was with his family should have told me that just being there stirred up emotions that he couldn't handle it." Crying, I fell into his warm hug. " I should have seen it!"

The next day, I was careful to keep the news of Damon's impending move quiet, but I'm sure he wondered why I hugged him more frequently than usual. With each squeeze, I felt more sure that I had made the only plausible decision I could. Damon couldn't continue living with me when he knew he had gotten away with such a tragic deed; he couldn't trust me, he had shown, and I couldn't look at him and see him in the same way. Oh, I loved that child though, and as I held him longer and longer with each hug, my heart was pulled further and further from my chest.

Trying to keep the routine as normal as possible (except that Damon didn't go to school) everyone completed their chores and wrote in their feelings book. I was saddened when I read that Damon's superficial feelings of madness about plugging up the toilet earlier that morning, or sad that he had missed school. There was no remorse for the deviance he had told us about the previous day. Before bed, as each child helped clean the kitchen after dinner, I asked Damon to take the kitchen trash out to the bear proof bin past the guest house. Smiling, he looked into my eyes and answered a happy, compliant, "Yes, mom!", before picking up the full bag and heading out. Five minutes later he came back inside asked to take a bath and prepared for bed.

As I gave him a hug, he sweetly looked up at me and said, "Good night Mom! I love you" and snuggled under the sheets. Switching on his alarm I noticed my hands were shaking and with each hug I gave to each child getting ready for bed, I realized an uneasy feeling settling in my gut. I knew it was the sadness I would feel at my son's departure. Despite all he had done, I still loved him. It was in my nature to love even the most disturbed child and as I couldn't turn my love on and off like a light switch, my heart throbbed with each beat. I couldn't stop loving him no matter what had happened, even if I had wanted to. It just wasn't possible.

The investigator was scheduled to meet with Damon in the morning and I wasn't mentally prepared for the emotional drain that would cause. Setting out the dinner to thaw for the next evening, I pulled Jerry from his evening reading and sunk into his waiting strength; it seemed like I had been doing that a lot lately. Absorbing his valor, stamina and power, I gained peace knowing that he was there with me for each step of that painful path. That night, after many sleepless nights, I descended into a restless slumber.

The next morning, I was awakened by Jerry's loving hand on my shoulder with yet another nightmare. The guesthouse was ashes, and Terena's belongings were nothing but smoke and ashes. The fire had consumed everything in that part of the yard and what little strength I had left was consumed by the enormity of the situation. Emotionally, physically and mentally, I was burned out. Now we were also literally burned up.

The investigator was already prepared to speak to Damon about his sexual indiscretions, but since the fire had occurred he questioned the boy about that instead. When no confession was made, I drove the three hours to Denver and left Damon with Lori. It wasn't until I got home that I learned how Damon had proceeded to spill his guts about starting the fire. Using a stolen lighter he had snuck into the small house and lit a blanket when taking the trash out the night before. He said he had fanned the flame until it was strong before closing the door. He didn't mean for the storage shed or the cars to get destroyed and was saddened at the thought of Terena's loss.

Damon then explained how he had picked the lock to Jerry's gun cabinet when he was downstairs folding laundry in order to access the rifles. As the investigator was upstairs questioning the girls and myself, and the firefighters continued snuffing out any flare-ups, Damon was pulling the antique guns from their secure holder and searching for bullets. Breaking into the locked ammunition box below the cabinet, he began shuffling through the different shells before he found one that looked like it would fit into the chamber. Loading the rifle, he planned on killing all of us before fleeing into the mountains with the horses. Luckily for us, he had loaded a 30 caliber shell into the 30-06, and jamming the wrong sized bullet into the chamber made the weapon useless. Frustrated, he had thrown all the weapons back into the broken cabinet and returned to his scheming while folding the laundry. I came and got him before he could come up with another plan.

While we were reminded of the disaster each time we stepped from the front door, Damon was taken into custody and placed in a juvenile detention center in Denver. Within two days he had been moved from that facility to a holding room in Grand Junction, and a few days after that he was transported to Glenwood Springs. The boys ranch in southern Colorado was ready for him and within a few days after arriving in Glenwood, he was on his way to the town of Pueblo for his last and final move.

I heard about each of his transitions as they occurred and worried that Damon would be scared and confused, his fuse becoming shorter and shorter with each change. Emotionally disturbed children didn't handle shifts easily, and as a result they became more prone to violent outbursts. I fretted about what all the moves were doing to him and what they would do to his ultimate rehabilitation. Thinking that he was safe and unable to harm himself or others was the only way I could put him out of my mind long enough to function.

Damon wasn't the only thing I worried about. Terena was a mess, with the fire having wiped out her entire past. She had little left except for some clothes and at nineteen years old, she struggled to make sense out of any of it.

She had loved Damon and knowing that he was responsible for her current distress caused her even more grief. She dropped out of college and began her search for healing. Her German Shepherd, I.Q., was fine and helped her stay in the present. Quest was still in the field to offer her a loving ride if she chose, but the occasional nicker for her rider went unheeded. Chucky, back from fishing above the Arctic Circle was there to distract her from her pain, while Beth showed her that the family was still there with love and understanding.

The many elements which added to my already existing guilt regarding Daniel were magnified tenfold. The unbearable weight of responsibility hung from my exhausted shoulders as if a yoke around my neck was attached to train holding a full load of coal; I felt like I couldn't move under the oppressive pressure.

Night after night, I would try fighting off insomnia, resentful of its grasp upon my life. And each morning, I would step from my bed having slept very little, with a sense that I was being literally dragged down into a pit of despair. The unity of my family was fractured and I, being the epicenter, cracked with it. I hit the bottom of clinical depression.

Staying home from work, Jerry brought me food and made arrangements for the foster children in my care to go to other homes. He would come into my room and hold me for hours as I drenched his Wrangler shirts in heartache. My brain wouldn't work. The circuits were fried.

My amazing husband, the one who was totally logical, then did the most illogical thing as he tried pulling me from the mess I had become. Walking into my room, he held a teddy bear in one hand and a new box of tissue in another. A huge part of my healing occurred when he handed me the token of his love and support; I hugged that bear filled with love the whole time allowing it to comfort my broken spirit.

Mentioning my fear to Jerry, we started discussing what options I had. We agreed that I needed to go to a therapist and to our family doctor.

After visiting Dr. Kelly, with antidepressants in hand I went home and slept for two weeks, only getting up long enough to eat and use the bathroom. In the end I felt functional at least. A local therapist helped me process the overwhelming sense of loss and grief I felt.

I thought that I was strong because I could handle living with a house full of psychopaths, while loving, and caring for them all. I thought I could push my body and mind to the limit with no consequences. I was wrong!

Not only was I learning about pushing myself too hard, but also about understanding what others went through when suffering with depression. I had heard about women who couldn't get out of bed to feed their families and I always thought they were wimps and making excuses for their laziness. Now

I knew. The moms that called me day after day, the moms that brought their kids to me, the moms who had written the many letters and hundreds of emails seeking answers were now better understood by me. Their pain, their needs and their real level of exhaustion was now much more comprehensible. My ability to listen with empathy and compassion had been expanded and developed further than ever before.

I started being more thankful for the opportunity to rest and for the fresh new start I was given. My memory was making a comeback as was my ability to think straight and logically. Energy began to fill my body. Slowly, I was healing from something so intense that it felt like I had just undergone very invasive surgery; I had to be careful how hard I pushed myself or how much excitement I felt. Too much of anything could send me spiraling back into the deep depths of nothingness which I had just climbed from.

Jerry was great. He would cautiously walk up to me saying, "You look tired. You must need a hug" before opening his arms and letting me step into them. In my cowboy's arms, I felt safe and secure. It was the most peaceful place in the world for me and with each hug, I was recharged a little more. Every opportunity I had, I poured myself into Jerry's embrace. As a motivational effort, he called I.Q.'s breeder and had her ship a new Shepherd puppy to me.

Beth: The days, weeks and months following the fire seemed to trudge on. Every word from Terena and Mom's mouth seemed laden with sorrow. My heart yearned to take their pain and throw it away into the vast Universe. If only God could turn back time and Damon had not done his horrible deeds.

I could tell speaking about the fire and Damon's damage was too much for everyone; so it was at this time that I turned to my buddy Rollie, the Golden Retriever. His soft liquid brown eyes seemed to emit understanding. It reminded me of the Golden I'd been so cruel to as a little girl. We could have had fun as well. It made me so sad to realize I'd ruined it then, but I wasn't going to sabotage my chances with Rollie.

Everyday I would take off into the woods on some adventure and each time he was by my side. I couldn't stand being around the house full of so much pain, so we would hike for hours. I would horseback ride to the reservoir nearby to swim and Rollie and I would paddle around together in the cool refreshing water. I would wash the gloom from me in the crystal mountain lake. A day didn't go by that we weren't side by side.

Rollie could sense my feelings of sadness and would encourage me by nudging me and laying his sweet head in my lap. With his tail fanning me, I would wrap my arms around his satin gold fur and sob into his warmth. His gentle heart accepted my grief and replaced it with his unconditional love and joyful spirit filling me with laughter and joy again.

He would pick up big logs and branches and while carrying them gingerly in his mouth, he'd bound around the field begging for me to follow him.

I was never far behind. Times were heavy then, but thanks to God and Rollie they were bearable. I knew we would all get through this.

Nancy: The love and support I was getting from my husband certainly helped, but I knew how changed the physical structure of my brain could become from depression, and so I searched for more help. I had heard about a program in Denver, developed by Dr. Alfred Tomatis, that had a very high success rate with healing the brain from the damaging effects of depression. I called them for help.

Terena was also suffering from depression, so the two of us packed our bags, packed up the teddy bear and puppy and drove into the big city together. The program used filtered Mozart music to heal the damaged areas. It sounded pretty hoaky to me, but they had scientific research to back up their methodology and several friends had recommended it highly. We both needed help. We decided to give it a try.

Each day, for two weeks, we spent hours in special bone conducting headphones while working on art projects. We allowed the sound to soothe our minds and do its healing work. Each night, as we finished with the program, we played with the growing puppy. Her ears were still droopy, so when one would accidentally stand straight before flopping back over, we both laughed and cheered our approval. The wet, unconditional kisses the black and silver dog shared with us lifted our spirits and filled our hearts with hope.

The entire environment was therapeutic, so when we laughed and sang together in the car on our way back home, we weren't surprised. We both were relieved to have found such a powerful solution to such a dreadful situation. What the Tomatis program didn't 'fix', the puppy did.

Terena and I were on our way back to a healthier life. Things were looking up for us and things were going to be different. I had hit rock bottom, so for me, the only direction I could move was upward. I was planning on scaling the ominous wall of depression like a skilled rock climber.

Chapter 21
The Seeds of Hope

Engulfed in the loving energy of my home, I focused on becoming stronger and happy again. I had come a long way from where I had been a few months earlier, but I still didn't feel like I was capable enough to handle the stresses and concerns involved with raising high risk children. Much to the dismay of the agency, I asked to place my other two emotionally disturbed children into long term care with the family providing their respite. I was taking a year long sabbatical. They needed more stability than I could offer.

As the time blitzed past, I starting think of my other options. The exhaustion, loss and grief caused by each child's leaving had caused my unraveling and I knew I couldn't do it again. I wanted to continue helping children, but I had to work in a way that didn't destroy me or my family, so I hit upon the idea of inviting the entire family to come stay in our home to learn the techniques required to help their children.

I could support the mom in bonding with the child. I would provide the structure and support of a healing environment so the parents could rest before learning all the specialized parenting skills. All this could be accomplished while keeping the family unit intact so the child didn't have to suffer the trauma of being separated from them. I wouldn't have to bond to the child and would instead connect with the moms and dads, and I could gain friendships with the many special parents who loved their challenging children.

I was so excited by this new concept and business plan that I decided to let go of the old by bringing in the new. I planned a two day fiesta and invited all the children who had lived with us, as well as the rest of our family, friends and neighbors. I was going to celebrate by surrounding myself with all the children who owned a piece of my heart and in doing so, rebuild my shaky confidence.

A few weeks later, on the morning of the party, they began arriving. By train, plane, bus and car, from all across the United States, the young men and women, who were children when I had seen them last, walked through our front door. I was greeted by hug after hug from powerful, loving arms. Jerry, Terena, Beth, Chucky and I greeted each guest.

The fields in front of our home, as well as out back the woods along the creek the teepee and campfire ring, all became a sea of smiling and laughing faces of those I loved. Everyone was there. Everyone except Will and Damon. Talking for hours, I caught up on all the news of each of their lives as they had grown. All were in school except for those who had already graduated. Their parents were happy with them and they had learned how to cope confidently and successfully with the trials and frustrations of life.

Pride swelled in my heart when I listened to each and every child tell their story. I felt as if my heart were so happy and filled with love, that it would soon burst from my chest in order to be relieved from the constraints of my body. With each young person's dreams and aspirations that I heard, happiness lifted my spirit. I knew they were succeeding in their lives and were strong enough to accomplish any dream they chose to fulfill. I was filled with more hope for the future than I could remember: hope for their futures as well as hope for my future.

With the day progressing into evening, we started preparing for the arrival of the neighbors and friends. Pulling two dozen watermelons from the creek where I kept them to stay cold and fresh, the kids started the task of carving them. Wielding sharp knives, I knew that each had been healthy long enough to act responsibly with the potential weapons. There were no more knives hidden under any of their pillows and it had been years since any had even thought about one that way.

Some carved their own melons and others in teams of two and three, and soon our table was decorated with melons shaped like parrots, baskets, swans and other forms. Melon balls were made from the juicy flesh. Jerry started up the grill where teriyaki chicken sizzled and shish kebabs required an occasional turn. Alicia was in the kitchen making several huge crusts and homemade tomato sauce for her famous pizza. Without my asking, the tables were set with silverware and the napkins folded into pretty fans. Two children dragged around the five hundred gallon horse watering trough and started dumping the many bags of ice around cases of frosty beverages. Cheese cubes were cut, the salad tossed, chips and dips laid out and the music started. With little orchestration from me, my many children did what needed doing, just by the very nature of their healthy work ethic they had learned so many years before. It brought a smile to my face.

Within an hour, the festivities began and more guests arrived. With more than one hundred party goers, the many plates making up the feast soon became empty and on full stomachs, six or seven large groups formed conversation rings. Laughing until my sides nearly split, we talked together until the wee hours of the morning as adults. We remembered the fun of the mud fights, the splashing in the creek, the silly things each had said and done as children in my care. The memories of the evil, hatred and destruction each had suffered through was never mentioned because those wounds had healed. They no longer carried the burden of them.

That night, when all had become quiet and every bit of party fever was squeezed out of my guests, I tiptoed around the many sleeping bags across the living room. Each bedroom was at capacity and the teepee had six kids sound asleep within its canvas cone. My neighbors and friends had long left.

The next morning, over a huge pancake breakfast, we discussed the various plans for the day. Some wanted to ride horses, others wanted to hike to the cave while a few wanted to just kick back and relax, allowing the day to bring whatever opportunities arose.

While I watched each little group prepare for their adventures as adults, I was reminded of them getting ready for the same activity as children. Standing there, smiling, the grown people in front of me transformed into the little kids I remembered them being. Laughter echoed throughout the rooms while jackets were put on and water bottles filled. My mind was pulled from the past when one asked, jovially, if I could help him zip up his coat. A happy nostalgia was creeping into my heart.

Tromping off in different directions, the many groups glowed under the Colorado sun. Those young men and women were beautiful on the inside and I couldn't help but think that the radiance showed through in their outer beauty. Each one was striking! What was more important, their gentle hearts and loving ways were a triumphant testimony to the work each had done in therapy and in their lives.

In the afternoon, the house and yard hummed with laughter and joy. Many of the children had never met one another, and those who had, hadn't seen each other in years, but they all shared a camaraderie of healing here in our home. As was the custom when they were younger, each child offered his or her services in preparing the house for the second day of festivities. Remembering the old vacuum, the same beat up broom, the familiar wheelbarrow and the same abused furniture needing dusting, the children laughed and talked as they worked. Together, as a huge work force moved joyfully in unison, the aftermath of the previous evening's celebration quickly became a thing of the past.

As we all sat in the garden sipping cold drinks, I went into my closet to get the bubble wands. I pulled out the soapy mixture, and as I did so a yellow note fluttered to the floor; on it was written, " I will always love you! Love, Damon". Smiling sadly, I thought back to his homework in therapy when he had to be sneaky in a loving way. Four years after that note was hidden I had found it, and on any other day it would have been special, but on that day, it was a message from God. Damon was still at the boys ranch, and although he could never come to the party, his spirit was there instead. I could now let go of the guilt and responsibility regarding his life with us, his message, placed there years before, appeared at the perfect moment. With a deep breath, I got the rest of the bubble hoops and wands while folding the little note into my pocket. "Damon, I will always love you too," I thought as I walked out to the garden.

Filling the tub with bubble mixture, I was reminded of Will and our Rubber Ducky adventure in the bathtub. Pulled from the past when ripples broke up the glassy surface of the bubble water, each youth dipped their wand into it carefully. Bubbles began floating in the air. The reflection as each delicate sphere danced past the garden with its roses brought with it the hope and promise of the vibrant future each of these young people had.

Alicia, knowing her pizza sauce and crust dough were ready, left early to start the preparations. Shredding the cheese and slicing the pepperoni, sausage, and olives, she placed each bowl on the counter while she returned to the garden to ask when the rest of the guests were expected. Twenty minutes later, as our neighbors started to descend on our home, she went back inside. In the kitchen she found her bowls, once filled with pizza toppings, empty and on the floor. CJ's German Shepherd had a few shreds of cheese on her nose and a very guilty expression on her face. She had consumed everything but the dough and sauce.

Alicia, with her head low, stepped from the back door. Seeing she was sad, I called to her from the garden. "The dog ate all the pizza toppings", she mumbled as she opened the gate. Without anger or frustration, the young lady, pointed to the culprit and started laughing. "See her guilty face? She should do some strong sitting to think about her behavior!" And with that, everyone started cracking up. We wouldn't be having pizza, but in Alicia's brilliant problem solving, she made bread sticks and used the sauce for dipping instead. Everyone loved it!

Once the night progressed, the company was great and the food was delicious. Conversations were interesting and filled with suspense and hilarity as tales were woven and facts revealed. It was a fabulous night and the moon shown down upon us all.

Each child had come to me like battle scarred caterpillars, and I had watched the magical process of their metamorphosis into beautiful butterflies. All were ready to spread their wings to fly, and I was ready to let them go. As the time came for each one to depart, they came to me, smiled into my eyes and thanked me. I gave each a great big hug that was returned with much love. I filled each of my precious children, now grown into young adults, with love as I sent them off into the world. My heart and mind were completely at rest and peace at knowing they no longer needed me. They were healthy; their hearts were healed. They had lives filled with love and enough love in their hearts to share with others.

That night, as I bathed in the joy from one of the happiest weekends in my life, I pulled my bedspread back to reveal a little golden dandelion flower that had begun to mean so much. Being greeted by such a heartwarming surprise from one of my children made me wonder who was secretly smiling in their bed anticipating my delight. With more joy and pride in my soul, I was filled with a feeling of peace and happiness at how extraordinary each one had become. The children, who had started as the weeds of society, unwanted and stepped on, had become the seeds of hope for future generations.

Tucking the precious yellow flower safely next to my pillow, I rolled over into my cowboy's loving embrace. Closing my eyes, I let my dreams for the children float up and away like seeds of a dandelion on the wind dancing to the melody of each child's future. With my husband's rough, work worn hands gently rubbing my back, I knew I had made a difference and was finally able to sleep.

Epilogue

Alicia graduated from high school and is currently attending business school. She wants to open an Italian restaurant specializing in gourmet pizza. She is engaged and plans on adopting her fiance's daughter.

Beth graduated from high school with honors and is a student at the University where she is studying to be a Pediatric Nurse. She is still very active in church and is learning to play the guitar to accompany her gift of song.

Chucky is a successful businessman. He and his loving wife, Laura, are expecting their first child.

Dr. Foster Cline is retired from treating patients. He teaches workshops on parenting that should not be missed! He has also written nine books filled with great information.

C.J. Cooil is retired and spends her spare time playing with her grandson.

Damon received his diploma while at the boys ranch and upon his release rented an apartment and is living independently. He won the state championship with his miniature horses before leaving the boys ranch.

Gabriel graduated from high school and finished his active duty with the Army. He is now at a local college preparing to become a state trooper.

R.B. and his amazing wife Kymm are raising their five children with love, honor and respect. He is an officer in the Marine Corps with a bachelor's degree in the social sciences. She is attending classes to complete a degree in early childhood education. Their children are beautiful, well behaved and brilliant!

Terena attained her Bachelor's of Science degree and is attending graduate school. She has a research project in the process of being published and is happily engaged to be married. She wants to adopt a child when the time is right.

Theodore (Teddy) graduated from high school and is currently attending a University where he is studying to become a radiologist.

Wilhelm (Will) finished his high school and work program, but failed to live by the law. He is currently serving time in a Utah state prison.

What can you do to help?

* Be a stay at home Mom until your child is at least three years old.
* Read this book and pass it on to a friend.
* Gain further insight into the symptoms and causes of Attachment Disorders.
* Realize parents of emotionally disturbed children are in a painful situation and need your support and understanding.
* Pray for the traumatized children of the world.
• Volunteer in your community.
• Help teach children to be respectful, responsible and fun to be around.
• Don't allow kids to manipulate you.
* Donate to the nonprofit organization SAVY (Stop Americas Violent Youth).

If you know a mom of a child with RAD what can you do to help?

* Listen to her with open ears and a nonjudgemental heart.
* Make short, loving, uplifting phone calls to her offering to listen, not to advise.
* Take her to lunch or dinner, or bring over a prepared meal for the family.
* Share anything funny with her, laugh together.
* Send her flowers, chocolate or cards with love and a smile in it.
* Give her a hug!
* Do not give unasked for advice.
* Take all information she shares with you in confidence.
* Run errands for the family.
* Learn how to be a respite provider to watch her child without causing any healing delays.
* Give her a gift certificate for a massage, hair salon or spa visit.
* Give her Mozart's music or other soothing, uplifting tunes.
* Give her a stuffed animal filled with love for her inner child.
* Remind her of her special traits and talents.
* Tell the child often, in front of her, how lucky they are to have a mom like her.
• Never tell her to 'just love the child more'!

To donate to SAVY, Inc. to help Stop America's Violent Youth, please send your donation to: SAVY, PO Box 421, Glenwood Springs, CO 81602

Risk Factors

Any occurring during the first 36 months of life puts a child at high risk for developing RAD:

- ➢ Maternal ambivalence
- ➢ In-utero trauma, drugs, alcohol
- ➢ Abuse (physical, emotional, sexual)
- ➢ Neglect
- ➢ Separation from primary caregiver
- ➢ Ongoing pain
- ➢ Poor day care
- ➢ Chronic maternal depression
- ➢ Several moves and/or placements
- ➢ Poor parenting

High Risk Signs in Infants

- ➢ Weak crying response or inability to settle
- ➢ Developmental delays
- ➢ Tactile defensiveness
- ➢ Poor clinging and extreme resistance to cuddling: seems "stiff"
- ➢ Poor sucking response
- ➢ Poor eye contact, lack of tracking
- ➢ Self abusive behavior (head banging, self biting, hair pulling)

Attachment Disorder Symptoms in Children

1. Superficially charming
2. Lack of eye contact on parents' terms
3. Indiscriminately affectionate with strangers
4. Not affectionate on Parents' terms (not cuddly)
5. Extreme control problems (sneaky)
6. Destructive to self, others and material things
7. Cruelty to animals
8. Lying about the obvious (crazy lying)
9. No impulse control (hyperactivity or stealing)
10. Learning Lags
11. Lack of cause and effect thinking
12. Lack of conscience
13. Abnormal eating patterns
14. Poor peer relationships
15. Preoccupation with fire, blood & gore
16. Persistent nonsense questions & chatter
17. Inappropriately demanding & clingy
18. Abnormal speech patterns
19. False allegations of abuse
20. Triangulation of adults
21. Presumptive entitlement issues
22. Parents appear hostile & angry

RECOMMENDED READING

Adopting the Hurt Child, by Keck and Kupecky Pinon Press 1995

Attaching and Adoption, Deborah Gray 2002

Attachment, Trauma and Healing by Levy, and Orlans, 1998, CWLA Publish.

Becoming Attached by Karen, 94, Oxford, NY: Oxford University Press

Broken Hearts, Wounded Minds, Elizabeth Randolph, PhD (970-984-2222

Can This Child Be Saved? by Foster Cline, M.D. & Kathy Helding

Facilitating Developmental Attachment by Hughes 1997

Ghosts from the Nursery by Robin Karr-Morse

High Risk: Children Without a Conscience, by Magid & McKelvey, Bantam '89

Holding Time, by Martha Welsh M.D. Simon and Schuster 1988

Parenting Teens with Love and Logic, by Cline and Fay, Pinon Press 1992

Parenting with Love and Logic by Foster Cline, M.D. & Jim Fay, Pinon Press '90

The Family Virtues Guide, by Linda Kavelin Popov, Penguin Books

The Handbook of Attachment Interventions by Levy, Academic Press 1999

The Miracle Worker, by William Gibson Bantam Books/Perma 1962

The Secret Life of The Unborn Child by Thomas Verny M.D. Dell 1981

Therapeutic Parenting it's an Attitude, by Deborah Hage, 970-984-2222

Touching (the Human Significance of the Skin), by Ashley Montagu
Harper and Row Publishers

When Love Is Not Enough by Nancy Thomas, 970-984-2222

Who's the Boss? Love, Authority, and Parenting by Nelson & Lewak

99 Ways to Drive Your Child Sane by Brita St. Clair (970) 984-2222

Order Form

Name _____

Address _____City _____State_____

Zip _____Telephone _____

____copies of the book **When Love is Not Enough** at $12 _____
     A guide to parenting children with Reactive Attachment Disorder

____copies of the video set **Rebuilding the Broken Bond** at $30 _____
     4 hours of humorously presented parenting plan for RAD

____copies of the book **Dandelion on My Pillow, Butcher Knife Beneath** $19.95_____
     True story of an amazing family that lived with and loved kids who killed!

____copies of the 60 minute video **Circle of Support** at $15 _____
     Explains RAD & gives great support ideas for friends and family

____copies of **Healing Trust: Rebuilding the Broken Bond** audio at $18.95_____
     Two humorous cassettes, 3 hours, explains RAD & many "how to's"

____copies of the 3 1/2 hr DVD set **Captive in the Classroom** at $30 _____
     Presents powerful techniques & tools to ID and redirect disturbed students

____copies of the 2 1/2 hr video set **Give Me A Break** at $29.95_____
     Information baby sitters need to be highly effective to provide relief.

____copies of the 60 min. video **Building Brilliant Brains** at $15 _____
     Understanding and healing traumatized childrens' brains. Shows PROOF!

____copies of **Ask Nancy** –DVD - answers to 30 most urgently $15 _____
     asked questions from parents and teachers

____copies of **Mastering Steps to Reach Children with RAD** / at $79.95_____
     When Love Is Not Enough - Changing parenting from Mystery to Mastery

____copies of **It's Not Just Horsing Around with Defiant Kids!** at $89.95_____
     Three DVD's & 175 pg manual w/ full lesson plan for horseback interventions

____copies of the Audio cassette set **Biology of Behavior** at $18.95_____
     Shares effective nutrition treatment ideas for attention and aggression.

____copies of **99 Ways to Drive Your Child Sane** booklet by St. Clair at $10 _____
     Wild ideas to add hysterical humor to a home with a disturbed child

____copies of **Therapeutic Parenting** book by Deb Hage MSW at $7 _____
     Wisdom from experienced Mom and Attachment Therapist

____copies of **Me and My Volcano** workbook at $5 _____
     Anger management workbook by Deborah Hage, MSW

____copies of **So You Want To Be A Princess?** book at $4 _____
     Clever insightful children's book for girls by Deborah Hage, MSW

____copies of **So You Want To Be A Prince?** book at $4 _____
     Clever insightful children's book for boys by Deborah Hage, MSW

____copies of **Neurofeedback & QEEG Questions & Answers** at $4 _____
     Audio CD by Attachment Therapist, Larry Van Bloem, LCSW

____copies of **Broken Hearts; Wounded Minds** book by Liz Randolph PhD $34.95_____
     . 250 pgs of past and current research in a power packed manual

____copies of **Children Who Shock and Surprise** booklet $10 _____
     by Liz Randolph, MSN, PhD, leading researcher, parenting & treatment ideas.

Order totals	Add
Up to - $30	$ 4
$31 - $45	$ 7
$46 - $90	$ 10
$91 - $150	$14
$151-$300	$17
$301 - $600	$20

Payable to: Families by Design   sub total _____
    PO Box 2812
    Glenwood Springs, CO   S & H _____
    81602
    970-984-2222   Total enclosed _____